Shaw, Synge, Connolly, and Socialist Provocation

THE FLORIDA BERNARD SHAW SERIES

UNIVERSITY PRESS OF FLORIDA

Florida A&M University, Tallahassee
Florida Atlantic University, Boca Raton
Florida Gulf Coast University, Ft. Myers
Florida International University, Miami
Florida State University, Tallahassee
New College of Florida, Sarasota
University of Central Florida, Orlando
University of Florida, Gainesville
University of North Florida, Jacksonville
University of South Florida, Tampa
University of West Florida, Pensacola

Shaw, Synge, Connolly, and Socialist Provocation

NELSON O`CEALLAIGH RITSCHEL

Foreword by R. F. Dietrich, Series Editor

University Press of Florida
Gainesville · Tallahassee · Tampa · Boca Raton
Pensacola · Orlando · Miami · Jacksonville · Ft. Myers · Sarasota

Copyright 2011 by Nelson O'Ceallaigh Ritschel
All rights reserved
Printed in the United States of America. This book is printed on Glatfelter
Natures Book, a paper certified under the standards of the Forestry Stewardship
Council (FSC). It is a recycled stock that contains 30 percent post-consumer
waste and is acid-free.

First cloth printing, 2011
First paperback printing, 2012

Library of Congress Cataloging-in-Publication Data
Ritschel, Nelson O'Ceallaigh, 1959–
Shaw, Synge, Connolly, and Socialist provocation / Nelson O'Ceallaigh Ritschel;
foreword by R.F. Dietrich, series editor.
p. cm. — (The Florida Bernard Shaw series)
Includes bibliographical references and index.
ISBN 978-0-8130-3651-9 (cloth: alk. paper)
ISBN 978-0-8130-4440-8 (pbk.)
1. Shaw, Bernard, 1856–1950—Political and social views. 2. Synge, J. M.
(John Millington), 1871–1909—Criticism and interpretation. 3. Connolly, James,
1868–1916—Criticism and interpretation. 4. Socialism and literature—Ireland.
5. Theater and society—Ireland. I. Title.
PR5368.P6R58 2011
822'.912—dc22
2010054038

The University Press of Florida is the scholarly publishing agency for the State
University System of Florida, comprising Florida A&M University, Florida Atlantic University, Florida Gulf Coast University, Florida International University,
Florida State University, New College of Florida, University of Central Florida,
University of Florida, University of North Florida, University of South Florida,
and University of West Florida.

University Press of Florida
15 Northwest 15th Street
Gainesville, FL 32611-2079
http://www.upf.com

To Don B. Wilmeth

Funding to assist in publication of this book was generously provided by the David and Rachel Howie Foundation.

Contents

Foreword	xi
Acknowledgments	xv
Introduction	1
1. A Dublin Socialist and an Irish Theatre	7
2. Answering *John Bull's* Provocation—Synge	50
3. Toward 1913 and the "Most Distinguished Irishman"—Shaw	93
4. Lockout—Shaw, Connolly, Synge, and the Red Guard—ICA	133
5. War and Revolution: The Convergence	169
Epilogue: Shaw and Execution	217
Notes	225
Bibliography	247
Index	259

Foreword

Much of today's cultural and political establishment in Ireland barely seems to recognize Bernard Shaw as Irish at all or simply dismisses him as "Anglo-Irish," and the amount of attention paid to Shaw in today's Ireland, especially in the schools, is slight compared to that given to his literary co-equals and contemporaries, James Joyce and William Butler Yeats, Shaw being to the drama what Joyce was to the novel and Yeats to poetry.

The reasons for this neglect of what is arguably "Ireland's Shakespeare" are many, but, to begin with, Shaw gladly abandoned Ireland when a teenager, lived another seventy-five years or so in and around London, and returned to Ireland for only a few visits. Although Joyce was equally as, if not more, alienated from Ireland, living in Europe his entire adult life, and Yeats spent much time abroad as well, these two made up for their physical absence from Ireland by writing about almost nothing but Ireland. Shaw, on the other hand, compounded his physical absence from Ireland with a seemingly spiritual absence as well, inasmuch as relatively little of what he wrote was explicitly about Ireland and what he did write was not in the preferred nationalist vein.

Believing that Shaw had created a false impression of not being much interested in Ireland by focusing his writing on the British Empire and the problems of Western democracy as seen from London, some scholars have tried to correct that false impression by collecting and commenting on the many essays Shaw wrote on Irish subjects (see, for example, Dan H. Laurence's *The Matter with Ireland*), which show that Ireland was more on his mind and more cared about than many thought. But what has been lacking in this attempt to reconnect Shaw to his native land is a convincing demonstration that, like Joyce and Yeats, he wrote *always* as an Irishman and that, perhaps even more to his credit in the eyes of the Irish, he conducted, however indirectly, ironically, and good-humoredly, a reverse Irish colonization of England!

That realization may come in time, but for now Nelson O`Ceallaigh Ritschel has begun the task of reconnection by focusing, in his *Shaw, Synge, Connolly, and Socialist Provocation,* on a particularly crucial part of the Shaw-Ireland relation, showing that there was an ongoing physical as well as spiritual Shavian presence in the burning issues of the day, in the two great revolutions of the struggle of Ireland for independence from "Great Britain" and the struggle of the Irish working class to connect their cause with an international uprising.

These two causes were interrelated in the militant Irish socialist movement of the early 1900s partly because generating of tension between nationalist and internationalist tendencies within the movement, Shaw taking the side of the latter. Perhaps the greatest value of Ritschel's study is in its revelation of how often things Shaw said, wrote, and did *really mattered* to the Irish in Ireland who had revolution on their minds and were responded to in ways that directly affected the outcome of events, most particularly in the works and deeds of two of Ireland's major cultural leaders of the early twentieth century, John Millington Synge and James Connolly.

This study is notable not just for its considerable amount of original research but also for how well the research supports an extraordinary analysis of major documents leading to fresh interpretations that leave little doubt that Shaw was listened to and argued with at key points in Ireland's history, with consequences great and immediate. Thus this study, while valuable enough in its making a major contribution to the scholarship in the field, should also have some impact on Shaw's standing in Ireland by showing him as far more engaged in historically monumental Irish concerns and more influencing of them than anyone has heretofore realized. Shaw's impact on "radical Irish socialism" has never been explained with such a clear drawing of connections between Shaw in London and the Dublin revolutionaries.

Another reason this book is worthy has to do with the zeitgeist. I was at first taken aback when Ritschel's manuscript appeared, for it was the third in a row in this Shaw Series focused on Shaw's socialism (Alexander's *Shaw's Controversial Socialism* and Carpenter's *Bernard Shaw as Artist-Fabian* immediately preceding it), and I wondered if the world, not to mention the publisher, was ready for another. But the more I look at this trio, the less this seems a coincidence, for aren't we all these days wondering about capitalism and taking a second look at socialism? Or at least at what the socialist pioneers had to say about capitalism's boom-and-bust pattern? So far from Ritschel's topic being a bit too much of the same thing, he may be just hammering home a point that needs hammering these days, as he reminds us of three Irishmen from an earlier time caught up in much the same problematics and passionately determined to address them, however much they may have disagreed about the ways and means.

R. F. Dietrich

Acknowledgments

In some respects, this book became possible by prodding from Don B. Wilmeth, to whom this work is dedicated. On two occasions, once while a doctoral candidate and the other in the wake of my first Synge book, Dr. Wilmeth suggested a Shaw direction. The first set me on the road to Synge, and the second sent me presenting a Synge paper, with Shavian relevance, at the first conference of the International Shaw Society (ISS). Over the next four years, I was contemplating Shaw within Shaw's Irish context. So, given such prodding, this book, as well as my earlier publications, became possible. A greater mentor has not existed.

Two years after the first ISS conference, while researching Irish socialist James Connolly, I returned to Brown University for the ISS's second conference, "Sesquicentennial Shaw," which Don Wilmeth hosted. Two years after that, I began working on this book.

Through the ISS, I made the acquaintance of Richard F. Dietrich, then ISS president and editor of the University Press of Florida's Shaw Series. So while I thank Professor Dietrich for his enthusiasm for Shaw through the ISS, I am greatly indebted to him as the Shaw Series editor. He read a draft of this book and promptly sent me superb editorial recommendations that allowed the book to fully emerge as a study of Shaw within Irish socialism.

I wish to thank Irish Shaw scholar Peter Gahan, whom I met at the first ISS conference. Our conversations led me to see Shaw further in relation to Ireland. Also, I thank Peter, as guest editor of *Shaw: The Annual of Bernard Shaw Studies*, volume 30, for publishing my article "Shaw and the Syngean Provocation," which was a forerunner for a section of my book's chapter 1. Peter's comments during the essay's writing process helped sharpen a number of key points. In this vein, I thank the Pennsylvania State University Press for permission to reprint part of that essay.

Great thanks are extended to the Society of Authors, on behalf of the Bernard Shaw Estate, for permission to quote extensively from Bernard Shaw's works and letters. In addition, I equally thank the Board of Trinity College Dublin for permission to quote profusely from J. M. Synge's works and letters. The Board of the National Library of Ireland is similarly thanked for their permission to quote from Joseph Holloway's "Impressions of a Dublin Playgoer."

Also, and importantly, I thank Admiral Richard Gurnon and Captain Bradley Lima, respectively the president and the academic dean of Massachusetts Maritime Academy, for approving and fully funding my sabbatical in spring 2009 so I could complete this book. Their support of my scholarly publications in this instance, and in all others, is greatly appreciated. I also acknowledge professional development funds in 2010 from Massachusetts Maritime Academy that have defrayed some of this book's production costs.

I also thank my department colleagues who on occasion listened to my ideas on Shaw and have spiritually supported my scholarship. In addition, I thank my former colleague Nora Bicki, who read drafts of the first four chapters of this book. Her comments were most helpful.

Thanks are also offered to additional Shavian and Irish Studies scholars who, over the years, have contributed, directly or indirectly, to the mindset that has composed this book. They include, but are not limited to, Bernard Dukore, Martin Miesel, Declan Kiberd, Ann Saddlemyer, Stephen Watt, and Lucy McDiarmid.

I also thank Amy Gorelick, the acquisitions editor at the University Press of Florida, who professionally led this book through submission and peer review to acceptance. In addition, I thank Ms. Gorelick for her patience in carefully, and quickly, answering my various questions along the way. Thanks are also extended to Catherine-Nevil Parker, this book's project editor at UPF, for guiding the project through publication.

Finally, I thank my partner and wife, Carolina, for helping this work through its formulation and completion. Her unconditional support and loving assistance, demonstrated in every step of this book's realization, are gratefully acknowledged. I remember my late parents, Brenda and Frank, who, in their respective ways, always encouraged my endeavors, with Brenda instilling a historical Irish consciousness. I remember as well our late Casey; never were my papers more organized on desk or table. I thank Deirdre for insisting on necessary breaks during the final year of writing this book. Thanks also to our nieces, Alex and Sasha, who prompt much love from their aunt and uncle.

Introduction

Shaw, Synge, Connolly, and Socialist Provocation explores Bernard Shaw's presence in the developmental progression of militant socialism in Ireland from the 1890s to nearly 1920. Shaw's participation was an integral presence during the key developments toward Irish revolution. His participation included the mere influence of his reputation, his direct contributions, and—perhaps key to the study—the effects they provoked from others. In other words, Shaw's presence in Irish radical debate was felt through not only his contributions, but also through the way he and his efforts were engaged by others. This book, then, details Shaw's impact on the development and evolution of what became militant socialism in early twentieth-century Ireland. Shaw's participation in the radical debate in Ireland proved critically provocative, even when developments, that is, the militant road, disagreed with his approach and stance.

However, this is not to insist that Shaw's works, especially his plays, are socialist propaganda in the usual sense, regardless of anything Shaw might have said to that effect. The intent here is to study the extent to which certain people took Shaw's works as such and acted accordingly. It has been well demonstrated that Shaw's plays are dramatizations of universal human problems, and few of them suggest that socialism is the solution to such problems. Most of his plays end problematically, without any resolution and without socialism being directly offered as a solution. Yet it is historically true that many people, knowing that Shaw was a professed socialist, *received* his works as socialistic, and that was particularly true of those in or related to the socialist movement in Ireland.

The book's first two chapters begin in the late 1890s while Shaw was engrossed in developing his Fabian philosophy and playwriting career in London, when he had little thought and seemingly no concern for provincial Ireland. Nonetheless, Shaw's emerging London reputation was brought to Dublin by an Irish journalist named Frederick Ryan. Ryan promptly lectured the recently formed and exceedingly obscure Irish Socialist Republican Party (ISRP) on Shaw's Fabian essays, lectures, views on Ibsen, and plays. Present, in an audience that may have been as few as fifteen, was the young socialist agitator and laborer James Connolly. Connolly's encounters with Shavian politics and participation would, over seventeen years, help propel Connolly to the realization of his life's work.

Emerging from the 1890s Dublin ISRP lecture on Shaw was a Shavian-influenced play, Ryan's *The Laying of the Foundations*, which introduced a socialistic precedent to the Irish National Theatre Society's (INTS's) first bill, in October 1902. It was a production that foretold much, as it drew on Shaw's *Unpleasant Plays* while including a character based on Connolly. Shaw and Connolly would become the two most highly profiled Irish socialists prior to 1920, and they were being represented in a Dublin theatre that would foster the day's political debates.

Yet soon after Ryan's play, Connolly left Ireland for America, where he developed himself through voracious reading and experience, returning in 1910. Therefore, the bulk of the book's first two chapters explores the gestation of leftist social thought in Dublin following Connolly's departure as continued in Dublin theatre. During its first decade, the INTS was attended by Dubliners involved in political debate, including the socialists who became Connolly's colleagues in 1910. It was in its second year that the INTS staged the first performed play by John Millington Synge, *In the Shadow of the Glen*, which clashed with the INTS's conservative audience members. Upon seeing the INTS for the first time in March 1904, including Synge's play, Shaw began writing his Irish masterwork, *John Bull's Other Island*, thought by some with socialistic leanings to be a direct contribution to socialistic thought in Ireland. An Irish contextual re-evaluation reveals the play to be a reconfiguration and expansion of Synge's play.

Even though *John Bull's* was not performed in Dublin until November 1907, it arguably had a presence in Ireland ten months earlier. Synge's response to Shaw's play (which he read in 1904) was to reconfigure the play into *The Playboy of the Western World*, premiering in January 1907, causing a riotous audience to explode. In contrast, Shaw's play was well received during its Dublin premiere, as many of his non-Irish plays had been. As *John Bull's* and *Playboy* are explored, their ideological similarities emerge as significant, yet the plays are quite different in their effect on their audiences. Essentially, the difference is philosophical, namely in the way their perceived socialistic considerations of Irish society were expressed to a middle-class Dublin audience. One courted popularity in making its case for gradualist social change, and the second, snubbing popularity, demanded immediate change in its audience. These differences marked a debate between international and national considerations by Shaw and Synge, and led to additional leftist Irish plays by other writers who followed Shaw, and eventually Synge. This debate anticipated the socialistic approaches that moved onto the streets as Synge's final illness neared him to death in 1909. A year after Synge's death, and after the Dublin premier of the playboy-ish *The Shewing-up of Blanco Posnet*, Connolly returned to Ireland and began his crusade. The march from theory to practice in Irish socialistic thought was advancing.

Chapters 3 and 4 move out of Dublin theatres, in part, as Shaw delivered his lecture "The Poor Law and Destitution in Ireland" to Dubliners in the context of Connolly's elaborate reply to the Catholic Church's effort to stifle socialism, *Labour, Nationality, and Religion*. The difference between Shaw's lecture and Connolly's Church response touched on the very debate fostered by Shaw and Synge. Connolly then became involved in the Irish trade union movement, uniting it with socialist theory. The period was peppered with Shavian-influenced plays, entering themselves into the socialist debate. As the bourgeois Dubliners whom Shaw satirized, who were also the enemies of Synge's plays, moved against trade unionism, the 1913 Dublin Lockout commenced. The colossal Dublin struggle of labor against capitalism was under way, and Shaw's presence was at hand.

Shaw, the now deceased Synge, and Connolly were united by their common opponents as events brought Shaw and Connolly together in a London rally for Dublin labor and the release of the imprisoned Irish trade union leader James Larkin. While both Connolly and Shaw delivered remarkable speeches, Shaw called for the arming of Dublin labor in order to stop the police brutality aimed at locked-out workers. In two weeks' time, Connolly called for the formation of Europe's first Red Guard, the Irish Citizen Army (ICA), which began training with words from its drill instructor on Shaw. As the ICA was forming, a bourgeois nationalist, Padraic Pearse, began to reconsider Synge, seeing him as a lost voice for Irish labor during the current Lockout. Pearse had come to recognize Synge's leftist stance in the rural *Playboy* at the very moment he publicly sided with Dublin labor. Pearse was now on track toward Connolly's ideology through *The Playboy of the Western World*, written in response to Shaw.

Following *The Shewing-up of Blanco Posnet*, socialistic and labor theatre made its appearances in the Shavian-inspired form, along with intriguing Shavian revivals. The Dublin Repertory Theatre staged *The Devil's Disciple* in one of Dublin's commercial middle-class theatres using recently unionized laborers as the American extras for a provocative production. But when Dublin labor leaders Larkin and Connolly called on British labor to strike in sympathy with Dublin labor throughout Britain, British labor refused, leaving Dublin labor in 1914 in defeat.

Chapter 5 encounters the effects of the Great War through the shambles of defeated Irish labor and considers how war divided Irish socialistic thought as epitomized by Shaw and Connolly, just as *Playboy* had earlier divided nationalists into conservatives and radicals. Committing himself to the defeat of German militarism, in which he tied the hope for a democratic victory leading to social justice, Shaw argued for Irishmen to enlist in the British military. The nationalized Connolly instead viewed the war as the collapse of socialist internationalism, as laborers and socialists throughout Europe enlisted in the imperial and capitalist armies. Consequently, Connolly called on Irish labor not to enlist in Britain's war. In this context, Shaw wrote his second Irish play, *O'Flaherty V.C.* As he had countered a Synge play in 1904, and in turn was countered by another Synge play, Shaw turned again to Synge in 1915, writing a Syngean-structured un-Syngean ideological play. Arguably, *O'Flaherty V.C.* in 1915 rivaled *John Bull's Other Island* for its supreme Shavian joke which, had it premiered in 1915 Dublin, would have brilliantly satirized Synge's foes—the enemies of social liberal advancement in Ireland.

But as *O'Flaherty V.C.* presented an Irishman content in the British army who recruits other Irishmen, Connolly, through Abbey Theatre actors who were his close ICA associates, was provoked by Shaw's play to respond by writing a play of his own. Connolly's *Under Which Flag?* attempted to counter Shaw's play point by point (including Syngean ties), hence creating a Shavian-provoked production, while Connolly produced his play amidst his preparations for Irish revolution. He had committed the ICA to achieving Irish independence to gain social justice in Ireland and, he thought, advance socialist revolution throughout Europe. Joining Connolly was the Synge-*Playboy*-inspired Pearse, with his middle-class nationalist militia.

The Shavian presence in the 1916 Irish revolution existed in the ways some perceived Shaw from 1899 to the provocation that created *Under Which Flag?* It was in Shaw's legitimizing of the ICA in 1913, and it was in Connolly's efforts to use Shaw's help in London during the weeks leading to revolution. These were weeks filled with preparations designed to portray British militarism as the aggressor in Ireland and attract support from Irish populations in Britain. After the revolution's collapse, as many surviving Irish writers scampered to eulogize and understand those who had led Dublin rebels to revolution, Shaw wrote immediately to check the ferocious military response he anticipated. Shaw then wrote to spare Connolly's life. The result of this book, then, is to bring to the surface Shaw's direct and indirect presence and provocation in what became militant Irish socialism.

The scope of the book is vast, as it contextualizes Shaw's involvement in ways not previously encountered in Shaw Studies. In parts, the work is critical literary examination and theatre history, rereading playtexts and play productions, and in other sections, the work is a historical exploration through a socialistic reading. Although the focus is on Shaw, Synge and Connolly are heavily considered, as their Shavian contexts present significant unexplored insight into both, as much as into Shaw. And other participants are considered as they too played their parts. These range from Frederick Ryan to William O'Brien, W. B. Yeats, Constance and Casimir Markievicz, Sean Connolly, Helena Moloney, James Larkin, Delia Larkin, Padraic Pearse, Thomas MacDonagh, Francis Sheehy-Skeffington, and others. In part, this is an examination of early modern leftist Irish theatre, Irish labor, and militant revolution—but above all, it is a study of Shaw.

Many important Syngean critics have made the leap to Shaw, becoming Shavian critics as well—such as Nicholas Grene, Ann Saddlemyer, and Declan Kiberd. Nevertheless, the socialistic bridge linking Shaw and Synge, and ultimately Connolly, has not been previously crossed. I bring to this work significant Syngean publications that have increasingly revealed a leftist, socially liberal Synge. This work has emerged from my various publications on the connections between *John Bull's Other Island* and *The Playboy of the Western World*, revealing a hitherto and exceedingly crucial unexplored portion of Shaw's professional life. My study is not a study of Shaw's complete participation in and with Ireland, which would be an entirely separate but also crucial study. Rather this is a study of Shaw's socialistic endeavors in Ireland and, most importantly, a study of how Shaw was perceived, received, and reacted to and against, in the intellectual and physical development of what evolved into militant Irish socialism. It is the study of Shavian provocation—Shaw's legacy in Irish socialism.

1

A Dublin Socialist and an Irish Theatre

G. B. Shaw's participation in Irish socialism was both direct and indirect, and it made an indelible mark. His persona as a socialist in Britain during the 1890s indirectly made Shaw's first impact on socialism in Ireland, emerging through the Dublin theatre movement that began solidifying in 1902. Ultimately, his socialistic impact reveals that Shaw's role in Dublin theatre of the early twentieth century was far more than a mere passing moment or two. Shaw's impact or influence introduced socialistic writing into the new Irish theatre, which engaged the few radical-leaning playwrights who emerged during this theatre movement's two decades, the most noted being John Millington Synge. Synge's early leftist leanings were expanded in reaction to Shaw's first direct effort in Irish theatre as Shaw contributed his major Irish play, *John Bull's Other Island*, in 1904. A socialistic presence in the Dublin theatre movement was highly significant in that this theatre functioned as a launching platform for the debates that anticipated and led to Irish revolution.

Shaw's involvement in the introduction of socialism into Irish theatre also began the connection, if obscurely at first, between Shaw and James Connolly—the militant working-class socialist who led Irish rebels in Dublin's 1916 Easter Rising. Eventually, Shaw would be highly instrumental in Connolly's development and emergence as the leading socialist activist in Ireland, even recalling Connolly after his execution. In fact, the introduction of Shaw-inspired socialism in Irish theatre as early as 1902 placed Shaw and Connolly, with Syngean echoes, on two separate tracks that would ultimately converge. In 1913, Shaw's provocative contribution during the Dublin Lockout, when Dublin workers and employers were engaged in a monumental clash that seemed poised to either further the enslavement of Irish workers or crush capitalism in the British Isles, proved a flash point for Connolly and his vision for Irish workers. Shaw's participation in the debate of Ireland and the Great War helped propel Connolly and the agenda of radical Irish socialism. By 1915–16, Shaw and Connolly each wrote plays for Ireland that galvanized the debate and emphasized the choices that then faced Irish socialists. Shaw's *O'Flaherty V.C.* and Connolly's *Under Which Flag?* advanced Connolly's militant socialism into revolution. Yet the ideologies of these two plays, and the socialist commitments behind them, were anticipated a decade earlier between Shaw and Synge.

Fabians, Frederick Ryan, and a New Irish Theatre

Shaw's socialist persona began with the Fabian Society in England during the 1880s. Tracy Davis writes that Shaw was taken with the Fabians' "middle-class, tolerant, educated clique that sought to reform society by argument, brain power, and superior organization rather than working-class revolt" (*George Bernard Shaw*, 17). A non-confrontational style is what one would have expected from Fabians, given that few members had "working-class affiliations" and the anger of the slums. Essentially, at the risk of oversimplification, the Fabians sought to promote socialist change from outside the working-class/employer-class battlefields. During London's Bloody Sunday in 1887, when English workers marched on Trafalgar Square with labor leaders for better working conditions and were attacked by London's police, Shaw was present. He "reported that he and others had to beat a rapid retreat from the police charge" (Gibbs, *Bernard Shaw*, 129). Davis suggests that the Fabians' approach helped Shaw to develop the nature of his plays, enveloping Shaw's belief in what "gave life to literature," namely "a criticism of society," as Stanley Weintraub remarks (Weintraub, *Unexpected*, 137).

Peter Gahan writes that when Shaw joined the Fabian Society he quickly established himself as "a leading member involved in committee work, lecturing, and writing on economics and, later, international politics, [and] he became one of the most active socialists of his generation" (*Shaw Shadows*, 46). Within a year of joining the Fabians, Shaw articulated a Fabian philosophy and tactic, while revealing a Dublin consciousness: "If socialism be not made respectable and formidable by the support of our class—if it be left entirely to the poor, then the proprietors will attempt to suppress it by such measures as they have already taken in Austria and Ireland. Dynamite will follow. Terror will follow dynamite. Cruelty will follow terror . . . If, on the other hand, the middle class will educate themselves to understand this question, they will be able to fortify whatever is just in socialism, and to crush whatever is dangerous to it" (Shaw, *Christian Socialist*, 40, as quoted in Kiberd, *Irish Classics*, 343). The Fabian effort "to reform society" by educating the middle class to socialist ideas is evident. In 1889, Fabians published *Fabian Essays*, including two by Shaw: "one of the most influential of all English books on socialism" (Gahan, *Shaw Shadows*, 46).

Shaw's essays were "Economic" and "Transition." In the former, Shaw takes aim at capitalism's effect on the proletariat. He argues that English laborers "are no longer even dirt cheap: they are valueless, and can be had for nothing." The proletariat's wage "is not the price of themselves: for they are worth nothing: it is only their keep. For bare subsistence wages you can get as much common labour as you want, and do what you please with it within the limits of a criminal code which is sure to be interpreted by a proprietary-class judge in your [the capitalist's] favour" Adding to this process, Shaw suggests that capitalism horridly "produces a delusive promise of endless employment which binds the proletariat to . . . disastrous consequences" (Shaw, "Economic," 51–53). Shaw would later continue these arguments in relation to Ireland.

In 1890, Shaw lectured the Fabian Society on Ibsen "as a campaigning socialist and cultural critic in a series called 'Socialism in Contemporary Literature'" (Gahan, *Shaw Shadows*, 46). These lectures resulted in Shaw's *The Quintessence of Ibsenism* (1891), of which he described its writing process as "an eminent socialist critic . . . [making Ibsen's] plays the text for a free attack on the idealist section of the English social Democrats" (as quoted in Gahan, *Shaw Shadows*, 22). Shaw viewed Ibsen's plays as undermining the "ideals and idealism" of the conventionalized middle class that saw itself as liberal minded but maintained and profited from capitalism. The socialist in Shaw had discovered how he could use literature to teach—ultimately to further a socialist vision. He moved into playwriting, delivering *Widowers' Houses* (1892) in which he indicts the middle and upper classes that profited on the obscene slum houses where the working classes were condemned to live.[1] Shaw as a playwright in Britain who could be counted in the socialist camp was emerging.

As Shaw developed his voice, an Irish journalist named Frederick Ryan attended Shaw's Fabian lectures in London, read Shaw's Fabian essays, embraced Shaw's assessment of Ibsen, and then read Shaw's early plays and saw some in performance. By 1899, Ryan had returned to Dublin and delivered a number of lectures on Fabians and modern drama to the Irish Socialist Republican Party (ISRP), which numbered fifty members or less.[2] The ISRP was founded in 1896 by James Connolly, and it was with the ISRP that Shaw's impact among Irish socialists began—and it was in Ireland, Declan Kiberd maintains, that Shaw's influence would be great, "far, far greater than he ever seemed to realize" (*Irish Classics*, 345).[3]

William O'Brien, who became a constant figure in Irish socialism for most of the twentieth century, recalled that as a young man in the ISRP he attended Ryan's lecture on modern drama. O'Brien remembered that the occasion was his first encounter with Shaw (*Forth*, 15). In his lecture, "Word on the Democratic Drama," delivered in February 1899, Ryan read "extracts from the plays of Ibsen and Bernard Shaw" (Nevin, *Connolly*, 70). O'Brien came to admire Ryan, stating, "I would say he was one of the finest type I met in my long career in the socialist and labour movement" (*Forth*, 15).

Ryan's interest in the use of literature to teach a socialist philosophy, which he saw in Shaw, expanded. In 1901, while writing of literature's ideal role, Ryan stated: "if a people be degraded so that they prefer impurity, . . . they can be redeemed . . . only by education—an education which will lead them spontaneously to prefer the best" ("Censorship and Independence," 3). Ryan embraced the Shavian view that literature and theatre can educate. As Ryan elaborated on Fabians for the ISRP, his most important contribution to Irish socialism was in theatre, particularly Shavian-inspired socialist theatre.

Ryan, a socialist, radical journalist, and former civil servant in London, became involved in the Irish National Theatre Society (INTS), formed in Dublin in 1902 after the April premiere of William Butler Yeats's *Kathleen Ni Houlihan* (written with Lady Augusta Gregory) and George Russell's (Æ's) *Deirdre*. Ryan was the INTS's first secretary and his play *The Laying of the Foundations* premiered on the society's original bill, presented in October and November 1902. The play not only introduced socialist views to emerging Irish theatre, it also carried the influence of Shaw, mostly from *Widowers' Houses*.[4]

Like *Widowers' Houses*, *The Laying of the Foundations* takes aim at the classes that maintained and profited from the urban slums where the proletariat was forced to live in squalor. Ryan's play was performed as a two-scene work.[5] Set in an Irish city, *The Laying of the Foundations* follows Michael O'Loskin, the son of a wealthy publican, who, unbeknownst to Michael at the play's beginning, is also a part owner of a series of deplorable tenement houses. Michael's father, Mr. O'Loskin, and his business partner, a city alderman named Farrelly, arranged to have Michael appointed as the city architect. Essentially, the duties of the position involve the overseeing of construction projects and inspecting existing buildings. Michael learns that his father and Farrelly expect him to look the other way regarding their tenements and building projects. Michael relates that during an inspection he discovered that Farrelly's construction firm is building a new city asylum, to house the poor consigned to such, with a concrete foundation of only four feet while the approved plans call for an eight-foot foundation. Michael not only intends to halt construction, he also plans to condemn the tenement houses that Farrelly and his father own, which Michael proclaims are "unfit for beasts" (*Laying*, 27).

Michael's parents, "respectable" middle-class citizens, are disgusted with Michael's idealistic behavior as city architect. The father relates to his wife that Michael is going to condemn the tenements they own with Farrelly: "Michael says they're rotten. I suppose it's all those people that got typhoid in them" (*Laying*, 27). The parents believe Michael's fiancée, Eileen McFadden, is a bad influence since she recently has been speaking at pro-labor rallies and writing in a labor newspaper edited by a character named Nolan. Michael's mother interrogates McFadden: "Is it a fact what they say Eileen that you are mixing yourself up with those common tradesmen? . . . Is it true that you are making speeches down in some low quarter of the town?" (*Laying*, 28).

Michael meets with the socialist editor Nolan, who informs him that Farrelly's company is the worst employer in the city, yet it receives lucrative city contracts because Farrelly is an alderman. Nolan further asserts that the iron being used in the asylum is from another Farrelly-owned company, a foundry where workers' wages are being cut under threat of replacement with foreign labor. Farrelly is presented as an all-controlling capitalist, not unlike Dublin's William Martin Murphy, who would clash with Dublin labor in 1913. By play's end, Michael labels Farrelly "a swindler, a corrupter, a liar" (*Laying*, 33).

Ryan's play climaxes when Farrelly attempts to bribe Michael, who rejects the bribe, stating he will stand up to Farrelly's capitalizing corruption.

Michael proclaims, "I do not compromise. I do not sell myself," to which Farrelly replies, "Then let it be war." The play ends with Michael's words, "The city of the future demands it. It can be nothing else but war" (*Laying*, 37).

The similarity in focus between *The Laying of the Foundations* and *Widowers' Houses* is evident. Davis's description of Shaw's play as a "critique of slum landlords and capitalist complicity" also accurately describes Ryan's play (*George Bernard Shaw*, 37). Davis notes, "Shaw concentrates on the class that necessitates and perpetuates . . . [the] misery [of the poor]" (*George Bernard* Shaw, 38), and clearly, this too is Ryan's concentration. Both plays also present their respective capitalist masters as seeking schemes to profit out of demolitions of some of their slum tenements. In *Widowers' Houses*, Shaw's Sartorius becomes involved at play's end with a plan that hopes to capitalize on the City of London's intention of knocking down blocks of housing to make room for a wider roadway. In Ryan's play, Farrelly concocts a scheme for Michael to condemn some of his tenement housing and then arrange for the city to purchase the cleared land at an inflated price. These two schemes echo Shaw's "Economic" essay, which states that the capitalist works within a "criminal code" judged in the capitalist's favor by "a proprietary-class." Clearly, Sartorius and Farrelly maximize profits at the expense of the poor.

Davis indicates that Shaw's first play was "originally aimed at instructing voters for an upcoming municipal election, reflecting the Fabian's platform and gradualist reform tactics" (*George Bernard Shaw*, 40). Ryan intended the same with his play in relation to Dublin municipal elections for seats on the City Corporation, the assembly that governed the city and had been complicit in the slum housing crisis in 1902. The ISRP had been running candidates for such seats since 1899. The party had presented James Connolly for the corporation months before Ryan's play premiered, and would do so again two months after the premiere. Ryan also hoped his play would instruct Dubliners how to vote.

There are differences, of course, between *Widowers'* and *Foundations*, most notably in the idealistic young men of each. Shaw's Trench, forced to realize that his yearly income is based on Sartorius's slums, is unable to effectively respond and continues in the complicity of "screwing, and bullying, and threatening" the slum dwellers for profit (*Widowers,'* 40). Ryan's idealistic Michael O'Loskin, on the other hand, realizes the horror of his family's involvement with Farrelly and is propelled to act by the injustice of Farrelly's machinations. In this regard, Michael O'Loskin is similar to Vivie in Shaw's *Mrs Warren's Profession* (1893). Unlike Trench of *Widowers*,' Vivie realizes that she has profited from her mother's brothels, profiting, as Davis notes, from the labor of others—namely of the powerless (*George Bernard Shaw*, 47). Similar to Ryan's Michael, Vivie breaks from her mother's world and profits, and enters into work in an actuarial office. Vivie, as Davis writes, "becomes part of the competent administrative middle class Fabians needed for bringing about social change" (*George Bernard Shaw*, 47). This is exactly what Michael represents and becomes during the course of his play, namely, a member of the reformed "competent middle class" that will deliver "social change," and in this he is assisted by his enlightened, socialist-leaning middle-class fiancée Eileen McFadden. The lessons offered in *Widowers' Houses* and *The Laying of the Foundations*, along with *Mrs Warren's Profession*, were presented by reasonable argument in an audience-friendly manner in emerging theatres that Shaw and Ryan viewed as playing to middle-class audiences with the potential to be enlightened: the Independent Theatre Society of London and the INTS, respectively.[6] In this regard, the presence of Shaw is unmistakably part of *The Laying of the Foundations* and the INTS.

Given his Shavian-Fabian-like approach in *The Laying of the Foundations*, Ryan struck a positive response from his primarily nationalist audience during the play's premiere. The reviewer for the nationalist *United Irishman*, edited by Arthur Griffith, responded favorably. The reviewer was moved by Michael's stance against the city's corruption: "He has taken his line, he will compromise nothing. If he succeed in defeating his adversaries, well; if he fail, if he be defeated, disgraced, dismissed, well also; for we know he will go down fighting, with his colours flying and his soul unconquered" (Seumar, "Irish Drama," 1). The reviewer is struck by Michael's firm and just stance against the character Farrelly. Indeed, how can a reasonable person view Ryan's play and not see Farrelly as unsavory and not admire Michael for his stance? Hence, this is the essence of Ryan's potentially pleasing approach. The socialist message is presented in a manner that courts audience members to Ryan's position against those ruthlessly profiting from slum housing. Such an approach ideally should be able to work, eventually transforming society. However, when socialist-leaning issues were presented in a way that sought to antagonize certain Dublin audience members, those members, like the *United Irishman*'s Arthur Griffith, responded with vehement hostility. *The Laying of the Foundations* seemingly worked well with its premier audience as *Widowers' Houses* had worked with its own first audience.

Tracy Davis notes that *Widowers' Houses* "is a socialist play without a socialist in it" (*George Bernard Shaw*, 39). If Ryan also saw the lack of a socialist in *Widowers'* he was careful to insert one in *The Laying of the Foundations*. Rather than the capitalist's agent, Likecheese, in *Widowers'* being the one to fully illuminate Trench to Sartorius's rack-renting, Ryan's Michael is educated about Farrelly by the socialist editor Nolan. The inclusion of such a socialist in a Shavian-inspired play was intriguing for Irish socialism in 1902, especially in regard to the ISRP's leader, the working-class James Connolly. Like Nolan, Connolly edited a socialist paper, the ISRP's *Workers' Republic*.[7]

Connolly's fellow ISRP member William O'Brien recalled of Ryan's play: "[Nolan] described as the editor of a labor paper . . . [is] meant [to be] James Connolly. In the play this character in discussing something with another repeated Connolly's dictum about there being two Irelands. . . . Ireland, as distant from her people, is nothing to me; and the man who is babbling over love and enthusiasm for Ireland and can yet pass unmoved through our streets and witness all the wrongs and the suffering, the shame and degradation wrought upon the people of Ireland—yea, wrought by Irishmen upon Irish men and women and without burning to end it, is in my opinion, a fraud and a liar in his heart, no matter how he loved that combination of chemical elements he is pleased to call Ireland" (*Forth*, 17–18). This position reflects Connolly's socialism in 1902 Ireland, which, as Donal Nevin suggests, is echoed by the character Nolan (*Connolly*, 747): "Patriotic! Oh! Yes, he's [Farrelly] patriotic enough. . . . Patriotism to the capitalist, is for use only at election times. . . . I believe in freedom for all and the rule of Labour. . . . [The owners of capital] have no rights against the common-weal. . . . Not if it means the robbing of other men's property, the taking away of other men's freedom. . . . There are two classes of men in every nation—the workers . . . and the drones, the landlords, capitalists, governors and loafers who take without rendering service. . . . The drones have no rights against the rest. Those who desire to live without working can have no claim to consideration from those who work and often only exist" (*Laying*, 31–32). Ryan drew on both Shaw and Connolly in his one play.

Connolly echoed Ryan's play in his 1903 address to the Wood Quay Ward electors in the *Workers' Republic*, recalling his previous year's defeat. In this address, Connolly reiterates Ryan's portrait of corrupt politics and its effect on the working class: "Let us take lesson by the municipal election of last year. Let us remember how the drink sellers of the Wood Quay Ward combined with the slum owners and the house jobbers; let us remember how Alderman Davin, Councilor McCall and all their fellow publicans issued free drinks to whoever would accept. . . . Let us remember the threats and the bribery, how Mr. Byrne of Wood Quay told the surrounding tenants that if "Mr. Connolly was elected their rents would be raised." . . . You will understand that there can never be . . . clean, healthy or honest politics in the City of Dublin, until the power of the drink sellers is absolutely broken—they are positively the meanest and most degraded section that ever attempted to rule a city" (quoted in Daly, 218). In Ryan's play, Michael O'Loskin's father is a publican allied to Alderman Farrelly, as the two attempt to control Michael in their efforts to profit at the expense of the poor. Ryan was most likely hoping to influence the 1903 Wood Quay Ward election, where Connolly ran as the ISRP's candidate.

Ryan's portrayal of Connolly as the socialist Nolan blended the universal qualities of the socialistic leanings of *Widower's Houses* with the specific socialism of Connolly within Dublin. The Nolan representation of Connolly also must have had a dramatic effect on Connolly and his colleagues within the ISRP. The small party was in great financial difficulty in 1902, when Ryan's play premiered. At that time, Connolly was in America endeavoring to raise funds, through subscription sales for the *Workers' Republic*, and consequently did not see Ryan's premiere. William O'Brien did attend, adding, "a number of us in the Socialist party [ISRP] attended and the play was quite successful" (*Forth*, 14). However, some attending ISRP members may have resented the portrayal of Connolly. It was at this time that Connolly became increasingly aware that his fellow party officers resented his leadership position, which he partly interpreted as having to do with their resentment that he was in the United States. He wrote to a party officer from America, "You people think no doubt that I have quite a picnic on but I have not" (as quoted in Nevin, *Connolly*, 202). Connolly's American tour, with addresses to socialist organizations in cities from New York to San Francisco, was grueling. In October 1902, Connolly angrily wrote to his ISRP colleagues: "Here I am . . . canvassing hard for subscriptions and in order to get them telling everybody that the [*Workers' Republic*] . . . will appear more regularly in future . . . , and you people at home have not the common manliness to try and stand my word by getting out the paper as promised. You may think it all a joke, but I think that you all ought to be damned well ashamed of yourselves. Is it so hard a job for you to get together enough matter to fill a paper once a month—such a terrible strain on your nerves! I am ashamed, heartily ashamed of the whole gang of you" (*Between Comrades*, 192).

Connolly did not know, when he wrote the above, that Murtagh Lyng, the acting editor in Connolly's absence, died on 26 October (Lynch, *Radical*, 125). But the paper remained dormant well after October, as there was no effort to replace Lyng, despite the American subscriptions Connolly was selling. Rather than his fellow ISRP officers using the money Connolly sent from America for the paper, they used it toward paying the large debt they had accumulated with the licensed bar in the ISRP's rooms (Nevin, *Connolly*, 209). Angered by this, Connolly made a motion in February 1903 on his return to Dublin to immediately settle the paper's outstanding printing bill. The motion was defeated, and Connolly resigned his leadership position (Nevin, *Connolly*, 209).

One of Connolly's last acts before his resignation was to arrange for a performance on 30 March of Ryan's play, by the INTS, as a fund-raiser for the ISRP. O'Brien, who attended this revival with Connolly, recorded that Connolly was "impressed" with the play and, presumably, with the Nolan character (Morrissey, *O'Brien*, 17). Still, Connolly's ISRP resignation held and, as a consequence, the party collapsed by summer of 1903.

As the ISRP ended, Connolly became a socialist agitator without an organization. Ryan's portrayal of Nolan seemed to be suspended in midair with the ISRP's collapse. The excessively poor proletariat Connolly left Ireland. He emigrated to America in what he thought would be a permanent condition for himself and family. Nevertheless, *The Laying of the Foundations* had introduced a socialist presence in Irish theatre, through Ryan's admiration for Shaw and Connolly—two socialists differing in class and strategy. But a socialistic presence would be carried further in Irish theatre by J. M. Synge, who would set the stage for Shaw's first direct contribution to Irish theatre, and to what would be perceived as Irish socialism.

Synge and an Irish Nora

Shaw's shadow in *The Laying of the Foundations* is difficult to dispute. However, Shaw's influence in 1902 was indirect. In addition, there is little evidence to suggest that Shaw knew Ryan's play, and Shaw, who was in Italy at the time, did not see the INTS when it made its first appearance in London on 2 May 1903, with Ryan's play among those performed.[8] But Shaw was not oblivious to the INTS, as indicated by his offering three plays in January 1903, including *Widowers' Houses* (Yeats, *Yeats Letters*, III, 302).[9] Perhaps the offer of *Widowers'* was in response to *Foundations*, or maybe Shaw remembered his former rent collecting from Dublin tenement dwellers before his emigration. While Yeats claimed in a December 1902 letter to Lady Gregory that Shaw mentioned to him that he would write an Irish play for the new Dublin theatre, Shaw would not do so for another two years (*Yeats Letters*, III, 268). Outside of conversations with Yeats, it seems Shaw had limited interest in Dublin theatre until he wrote *John Bull's Other Island*. Yet to fully determine and appreciate Shaw's major Irish play and its role in Irish socialism, we must briefly examine the left-leaning Synge and the play he introduced to the INTS which largely prompted Shaw's direct involvement in 1904.

One cannot suggest that Synge took up a socialistic slant in his writing due to *The Laying of the Foundations* or due to influence from Shaw. Synge formulated his own politics via a different route, although it was a route not without similarities to Shaw's. Davis notes that "ownership was the topic that turned . . . [Shaw] into a socialist writer" (*George Bernard Shaw*, 37). The same can be said for Synge. While Shaw's socialist focus grew from his knowledge of socialist theory, accented by urban experiences and knowledge, Synge also studied Marx and had an early awareness of injustices enacted on the urban proletariat. Synge recalled children of poverty playing outside Dublin's St. Patrick's Cathedral while the comfortable class inside worshipped the New Testament with no concern for the poor (McCormack, *Fool*, 143, 55). But the angle of Synge's focus differed from Shaw's.

Anglo-Irish and Protestant like Shaw, although from a family with more means than Shaw's, Synge developed into what Bruce Arnold describes as "that unusual Irish political creature, an Anglo-Irish Ascendancy radical, with views which wavered between socialism and communism" (*Jack*, 136). Similarly, Ben Levitas argues that Synge was heavily on the "left" with his plays and writing (*Theatre*, 105).[10] But unlike Shaw, Synge would become a direct part of the new Irish theatre when his play *In the Shadow of the Glen* premiered in October 1903. As such, Synge would become focused on the re-imaging of Ireland, and his socialistically leaning views would be in service to this focus. In 1898, Synge noted, "I had relinquished the Kingdom of God . . . to take a real interest in the kingdom of Ireland" ("Autobiography," 13). Synge was not an internationalist.

The emergence of Synge's socialistic leanings, as with his development as a writer, was prompted by his four visits to the Aran Islands from 1898 to 1901. These visits led Synge to write six plays and *The Aran Islands*. Synge's direct experiences in the rural west were intensely different from Shaw's primarily urban existence by 1900. While at Aran, Synge was much taken with the mixture of Gaelic traditions and outside influences, like Christianity and Gaelic, with native pagan traditions seemingly having the upper hand. The islands, especially the less-developed Inishmaan Island, allowed Synge an escape from conventionalized, capitalistic middle-class society and the conservative morality which that class was infecting all classes with throughout Ireland's mainland. As with Shaw, Synge disliked this class, a feeling that grew with each of his plays. On Inishmaan, Synge became intensely aware of the way island peasants worked—as opposed to most of Ireland. As various people worked in thatching a cottage roof, Synge noted, "the man whose house is being covered is host instead of an employer, he lays himself out to please the men who work with him" (*Aran*, 75–77). Synge went on: "It is likely that much of the intelligence and charm of these people is due to the absence of any division of labour, and to the correspondingly wide development of each individual, whose varied knowledge and skill necessitates a considerable activity of mind" (*Aran*, 77).

On Inishmaan, Synge found workers not destroyed, or alienated, by their work. Due to the remoteness of the islands, no real industry existed, and even landlord agents were absent, as well as any who could be called "bosses" of labor.[11] The workers Synge observed were not "valueless" in their work and lives, unlike the urban proletariat Shaw theorized about. The Inishmaan islanders Synge came to know were not ground into a dehumanized existence by a modern capitalist system, nor did they bear the stifling morals of a conservative capitalist middle class. However, the cost for the island's inhabitants was high, as fishing offered much danger and could only feed so many; hence, death and emigration were significant, as were the realities imposed on islanders from the mainland's economy. Nevertheless, Synge was so taken with the life he witnessed, a life that seemed to owe more to the past than to the present, that he used it as the basis for his women protagonists, while the greed he encountered in other sections of rural Ireland led to his less admirable portraits. On Inishmaan's pier, Synge observed a young woman much different from those in domestic slavery in most of Ireland: "I noticed one extraordinary girl in the throng who seemed to exert authority on all who came near her" (*Aran*, 19). As if from past Ireland, she became a model for Synge's women protagonists, using Ireland's past to create a more liberal, new Ireland.

Synge's first performed play, *In the Shadow of the Glen*, is crucial to Shaw's participation in Irish socialism. Like Shaw, Synge also found inspiration in Ibsen for exposing the conventionalized middle class, even though Synge dismissed Ibsen in his preface to *The Playboy of the Western World* in 1907, in which he wrote that Ibsen deals "with the reality of life in joyless and pallid words" ("Preface," 96). Synge's 1907 dismissal of Ibsen was a dismissal of the popular problem plays that sprang up in Ibsen's wake, like Arthur Pinero's *The Second Mrs. Tanqueray* of the London stage. Ibsen's *A Doll's House* pointed toward a modern and radical woman for Europe, as its protagonist Nora, by play's end, seeks to be no man's property. *In the Shadow of the Glen*'s Nora delivered a radical image of a new woman for Ireland. As women's suffrage and equality was part of Shaw's socialism, it was part of Synge's as well.

After witnessing a rehearsal for *In the Shadow of the Glen*'s premiere, the portrait painter John B. Yeats, father of W. B. Yeats, remarked that the play began Ireland's "work of self-examination and self accusation" ("Ireland Out of the Dock," 2). Indeed, Synge was embarking with *Shadow* into the process of forcing Ireland to do exactly that. Arguably, this was similar to what Shaw was perceived to do with his play *John Bull's Other Island*. However, Synge's approach in *Shadow*, and his following plays, was much different from the audience-friendly approach of Shaw and Ryan. Davis points out that in 1897, "Shaw warned against regarding all socialists as united in philosophy as well as tactics" (*George Bernard Shaw*, 135). As a Fabian, Shaw was content to pursue the gradualist tactic, which well suited his sense of international social reform. Synge, on the other hand, being concerned with Ireland nationally, focused on a smaller "canvas" than Shaw, and practiced a tactic that sought immediate results. Presumably due to his direct experiences with many rural Irish peasants, Synge had no patience for gradualism. Instead, his work can be seen as aggressively assaulting those audience members complicit in the conditions of the Irish proletariat. That Synge was antagonistic in his plays to the majority of his original audiences consisting of conservative, conventional middle-class individuals goes a long way in explaining the volatile receptions most of Synge's plays received during their premier runs in Dublin. This contrast in approaches between Shaw in particular and Synge was epitomized by audience reactions in 1907, when Synge's *The Playboy of the Western World* premiered and Shaw's *John Bull's Other Island* first played Dublin. Of the two searing plays, one was met with audience disruptions, the other warmly applauded. This contrast began with *In the Shadow of the Glen*, to which Shaw responded.

In the Shadow of the Glen's one-act plot follows its protagonist Nora, a young woman who believes her much older husband, Dan Burke, has died. A wandering stranger, the Tramp, seeks shelter in the Burkes' small isolated cottage in Ireland's Wicklow Mountains. Nora steps out to bring in a neighboring herd, and during her absence Dan reveals to the Tramp he is not dead. Dan re-assumes his pretense when Nora returns with Michael Dara. As Michael counts the money Nora has, believing it is now hers given Dan's supposed death, Nora relates her lonely existence as Dan's wife. Dan, believing he is going to catch Nora accepting Michael as her new husband, reveals himself alive only after Nora rejects Michael's plans to marry her—the opposite of what Dan was expecting. Still, Dan orders Nora to leave his house. After the Tramp reveals to Nora the wonders of living in the open air, she leaves her husband, walking out with the Tramp. The play closes with Dan and Michael sharing a drink.

While Synge's play questions prolonging the loveless marriage, as in the case of the young Nora and her old husband Dan, it attacks the subjugation of women within horrific marriages in Ireland. In 1903, Ireland, legally and morally, allowed no recourse for such trapped women who were only their husband's drudges. Nora describes her constant routine of "boiling food for himself and food for the brood sow, and baking a cake when the night falls" (*Shadow*, 41). To compound Nora's trapped position, Dan works to keep her isolated from others and treats her in an alienating fashion devoid of emotional attachment. Early in the play, Nora remarks that Dan "was an old man, and an odd man. . . . Maybe cold would be no sign of death with the like of him, for he was always cold, every day since I knew him . . . and every night" (*Shadow*, 35). Dan treats Nora as less than an abused employee. In an attempt to relieve her isolation, Nora tries to talk with occasional passing farmers and strangers, a behavior Dan sets himself to end with his scheme of appearing dead.

To emphasize Dan's attempts to master Nora as he enforces her isolation and entrapment, Synge portrays Dan's physically and psychologically abusive behavior through his dialogue with the Tramp: "bring me a black stick you'll see in the west corner by the wall. . . . it's a long time I'm keeping that stick, for I've a bad wife in the house." The Tramp interestingly responds to the order by asking, "Is it herself, master of the house, and she a grand woman to talk?" (*Shadow*, 39). The implication is that Dan does not want his wife to talk, preferring her to remain silent. It appears that talking, which the Tramp appreciates in Nora, revealed by his vexation in asking the above, represents Nora's freedom to think. Silencing Nora maintains her subservient position.

When Dan is believed dead, Michael attempts to continue Nora's subjugation. Once Michael is in the cottage, Nora speaks of her isolation as Dan's wife, as if now, with Dan's supposed death, she is free to contemplate her existence—in essence, to begin a process of increasing her human worth. Nora admits she married the older Dan because he had a farm and livestock, but now realizes her grave folly: "I do be thinking in the long nights it was a big fool I was that time, Michael Dara, for what good is a bit of farm with cows on it and sheep on the back hills, when you do be sitting looking out from a door the like of that door" (*Shadow*, 40). As Nora speaks of what she believes was her former enslavement, Michael makes his move. Rather than listening to Nora, he has been greedily counting Dan's money, which he believes is now Nora's. Once he completes his counting, Michael exploitatively announces his plan to marry Nora, without asking her, and his moving into the cottage, with its land and livestock (*Shadow*, 41). In this, Synge portrays the "crass bourgeois moralism" that had made its way into rural Ireland, as Michael desires "to marry for money rather than love" (Kiberd, *Inventing Ireland*, 485). Michael wants to do that which Nora had done when she married Dan but now knows it to have been a horrific mistake. To Michael's marriage plans, Nora responds: "Why would I marry you, Michael Dara?" (*Shadow*, 41). Nora's rejection proclaims a new self that desires her human value and is a first step toward casting off the conventional middle-class values infecting the Irish peasant class by 1903. Synge's play was expanding a leftist take on Irish life into a pro-woman's direction that mirrored and anticipated the growing position of socialists who grafted gender equality into their agenda for social justice. Such a development would attract Shaw's attention.

In response to Nora's rejection of Michael, which Dan does not anticipate, Dan reveals himself alive and promptly orders Nora to leave his cottage in an attempt to stifle Nora. Dan's attempt fails, as she decides to go out with the Tramp, saying "you've a fine bit of talk, stranger, and it's with yourself I'll go" (*Shadow*, 43).

If Synge had not presented Nora as walking out of Dan's marriage, *In the Shadow of the Glen* would have been considerably less antagonistic. It might have only exposed its audience to a battered, entrapped woman valued only as her husband's drudge, which might have led an audience to see the need to view women more sympathetically as human beings, not a man's property, but nothing more than that. Instead, Synge's play, as written and premiered, prompted strong audience objections.

The main attacks against *In the Shadow of the Glen* were led by Arthur Griffith and his nationalist weekly the *United Irishman*, the same paper that praised *The Laying of the Foundations* the year before. The conservative Catholic Griffith was unable to see Nora's entrapped position. All he could see was her act of leaving her husband. His paper's review of the play, which he wrote himself, stated: "[T]his play of his [Synge's] shows him to be as utterly a stranger to Irish character as any Englishman who has yet dissected us for the enlightenment of his countrymen. . . . Some men and women in Ireland marry lacking love, and live mostly in a dull level of amity. Sometimes they do not—Sometimes the woman lives in bitterness—Sometimes she dies of a broken heart—but she does not go away with the Tramp. . . . It is not by staging a lie we can serve Ireland" ("All Ireland" [17 October 1903], 1). Since the objection was to the fact that Nora leaves her husband, despite Dan's vocal banishment, Griffith and his fellow detractors expected Nora to plead, or beg her husband to remain regardless of Dan's stick. Such an expectation is an expectation that Nora's only course is to beg and take the beating. This enslaved existence for Nora is what Dan desires, since spousal abuse is about power and control.[12] Therefore, Nora's act of leaving her husband was radically and directly confrontational to her husband and, more importantly, to the conservative audience members, as Nora's exit ends her position as her husband's domestic slave. The conservative middle-class audience craved respectability, and a woman leaving her husband, no matter what her circumstances, violated this sense of moral respectability, even if such morals devalued and imprisoned women. Of course, by being antagonistic, Synge exposes his play's moral detractors as wanting Nora to remain in an abusive marriage—that was the real immorality. It was an immorality that echoed Connolly's above-quoted anger at the degradation "wrought by Irishmen upon Irish men and women."

One might see *In the Shadow of the Glen* as more of a gender play than one with socialistic leanings. However, many male socialists at this time, such as Shaw and Connolly, in and out of Ireland were committed to equality for women as a socialistic issue. This commitment usually manifested itself in support for women's suffrage, a movement that had been gaining momentum since Ibsen's *A Doll's House*, a play in which another Nora leaves her husband by play's end. As early as 1892, Shaw strongly argued for women's suffrage in a London speech (Gibbs, *Bernard Shaw*, 293). In the theatre, the women's question was dramatically expressed through the calls for accessible marital separation or divorce. This was particularly apparent in Ireland. Following Synge's *Shadow*, an Abbey Theatre rival, Cluithcheoiri na hEireann, staged, in 1911, a production of Aleksandr Ostrovsky's 1859 Russian play *The Storm*, which also called for a woman's right to easily escape an imprisoning marriage that devalues the wife. Five years after Synge's *Shadow*, Shaw wrote his own women's play calling for accessible divorces for women, *Getting Married*.

Getting Married, in publication form, was brought into the debate on divorce in Ireland three months after the above production of *The Storm*. In the May 1911 issue of the high-minded *Irish Review*, founded in March 1911 by Thomas MacDonagh, Padraic Colum, and Mary Maguire as "A Monthly Magazine of Irish Literature, Art and Science," the socialistic journalist Francis Sheehy-Skeffington reviewed the publication of Shaw's latest book, which included, with prefaces, *The Doctor's Dilemma*, *Getting Married*, and *The Shewing-up of Blanco Posnet*. Of particular interest to Sheehy-Skeffington is Shaw's preface to *Getting Married*, "On Marriage." While not mentioning Synge's *Shadow*, Sheehy-Skeffington sees Shaw's preface as addressing the issue of divorce for loveless marriages: Shaw "shows how by making divorces as cheap, as easy, and as private as marriage, one can eliminate from the present social system some of its worst features" ("Reviews," 154). Sheehy-Skeffington notes that all Irish people who wish to redress the marriage law that "places a married woman's person absolutely at the disposal of her husband . . . must read Shaw as their first text-book" ("Reviews," 154–155). Of course, Shaw's arguments in favor of divorce in *Getting Married*, and its preface, address an audience, which Sheehy-Skeffington expanded to include an Irish audience with his review, in a manner that was perhaps more agreeable to most than Synge's play of eight years earlier.

The antagonizing aspect of Synge's play, that a woman boldly leaves her abusive husband, was also why others praised the play. John B. Yeats wrote: "Mr. Synge has attacked our Irish institution, the loveless marriage," adding that the play's "lesson enforced [the idea] that rent contracts are not the only ones that stand in need of revision" ("Out of the Dock," 2).[13] J. B. Yeats saw the hypocrisy of conservative middle-class nationalists who could support reforms of landlord tenant contracts to benefit middling-class farmers but not the right for an Irish woman to escape her demeaning, dehumanizing, devaluating enslavement. In response to Griffith's initial attacks on *Shadow*, and attacks by others, J. B. Yeats further defended the play: "The outcry against Mr. Synge's play seems to me largely dishonest; the objection not being that it misrepresents Irishwomen, but that it is a very effective attack on loveless marriages—this most miserable institution. . . . My complaint . . . is that it does not make it quite clear that the wife will not return to the house in which she should never have entered" ("Correspondence," 7). But those who praised the play in 1903 were in the minority.

While Shaw's *Getting Married* addressed illiberal divorce laws (and conservative social attitudes) in Britain, the situation was much different in Ireland. Although the Divorce Act of 1857 legalized divorce in England, making it somewhat less difficult, the act did not make any divorce, difficult or otherwise, legal in Ireland. Terence Brown suggests that this was "an attempt [by the British government] to placate Catholic [conventionalized] opinion [in Ireland]" ("Notes," 267). While Synge may not have been directly attacking the divorce law in Ireland, he was attacking the restrictive conservatism that made accessible marital separation impossible and the continual enslavement of women possible. Knowing that he was being antagonistic toward his conservative audience by presenting an Irish wife leaving her husband, Synge rooted *Shadow* in pagan Irish traditions that surprisingly were perceived as having provided some rights to unsatisfied wives. Utilizing Irish traditions was natural for Synge, given that much of the culture he observed in remote sections of rural Ireland, as in Aran, was based in pagan native traditions. Of course, by tying his play to such traditions, Synge was bracing his play to withstand attacks from conservatives who would charge that *Shadow* was un-Irish. In fact, the very topic of accessible marriage separation was present in ancient Gaelic Ireland and was, presumably, natively Irish.

Gaelic law in Ireland had allowed for the legal dissolution of marriage. S. J. Connolly and Ni Chonaill explain that the grounds for divorce included "domestic violence, infertility/sterility, or failure of maintenance" ("Divorce," 151).[14] Such a liberal divorce law recognized a woman's human value, or at least did not overtly devalue women. In the context of this assessment of native Irish tradition, Synge's Nora is within her traditional rights to leave her husband. Ending her marriage and her subjugation politically rebuked foreign law and influence, in addition to affirming women's rights. Certainly, the distaste of foreign influence was paramount with Synge, epitomized by the socialistic working conditions of the island peasants he observed in Aran.

The Irishness of *In the Shadow of the Glen* was furthered by Synge by presenting the Tramp as being in the tradition of native itinerant, possessionless bards, as in the late eighteenth- and early nineteenth-century poet Antoine Raftery (1778–1835). Raftery represented a native ideal for Synge, being connected to Ireland's nature and landscape. The Tramp's speech, when outlining an option for Nora near play's end, echoes the native poetic traditions of Raftery's verse in a speech that captures the Irish pagan ideal of nature: "[Y]ou'll be hearing the herons crying out over the black lakes and you'll be hearing the grouse and owls with them, and the larks and the big thrushes when the days are warm" (*Shadow*, 43). Raftery's "Killeaden" poem celebrates cuckoos and thrushes singing among blackbirds, goldfinches, and woodcocks ("Killeaden," 725).[15]

In this Irish vein, when Synge's Nora is trying to decide what to do after Dan has ordered her out and she does not plead to stay, the Tramp suggests that she could live with Michael. Nora responds, "What would he do with me now?" The Tramp answers, "Give you half of a dry bed, and good food in your mouth" (*Shadow*, 43). The Tramp is free of the conservative, conventional middle-class moral values of the audience members who attacked the play in that half of a bed obviously implies a marriage-like relationship, even though Nora would still be married to Dan in the eyes of English law and the Catholic Church. Since Michael does not respond to the Tramp's progressive but natural suggestion, Michael is revealed as adhering to the stifling morality. The unconventional and socially free

Tramp sees Nora's value as a person and does not try to devalue her, but instead invites her to a world of nature free of divisions of labor and enslaving values.

Being without economic wealth and possessions, Synge's Tramp was far from an ideal person for the play's original conventional middle-class audience. This was a further confrontation from Synge's play that exposed the first audience's class snobbery, which is noted in Griffith's above-quoted attack on the play: "she does not go away with the Tramp." Not only does Synge's Nora leave her husband, she leaves with a person the conservative audience saw as possessionless and poor—despite the fact that Synge depicts the Tramp as being free in Ireland's nature and helps Nora toward such freedom and, therefore, toward her empowering new self.[16]

Nora's empowering self-value, realized when she leaves her husband with the Tramp, led Synge's contemporary Oliver St. John Gogarty to consider Nora in 1903 as "capable, quick, intelligent" ("A Word," 6). Nonetheless, Dan appears triumphant at play's end, as Nora departs with only the clothes she wears, indicating that a wife legally owns nothing. But her parting words scathingly confront his smugness: "You think it's a grand thing you're after doing with your letting on to be dead, but what is it at all? What way would a woman live in a lonesome place the like of this place . . . ?" (*Shadow*, 43). This is the play's question: how could a thinking, passionate woman, who does not beg to stay but reclaims her human worth, remain in such a place? The victory is Nora's in her escape.

In *In the Shadow of the Glen*, Synge advocated a social change for Ireland that confronted the conservative, middle-class Dubliners who impeded liberalizing social reform. Nora's act of leaving her husband decidedly casts off the values of such Dubliners and undermines their stranglehold on Ireland. While framing his social agenda within native pagan traditions, as then perceived, Synge further exposed his detractors as empty or hypocritical nationalists, ultimately pseudo-nationalists, with little sense of their country's native traditions. Synge's battle lines had been drawn by his hostile approach. George Roberts, who would become an important editor of Irish works (including Synge's in 1907 and a Shaw work in 1918) and had played Dan in *Shadow*'s premiere, recalled that following the play's first performance Synge nervously faced the audience when the author was called for, but "when he heard the hisses a glimpse of defiant pleasure came over his face. I think the hisses pleased him much more than the applause" ("J. M. Synge," 120). Synge relished his antagonistic and, perhaps, impatient and hostile approach. Indeed, that approach, which presented a strong Irish woman offensive to many of the play's original audience, eventually reached Shaw, who would, in turn, offer not only a different Nora, but also his first direct effort to be viewed as socialistic on behalf of Ireland.[17]

John Bull's Takes Shape

Shaw's process toward writing *John Bull's Other Island* began not when he and Yeats first discussed his writing an Irish play in 1899, but when the INTS made its second visit to London. On 26 March 1904 the INTS, as it did the previous year, performed for one day, with matinee and evening performances. The brief engagement attracted much attention from London critics and some of the Irish living in London. Critics like Max Beerbohm, who had replaced Shaw as critic for the *Saturday Review*, and William Archer generally wrote favorably on the engagements. However, Archer did strike one condescending note in his review: "As yet the Irish theatre has given us only dramatic sketches—no thought-out pictures with composition and depth in it" (as quoted in Saddlemyer, "Notes," 83). Synge, whose *In the Shadow of the Glen* and *Riders to the Sea* were performed during the matinee, was put off by "Archer's . . . snub at our short one-act plays" (*Synge Letters*, I, 81). Synge noted in a letter to Frank Fay, "I believe . . . that our real critics must come from Dublin. It is only where an art is native, I think, that all its distinctions all its slight gradations, are fully understood" (*Synge Letters*, I, 81). However, Synge knew Archer was correct; if the INTS was to make its mark it would have to produce full-length plays. Synge was already writing *The Well of Saints*, which would become the INTS's first full-length play. Shaw also knew that Archer's view was accurate, and being a Dubliner he understood the Irish plays performed.

The March 1904 London appearance by the INTS was largely orchestrated by Yeats. The performances' public purpose was to expand the critical response to the emerging theatre, while its private purpose was to solidify the financial backing of Annie Horniman toward securing and renovating a permanent Dublin theatre. Horniman had backed Florence Farr's Avenue Theatre project in 1894, which premiered Shaw's *Arms and the Man* and Yeats's *Land of Heart's Desire*. As early as October 1903, Yeats had been courting Horniman as a steady sponsor for the INTS. In little more than a week after the Dublin theatre's London performances, Yeats officially announced to company actors on 8 April 1904 that Horniman was going to back their theatre and provide a building. Shaw's interest in the INTS may have been piqued by the knowledge that the society was to get its own theatre, and, perhaps by Shaw's desire to see for himself what the Dublin theatre was producing. Shaw attended the 26 March London INTS performances (Holroyd, *Bernard Shaw*, 82; J. Kelly, "Notes," 563), the result of which was *John Bull's Other Island*.

There is evidence to suggest that within weeks, or even days, of seeing these London performances, Shaw began contemplating a full-length Irish play for the INTS. He was also intending for his Irish play to open the theatre that Horniman was buying and renovating into the Abbey Theatre for the Yeats-led INTS. In a 2 April 1904 letter to John Quinn, Yeats partially described the success of the London performances by revealing that Shaw had begun a play for the INTS (*Yeats Letters*, III, 563). Nearly two weeks later, Yeats added to Quinn that they, the INTS, were thinking of opening their fall season with Shaw's new play *(Yeats Letters,* III, 580).[18] The expectation, in April was that the Abbey Theatre would be ready to open in the autumn rather than December. It is remarkable that the egotistical Yeats was entertaining, or even pretending to entertain, the idea of opening the Abbey Theatre with a play other than his own *On Baile's Strand*, which he was readying for the purpose.[19] But Yeats's admission here suggests that Shaw and he had discussed the possibility, and Yeats may have assumed that Shaw's play would be one act. A month later, Yeats mentioned in an 18 May letter to George Roberts, who was then still a company actor, that, after talking to Shaw, he was sure the new play would be humorous, but added that he (Yeats) did not know whether the play's subject would allow it to be performed (*Yeats Letters*, III, 600). Yeats was already hedging his way toward not opening the Abbey with the play Shaw had not yet even started in May 1904. Shaw began writing it in June, finishing a draft he first titled *Britannia Rule* by the end of the summer.

The title of Shaw's major Irish play, *John Bull's Other Island*, reflects Shaw's most discussed effort in the play, the undermining of what he perceived as the growing feverish nationalism then in Ireland. This undermining was still on Shaw's mind when he wrote his preface for the play in 1906, "Preface for Politicians" (Holroyd, 387). In the preface, Shaw asked, "What Is an Irishman?" He answered with himself as example. As a Protestant Irishman, he defines himself as a "genuine typical Irishman of the Danish, Norman, Cromwellian, and (of course) Scotch invasions" ("Preface," 474). Despite the veil of Shaw's Anglo-Irish background, he was not far from the reality of most Irish people at the time, who, at the very least, had backgrounds composed of numerous elements from the many invasions and immigrations into historical Ireland, a point that for Shaw undermined much of the rhetoric of nationalism in 1904–07 Dublin that tied its beliefs of independence to a sense of a pure Irish identity and race. In *John Bull's*, the Irish Larry Doyle responds to hearing about Ireland's Celtic race: "That sort of rot does more harm . . . why Ireland was peopled just as England was; and its breed was crossed by just the same invaders" (*John Bull's*, 80). Of course, given this primary direction in "Preface for Politicians," much of the critical discourse on the play has focused on the play's discussion of national identities, Irish and British.

Shaw's consideration of national identities in the play, mixed up in a mock trinity composed of the British civil engineer Tom Broadbent, Broadbent's Irish-born London partner Larry Doyle, and the contemplative defrocked Irish priest Peter Keegan, is part of the play's effort to unravel the Irish nationalism that was, in Shaw's belief, feverish in 1904. In his preface, Shaw maintained that the nationalist rouser was a windbag that required no "knowledge, character, conscience, diligence in public affairs, nor any virtue, private or communal" ("Preface," 486). Yet Shaw clearly knew that the INTS in 1904 was playing within various forms of Irish nationalism. In fact, the society owed its existence to Yeats's nationalist *Kathleen Ni Houlihan*. In Act I of *John Bull's*, Larry Doyle complains that an Irishman in Ireland "can't be intelligently political; . . . If you want to interest him in Ireland you've got to call the unfortunate island Kathleen ni Hoolihan [*sic*] and pretend she's a little old woman" (*John Bull's*, 81). This is exactly what *Kathleen Ni Houlihan* does, portraying Ireland as an old woman calling young men to fight and die for her. The decisive jab at Yeats was searing.

Obviously, Shaw's *Kathleen Ni Houlihan* allusion was meant to ridicule Yeats's play and the mystical-romantic nationalism Yeats was fostering in 1904. This was a more serious jab at the time than it appears now. Being the credited author of *Kathleen Ni Houlihan* was an integral part of Yeats's persona or identity that he assumed among nationalists in Dublin. When he defended Synge's *The Playboy of the Western World* in 1907, Yeats silenced the nationalist detractors by saying, "The author of *Cathleen Ni Houlihan* addresses you" (as quoted in Ellman, 179).[20] Of course, Yeats's Anglo-Irish, Protestant background was similar to Shaw's, but he sought to make himself part of the ideal of an Irish race, whatever that might be. But potentially undermining Yeats in Dublin was going to work against *John Bull's* opening the Abbey—and Shaw undoubtedly knew this. As Shaw was preparing to submit *John Bull's* to Yeats in early September 1904, he simultaneously arranged for a London premiere with the newly formed Granville-Barker and Vedrenne management of the Royal Court Theatre. As an effort to explain why his play did not open the Abbey, Shaw stated in his preface, "my play is a very uncompromising presentment of the real old Ireland," inferring not only that the INTS was presenting an unreal Ireland but that *John Bull's* was rejected by Yeats and company because Shaw's portrayal of Ireland was uncompromisingly real ("Preface," 473). As *John Bull's Other Ireland* undermined and negated the Dublin middle-class focus on Irish nationalism in 1904, it also, and more meaningfully, countered *In the Shadow of the Glen*'s socialistic leaning by considering international modern capitalism in an Irish setting. In essence, Shaw was to differ with Synge not on strict socialism, but on their approaches to socialism as Synge's was nationally based and Shaw's was more international, and, as such, Synge's immediacy of confrontation was not for Shaw.

Despite Shaw's and Synge's respective approaches to socialistic leanings, *John Bull's Other Island* was not fully opposed to the ideology found in *In the Shadow of the Glen*, yet endeavored to offer, in response, an "uncompromising" and more truthful (in Shaw's opinion) view of Ireland. The opening scene of Shaw's Act II, depicting Peter Keegan conversing with a grasshopper, directly mocks Synge's effort to use the Irish native literary and cultural traditions of embracing nature. By using such traditions in *Shadow* to support Nora's leaving her husband, Synge challenged the Catholic Church's view on divorce and marital separation. The Church was an integral part of the respectability obsessively craved by Dublin's conservative, middle-class, capitalistic nationalists. But for Shaw, who would also critically portray the Church in Ireland, not only was the use of such native traditions antagonizing in Synge's hands, they were distracting in regard to a modern view of Ireland. Shaw preferred to leave ancient Ireland in the form of an abandoned round tower, produced originally by the early Catholic Church, which is enjoyed by a marginalized madman and is romanticized by an Englishman who will reduce and negate it into a future tourist attraction.²¹ Shaw most likely thought *In the Shadow of the Glen*'s positively presented, non-materialist, nature-loving Tramp was problematic for a truly modern portrait of Ireland, especially since Synge's Nora leaves her husband to live in nature in the Tramp's company—a character type that was clearly the antipathy of the middle class Shaw's play might teach and reform. We know that Synge recognized the grasshopper jab at his expense from a letter Yeats wrote to Shaw explaining why the INTS could not produce *John Bull's* in 1904. In the letter, Yeats mentions Synge's objections, including Synge's suggestion that the Keegan-grasshopper scene be cut (*Yeats Letters,* III, 662). Shaw's Irish play, then, was written in much opposition to the Dublin theatre movement as it existed in 1904 in regard to some of its ideological focus and some of its approach. But an integral part of Shaw's play is the presentment of a vivid socialistic view of Ireland that is a reconfiguration and expansion of the socially liberalizing portrait presented in Synge's *In the Shadow of the Glen.*

The assertion that Shaw wrote plays that reconfigured or expanded another playwright's work is detailed by John Bertolini, in "Wilde and Shakespeare in Shaw's *You Never Can Tell.*" Specifically, Bertolini argues that Shaw competed during the 1890s with Oscar Wilde, the other important Irish-born dramatist writing then for the London stage. Bertolini argues that Shaw's Unpleasant Plays, like *Widowers' Houses* and *Mrs Warren's Profession,* were built on Shaw's reaction to Ibsen, while Shaw's Pleasant Plays from 1894 to 1896 reveal "Shaw trying to define himself in the shadow of Wilde's success." Bertolini argues that Shaw's *Arms and the Man, The Man of Destiny, Candida,* and *You Never Can Tell* challenge Wilde's *An Ideal Husband* and *A Woman of No Importance* ("Wilde," 157). Furthermore, Bertolini asserts that by drawing on Shakespearean comedy in *You Never Can Tell,* Shaw also challenges and attempts to surpass Wilde's masterwork *The Importance of Being Earnest*: "Thus does Shaw seek to compete with his rival Shakespeare and to defeat his rival Wilde" (162). If Shaw truly wrote his early plays in response to Ibsen, Wilde, and even Shakespeare, Shaw arguably and logically turned his attention to Dublin in 1904 and wrote in rivalry to the Dublin playwrights to compose a real portrait of Ireland.²² In this process, Shaw naturally addressed the most socialistically leaning Dublin playwright who was performed in London in March 1904, and who philosophically challenged his international Fabianism—Synge.

John Bull's Other Island

The premise of *John Bull's Other Island* is established in its first act, which is longer than any of the individual one-act plays the INTS presented in its 1904 London appearance. Shaw's play is set into motion by Tom Broadbent's decision to visit Ireland on behalf of the business syndicate he and Larry Doyle, as civil engineers, represent. In the opening moments, Broadbent informs his valet Hodson to pack his revolver, as they are going to Ireland. From then on, the act thoroughly establishes Broadbent as a foolish liberal Englishman in the spirit of the Liberal prime minister William Gladstone, who had presented various unsuccessful Irish Home Rule efforts during the 1870s and '80s. Nicholas Grene observes that Broadbent is "one of the greatest comic stage-Englishmen ever created" (*Politics*, 21). Indeed, this is certainly the case as Broadbent attempts to hire Tim Haffigan as a guide. Haffigan appears as a grotesque colonial-created Irish stereotype, which allows Broadbent to make his absurd declarations. On announcing his intention to go to Ireland, Broadbent declares, "I am an Englishman and a Liberal, and now that South Africa has been enslaved and destroyed, there is no country left to me to take an interest in but Ireland" (*John Bull's*, 72).[23] Once the Irish-born Larry Doyle enters, it is quickly realized that Haffigan, a Scotch-born Irishman never in Ireland himself, is playing the Irish stereotype for whatever he can take the apparently foolish Broadbent for. Behind the veil of Shaw's amusing playing of national stereotypes is the fact that a person of the laboring class is reduced by a social and economic system to pander to the comfortably middle-class Broadbent. But if Tim Haffigan can play at being an Irish stereotype for the Englishman, perhaps the capitalist Broadbent can play the reverse for the Irish.

Given Shaw's comedic approach, the seriousness of the play is presented to an audience either appreciative of or disarmed by the satirical comedy. Once Tim Haffigan has been exposed, the dialogue between Broadbent and Doyle begins to hint at the real purpose behind the visit to Ireland. Doyle states to Broadbent: "Your foreclosing this Rosscullen mortgage and turning poor Nick Lestrange out of house and home has rather taken me aback; for I liked the old rascal when I was a boy and had the run of his park to play in. I was brought up on the property." Broadbent responds, "But he wouldn't pay the interest. I had to foreclose on behalf of the Syndicate. So now I am off to Rosscullen to look after the property myself."

To which Doyle states: "That's it. That's what I dread. That's what has upset me" (*John Bull's*, 78–79). By the end of the play, Doyle's Act I reluctance to return to Ireland with Broadbent will be seen to have much to do with Broadbent's plans and his (Doyle's) complicity in such plans. Yet clearly, at this point in Act I, Broadbent is presented as going to Ireland as an Englishman representing a syndicate, or absentee landlords from an Irish rural perspective, on a foreclosure and eviction. The old issues of rural Ireland are being spun by Shaw in the context of land reform in Ireland of the late nineteenth century. But interestingly, Shaw reveals that such land reform provided equal-opportunity to become dispossessed by efficient capital, as Lestrange had been a landlord but now is like an evicted peasant—equal at last.

Norma Jenckes writes that Broadbent's repeated slogans of reform for Ireland see "no further than Gladstone and his call for 'efficiency' aims at eliminating the Irish small farmer." Jenckes further explains that Gladstone's acts of conciliation toward Ireland, namely his efforts to placate the Irish members of Parliament that supported Gladstone's coalition governments, was through proposing acts "which made it possible for tenants to purchase their lands" ("*John Bull's Other Island*: A Critical," 46). While these land reforms were attractive on paper, they led to new dangers and consequences for Ireland. Jenckes quotes Friedrich Engels, who in 1888 foretold of the coming problems of forcing the landlords in Ireland to break up their estates so their tenants could purchase their land holdings at a price they could afford: "People there want first of all to become peasants owning a plot of land, and after they have achieved that mortgages will appear on the scene and they will be ruined even more. But this should not prevent us from seeking to help them to get rid of landlords, that is, to pass from semi-feudal conditions to capitalist conditions" (as quoted in Jenckes, "*John Bull's Other Island*: A Critical," 46). This process is mirrored as Shaw's play portrays the modernizing of Ireland into a more modern capitalistic system that "eliminates" and destroys the Irish rural laborer. As Shaw's "presentment of the real old Ireland," the play is on target. Once owning land, the rural Irish laborers became as capitalistic as their former landlords, succumbing to dangerously accessible mortgages.

In *John Bull's Other Island*, the former tenant farmer Matthew Haffigan is presented as an example of such an Irish peasant who now owns a small holding of land. He is portrayed in Act III meeting with other

Rosscullen men who seek a candidate to represent them in the British Parliament, one who will prevent further land reform that would allow more laborers to acquire land. Matthew Haffigan is particularly against the poor, like Patsy Farrell, from becoming landowners. Larry Doyle rips into Haffigan: "What call have you to look down on Patsy Farrell? . . . Do you think because you're poor and ignorant and half-crazy with toiling and moiling morning noon and night, that you'll be any less greedy and oppressive to them that have no land at all than old Nick Lestrange, who was an educated traveled gentleman that would not have been tempted as hard by a hundred pounds as you'd be by five shillings? Nick was too high above Patsy Farrell to be jealous of him; but you, that are only one little step above him, would die sooner than let him come up that step; and well you know it" (*John Bull's*, 118–119).

Indeed, grotesque capitalism was the result of breaking the feudal-like landlord system in Ireland—the truth of rural Ireland in 1904. Shaw was right in that the truth was not in Yeats's mystical, romantic *Kathleen Ni Houlihan,* where materialism is shunned in favor of sacrificing one's self for Ireland.[24] The truth in rural Ireland at the beginning of the twentieth century was the dominating infection of capitalism into rural Ireland, into the Irish peasant class from the middle class, following the infection that had been festering in the urban centers since the Great Famine of the late 1840s. This was the truth as presented in Synge's *In the Shadow of the Glen*. Declan Kiberd writes, "As if to vindicate Shaw's diagnosis, Synge also found a landscape riven with growing class tensions and a crass bourgeois moralism. *In the Shadow of the Glen* offered an astringent critique of the new respectability among country people" (*Inventing Ireland*, 485). This is particularly portrayed in Synge's *Shadow* by Michael as he counts the money he believes is Nora's, telling her he will marry her and move into the cottage and land that had been her husband's. While Kiberd is accurate in this assessment, his phraseology suggests that Synge verified Shaw's view, but Synge's *Shadow* preceded Shaw's *John Bull's Other Island*. Instead, one can only say the opposite, that Shaw verified Synge. But as Shaw was countering Yeats's portrayal of a romantic nationalist Ireland, Shaw was also reacting to Synge's *Shadow*, not to necessarily dismiss Synge's entire socialistic view of rural Ireland, but to present a wider socialistic take that Shaw believed had a greater relevance and a better chance to succeed over time.

Most significantly for Shaw and Synge is the fact that they are both seeing and detecting, Synge from mostly direct observation in rural Ireland and Shaw from socialist theory, that rural Ireland, like urban Ireland, was by 1903–04 infected with class greed and its by-product of an ugly craving for social respectability. The connection between capitalism and the desire for moral respectability was cast in Ireland in 1890 when the Home Rule leader Charles Stewart Parnell was ruined by powerful capitalists, like William Martin Murphy, who used Parnell's adultery to maneuver their personal gain, all despite Parnell's enormous unselfish efforts for Ireland and the politics the captains of Dublin industry publicly supported. This was mimicked by a greedy Church that preached conservative morality that favored wealth, not the poor. All of which trickled through the Irish classes to rural peasant Ireland. It was rural Ireland that the conservative pseudo-nationalists in Dublin romanticized to create their sense of a real or truthful (but in reality fanciful) Ireland. This reverberates in Griffith's objection to Synge's *In the Shadow of the Glen*: "It is not by staging a lie we can serve Ireland." By "lie" he refers to an ideological objection to the fact that Synge's reality contradicts a fantasy of the conservative imagination.

P. J. Mathews details the obsessive need for Dublin middle-class nationalists, pseudo or otherwise, to portray a respectable Ireland as accelerating from the 1899 Gaelic Language controversy. The controversy involved two Trinity College professors, John Petland Mahaffy and Robert Atkinson, who testified before British-sponsored hearings on whether Gaelic language should be taught in Ireland's secondary schools. The professors asserted that the language was immoral (Mathews, *Revival*, 37).[25] Atkinson specified that "no human being could read through [a Gaelic] . . . book, containing an immense quantity of Irish matter, without feeling that he had been absolutely degraded by contact with it—filth I will not demean myself to mention . . . I would not allow any daughter of mine to study it" (as quoted in Mathews, *Revival*, 39). The response from many nationalists was "the need to prove at all costs the morality of Irish culture" (Mathews, *Revival*, 43). This was especially the case since Gaelic had, during the 1890s for Dublin middle-class nationalists, come to symbolize Ireland's west, a west that was being romanticized by the Gaelic League (formed in 1891) and the Celtic Twilight writers, most notably Yeats, into the symbol for a true Ireland. To condemn the native language as amoral, which was only spoken as a primary language in remote western sections of 1899 Ireland, was to condemn Ireland as amoral. Mathews notes that the effort to prove Ireland's morals through western Ireland "would prove to be almost as restrictive as the colonial attempts to degrade it" (Revival, 43). Specifically, the conservative bourgeois Dublin nationalists who took offense at the Trinity College professors sank into their class's obsessive desire for respectability.

Falling into this effort to present Ireland's respectability is Yeats's *Kathleen Ni Houlihan*, set in Ireland's west on the north County Mayo coast. At one point in the play, the Old Woman states, "With all the lovers that brought me their love, I never set out the bed for any" (*Kathleen*, 29). Since the play's mystical nationalism and plot can still be presented without this line, there is no reason for its inclusion other than to testify to Kathleen's respectable purity, hence placating middle-class Dubliners who wanted to believe in Ireland's respectability and, most importantly, their respectability. The capitalist middle-class nationalists in Dublin celebrated the 1902 premiere of *Kathleen Ni Houlihan* and made it the most revived play in the repertoire of the INTS (called the National Theatre Society Ltd. after 1905) from 1902 to 1916. Arthur Griffith championed the play in his *United Irishman*, predicting that via the play the Irish "may recover their lost souls" ("Editorial," 12 April 1902, 3). A few years later, Shaw would dismissively, and perhaps sarcastically, state to Lady Gregory, "when I see that play I feel it might lead a man to do something foolish" (as quoted in Gregory, *Seventy*, 444). Thirty years later, Yeats asked if his play had sent "out" men to die for Ireland's independence ("Man and the Echo," 337). Given the moral conservatism of the play's mysticism, plus the fourteen years between the play's premiere and political insurrection in Ireland, the answer is emphatically no. It would take different words from a different perspective to arm Irish men and women for their own cause.[26]

Yet, given the obsessive desire to prove and believe in Ireland's respectability among conservative middle-class Dublin nationalists, with their expectations defined by *Kathleen Ni Houlihan*, one can see how such an audience objected to Synge's portrayal of a woman leaving her husband— especially so when she walks out with a tramp. From Shaw's perspective, Synge's Nora, a woman devalued by her enslavement as an abused drudge within a rural Ireland embracing capitalistic greed, is negated by the non-respectable act of her leaving her husband. Again, Synge's desire to portray Nora in a defiant act at play's end, perhaps satisfying an optimism in Synge that Nora can find independence and value, vehemently opposed most of the original Dublin audience's sense of respectability. All that such an audience could see was Nora leaving her husband and marriage vow, not Nora's devalued position in Dan's house. This was the same for conservative Irish middle-class nationalists who saw the play performed in London in March 1904. One such audience member, poet Delia O'Dwyer, attacked the play in Griffith's *United Irishman,* charging that because Nora walks out of her marriage she "is not Irish" ("Irish National," 6). In *John Bull's Other Island,* Shaw presents his Nora, and his play, differently, yet like Synge, presents a rural Ireland (hence Ireland) as imbued with class greed. But Shaw's major Irish play was not antagonistic to a Dublin audience like Synge's, and while being a full-length play, Shaw presented a wider portrait of 1904 Ireland that could be seen as a portrait of capitalism in Ireland.

When *John Bull's* was eventually first performed in Dublin, in 1907, there were no objections to Larry Doyle's Act I dismissal of Irish nationalists as only being able to consider Ireland seriously by thinking of the country as Kathleen Ni Houlihan. There were no objections when Larry went further about Irishmen being unable to see reality: "At last you get that you can bear nothing real at all: you'd rather starve than cook a meal; you'd rather go shabby and dirty than set your mind to take care of your clothes and wash yourself; you nag and squabble at home because your wife isn't an angel and she despises you because you're not a hero; and you hate the whole lot round you because they're only poor slovenly useless devils like yourself" (*John Bull's,* 81). While such a speech is intensely critical, Shaw removes its antagonistic potential as soon as it is delivered by means of Broadbent's quick response: "Never despair, Larry. There are great possibilities for Ireland. Home Rule will work wonders under English guidance" (*John Bull's,* 82). The absurd comedic remark allows Larry's comments to pass without objection from a bourgeois Dublin audience. In addition, Larry's remarks which touch on the loveless Irish marriage intimates that miserable couples do not separate but rather remain together in misery, unlike Synge's Nora. Of course, Larry is stating what he believes is the norm (with the play's hope for future change), whereas Synge is projecting a call for Ireland to immediately change to become more socially just.

By the end of Act I, Shaw prepares for the introduction of his Nora, a delicate heiress who has been waiting eighteen years for Larry to return for her.[27] Furthermore, Larry explains to Broadbent Nora's ridiculous and petty sense of class: "When you go to Ireland, just drop talking about the middle class and bragging of belonging to it. . . . If you want to be particularly offensive to Nora you can call her a Papist; but if you call her a middle-class woman, Heaven help you!" (*John Bull's*, 88–89). While Nora's father had been a landlord, she clearly is middle class in the play despite her pretensions. Shaw envelops his background information on Nora through Broadbent's absurdities as he begins falling in love with her before leaving London: "There is something very touching about the history of this beautiful girl" (*John Bull's*, 89).

Before Act I ends, Shaw, through Larry, warns his audience of Broadbent's foolish façade that disarms all, including most of the audience. Broadbent, who for most of the act has been proclaiming himself as an advocate for reform in Ireland, is likened to a caterpillar by Larry: "the Englishman does what a caterpillar does. He instinctively makes himself look like a fool, and eats up all the real fools at his ease while his enemies let him alone and laugh at him for being a fool like the rest. Oh, nature is cunning!" (*John Bull's*, 86). Act II continues Broadbent's absurdities while moving along what could be perceived as the socialistic portrait of the all-consuming capitalist.[28]

Shaw's stage description of Nora Reilly in Act II, when she first appears, notes that for an Irishman like Larry she is "helpless, useless, almost sexless, an invalid without the excuse of disease" (*John Bull's*, 94). Shaw's Nora is the opposite of Synge's Nora at the end of his play. Given such seemingly conscious opposite natures, it can be no coincidence that Shaw named his main Irish woman-character Nora three months after seeing Synge's Nora in London, as both Noras leave with intruding strangers. While Larry's view of Nora Reilly is "an incarnation of everything in Ireland that drove him out of it," she was welcomed and accepted by the Dublin respectable middle-class nationalists when the play first appeared in Dublin (*John Bull's*, 94). Arthur Griffith found the submissive Nora to be "an Irish lady" and could only cite her in his review for humming an old English music hall song before a round tower ("Shaw at Home," 3). She was far more acceptable and admired by such Dubliners as Griffith than Synge's Nora, who ends her abuse, even though Nora Reilly leaves not with a tramp but with an invading, land-devouring Englishman whom she agrees to marry. Curiously, and humorously, Dubliners like Griffith seemed to view Nora Reilly as the English Broadbent does, "an attractive woman" (*John Bull's*, 94), missing Shaw's satire.

Like Synge, Shaw labels the Dublin conservative, conventional middle-class nationalists as pseudo-nationalists. In fact, *John Bull's* original Dublin audience enjoyed the play. There are no accounts of the play's 1907 Dublin audience protesting anything in the play, even though the manager of the Theatre Royal, where the English Vedrenne-Barker touring company performed the play for its Dublin premiere, had sixty police constables on hand in the anticipation of audience trouble. Nine months earlier, audience disturbances were intense when Synge's *The Playboy of the Western World* premiered at the Abbey Theatre and police were called in by Yeats and Lady Gregory. Shaw's Nora was not as inflammatory as Synge's women-characters. But clearly, the conservative Dublin nationalists who objected to Synge's Nora but enjoyed Shaw's Nora put their middle-class respectability before their nationalism. Shaw's joke in this, of course, is that Nora Reilly agrees to marry Broadbent while knowing him for only twenty-four hours—ultimately, not so respectable when the surface is scratched. This, of course, points to Shaw's ultimate joke in the play. As he satirizes the petty, greedy Irish characters and the capitalist Broadbent, the joke is on the conservative middle-class nationalists who laughed but missed the satire on themselves. While they boisterously protested Synge's play(s) as Synge aggressively held a mirror to their own images, they enjoyed Shaw's play, proving themselves ignorant and non-nationalists, as they did not protest the Englishman acquiring the Irish heiress, hence Ireland itself.

When Nora first appears in Act II she is positioning herself to receive the returning Larry, for whom she has been waiting eighteen years. She engages in conversation with the defrocked priest Keegan, trying to see if he thinks Larry is returning for her. Rather than meeting Larry later in the act, she encounters, before the round tower, Broadbent, who seemingly falls immediately in love with her and absurdly proposes marriage. In Act IV, when Nora is finally alone with Larry, she admits to thinking of little else over the years but him. He asks her, "Why didn't you give it up? Why did you stay here?" She responds, "Because nobody sent for me to go anywhere else, I suppose. That's why" (*John Bull's*, 143). In many respects, Nora's response epitomizes her character. After her father died she moved in with Larry's family, then waited for Larry's return, and, in the end, agrees to marry Broadbent. She can only identify herself in relation to men, her father's daughter, Larry's unofficial fiancée, and then Broadbent's official fiancée. In this regard, she is the opposite of Ibsen's Nora, who breaks from such identification at the end of her play, and Shaw's Nora takes no initiative nor gains any independence as Synge's Nora does. But like Synge's Nora, Nora Reilly has borne a lonely existence in rural Ireland during her long years of waiting.

Later in Act IV, Nora Reilly tells Broadbent she is ashamed of campaigning for his candidacy to the British Parliament representing Rosscullen. Broadbent begins to reveal his modern, calculating capitalism during this exchange with Nora. She asks: "Oh, how could you drag me all round the place like that, telling everybody that we're going to be married, and introdoocing me to the lowest of the low, and letting them shake hans with me, and encouraging them to make free with us? I little thought I should live to be shaken hans with Doolan in broad daylight in the public street of Rosscullen" (*John Bull's*, 152). Nora displays her sense of class and respectability that came with her father's landowning semi-feudal aristocracy. But Broadbent is more efficient with his capitalism as he instructs Nora to call on the publican's wife, to which she replies: "Is it me call on Doolan's wife!" Broadbent answers her: "Yes, of course: call on all their wives. We must get a copy of the register and a supply of canvassing cards. No use calling on people who havnt votes. You'll be a great success as a canvasser, Nora: they call you the heiress; and they'll be flattered no end by you calling especially as you've never cheapened yourself by speaking to them before—have you? . . . I get engaged to the most delightful woman in Ireland; and it turns out that I couldn't have done a smarter stroke of electioneering" (*John Bull's*, 152).

At this point, even Nora begins to see the calculating opportunist, rather than total fool, that Broadbent is. She asks, "An would you let me demean meself like that, just to get yourself into parliament?" He patronizingly assures her, "it's all right: do you think I'd let you do it if it wasn't?" She answers, "Well, praps you know best" (*John Bull's*, 152–153). Nora is letting herself be defined by a man she not only does not love, but does not know. When she and Larry speak afterwards, Larry tells her she has made a fine match: "Mrs. Tom Broadbent will be a person of very considerable consequence indeed. Play your new part well, and there will be no more regrets, no more loneliness, no more idle regretting and vain hopings in the evenings by the Round Tower" (*John Bull's*, 154). The insinuation is that Nora's match to Broadbent will be profitable, marrying for wealth and attention. This is similar to the marriage Michael Dara proposes to Synge's Nora and the marriage she walks away from with her husband. While one

Nora is blatantly antagonistic to the audience incapable of seeing her as worthy of her freedom, the other is accepted and found attractive by those unable to see Shaw's satire. Intriguingly, Shaw and Synge both present the loveless marriage, reaching the same conclusions but with differing approaches. But Shaw envelops his scenario by suggesting that aristocratic Noras do not leave with Tramps, but with entrepreneurs, which was more satirically comical—especially when portions of the audience did not get the joke but saw nothing wrong with marrying for position, even if to a conquering Englishman.

As important as Nora Reilly is to *John Bull's Other Island*, she is not the central character, which is perhaps another indication of Shaw steering away from *In the Shadow of the Glen*'s Nora. Broadbent remains the central character throughout the play, and like Larry's likening him to a caterpillar in Act I, Broadbent proves the "efficient" capitalist by play's end. However, to reach the play's full socialist take on Ireland, Shaw, like Synge, strikes at the Catholic Church within Ireland, a foe both would tangle with again.

Both Shaw and Synge recognized the Church's direct role in the capitalism that infected rural Ireland in 1903–04, or at least its willful complicity. In this, they saw the Church failing the Irish, serving itself rather than the people. Synge's attack on the Church-sanctioned respectability in *Shadow*, through marital separation, hit its mark with its 1903 detractors who were mostly, or exclusively, Catholic.

Synge took an aggressive aim at the Church in *Riders to the Sea*, which portrays an Aran Island woman turning away from the Church at play's end in favor of embracing the pagan Irish tradition of keening when the last of her sons has died. Not only had the priest serving the island failed to intervene and stop the last son, Bartley, from going to sea, he is absent when Bartley's dead body is brought to his mother. More blatantly confrontational, Synge's *The Tinker's Wedding*, written at the time when *Shadow* and *Riders* were, portrays a greedy capitalistic priest who sells his Church's supposed respectability and resorts to violence when he is not paid the money he demands. *Tinker's* was so potentially antagonistic because of its priest that the INTS did not produce it. But since the play was first published in 1907, Shaw did not know of it when writing *John Bull's*. Nonetheless, Shaw had witnessed Synge's attacks on the Church in *Shadow* and *Riders* in 1904.

In a less openly aggressive manner, *John Bull's Other Island* criticizes the Catholic Church in Ireland subtly. In Act II, Father Dempsey, like the land agent Cornelius Doyle, partakes in class superiority. When the laborer Patsy Farrell is "intolerably overburdened" by carrying Dempsey's hamper, Con Doyle's goose, and Broadbent's luggage, he stumbles, dropping his burden; Dempsey scolds him with class contempt: "Are you drunk Patsy Farrell? Did I tell you to carry that hamper carefully or did I not?" (*John Bull's*, 98).[29] Dempsey is also present in Act III when Matthew Haffigan, Con Doyle, and Barney Doolan conspire to find a candidate to represent their district in the British Parliament who will prevent further land going to laborers like Farrell. Dempsey is in fact a conspirator in this pack, shamelessly and capitalistically looking out for the Church's financial interests instead of helping the poor: "When too much money goes to politics, it's the Church that has to starve for it. A member of parliament ought to be a help to the Church instead of a burden on it" (*John Bull's*, 117). But the hint of a negative portrait of a priest in 1904 (or 1907) is partnered with the comedy of the Act which sees the conspirators giving the candidacy to Broadbent. Even Matthew Haffigan, who rants on about the hardships he suffered under the British landlord system, agrees to Broadbent. In subtle fashion, Shaw presents these Irishmen putting their capitalistic cravings before any sense of Ireland for the Irish, proving their very nature. Unfortunately for them, they are the fools the caterpillar Broadbent, the more "efficiently" modern capitalist, is devouring.

To fully unveil Broadbent's machinations, Shaw creates the defrocked priest Peter Keegan. Through Keegan, Shaw further undermines the Catholic Church in Ireland. Keegan was defrocked because he dares to think and he contemplated the value of another faith for one of its believers:

> I heard that a black man was dying . . . When I went to the place I found an elderly Hindoo, who told me one of those tales of unmerited misfortune, of cruel ill luck, of relentless persecution by destiny, which sometimes whither the common places of consolation on the lips of a priest. But this man did not complain of his misfortunes. They were brought upon him, he said, by sins committed in a former existence. Then, without a word of comfort from me, he died with a clear eyed resignation that my most earnest exhortations have rarely produced in a Christian, and left me sitting there by his bedside with the mystery of this world suddenly revealed to me . . . This world sir, is very clearly a place of torment and penance, a place where

the fool flourishes and the good and wise are hated and persecuted. (*John Bull's*, 140)[30]

Of course, the philosophical nature of the defrocked Keegan is a scathing commentary on the Catholic Church in Ireland as he contrasts significantly with the respectable priest Father Dempsey. This is particularly set up by Shaw in Act II, when Dempsey is asked by Broadbent if he has a theory on Ireland's round towers, to which he answers: "A theory? Me!" Con Doyle explains, "Father Dempsey is the priest of the parish, Mr. Broadbent. What would he be doing with a theory?" (*John Bull's*, 97).

The philosophical, contemplative Keegan is thoroughly distanced from the Church in Ireland, even going back to Keegan's seminary education, which took place in western Spain, rather than in Ireland (*John Bull's*, 94). The distancing is clear, but subtle. It is the defrocked priest, not the conventional, respectable Father Dempsey who cares about Rosscullen's people, placing Keegan in the mock trinity within the play's conclusion.

In the play's final scene, after Larry learns of Nora's engagement, Keegan, Larry, and Broadbent come together in the Rosscullen open air. During the previous scene, the last between Nora and Larry, Keegan and Broadbent conversed out-of-sight but now join Larry. After mentioning the engagement, Broadbent states, "Well, Mr. Keegan, as I said, I begin to see my way here. I begin to see my way." Keegan responds, clearly emerging now as the only rationally thinking person living in Rosscullen: "The conquering Englishman, sir. Within 24 hours of your arrival You have carried off our only heiress, and practically secured the parliamentary seat. And you have promised me that when I come here in the evenings to meditate on my madness; to watch the shadow of the Round Tower lengthening in the sunset; to break my heart uselessly in the curtained gloaming over the dead heart and blinded soul of the island of the saints, you will comfort me with the bustle of a great hotel, and the sight of the little children carrying the golf clubs of your tourists as a preparation for the life to come" (*John Bull's*, 155).

Perhaps flattered by the label of "conquering Englishman," Broadbent emerges as the efficient, opportunistic (therefore ruthless) capitalist. Significant is the fact that Nora is not present at this point in the play. By touching on the centuries-old tradition of portraying Ireland as a woman, as Yeats-Gregory do in *Kathleen Ni Houlihan* and Synge in *In the Shadow of the Glen*, Shaw uses his Nora's departure and absence from *John Bull's* climactic scene as a further indication that what has been previously thought of as Ireland is irrelevant in 1904 to what is really transpiring. She, Ireland, is now only a voiceless means toward profits for the "efficient" capitalist. Broadbent reveals his plan for the resort which is being admirably supported by his engagement to Nora and his upcoming parliamentary seat. Keegan now engages Broadbent, as no one else can in Rosscullen, about his plans. The others, like Larry's father, are blindly mesmerized by the mortgages Broadbent has offered. Keegan questioningly states, "you will not lend them more on their land than the land is worth, so they will be able to pay the interest." Larry answers, stepping up as Broadbent's lieutenant, "We will lend every one of these men half as much again on their land as it is worth, or ever can be worth, to them" (*John Bull's*, 156). As the properties are foreclosed, Broadbent and Larry, on behalf of the Syndicate, will acquire the land for the resort. The nightmarish capitalistic Rosscullen future is, as Broadbent states, not "in the hands of your Dorans and Haffigans" (*John Bull's*, 156).

Prodded further by Keegan, Broadbent, through a cold capitalistic vision, explains that there are only "two sorts of people: the efficient and the inefficient. It don't matter whether they're English or Irish" (*John Bull's*, 157). In such a Shavian vision of hell on earth, national identity succumbs and submits to "efficient" capital. Engels's theory emerges.

When Keegan asks of what will happen to Matthew Haffigan, with Shaw mimicking the INTS's other well-used convention of symbolizing Ireland through the rural Irish, Larry says Haffigan will be employed somehow but is immediately overruled by Broadbent: "No, no: Haffigan's too old. It really doesn't pay to take on men over forty even for unskilled labor, which I suppose is all Haffigan would be good for. No: Haffigan had better go to America, or into the Union [workhouse]" (*John Bull's*, 157). Now Keegan grasps the full extent of Broadbent's scheme that will "efficiently" acquire the resort from the original investors, secure new investors, and reap profits upon profits "when at last this poor desolate countryside becomes a busy mint in which we shall all slave to make money for you" (*John Bull's*, 160). After Broadbent boasts that English tourists, or "idlers" as Keegan labels them, will bring money to Ireland, Keegan answers with a response that reverberates with the Industrial Revolution in England: "Just as our idlers have for so many generations taken money from Ireland to England. Has that saved England from poverty and degradation more horrible than we have ever dreamed of?" (*John Bull's*, 161).

This discussion among the trinity of Broadbent, Larry, and Keegan (a bastardization of the Holy Trinity: the Father, the Son, and the Holy Ghost, which also echoes the trinity in *In the Shadow of the Glen* through Dan, Michael Dara, and the Tramp) reveals not only the despairing present of 1904 Ireland, with new landowners mortgaging themselves back into dispossession, but Ireland's bleak future with efficient capitalism. It is a capitalism that promises an Ireland as a tourist haven to enrich English and foreign investors, not the Irish. Interestingly, this becomes Ireland's reality for much of the twentieth century. Yet this three-character discussion allows Keegan, again not the conventionalized Father Dempsey, to express a true Catholic sense of community as an ideal in the place of capitalism, which, according to Shaw, should also replace nationalism: "Sir: when you speak to me of English and Irish you forget that I am a Catholic. My country is not Ireland nor England, but the whole mighty realm of my Church. For me there are but two countries: heaven and hell; but two conditions of men: salvation and damnation. Standing here between you the Englishman, so clever in your foolishness, and this Irishman, so foolish in his cleverness, I cannot in my ignorance be sure which of you is the more deeply damned" (*John Bull's*, 162). Larry dismisses Keegan's meditations: "your approval is not of the slightest consequence to us. What use do you suppose all this drivel is to men with serious practical business in hand?" (*John Bull's*, 162).

Keegan ends his presence in the play by sharing the remainder of his Catholic vision on the "efficient" capitalists—English and Irish: "In my dreams it is a country where the State is the Church and the Church the people: three in one and one in three. It is a commonwealth in which work is play and play is life: three in one and one in three. It is a temple in which the priest is the worshipper and the worshipper the worshipped: three in one and one in three. It is a godhead in which all life is human and all humanity divine: three in one and one in three. It is, in short, the dream of a madman" (*John Bull's*, 163). This view is not only a true Catholic vision spiritually, without the structure and administration of the Catholic Church, with its paternalized order of priests, bishops, cardinals, and a pope being the people's betters, but where all, priest and people are the same, worshipped and worshipper. In such a vision, the people, not the monetary interests of the Church, are served. In essence, this is an ideal socialist vision in 1904, borrowed by the Fabian Shaw from early Christianity.

In Keegan's socialistic ideal all are equal, socially, economically, politically, and so forth. Most significantly, in consideration of *John Bull's Other Island* being a response to *In the Shadow of the Glen*, is that this ideal vision is spoken not by one representing an ancient pagan tradition, but by a truthful Catholic priest, even if a defrocked one.[31] For Shaw, Keegan is more relevant than Synge's Tramp. They both share a similar vision while belonging nowhere but everywhere within Ireland, although the internationally traveled Keegan is obviously on a much grander scale. Synge's Tramp, in his admiration for Nora's "grand talk" and his suggestions that she and Michael can live as wife and husband (regardless of the Church's preached middle-class respectability) if they desire to, reflects a vision of a socialistic-gender-type equality in the 1903–04 context, as he symbolizes native pagan Irish traditions, through the tradition of itinerant Irish bards he embodies. But Synge's Tramp was offensive to his original respectable audience. A wandering tramp was not in the least acceptable for such an audience and not someone for Nora to accompany when she leaves her husband, hence the flash point for many of *Shadow*'s original conservative audience members.[32] A defrocked priest like Keegan, on the other hand, and despite his "mad" mutterings, is still acceptable enough to be invited into respectable homes as in the opening scene of Act IV, when he is present in Con Doyle's parlor to hear the retelling of Broadbent's wildly humorous drive through Rosscullen in his motorcar with Haffigan's pig.[33] Undoubtedly, the voicing of a socialistic ideal through a character like Keegan emerges as part of Shaw's reconfiguration of Synge's *Shadow*.

The concept of Keegan is true to the Fabian philosophy of "gradualism," reforming society by slow, rational education of the body politic. Indeed, this approach epitomizes the entire comedic *John Bull's Other Island* through its extensive character discussions. Synge's use of his Tramp, in contrast, was the opposite of the gradualist approach. Synge assaulted his audience in an effort to provoke their immediate change, while Shaw sought to subtly prod his audience to understand the horror of a society without socialistically leaning values. A large part of Shaw's reconfiguration of *In the Shadow of the Glen* was that his socialistic image was grander and more encompassing with its take on the 1904 mortgage situation and Ireland's future in the hands of "efficient" international capitalists, whereas Synge's was more narrowly focused on Ireland from within an isolated peasant cottage.

Shaw deliciously ends *John Bull's Other Island* with Broadbent listening to Keegan's ideal vision and commenting after Keegan departs, "He's a real character, he'll be an attraction here." Indeed, in Shaw's bleak vision for Ireland under Broadbents and Larry Doyles is the sense that a socialistic-type visionary like Keegan is an antiquated, meaningless tourist curiosity, like the round tower, even before his ideas can ever be heard by reasonable individuals. In fact, if no one listens to Keegan—and no one will, since all view him as mad—"efficient" capitalism will always carry the day. Broadbent emphasizes the play's bleak moral by closing the play onstage with only himself and Larry, recalling the closing moment of *In the Shadow of the Glen* when Dan and Michael Dara drink alone to the continuation of the respectable bourgeois values they embrace. Broadbent states: "I feel sincerely obliged to Keegan: he has made me feel a better man: distinctly better. . . . I feel now as I never did before that I am right in devoting my life to the cause of Ireland. Come along and help me to choose the site for the hotel" (*John Bull's*, 163). Shaw's last joke of his play switches the nationalists' preached sentiment of giving one's life to the cause of Ireland with Broadbent's capitalist cause in Ireland, which is indeed a hell on earth. It is this imaging that represents Shaw's perceived first direct participation in socialistic thought in Ireland, which would lead to much more in many differing ways.

So while Shaw's plays in general examine universal experiences and behavior, *John Bull's Other Island* offered enough socialistic leaning commentary to inform Synge's further canon, to become, over time, provocative for Irish radicals to act on. But the writing of *John Bull's* was only an early step.

John Bull's Other Island: Prompting and Provoking

A. M. Gibbs writes that *John Bull's Other Island* "marked the first real step on the ladder in his [Shaw's] ascent to real success and fame in the professional theatre in England" (*Bernard Shaw*, 247). In Dublin, the play was rejected for both opening the Abbey Theatre and joining its repertoire in 1904. Shaw noted in his preface to the play, "Like most people who have asked me to write plays, Mr. Yeats got rather more than he bargained for" ("Preface," 473). Indeed so; *John Bull's* harshly dismissed Yeats's *Kathleen Ni Houlihan* and the nationalism it appealed to, while reconfiguring and expanding *In the Shadow of the Glen* into a broader, international-leaning socialist statement on Ireland that played to significant audiences. Before *John Bull's* played in 1907 Dublin, it established Shaw's popular success in London.

London's Royal Court Theatre's 1904–05 production of *John Bull's* was enjoyed by audiences appreciating its grand humor. The popularity prompted the attendance of Britain's king and prime minister. Davis writes that, "When King Edward VII ordered a command performance of *John Bull's Other Island* in 1905, Shaw was suddenly news" (*George Bernard Shaw*, 67). Of course, the play's Keegan would consider Edward VII to be the grandest of idlers, living on the work of others. Nevertheless, Shaw created a play that was the opposite of the unpopular *In the Shadow of the Glen* in most respects except for the shared socially liberalizing vision in both plays. It remains a matter of opinion as to which play was more effective in presenting their treatments of Ireland to the Irish.

Despite the stamp of approval from London's most respectable idlers, *John Bull's Other Island* enjoyed its success when it first played Dublin, even among Irish nationalists. Seemingly, conservative nationalists, like Arthur Griffith, missed the play's dismissal of themselves when they had clearly seen the attacks from *In the Shadow of the Glen*, or they recognized the satire but were not offended. Why had Griffith not been suspicious of the play given its phenomenal London popularity, especially among Britain's rulers? While the king and prime minister laughed at the end of *John Bull's*' Act III, when Matthew Haffigan is accosted by Broadbent's valet Hodson in his native Cockney accent asserting that urban British economic oppression was worse than Irish rural economic oppression, did such idlers see the satire that confronted the means of wealth they lived on? While Shaw's humor allows the play's scathing jabs to go before its audience without retaliatory hostility, are we to wonder if Shaw's warning of the hellish capitalist world, where national identity is useless, was heeded over time, or if Synge's audience antagonism in *In the Shadow of the Glen* led to social change within Ireland? Of course, both Shaw and Synge were playing for an intellectual elite section of the audience(s) that would understand, but which one could sway the others or the non-elite? Certainly *John Bull's* was more nurturing to its overall audience than *Shadow*, helping to lead them to change. Undoubtedly, Shaw's tactic would play better over time, but could it appease the impatient? What was emerging between Shaw and Synge in 1904, and for others later, were two distinct philosophical tracks to socialism in Ireland, but *John Bull's* did not play Dublin until 1907.

When *John Bull's Other Ireland* came to Dublin in November 1907, the Irish socialist movement was still unorganized. James Connolly had not yet returned from America and would not do so until 1910, but well before that, Shaw's *John Bull's* made a highly significant impact on Irish socialistic radicalism that would be realized within the decade following the play's first Dublin run. The year 1907 marked the beginning of the next act of Shaw's participation in socialism in Ireland. Numerous productions of Shaw's plays, in addition to *John Bull's*, came to Dublin in 1907 by touring British companies. But most importantly, 1907 also saw Synge's response to Shaw's comedic Irish masterpiece, which was itself an Irish masterpiece.

2

Answering *John Bull's* Provocation— Synge

When *John Bull's Other Island* first played Dublin, in November 1907, Synge wrote his fiancée Molly Allgood: "I do not feel the slightest inclination to go and see Shaw—I'd rather keep my money for [an Irish] concert tomorrow and hear something that is really stirring" (*Letters to Molly*, 217).[1] Synge clearly felt disdain for Shaw's master Irish play, despite that he and Shaw were not entirely opposed to one another intellectually in their considerations of Ireland's condition at the start of the twentieth century. Perhaps angered by Shaw's jab at his plays' connections to nature, through Keegan's grasshopper conversation, and/or strongly opposed to Shaw's Fabian international approach, Synge was moved against *John Bull's Other Island* as soon as he read it in 1904.[2] The result was a play responding to *John Bull's* that cemented a Shavian presence in the further development of the coming socialist Irish debate, including *Blanco Posnet*.

Synge, like Yeats, may also have resented Shaw's audacity for writing a play intended to open the Abbey Theatre, which was being built for the plays of Synge, Yeats, Gregory, and their fellow dramatists in Dublin while Shaw had been making his name in London. Yeats recalled the effects of Synge's temper after Synge's death: "He knew how to hate" (*Memoirs*, 201).[3] All of these factors led Synge toward his reaction to *John Bull's*, along with his adamant belief: "I write of Irish country life I know to be true and I most emphatically will not change a syllable of it because B. or C. may think they know better than I do . . . [and] I will not falsify what I know to be true for anybody" (*Synge Letters*, I, 91). Synge was unwilling to sway from his aggressive approach because certain people might be upset, and, arguably, he had little tolerance for Irish plays that either lacked his assessment of Ireland or differed from his approach. He rarely complimented other Irish playwrights; Yeats remarked of Synge, "I never knew what he thought of my work" (as quoted in Gregory, "Synge," 88). In fact, Synge responded to Yeats's play *Deirdre* as he responded to Shaw's *John Bull's*.

On 12 September 1907, Synge wrote to the Irish-born American journalist Frederick Gregg, that he was tempted to write a play on Deirdre (*Synge Letters*, II, 56). In 1906, Yeats had written *Deirdre* based on Irish mythology's Deirdre legend, which Synge intensely disliked. Seven days prior to his letter to Gregg, Synge had started his last play, *Deirdre of the Sorrows*. The play followed Synge's response to *John Bull's Other Island*. Shaw was not the only Irish playwright to write in response to another out of rivalry or competition. Prompted by Shaw's provocation, which was Shaw's reaction to *In the Shadow of the Glen*, Synge wrote *The Playboy of the Western World*. The opposing socialistic-leaning slants in Irish theatre were becoming more prominent and soon would involve additional writers of differing classes.

English Tommy or Irish Playboy?

September 1904 was an eventful month for Synge. On the 17th, he arrived for his first visit to County Mayo, on its north coast in the Belmullet area. According to Yeats's September letter to Shaw, Yeats had sent Synge the script Shaw had mailed him of *John Bull's Other Island*, and Synge read Shaw's play on the train from Dublin to Sligo, where he took a steamer to Belmullet (*Yeats Letters*, III, 660). The Belmullet area would become the setting of *The Playboy of the Western World*. In fact, Synge began drafting *Playboy* while in Mayo in September 1904, in other words, within days of reading *John Bull's* (Saddlemyer, "Appendix B," 293).

Synge's reworking of Shaw's play bears many similarities to the original, from the seemingly minutest point to the broadest strokes of each. As Shaw in Act I of *John Bull's Other Island* alludes comically to Britain's Boer War (1899–1901), so too does Synge in Act I of *The Playboy of the Western World*. The Boer War was viewed by many in Ireland and Britain as a callous display of capitalistic imperialism on the part of England. The war had been fought against Dutch settlers (Boers) for control of South Africa, rich with diamond and gold reserves. Some socialists saw the war as having been fought for the diamonds and gold, serving the designs of English capitalist Cecil Rhodes. In Shaw's play, Broadbent states, "where else can I go? I am an Englishman and a Liberal and now that South Africa has been enslaved and destroyed, there is no country left for me to take an interest in but Ireland" (*John Bull's*, 72). Synge's character Philly states of the stranger that arrives in Act I, Christy Mahon, "Maybe he went fighting for the Boers, the like of the man beyond, was judged to be hanged, quartered and drawn. Were you off east, young fellow, fighting bloody wars for Kruger and the freedom of the Boers?" (*Playboy*, 79). Kruger was the leader of the Boers' South African Republic. John MacBride was the man Philly refers to who had fought against the British and for the Boers. MacBride was, like the village inhabitants in *Playboy*, from County Mayo, specifically from Westport rather than Belmullet, hence, "the like of the man beyond." MacBride had fought with an Irish brigade, earning the rank of major. While not captured by the British during the war, he was wanted for treason, a crime in earlier times punishable in Ireland by hanging, drawing, and quartering, as in the case of Robert Emmet in 1803.

MacBride was eventually executed by the British in 1916 for treason for participating in the 1916 Easter Rising, but he was shot by a military firing squad.[4] In Synge's time, MacBride married Maud Gonne in 1903, but later she divorced him in France, where divorce was accessible. Gonne was the Irish nationalist Yeats had been infatuated with since meeting her in the 1880s, and her marriage to MacBride had been a bitter retort for Yeats. So while Shaw jabbed at Yeats's romantic portrayal of Ireland in *Kathleen Ni Houlihan* in Act I of *John Bull's*, Synge's allusion to MacBride did much more than merely rework Shaw's allusion to the Boer War. It delivered a searing jab at Yeats's romanticism. Synge, like Shaw, valued little the romanticizing of the conservative *Kathleen Ni Houlihan*. So Synge's Boer War allusion mimicked Shaw while jabbing Yeats *and* Gonne. The conservative Gonne had denounced *In the Shadow of the Glen* in the *United Irishman* over its portrayal of a woman leaving her abusive husband, an act Gonne had completed by 1907 by divorcing the physically abusive MacBride. In *Playboy*, Synge was following Shaw's lead, grinding more than one axe.

The broad strokes that Synge met, mimicked, and reconfigured from Shaw's response to *In the Shadow of the Glen* are highly evident when one considers *The Playboy of the Western World* in the context of *John Bull's Other Island*. Both plays present strangers visiting rural Irish villages who are quickly embraced as saviors. In Synge's first sketches for the play to become *Playboy*, the savior character, later named Christy Mahon, "is being elected county councilor"—reminiscent of Broadbent's rise to parliamentary candidate in Shaw's play (as quoted in Saddlemyer, "Appendix B," 295). The action in both the completed *Playboy* and *John Bull's* from Act II on, when Broadbent arrives in Rosscullen, transpires within twenty-four hours, with their respective savior characters reaching peaks of popularity after wild and celebratory activities that occur offstage. Broadbent's peak follows his motorcar drive through the village with Haffigan's pig, and Christy Mahon's high point follows his victories in all the fair games, including the mule race on the strand. Humor stems from both. Christy's father watches his son's victories, and says, "I never till this day confused that dribbling idiot with a likely man" (*Playboy*, 106), while the retelling of Broadbent's drive creates much comedy, a blueprint for the comedic car crashes popularized in silent films.

To solidify the peaks of Christy and Broadbent, both become engaged to the most elevated single women within the two plays, Pegeen and Nora Reilly, respectively. Pegeen is the publican's daughter and Nora her village's heiress. Christy and Broadbent also are susceptible to being perceived as idiots and fools. But here they begin to differ, as Broadbent is not quite the total fool, but plays at being one, and Christy may well be the fool his father believes. Interestingly, the initial appearances of these two characters into their play's Irish locales are each followed by the appearances of characters intricately connected to them and their true identities: Christy's father Old Mahon follows in Synge's play and Broadbent's partner Larry Doyle in Shaw's.

After the engagements are set, Synge follows Shaw's plot in presenting the disillusionment or truthful character revelations of the perceived saviors. Keegan presses Broadbent and discovers how the efficient capitalist will not save the villagers who will elect him to Parliament but will destroy them by confiscating their lands. Christy as false savior is unearthed when Pegeen realizes his tale of killing his oppressive father is untrue, reducing Christy to a mere braggart and liar.

Shaw's creation of Keegan as the only rational resident of Rosscullen is met by Synge's Pegeen, who becomes the person in her village who rationally speaks for most. Even Keegan and Pegeen have similar names. They do differ in that as Keegan discovers Broadbent's real plan for Rosscullen, he understands he is helpless against the "efficient" capitalist. Pegeen, on the other hand, is more proactive, as she decides that the false Christy has no place in her village. In Keegan's statement of his socialistic ideal of no nationalities, where "the priest is [among] the worshipper[s] and the worshipper the worshipped," he remains a Catholic, but perhaps in its truest communal way. Even though Keegan is separated from his Church's organization and administration, he is still Catholic. Synge's Pegeen, as her name suggests, is far closer to Synge's strong affinity for pagan Ireland, as seen in her poetic, Gaelic-based speech and in her rejection of the Church's influence as she rejects the pious Shawn Keogh. Synge clearly stays with his sense of pagan Ireland being a truer Ireland than Catholic and Christian Ireland, which he saw as instilling the bourgeois desire for respectability, undermining true Irish native identity.

One of the differences between *John Bull's Other Island* and *The Playboy of the Western World* is that Shaw saw one of Ireland's problems as seeing itself in provincial terms. So to present his Fabian criticism of the Irish capitalistic middle class, Shaw illustrates petty Irish capitalists being devoured by more efficient international capitalists, but makes his presentation through satirical comedy and by creating the most "efficient" capitalist as English. On one level, Broadbent reveals the insidious danger of efficient capitalism that can destroy the provincially minded Irish capitalists with ease, and on a second level, by his being English, the Irish bourgeois audience is made comfortable with an English enemy, a seeming comedic fool. They can, if able, see the dangers of what Broadbent represents without feeling insulted, while Broadbent's nationality suggests the internationalism of the real capitalist threat. Synge, on the other hand, expresses the capitalistic threat as very much an internal Irish problem. He may well have viewed Irish capitalism as having its origins in British industrialism, but its infiltration, its infection into rural Ireland, symbolizing the infection of all Ireland, becomes Synge's focus. And as such, he deals with the infection internally.

In *Playboy*, Synge aimed directly at the middle-class Dubliners, rather than appeasing them with an English fool, in order to drive them away from their capitalistic culture. He struck at the Irish capitalist moral obsession with respectability, the very mindset of the conservative, capitalistically thinking Irish middle class through that class's overly romanticized affinity for a pure Ireland. Such an assault from Synge, with only an Irish focus and without the appeasing nature of Fabian gradualism, shaped Synge's response to *John Bull's* into an impatient, antagonistic, nationally inclined socialistic take on Ireland. Synge's assault meant that he was essentially at war with much of the Abbey Theatre's middle-class audience, an audience that had tried to reject his approach, and therefore his radical and leftist take, in his earlier plays *In the Shadow of the Glen* and *The Well of Saints*.

Briefly, *The Well of Saints* is socialistically inclined, arguably growing out of what W. J. McCormack sees as Synge's interest in "the transformation of the medieval Christian hegemony into modern capitalism" (*Fool*, 185). The play portrays a blind couple given temporary sight by a wandering priest, giving Martin and Mary Doul full access to the society of the play's rural Irish village. The village, with its excessive devotion to the priest's religion, Catholicism, proves a harsher world than the imagined and real world Martin and Mary knew in their blindness. With sight, Martin must work and is employed by the smith Timmy. Consistent with Shaw's portrayal of class cruelty among small Irish employers toward Irish laborers as seen in the treatment of Patsy Farrell in *John Bull's*, Synge's Timmy is a hard work-master. Martin responds to Timmy's barking orders in Act II, sounding much like a labor union's demand for better working conditions: "It's destroyed I'll be whacking your old thorns till the turn of day, and I with no food in my stomach would keep the life in a pig . . . Let you come out here and cut them yourself if you want them cut, for there's an hour every day when a man has a right to his rest" (*Well*, 73).

Timmy's role in low-level Irish commerce, with his obsessive devotion to the priest, symbolizes for Synge the infiltration of capitalist middle-class values into rural Ireland by 1905, when *The Well of Saints* premiered. These values are accented by the young Molly, who moves to marry Timmy, despite hearing native-Irish-inspired love poetry spoken to her by an imaginative Martin: "I'm seeing you this day, seeing you, maybe, the way no man has seen you in the world" (*Well*, 78). Martin warns Molly that marriage to Timmy will be one of misery, as he will be in his forge, "sitting there by himself, sneezing, and sweating, and he beating pot-hooks till the judgment day" (*Well*, 81). Still, Molly, who thinks herself a "well-reared civil girl," is devoted to the bourgeois respectability poisoning Ireland and so chooses to marry the imaginationless Timmy.

By play's end, when the priest offers Martin and Mary permanent sight, symbolizing the permanent offer to be in the everyday, conventionalized Irish world, the couple rejects it, preferring their blind but masterless world. Martin defiantly states after the priest promises holy images of priests and their churches: "Isn't it finer sights ourselves had a while since we sitting dark smelling the sweet beautiful smells do be rising in the warm nights and hearing the swift flying things racing in the air . . . till we'd be looking up in our own minds into a grand sky, and seeing lakes, and broadening rivers, and hills are waiting for the spade and plough" (*Well*, 90). The priest responds to Martin's rejection of his religion and middle-class morality by damning and banishing Martin, in a rather un-Christian manner: "I'd put a black curse on him [Martin] would weigh down his soul till it'd be falling to hell . . . if you [Martin] won't go with your own will, there are those standing by will make you surely" (*Well*, 91) The villagers, like a mob, are happy to see Martin and Mary driven out and marginalized.

The original Dublin middle-class audience, for the most part, damned the play for its unflattering portrait of the priest and its rural villagers. The conservative, bourgeois constant playgoer Joseph Holloway recorded: "Probably the curtains have closed in on The Well of Saints [*sic*], Mr. Synge's harsh, irreverent, sensual representation of Irish peasant life, with its strange mixture of lyric and dirt, for the last time as far as Dublin is concerned . . . and I for one am not at all sorry. . . . I have never witnessed a play that repelled me so much as this same The Well of Saints [*sic*] written by one who has as much sympathy for the humbler Irish and their Catholic faith as a Maxim gun with an Englishman at the side of it has for a lot of unarmed savages!" (*Joseph Holloway's*, 53–54).[5] While Holloway's views are grounded in Dublin middle-class, capitalist values, he was right in noting Synge's attack on some of the rural Irish, specifically those who embraced grotesque bourgeois values. Within the arena of his antagonistic approach, Synge's attack was directed at the capitalist-minded Irish and what they were capable of against their fellow Irish, especially the economically "humbler Irish."

The Well of Saints, completed by Synge two months before he read *John Bull's Other Island*, followed Synge's earlier approach of antagonizing most of his audience. In Shaw's play, Synge encountered the gradualist international approach. Undoubtedly for Synge's nationalized vision, the direct capitalist threat being an Englishman was not what he observed in Irish life, country or urban. He was on a path while writing his response to *John Bull's* that would intensify his attacks, elevating the debate of socialism in Ireland within Irish theatre to a new level. Synge's *Playboy* would definitely not nudge.

While Synge was writing *Playboy* he was hired by the *Manchester*

Guardian to write a series of articles on the Congested Districts in Connacht (rural west Ireland in Counties Galway and Mayo) during the early 1905 summer. Manchester, a British industrial city, had a significant Irish population that had immigrated to work its factories, and the liberally minded newspaper took an interest in Ireland's west. The paper even sponsored relief programs in the Congested Districts, which was home to the severest rural poverty then in Ireland. Undoubtedly Synge set out to confirm what he already knew of capitalism in rural Ireland. Synge lamented in his first article, "From Galway to Gorumna," "that nearly all the characteristics which give colour and attractiveness to Irish life are bound up with a social condition that is near to penury" ("From Galway," 145). To Synge, the embracement of capitalist economic advancement among middle-class Irish stripped them of attractive "characteristics" that made them Irish. Synge ends the article by telling of a conversation with a man near the coastal village of Spiddal, County Galway, about whether the people are able to fish, to which the man replied: "there's little fishing in it at all, for we have no good boats. There is no one asking for boats for this place, for the shopkeepers would rather have the people idle, so they can get them for a shilling a day to go out in their old hookers [traditional Galway working sailing sloops] and sell turf in Aran and on the coast of Clare" ("From Galway," 130).

Repeatedly, Synge negatively notes in his *Manchester Guardian* articles the capitalistic Irish cruelly taking advantage of the poorer Irish. In his assessment of peasants selling kelp, Synge notes, "In some places the whole buying trade falls into the hands of one man who can then control the prices at his pleasure" ("Kelp Makers," 170). In effect, the poor locals not only had no way of knowing whether the price the buyer set for kelp was fair, they had no effective recourse. In other instances, Synge aims at the shopkeepers: "What is worse, the shopkeeper in out-of-the-way places is usually the only buyer to be had for a number of home products, such as eggs, chickens, carragheen moss and sometimes even kelp; so that he can control the prices both of what he buys and what he sells, while as a creditor he has an authority that makes bargaining impossible: another of the many complicated causes that keep the people near to pauperism!" ("Inner Lands," 203). Likewise, Synge noted that some shopkeepers bought out "the tenant right" holdings of some families and shipped the families to America with "what remained of the money" after paying off the debt to the shopkeeper: "This is probably the worst kind of emigration, and one fears the suffering of these families, who are suddenly moved to such different surroundings, must be great" ("Erris," 198).

Immediately following the completion of his *Manchester Guardian* articles, Synge privately wrote to his friend, the radical journalist Stephen MacKenna. He complained about the hypocrisy and practices of the above type of shopkeepers, who played up their airs of middle-class respectability and morality, all the while claiming to be nationalists, as they horribly misused and profited on the Irish poor: "[the] general-shop-man who is married to the priest's half-sister and is second cousin once removed of the dispensary doctor, . . . [and his like] are horrible and awful . . . while they're swindling the people themselves in a dozen ways then buying out their holdings and packing off whole families to America. The subject . . . [is] beastly" (*Synge Letters*, I, 116).

Interestingly, in his *Guardian* articles, Synge echoes Shaw on the issue of the Irish tenant farmers in the government scheme of being able to purchase the tenant land they worked. Shaw, as expressed by Larry in Act III of *John Bull's*, argues that a new small landowner like Matthew Haffigan would become a crueler landlord to the poorer Irish laborers than the old landlords had been. Synge: "A great deal has been said of the curse of the absentee landlord; but in reality the small landlord who lived on his property and knew how much money every tenant possessed, was a far greater evil" ("Smaller Peasant Proprietors," 193). Obviously, on this issue of the new small landlords and on the danger of the Irish being in debt to capitalists, Synge and Shaw were close in some of their thinking, and, as Synge's *Guardian* articles suggest, the two playwrights were ideologically very close on some Irish issues in 1905 as Synge moved his playwriting attention to primarily completing *Playboy*. Shaw and Synge agreed on the detrimental aspect of the landlord system, old or new, that discouraged tenants from bettering their holdings as improvements resulted in higher rents (*John Bull's*, 157–158, "Smaller Peasant Proprietors," 194). Yet as dramatists, the differences between the approaches of Shaw and Synge reflected their international and national bases, even though in *John Bull's*, Shaw had moved a little toward the national perspective, since he so specifically wrote of Ireland. Likewise, Synge's leftist leaning in the Congested Districts, and elsewhere, surely owed some to radical considerations with his friend MacKenna during their Paris days. Synge's mother reported in

1896 that her young son "has gone to Paris to study socialism" (as quoted in McCormack, *Fool*, 143).

Despite some of the international origins of Synge's socialistic leaning, it was, again, predominantly shaped by his direct observations of the rural Irish proletariat and their interaction with the usurious, capitalizing class, hence Synge's national direction. Likewise, his urgency over such conditions could not entertain a gradualist approach, perhaps accented by his own failing health. Synge had no confidence that the conservative, conventional, capitalistic, Irish middle class could be reasoned with over time. This was only reinforced by the objections leveled against *In the Shadow of the Glen* and *The Well of Saints*, the latter's February 1905 premiere restarting the press condemnations of the former. Less than one week before *Well*'s opening, Synge wrote to his English publisher Elkin Mathews about the first publication of *Shadow* and *Riders to the Sea*, with Synge primarily working out the royalties. He added that he did not think *The Tinker's Wedding* should be included in the volume: "As far as I am concerned, I would rather, I think, hold back this Tinker's Wedding for a while—if you do not absolutely need it to fill your volume—as there is a character or two in it that would displease some of our Dublin Catholic friends, and perhaps hinder the sale of the volume in Ireland" (letter in possession of author). Synge knew the response *Tinker's* would receive from Dublin's middle-class conservatives, yet, by the time of his *Guardian* articles, Synge was showing signs of becoming more antagonistic. In support of his attacks, in a nationally socialistic context, on Catholicism and its morality in *In the Shadow of the Glen* and *Riders to the Sea*, Synge provocatively quotes a poverty-stricken ferryman in his *Guardian* article "The Ferryman of Dinish Island": "I don't know what way I'm going to go on living in this place that the Lord created last, I'm thinking, in the end of time; and it's often when I sit down and look around on it I do begin cursing and damning, and asking myself how poor people can go on executing their religion at all" ("Ferryman," 168). Including this quote of a peasant contemplating how the poor can continue to practice Catholicism in light of their poverty was militantly antagonistic toward the bourgeois audiences that had objected to *Shadow* and *The Well of Saints*.

Generally, Synge's articles on the Congested Districts were openly critical of Irish capitalists contributing to the poverty of the poor, and attacked the romanticized views of Ireland's west that many Dubliners believed in

1905. In his letter to MacKenna about the *Manchester Guardian* articles, Synge privately thought about directly exposing in a play the Irish capitalists he encountered in Connacht, by "putting those lads on stage. God, wouldn't they hop!" (*Synge Letters*, I, 116–117). Synge indeed chose to expose them in his response to Shaw in *The Playboy of the Western World*, hopping and all.

The Playboy: Socialistically Nationalist

Since Synge's focus, antagonistic for some, was obviously far more national than Shaw's, some might see Synge's plays as being provincial in comparison to Shaw's. Of course, the playwrights like Synge who specifically wrote Irish plays for Dublin theatre in the first decade(s) of the twentieth century approached their focus within the shadow of Ireland's colonial status. Just as Shaw's Fabian background afforded him a gradualist and mainly international approach, his existence in London afforded him a distance from Ireland's nationalist question in *John Bull's*. Such was generally not the case for Synge, despite his Paris years, which mostly predated his playwriting.

Yet, as alluded to, Shaw and Synge wavered some from the strict classifications of international and national. In his direct Irish work, Shaw could at times be quite specifically national in focus. *John Bull's* was more national than most of Shaw's other plays. The play was uniquely Irish in its handling of crucial 1904 Irish national issues, like nationalism and land reform, but it was internationalized by Shaw's international response to such issues—his dismissing nationalism as foolish provincialism and seeing the danger of grotesque capitalism in current land reform. This internationalizing would be carried into Shaw's future forays into Ireland's national politics. On the other hand, Synge's canon was specifically national in its focus, and drew its proposed solutions from his perception of ancient and truthful Ireland, but the issues he tackles, like socialistic efforts for gender equality, were undoubtedly adopted by Synge from influences outside Ireland. But in overall contrast, Shaw was more international and Synge more national in their specific treatments.

In a 1928 letter to the *Irish Statesman*, Stephen MacKenna recalled that "Synge was intensely Nationalist; he habitually spoke with rage and bitter baleful eyes of the English in Ireland" ("Synge," 14). In my earlier books *Synge and Irish Nationalism: The Precursor to Revolution* and *Performative* and *Textual Imaging of Women on the Irish Stage, 1820–1920: M. A. Kelly to J. M. Synge and the Allgoods*, I argue that *The Playboy of the Western World* is a nationalist work with a radical, leftist leaning. Synge's plays in general had the ability to separate and define Ireland's nationalists in Dublin from 1903 to 1910, dividing nationalists into radicals or conservatives. The radical nationalists, like Thomas MacDonagh, favored Synge's plays from the outset, while socially conservative nationalists such as the editor Arthur Griffith strongly opposed the plays. This equation, of course, foreshadowed the Irish Civil War in 1922, when conservative and radical nationalists split over the 1921 Anglo-Irish Treaty. The conservative Free State that emerged, with Griffith as its first president, rejected much of the liberal radicalism promised by the Easter Proclamation of 1916, which included James Connolly's socialist input. The fact that Synge's plays drew heavily from ancient Gaelic culture undermined the "nationalism" of the conservative middle-class audience members who rejected the plays, especially when someone like Maud Gonne rejected *In the Shadow of the Glen*'s depiction of Nora leaving her husband as an example of the "destructive tyranny of foreign influence" ("A National Theatre," 2–3). As stated earlier, accessible marital separation was very much part of ancient native Irish Gaelic culture. When Gonne divorced her abusive husband in France, her popularity among conservative nationalists in Dublin was drastically diminished.

The nationalist direction of *The Playboy of the Western World* lies partially, simply stated, in the play's depiction of violence. When Christy Mahon arrives in the play, his tale of killing his abusive and authoritative father is celebrated by Pegeen and most of the play's villagers. Christy reinforces this perception of his violence by aligning his father to brutish, foul-mouthed British army officers: "I'd hear himself snoring out, a loud lonesome snore he'd be making all times, the while he was sleeping, and he be a man'd be raging all times, the while he was waking, like a gaudy officer you'd hear cursing and damning and swearing oaths" (*Playboy*, 84).[6] Christy's killing of his father is accepted and perceived as symbolizing a strike from the oppressed against the oppressor. One audience member, who defended the play in the press at the time of its January 1907 premiere, wrote of Christy: "has he not laid his father low with a lick of a spade, and Pegeen exalts him into a hero.—A sort of hero he is too . . . all his aspirations restrained unfilled, and his poetic feeling ground back into his heart to smoulder there till the time when his father's tyranny is brought to a head, and Christie [sic] turns after much provocation and strikes him down" (P.M.E.K., "A Plea," 3).⁷ This witness to the play's premiere understood why this parricidal action, from a nationalist-socialistic angle, is cause for heroism and celebration.

However, this heroism evaporates in the play when Pegeen sees Christy's father alive toward the end of Act III. She turns on Christy for being a liar, which prompts Christy to fight his father again, this time before Pegeen and all. When everyone again thinks he has killed his father, Pegeen and the villagers (all but the Widow Quin and Sara Tansey) remain against Christy. This time they reject his violence. The reason for this rejection is found in Christy's motives. With the "first" killing he was standing up for himself against a brute, which has symbolic meaning for a colonized and economically oppressed people. Following the "second" killing, Christy states: "I'm thinking, from this out, Pegeen'll be giving me praises the same as in the hours gone by" (*Playboy*, 114). Christy's second act of violence is committed solely for personal gain, it cannot symbolize anything for Ireland like a blow from the oppressed against the oppressor. When Christy turns to a Pegeen set on dismissing him, after the second killing, he asks, "And what is it you'll say to me, and I after doing it this time in the face of all?" To which Pegeen replies with the play's most poignant speech: "I'll say, a strange man is a marvel with his mighty talk; but what's a squabble in your backyard, and the blow of a loy, have taught me that there's a great gap between a gallous story and a dirty deed" (*Playboy*, 116).

The play defines violence in 1907 Ireland. That which can symbolize for Ireland the oppressed against the oppressor is celebrated and has relevance. Violence committed strictly for personal gain is condemned and has no relevance for Ireland. That many nationalists rejected the play was perhaps Synge's joke, in that his play's definition of violence is based on Yeats-Gregory's *Kathleen Ni Houlihan*, which Yeats publicly described in Arthur Griffith's paper the *United Irishman* in 1902 as thematically being "the perpetual struggle of the cause of Ireland . . . against private hopes and dreams" ("Mr. Yeats' New Play," 5). *Kathleen* was extremely popular among the very nationalists who opposed *Playboy*, yet they failed to see the same nationalist message when Synge did not clothe it in an allegorical character who conservatively maintains her respectability but not her land. Synge also presents that nationalist message as being not understood by the play's only potential male hero, Christy, a negative but potentially accurate portrait of Irish manhood in 1907 colonized Ireland. Ultimately, *Playboy*'s definition of violence would be embraced for revolutionary Ireland.

In describing Synge's nationalism, MacKenna noted that Synge hated the lying he observed in nationalist organizations ("Synge," 14). Exactly what Synge found to be a lie or lies among such groups we can only speculate. Perhaps it was the hypocrisy among self-proclaimed nationalists, like the pseudo-respectable shopkeepers he found in Connacht, who swindled the poorer Irish classes, swindling their own people for personal profit while espousing nationalism for Ireland. Specifically, Synge noted, like *John Bull's* argues, that these petty capitalists actively advocated the United Irish League, which was one of the supposedly nationalist organizations that promoted the land scheme of putting land ownership into the hands of peasants unable to afford it, hence leading to their economic ruin while the shopkeepers ultimately and eventually acquired the land for virtually nothing (*Synge Letters*, I, 116–117). Again Synge's mindset echoes a Shavian concern from *John Bull's*. These very Connacht capitalists were essentially the same as their counterparts in Dublin who had objected to Synge's earlier plays because their hypocritical "respectability" was offended. They were unable to see Synge's nationalist overtones in his portraits of true, native Ireland struggling against obscene bourgeois influence. Synge's view that the rural Irish capitalists were the same as the Dublin bourgeois nationalists was borne out by these very nationalists' turning against Irish labor during the disputes with Dublin employers in 1911 and 1913.

In 1911 when striking Irish workers were blocking the delivery of food into Dublin, Arthur Griffith, Synge's most outspoken opponent, called on "the [British] government to guarantee its . . . [the food's] transportation by using the services of its soldiers" (Glandon, *Arthur Griffith*, 100). During the 1913 Dublin Lockout, when the Irish Transport and General Workers' Union (ITGWU) members were locked out by Dublin employers trying to break the union (which was fighting for decent working conditions), Griffith wrote that the locked-out Irish workers should be "bayoneted" (Haverty, *Constance Markievicz*, 111). Griffith's call for British soldiers to move against his fellow Irish is vile, not to mention hypocritical for someone claiming to be a nationalist. Apparently, Griffith's class values came before his nationalism. To make these capitalists "hop" on stage, Synge attacked with *The Playboy of the Western World* as he responded to Shaw's "uncompromising" Irish play.

Another Uncompromising Irish Play

As Shaw wrote *John Bull's Other Island* to be, in a sense, a (or the) defining play on early twentieth-century Ireland, Synge attempted to do the same. Rather than work up the rural Irish petty capitalists, as Shaw does in *John Bull's*, as characters comically falling over themselves to put forward a British "efficient" capitalist as their candidate for Parliament, Synge moves directly into the petty class within its dirty dealings with the peasantry and their own relations. Shaw's grand plot portrays the petty capitalists scheming to keep the likes of Patsy Farrell from land ownership while the efficient Broadbent schemes to confiscate everything from all the Irish characters, showing how petty capitalists against efficient capitalism are only steps away from being peasants and are about to be returned to the dispossessed class. Synge's focus is directed on the Irish only. Synge's plays see Ireland's problems as being perpetuated by the Irish against the Irish, almost echoing Shaw's Larry Doyle, who chastises Matthew Haffigan for his oppressive efforts to keep Patsy Farrell poor. But rather than portraying such sentiment as coming from an Irishman in collaboration with a British capitalist in the international ruining of Ireland, Synge locates his play within the peasants' closeness to the land and its dirt. In Christy's tale of killing his father prior to the play's action, the supposed killing took place in a field of potatoes. Potatoes symbolized the poorest of rural Irish laborers. They also recalled the horror of the 1840s Famine, when landlords and government allowed so many Irish peasants to die of starvation or emigrate while other crops flourished. It is among potatoes that Christy claims to have been oppressed by his greedy father to the point of Christy's needing to kill him. Class, history, and brutality in Ireland are engulfed in Synge's *Playboy*, being his uncompromising vision.

Specifically, Synge does not use settings for his response to *John Bull's* that follow Shaw's lead. Shaw had set his major Irish play in the comfortable middle-class London flat and office of Broadbent and Doyle, the former land agent Con Doyle's respectable sitting room, and the romantic outdoor landscape of round towers that are reminiscent of Boucicault's Irish melodrama sets that played so successfully to London and New York middle-class audiences in the 1860s–80s. Rather, Synge focuses on what he witnessed in Ireland's west. An unrespectable, unromantic dirty pub was just as much a likely defining battlefield for Ireland's socialist humanity as Shaw's sets that catered to the bourgeois class. Such contrasting setting from Synge was meant not only to counter Shaw's sense that his play presented the "uncompromising real Ireland," but also to challenge the conservative, Dublin middle-class, self-proclaimed nationalists who held Ireland's west as a romanticized ideal of Ireland. Shaw too, of course, had set most of *John Bull's* in the rural west, but presented a rural west that a Dublin middle-class audience could find comfortable. Synge's *Playboy* set undermined such audience comfort by being a rural set that even contrasted with the idealized peasant cottage of *Kathleen Ni Houlihan*, where a family receives an enormous non-peasant dowry. Even *Playboy's* locale in Belmullet, on the north Mayo coast, was very close to the locale of *Kathleen Ni Houlihan* that had been so popular with the detractors of Synge's earlier plays.

Synge's assault on the capitalistic middle-class respectability, and his countering of Shaw, begins in *Playboy* with the set of Michael James Flaherty's pub, or country shebeen, as "very rough and untidy," with Michael's daughter Pegeen being described as "a wild-looking but fine girl of about twenty. . . . She is dressed in the usual peasant dress" (*Playboy*, 73–74). The implication of Synge's set description is that the pub is a very rural, run-down, poor establishment, the definition of a shebeen. Despite the pub's economic peasant condition, its owner sports a respectable name as Michael James Flaherty, as if one first name was not enough. Synge's stage direction reveals that Michael is a "fat jovial publican" (*Playboy*, 76). In his articles on the Congested Districts, Synge describes the location setting of the play, Belmullet, as "of the greatest poverty" ("Homes of the Harvestmen," 183). Presenting a set that visually touches the poor, rather than Shaw's bourgeois sets, transported a middle-class audience to a locale that many would have wanted to avoid. Given the poverty of the shebeen as Synge describes, it is obscene and vulgar that Michael is so well-fed. He is akin to the capitalist publicans and shopkeepers Synge observed in Connacht excessively profiting on the poor, the real capitalist threat to Ireland on a day-to-day basis, that is very unlike Broadbent. In his letter to MacKenna about his Congested Districts articles, Synge referred to such capitalists as having "a rampart double-chinned vulgarity" (*Synge Letters*, I, 117).

The hypocrisy of Michael's respectability is heightened by his shameful drinking. He leaves in Act I to attend Kate Cassidy's wake and becomes so drunk he must be carried home in an ass cart the next day. Nevertheless, to maintain his respectability, Michael and Shawn Keogh have made a bargain with the Catholic Church for Pegeen to marry Shawn, despite their being cousins, and despite Pegeen's contempt for Shawn. Michael desires the marriage since Shawn is the most propertied man of the play, with lands, heifers, and a "blue bull from Sneem" (*Playboy*, 111). Regardless of these respectable airs, Pegeen remains dressed as a peasant and is described at one point as having "a stale stink of poteen on her" (*Playboy*, 100). Pegeen clearly is like an heiress among the other inhabitants of the poverty-stricken area, in the sense of being a publican's daughter, but her dress and poteen stains contrast significantly to her father's well-fed status and to Shaw's respectable Nora. In fact, the reality of Pegeen and her father in the play's action is that she works his pub and his livestock while plump Michael James lives off her labor.

Shawn Keogh, like Pegeen's father, is detailed in Synge's stage description as "fat" as well as "fair" (*Playboy*, 74). Being fair complexioned at harvest time in a poor farming and turf bog area like Belmullet suggests that Shawn does little manual work himself, and the "fat" description also recalls the capitalist-minded greedy priest in *The Tinker's Wedding* as being "near burst with the fat" (*Tinker's*, 47). Synge creates Shawn as a capitalist farmer who in Act II attempts to rid the area of Christy by using the buy-out tactic of Connacht shopkeepers who bought out families and sent them to America. When this tactic does not work, Shawn quickly adapts and tries to buy help from the Widow Quin to keep Christy away from Pegeen. In addition to agreeing to give her a red cow, a mountainy ram, a right of way across his rye path, a load of dung, and the right to cut turf on one of his bogs, Shawn offers: "I'd give you the wedding-ring I have, and the loan of a new suit, the way you'd have him decent on the wedding day. I'd give you two kids for your dinner, and a gallon of poteen, and I'd call the piper on the long ear to your wedding from Crossmolina or from Ballina" (*Playboy*, 97). Shawn has everything covered from land to poteen. And like a true capitalist, Shawn first offered the Widow only a single ewe, but she capitalistically bargains for more. Given Synge's concern over petty capitalists in the Congested Districts, and his response to Shaw's then reputation in Ireland as a socialist, Synge's point here with Shawn and the Widow's bargaining was the capitalist infection of rural, and all, Ireland.

While Shaw's *John Bull's* criticizes Irish capitalists who attempt to keep Patsy Farrell dispossessed, the assault on such capitalists in a Dublin audience is through the satirical humor of the characters' interaction with the British Broadbent and his "efficiency." Even if conservative bourgeois audience members missed the satirical targeting of themselves, there is the gradualist hope they will recognize it over time. In the meantime, their ignorance of themselves as the "target" forms a joke, as they are comforted by the "villain" Broadbent, an apparent fool, being English. Synge's more volatile approach made it immediately and adamantly clear to his audiences who his targets were, expressed through characters like Michael James and Shawn Keogh.

Provocatively, the capitalistic nature of Shawn is emphasized by his obsession with pious, Catholic respectability. The hypocrisy he represents is paramount. When asked by Michael James to stay with Pegeen, the woman Shawn wants to marry and makes various bargains for, so she will not be alone in the pub while Michael attends the all-night wake, Shawn replies: "I'm afeard of Father Reilly; and what at all would the Holy Father and the Cardinals of Rome be saying if they heard I did the like of that?" (*Playboy*, 76). When Michael suggests that Shawn and Pegeen would be in separate rooms, Shawn replies again, "I'm afeard of Father Reilly, I'm saying. Let you not be tempting me, and we near married itself" (*Playboy*, 77). Shawn is so obsessed with being respectable in the eyes of the Church, he is useless as a suitor to Pegeen except for his money and middle-class "respectability," which appeal only to Pegeen's father.

While Shawn's materialistic capitalism should be incompatible with his pious respectability, that respectability is proven even more hypocritical in that Shawn willingly and easily lies. In Act II, in order to speak to Christy without Pegeen being present, Shawn lies to Pegeen about seeing her "mountainy sheep eating cabbages in Jimmy's field. Run up or they'll be bursting surely" (*Playboy*, 95).

The hypocrisy of Shawn's respectability is further exposed when Christy is hired as a pot-boy in the pub. Shawn: "That's be a queer kind to bring into a decent quiet household with the like of Pegeen Mike" (*Playboy*, 81). Of course, how can a shebeen pub ever be considered a "decent quiet household"? Shawn calls it such because he wants to marry Pegeen, the only heir to the pub, and simultaneously maintain his respectability. Shawn clearly wants the marriage to Pegeen, knowing she loathes him, to capitalize on the pub's profits despite the real disrepute that should have been attached to a pub in 1907 from the Church. The blatant and hostile joke from Synge was that the Church did not necessarily have to see a pub as non-respectable. Yet Synge further reveals Shawn's sham respectability through Shawn's allegiance to the area's priest, Father Reilly.

Father Reilly, like the priest in Synge's *Riders to the Sea*, is absent throughout the play regardless of the Church's contention in the early twentieth century that priests in rural Ireland were community leaders. In *John Bull's*, Shaw subtly contests this contention through the pious-appearing Father Dempsey, who looks out for the Church's financial interests rather than the poor, and the community-passionate, but defrocked, Peter Keegan. In *Playboy*, the absent Father Reilly has a voice through the capitalistic but pious-appearing Shawn, with whom he has an alliance. When Reilly learns from Shawn that a self-proclaimed murderer is staying with Pegeen in her father's pub, Reilly and Shawn consort with the Widow Quin and send her to intervene to save Pegeen's respectability and preserve Shawn's chance to marry Pegeen. The Widow, on gaining entrance into the pub, explains, "I'm after meeting Shawn Keogh and Father Reilly below, who told me of your curiosity man, and they fearing by this time he was maybe roaring, romping on your hands with drink" (*Playboy*, 85). The Widow Quin is a curious person for the priest and Shawn to turn to, given that she is anything but a respectable person, having "buried her children and destroyed her man" (*Playboy*, 86). When she alludes to having killed her husband, Pegeen charges: "She did not. She hit himself with a worn pick, and the rusted poison did corrode his blood the way he never overed it, and died after" (*Playboy*, 86). Pegeen elaborates further on Quin's character, which the Widow does not deny: "Doesn't the world know you reared a black lamb at your own breast, so that the Lord Bishop of Connacht felt the elements of a Christian, and he eating it after in a kidney stew? Doesn't the world know you've been seen shaving the foxy skipper from France for a threepenny bit and a sop of grass tobacco would wring the liver from a mountain goat you'd meet leaping the hills?" (*Playboy*, 87).

The pious airs of Father Reilly and Shawn are indeed negated by their association with Quin, given her bestiality (as a Christian) and her prostitution (implied by her shaving the French skipper). The amoral Quin is the only character, along with the violence-loving Sara Tansey, who tries to help Christy after he fights his father a second time before everyone and they all think he kills him.[8] The hypocrisy of Shawn and Reilly is completed with their affiliation with a Church that sells its own morality in a "bargain" to allow Shawn to marry his cousin Pegeen: "Aren't we after making a good bargain, the way we're only waiting these days on Father Reilly's dispensation from the bishops, or the Court of Rome" (*Playboy*, 74). The characters Shawn and Father Reilly expose the sham of the Church in Ireland that should have been serving the poor, not creating and backing Shawn Keoghs. Yet clearly Synge's assault on the Church's respectability and the capitalist middle-class Irish, like Shawn, was far more antagonistic than Shaw's confronting and satirical attack on the same target via his Dempsey and Keegan characters. Synge undoubtedly viewed his attack to be more direct, which worked to make his play an uncompromising portrait of Ireland.[9] His portrayal of the greed of Shawn and Michael, with Father Reilly's blessing, as examples of the capitalist infection in rural Ireland, is epitomized as they conspire to enslave Pegeen in a marriage they view as "respectable," but is against her will, which would financially profit both Shawn and Michael—profit being their bottom line.

Pegeen, as the publican's daughter, is, of course, a member of a lower middle class, but she is a character that is trapped, a prisoner of her class's crass social and material values. True, she too is referred to at times by two first names, Pegeen Mike. However, these names are very different from her father's Michael James. Pegeen's respectable name is Margaret but she does not use it, using instead a name that bespeaks of pagan, non-Christian Ireland (Innes, *The Devil's*, 67). This, of course, begins to distance Pegeen from the conventional Christian morality in Ireland that helped form middle-class capitalist respectability rather than carry out the socialistic teachings of the New Testament. In one of the reviews that attacked the play for being amoral during its premier run, the *Freeman's Journal* only referred to Pegeen as Margaret, purposely avoiding the character's non-Christian name that is used exclusively throughout the play.

Synge's description of Pegeen when the play opens as a "wild-looking" woman in "usual peasant" dress reveals that she is much closer to the true Irish culture or life usually found by Synge among the peasant class than among those like her "respectable" father. It is key to keep in mind that Synge, expressed in his article "From Galway to Gorumna," believed bourgeois infection robbed the Irish of their "colour and attractiveness"—or in other words, their Irishness ("From Galway," 145). It is true that early on in the play Pegeen dismisses the men in the Belmullet area, but this is not a dismissal of them as suitors in a class-snobbery context, but rather a dismissal of them for lacking heroics or any type of real spirit—in fact, dismissing them for lacking an Irish spirit. For example, she negates Jimmy Farrell's manhood by revealing Farrell's disturbingly vulgar greed as he tried to avoid paying for a new dog license: "Jimmy Farrell hanged his dog from the license, and had it screeching and wiggling three hours at the butt of a string, and himself swearing it was a dead dog, and the peelers [police] swearing it had life" (*Playboy*, 80). Farrell is also described as "fat," therefore financially above peasants.[10]

"Fat," and all it implies in the play's context, is not an attraction for Pegeen. Ultimately, Pegeen is willing to marry the nearly starved (from his travels) Christy Mahon, based not on his material wealth or pious respectability, as he clearly has neither when he arrives, but on his heroic, spirited tale of having killed his brutish, bullying father. In fact, the newly arrived Christy seemingly has an Irish spirit that has not been erased by the infection of bourgeois values.

In seeming contrast, Christy's father, Old Mahon, is infected with capitalist greed and also represents the class Synge loathed throughout Ireland. When asked in Act II what drove him to strike his father, Christy explains that Old Mahon was pushing him to marry the Widow Casey, whom Christy describes as a "walking terror." He adds that his father's motivation for insisting on this marriage was because "he'd have her hut to live in and her gold to drink" (*Playboy*, 91). Christy's tale of striking down his oppressor, "killing" his father prior to the play's action, takes on a new texture in that Old Mahon is not only tied to a British army officer, but also bound to middle-class capitalist greed, the greed that Synge saw as stripping the Irish of their Irishness. Christy, then, early in the play represents a real hero for Pegeen and her ticket to escape from the stifling middle-class values of her father and Shawn, hence his appearance as a savior.

Maurice Bourgeois's 1913 *John Millington Synge and the Irish Theatre* argues that in *Playboy*, Synge revisits *In the Shadow of the Glen*'s assault on loveless and arranged marriages in Ireland. Bourgeois believes that Pegeen is another example of a strong Irish woman rejecting a forced marriage arrangement being pushed on her by two men (believing that

Nora's marriage in *Shadow* was also an arrangement). Bourgeois writes that to illustrate the horror of Pegeen's situation, Synge portrays Shawn as "an exceeding prudish, pusillanimous, spiritless bumpkin weakly in body and mind, who has a farm and cattle, but no intelligence" (*John Millington Synge*, 195). He does everything but label Shawn a product of the infection of middle-class values in rural Ireland. Synge's contemporary, the journalist P. D. Kenny, who had authored a radical socialist-leaning book titled *Economics for Irishmen* in 1905, also saw *Playboy* as depicting the spiritually debilitating consequence of "arranged and loveless marriages" (but respectable) in Ireland (Mikhail, "Notes," 41). Certainly, the forced marriage to Shawn pushes Pegeen to see what she wants to see in Christy.

The notion of Pegeen being trapped by the capitalism that Synge viewed as infecting rural Ireland, and all Ireland, is consistent with Pegeen's thematic representation of pagan Ireland, Synge's ideal of Ireland that existed before bourgeois infection. Nationalistically, as I argue in *Synge and Irish Nationalism*, Pegeen's representation of pagan native Ireland, as her name suggests, thematically explains why she attempts to form an alliance with Christy, who must represent Christ or Christianity in Ireland, as his name and his savior-type status implies. Forming an alliance with Christy mirrors historical pagan Ireland's forged alliance with Christianized leaders to strengthen its position. The fact that Christy proves a false hero, a false savior, reflects Synge's sense of Christianity failing Ireland—the conservative Christian moral values that ruined Parnell but ignored the real message and teaching of the Christ myth in favor of monetary-instilled class respectable interests. This argument is only strengthened by Christy's appearance as a spirited, moneyless man for Pegeen in Act I, especially within the context of the New Testament's philosophy, the last shall be first. Since the Catholic Church failed to maintain this philosophy in Ireland, as Synge saw it, Christy's failure for Pegeen is further explained.

Of course, Pegeen is given a clue in Act I that Christy will fail her because of his true nature when he is asked if he committed thievery. He replies, "with a flash of family pride," "And I the son of a strong farmer ... could have bought up the whole of your old house a while since, from the butt of his tailcoat and not have missed the weight of it gone" (*Playboy*, 79). However, this clue to Christy's bourgeois pride, therefore the bourgeois values he really harbors, is stated before he tells his story of having killed his father while digging his father's potatoes, which overshadows his earlier comments. Ultimately, Christy represents the middle-class conservative nationalists who have promised much for Ireland, like Christy's "gallous" tale, but at heart were still harboring their bourgeois pride and values and deliver only talk.[11] Christy, like Shawn, is mindful of the pub that would become his should he marry Pegeen: "Half a hundred beyond. Ten there. A score that's above. Eighty jugs. Six cups and a broken one. Two plates. A power of glasses. Bottles, a school-master'd be hard set to count, and enough in them, I'm thinking, to drunken all the wealth and wisdom of the County Clare" (*Playboy*, 88).

Declan Kiberd also notes Synge's portrayal of bourgeois values infiltrating the community in *Playboy*, as it does in *In the Shadow of the Glen*. But, Kiberd believes that at play's end Pegeen "surrenders to . . . become a 'proper' country girl" when she rejects Christy's second attempt at violence (*Inventing Ireland*, 182).[12] However, as argued above, Pegeen rejects Christy and his second "killing" because he does it solely for personal reasons, which is foreign to the communal sense of pagan, or paganized Ireland, that Synge idealized and had found on Inishmaan. Plus, Pegeen at the play's very end, after she exiles Christy, boxes Shawn's ears and exclaims, "Quit my sight" (*Playboy*, 118). She passionately and adamantly rejects the "proper" respectable gentility in her final rejection of the wealthy, but hypocritical Shawn Keogh.[13]

In fact, Pegeen challenges and negates the Irish bourgeois paternal family structure by being or endeavoring to become an independent woman, much like *In the Shadow of the Glen*'s Nora. But unlike Synge's and Shaw's Noras, Pegeen does not leave with the intruding stranger at play's end when she finally rejects Shawn, leaving her on her own. Throughout her play, Pegeen alone decides to go against her father's wishes in early Act III when she wants to marry Christy, and at play's end she alone decides that the false Christy must leave. The Irish conventional middle class in Synge's time adamantly believed in the submissive domestic role for women. When Synge was writing his plays, Arthur Griffith published a series of articles by Mary Butler, a conservative nationalist, in the *United Irishman* calling for Irish women to serve Ireland within the domestic sphere of their home (Biletz, "Women," 67).[14] Pegeen is the constant antithesis of Butler's advice. She alone, not Christy, is the one who stops Old Mahon from beating Christy when he confronts Christy for the first time in front of Pegeen. It is Pegeen who puts the rope on Christy when the villagers think he has killed his father before them, and all the other men are too drunk or too weak to do it. And unlike Shaw's domestic Nora, who fails to find love with Larry, Pegeen expels Christy's love based on lies.

Pegeen strives to determine her own life and direction as she tries to see in Christy a hero and as she rejects her father's and Shawn's effort to trap her in a loveless marriage. This direction is the opposite of Shaw's Nora, who finds herself at play's end engaged to a man she neither loves nor knows. In her plight, and representing traditionally submissive Irish women, Shaw's Nora is unable to seek self-determination. So while a conservative Dublin audience accepted her in 1907, but amid Shaw's intention that her condition would gradually nudge that audience to see her entrapment, Pegeen was intended to offer a new and furthered image of Irish women, one grounded in pagan Ireland, to reject the Irish woman's enslaved domestic role with the intent of ushering in a new social Irish order. As a consequence, Pegeen was mostly not accepted by her original audience. This non-domesticity of Pegeen, or her independent spirit, is again a characteristic Synge observed in Aran and therefore he believed it was native to Irish culture that was free from bourgeois-infected desire for respectability that relegated women throughout Ireland as domestic slaves. Such women were neither expected nor wanted by the conservative Dublin middle class.[15]

Playboy's attack on the capitalist attitudes of Ireland's middle class was still carried further by Synge through the explosive audience disturbances and press attacks that greeted the play during its premier run. On the third night, the audience erupted into riot during Act III when Christy stated, "It's Pegeen I'm seeking only, and what'd I care if you brought me a drift of chosen females, standing in their shifts itself, maybe, from this place to the Eastern World?" (*Playboy*, 115).[16] The main objection from the audience was supposedly over the word "shifts." Such a reaction clearly revealed the foolish pious respectability of the audience members who objected. Synge himself told a reporter for the *Evening Herald* during the premier run that *shift* "was an everyday word in the West of Ireland" and that it had been "used without any objections in Douglas Hyde's 'Songs of Connacht'" ("Abbey Theatre Scene," 36). However, the real implication from Synge is more than an assertion that the detracting audience members did not understand their idealized *Love Songs of Connacht*, nor understood the West of Ireland; he was insinuating that his detractors did not understand the Irish mythic hero Cuchulain.

In the myth "The Cattle Raid of Cuailnge," a young Cuchulain is welcomed back from a battle by many naked or semi-naked women. This continues the allusion Synge makes between Christy and Cuchulain, namely in Christy's triumphs in the sports at the fair. Cuchulain's myth includes his great victories at all sports. The fact that the supposed nationalists did not see that Synge was presenting a false Cuchulain via Christy, as well as a false Christ, reveals that the detractors did not even know Cuchulain, whom they claimed to admire. Exposing such ignorance among the detractors, which Synge anticipated, exposed the detractors as pseudo-nationalists. Kiberd reminds us that "Synge was amused by the fact that the great deeds of Cuchulain were typically applauded by men too timid" to act them out (*Inventing Ireland*, 171). The difference between Christy and Cuchulain is that the latter always did his deeds for Ireland, not for personal gain. Ultimately, of course, Cuchulain was of a pagan myth and therefore of pagan Ireland. Synge knew the Catholic, respectable bourgeois class could not really appreciate Cuchulain's legend, which advocated the message of serving Ireland over serving one's selfish interests.

Objecting to "shifts" was beyond the ridiculous, which illustrated the play's detractors as being infected with the bourgeois obsession for respectability that they clearly placed before Ireland in that they allowed their supposed morality to blind them to the play's definition of violence; a definition that would resonate and re-emerge for a handful of Irish radicals in 1916, who faced the capitalist empire for Ireland while most of the Irish remained in their homes or in a British war. The play's definition of violence was crucial for 1907 Ireland, not to mention its prophesy and advocacy for 1913 and 1916, and it was being missed by most of the audience—it was almost as if Parnell's collapse and ruin were occurring all over again. In fact, a shift was thrown in Parnell's face by the moralizing bourgeois-infected mob that had turned on him, despite his work for Ireland, in 1890 (McCormack, *Fool*, 312). The *Freeman's Journal* alluded to "shift" by sympathizing with Sara Allgood, who played the Widow Quin, as "it was sure she would blush to utter [the word] even in the privacy of her bedroom" (Roberts, "J. M. Synge," 126). Such an absurd reaction reveals the detractors as being like the hypocritical Shawn Keogh, who, despite his obsession with pious morality, is willing to purchase help from the Widow Quin. That the hypocrisy of the play's detractors was not lost on Synge is revealed in Yeats's claim that during the play's second performance, while certain audience members were being disruptive, Synge came to him and said: "A young doctor has just told me that he can hardly keep himself from jumping on to a seat, and pointing out in that howling mob [objecting to the play on moral grounds] those whom he is treating for venereal disease" (as quoted in "J. M. Synge and the Ireland," 56).

The *Freeman's Journal* also stated that *Playboy* was "an unmitigated protracted libel upon Irish peasant men, and, worse still, upon Irish peasant girlhood" (as quoted in Hogan and Kilroy, *Abbey Theatre*, 125). The slander the paper saw to Irish women, which it demeaningly labeled "girlhood," was the play's portrayal of Irish women being fascinated with Christy.[17] Arthur Griffith specified in his review that the play portrays Irish women "contending in their lusts for the possession of a man who has appealed to their depraved instincts by murdering, as they believe, his father" ("All Ireland," 2 February 1907, 1). Griffith, it is remembered, objected to *In the Shadow of the Glen*'s Nora because she leaves her physically abusive husband. He believed that Irish women must not leave their husbands. Here with *Playboy*, Griffith again cannot see past his bourgeois morality and belief in a respectable Ireland. He cannot see how or why Christy appeals, through the perceived spirit and heroic tale that sets Christy above Pegeen's petty capitalist father, the bourgeois pious Shawn, and all the rest of the Belmullet locale's men. Christy as would-be savior appears to offer everything to Pegeen, and his failure at play's end represents the failure of Irish manhood, and Christianity as practiced, in capitalist-infected 1907 Ireland.

Pegeen, in the play's opening moments, clearly runs down the type of failing men found in Mayo, with Mayo representing Ireland.[18] The characters of Michael and Shawn, Jimmy Farrell and Philly Cullen all affirm Pegeen's assessment, which is not contradicted by Old Mahon's character, all of which literally opens the door for Christy in Act I. The exposure of Christy Mahon as a liar and then an advocate for selfish personal gain by his Act III act of violence against his father, reveals him to Pegeen, and the audience, to be an empty braggart. This is affirmed yet again near the play's very end, when Pegeen and the villagers, thinking he has now killed his father, are trying to tie Christy up; Christy threatens: "if I've to face the gallows, I'll have a gay march down, I tell you, and shed the blood of some of you before I die . . . If I do lay my hands on you, it's the way you'll be at the fall of night, hanging as a scarecrow for the fowls of hell.

Ah, you'll have a gallous jaunt I'm saying, coaching out through Limbo with my father's ghost" (*Playboy*, 116). But rather than carry out the violence he threatens, all Christy can manage is to bite the weakest among them, Shawn Keogh, on the leg: "My leg's bit on me. He's the like of a mad dog"—indeed (*Playboy*, 117).

Christy with his bourgeois pride is nothing more than a boaster with empty words. Shaw, more subtly, portrays the failure of Irish manhood in *John Bull's* via the petty Rosscullen capitalist men falling for Broadbent's offered mortgages, and Larry participating with Broadbent to efficiently confiscate Rosscullen from its inhabitants while knowing full well the ruinous implications for those inhabitants, including his father and aunt. Synge's *Playboy*, on the other hand, presents Ireland's failed manhood through the failings of Christy, Shawn, Michael James, and Old Mahon. Synge's attack on Irish manhood, without the buffer of a comical figure like Broadbent, directly casts the would-be nationalists in the Abbey Theatre's 1907 audience as being little more than Christys, all talk and no unselfish actions. Given Synge's abrupt labeling of his detractors as Shawns, Old Mahons, and Christys, it is no wonder audiences broke up over the play.

In the end, *The Playboy of the Western World* indicts the bourgeois nationalists who were obsessed, not with improving Ireland for all the Irish, but with their meaningless pious respectability and profits, who only offered empty words and empty actions and knew nothing of real Ireland. This was indeed a nationalist and socialistic confrontational indictment of 1907 Ireland, an Ireland that had witnessed many nationalists in Dublin talk and write about independence but offer nothing except for their unwillingness to improve the existence of the Irish proletariat. To Synge, the real Ireland was not "respectable" but rather free of pretentious respectability. It was the Ireland he observed in Aran when he returned for his second visit and shared photographs he had taken: "[A] young woman I had spoken to a few times last year slipped in, and after a wonderfully simple and cordial speech of welcome, she sat down on the floor beside me to look on also. The complete absence of shyness or self-consciousness in most of these people gives them a peculiar charm, and when this young and beautiful woman leaned across my knees to look nearer at some photograph that pleased her, I felt more than ever the strange simplicity of the . . . life" (*Playboy*, 52). In effect, it was an Ireland absent "of any division of labour" and therefore with no need for restricting class behavioral codes that reeked of hypocritical morality. The socialist leanings in *The Playboy of the Western World*, together with the play's presentment of a strong Irish woman in Pegeen, itself socialistic, was Synge's effort to re-image Ireland by attacking the capitalistic values that prevented liberalizing social progress and justice.

In essence, Synge chose to indict his conservative Irish detractors, whereas Shaw, when *John Bull's* first played Dublin, preferred to ridicule the same conservative nationalists who missed the Shavian satire but laughed rather than riot. One sought a changed Ireland, and the other to prod the world to change. As a consequence, *Playboy*'s premiere courted violence, provoking self-indicting rioters in the theatre and, interestingly and despite Synge's urgency, over time Irish revolution.

If Synge was pleased with the hissing amid audience applause that greeted him when called for following the premiere of *In the Shadow of the Glen*, how did he feel about the reaction to *The Playboy of the Western World*? In a letter to MacKenna after the play's premiere, Synge wrote about the play's reception: "the scurrility, and ignorance and treachery of some of the attacks upon me have rather disgusted me with the middle class Irish Catholic. As you know I have the wildest admiration for the Irish Peasants, and for Irish men of known or unknown genius—do you bow?—but between the two there's an ungodly ruck of fat-faced, sweaty-headed, swine. They are in Dublin, and Kingstown, and alas in all the country towns" (*Synge Letters*, I, 330).[19] The play's reception solidified Synge's view of the falsity of the Irish "respectable" middle class.[20]

In his letter to the American journalist Frederick Gregg, eight months after *Playboy*'s premiere, Synge states that the *Playboy* row invigorated him (*Synge Letters*, II, 56). His response to the provocation that started with Shaw's master Irish work *John Bull's Other Island* resulted in Synge's masterwork, but in a volatile form that exploded in the theatre. As the hostility of the 1907 audience reception of *Playboy* arguably prophesized the violent clashes that would erupt in Dublin in 1913 between labor and capitalists, and re-emerge in 1916 and again in 1922 civil war Ireland, *Playboy* and *John Bull's* had epitomized, perhaps with no turning back, the two tracks for Irish socialistic theatre that would help propel Ireland into revolution—with Shaw's presence in both.

The Playboy Blanco

In November 1907, Synge elected not to see *John Bull's Other Island* when it came to Dublin, but Shaw had seen *The Playboy of the Western World* when it played in London for the first time in June 1907. In 1911 when the Abbey Theatre first toured the United States, Shaw provided an article in support of the tour in New York's *Evening Sun*: "John Synge wrote a wonderful play called The Playboy of the Western World [sic], which is now a classic." But Shaw clarified his remark by adding that, "This play was not about an Irish peculiarity, but about a universal weakness of mankind: the habit of admiring bold scoundrels" ("The Irish Players," 73). Shaw did not appear to see Synge's play in necessarily Irish terms, or, if he did, he did so rarely.[21] But Shaw may indeed have come to recognize in *Playboy* Synge's specific indictment of the middle-class pseudo-nationalists who attacked his (Synge's) work, who, at least in regard to the bourgeois values of their class, were Shaw's target as well, even if Shaw chose to see them as not being "peculiar" to Ireland. However, Shaw's views on *Playboy* may have taken some time to develop into a recognition of Synge's specificity.

Shaw's sense that the issues in *Playboy* were universal, found in all countries, testifies to Shaw's grasp of universal conditions. His target was always larger than conditions in any one country, so seeing *Playboy* as a universal condition, despite Synge's intent, was to be expected from Shaw. He certainly was correct when he viewed *In the Shadow of the Glen* in 1904 as being limited by its national focus.

Shaw's opinion of *Playboy* evolved from his first exposure to the play, which was during the Abbey Theatre's 1907 London engagement. Shaw's immediate response to the play's first revival was reported by Ben Iden Payne to have merely been: "He shrugged his shoulders about the play and did not admire the acting" (as quoted in Laurence and Grene, "Introduction and Notes," xiii). The 1907 London production of *Playboy*, and subsequent Abbey Theatre stagings of the play, was significantly toned down from the play's January premiere. Some of the language believed offensive to the Dublin audience in January, as well as that thought to be potentially offensive to a London audience, was censored and altered. More significantly, the revival was played more as a broad comedy or farce than in the play's premiere. Dublin actor Maire Nic Shiubhlaigh recalled that the premier staging "was played seriously, almost somberly, as though each character had been studied and its nastiness made apparent" (*Splendid*,

81).²² Synge had actively participated in the staging of the premiere, attending all or most rehearsals. He had wanted the play's characters to clearly signify the character types from Ireland's rural west that they were intended to represent, and during the premiere's rehearsals, Synge resisted for the most part altering the antagonistic dialogue. While Synge labeled the play a comedy, he undoubtedly saw it along the lines of what is now called a dark comedy. However, Synge did concede to toning down *Playboy* for the first London performances, which he probably agreed to partly for the sake of his fiancée, Molly Allgood (who again played Pegeen), and partly because the English censor, the Lord Chamberlain, forced some of the alterations for the 1907 London performances. In fact, one month before its London premiere, the tour's chief architect, W. B. Yeats, who was visiting Venice at the time, was "summoned back to London" as the Lord Chamberlain "threatened to stop the production" if alterations were not made to the dialogue (Quin, Ni Dhuibhne, and McDonald, *W. B. Yeats*, 84). The exposure *Playboy* brought to the Abbey Theatre regarding censorship, from the Lord Chamberlain's power in England and from the attempts to censor through disrupting performances by the Irish bourgeois pseudo-nationalists in Dublin, opened a door for a Shavian premiere in Dublin.

Still, the general Shavian take on *Playboy* was that the play focused on a universal human trait, the admiration of scoundrels by the supposedly respectable middle class. To Shaw, this admiration exposed the hypocrisy of the bourgeois. So while Shaw saw Synge's Christy Mahon's popularity among Pegeen's villagers as exposing their hypocrisy, Synge had more in mind. After all, a real target for Synge was the Irish character-type represented by the respectability-obsessed Shawn Keogh, who does not admire the self-proclaimed parricide Christy Mahon. Synge's intent was to directly expose the hypocrisy in his play's original Dublin audience. This hypocrisy was revealed in the exposure of the bourgeois audience who claimed to be nationalists but were only pseudo-nationalists, illustrated by their objection to Synge's portrayal of them as obsessed with Catholic morality like Shawn, as obsessively drinking as in Michael James, as mimicking British bullying authority as in Old Mahon, and/or, in the ultimate exposure, as boasters with much talk but no action like Christy Mahon—all characters infected with bourgeois capitalist values. Again, if this was not enough, Synge cemented his indictment of 1907 Irish manhood by presenting an independently minded woman in Pegeen to undermine the men further by being more "manly" than the men. A contemporary audience member who saw *Playboy*'s premiere and publicly defended the play, wrote about the audience's objection, thinking that their excessive objections revealed their true natures: "[it is] only the thief who gets in a rage at being called dishonest, the honourable man merely smiles" (P.M.E.K., "A Plea," 3). Synge's indictment of the play's premiere audience was solidified in that the audience saw itself in Synge's expression of failed Irish manhood. The audience recognition of Synge's indictment of themselves was achieved by Synge's blatantly antagonistic approach.

The fact that Shaw eventually recognized the Irish specificity in Synge's confrontation is revealed when he wrote on hearing about the Irish-American audience disruptions against *The Playboy of the Western World* in New York and Philadelphia during the Abbey Theatre's 1911–12 American tour. Shaw revealed his recognition of the indictment leveled by *Playboy* on self-proclaimed respectable Irish nationalists who were obsessed with conservative Catholicism, drank too much, and/or were empty boasters: "The American Gaels are the real Playboys of the Western World, and they are naturally angry with Synge for showing them up" (as quoted in Laurence and Grene, "Introduction and Notes," 67). In tune with his views of *Playboy* is Shaw's play *The Shewing-up of Blanco Posnet*, which premiered in Dublin by the Abbey Theatre in August 1909, five months after Synge's early death from cancer.

In the Shavian canon, *The Shewing-up of Blanco Posnet* is remembered as being a blow against theatre censorship in Britain in the form of clashing with the Lord Chamberlain. When the Lord Chamberlain banned the play in England on moral grounds, the Abbey Theatre's remaining directors Lady Gregory and W. B. Yeats, fresh from their own experiences with censorship over *Playboy*, offered to stage *Blanco Posnet* in Dublin.[23] The Abbey Theatre's premiere of the play, given that the Lord Chamberlain's authority did not extend to Ireland, is now famous. Shaw used the play and its first production to argue against theatre censorship, which then and now dominates thought on the play. Nonetheless, the play echoes Shaw's views of *Playboy* and takes its spot within socialistic debate in early modern Irish theatre.

Shaw presents his audience with a seeming scoundrel, Blanco Posnet, who stands accused of horse-stealing and faces what appears to be his inevitable hanging. Yet Shaw clearly directs the audience to sympathize with

Blanco, as the respectable people who want to hang and shoot him are anything but respectable. Lucy McDiarmid points out that Shaw "tantalizingly" uses the supposed moral "blasphemy" to reach his religious-like sermon, mixing scoundrel with the heroic (*Controversy*, 93). The audience's liking of Blanco, for Shaw, is similar to his view of Synge's Christy Mahon being celebrated, not by his original audience but initially by Pegeen and her village, because he is perceived as a scoundrel who has murdered his father. While Synge would not have agreed with such a reading of *Playboy* given Christy as a false savior, Shaw portrays those who would judge Blanco to be like those who judged Synge and his play. They are revealed as scoundrels in their own right. Blanco charges his brother Elder Daniels, a pillar of pious respectability, "All you ever did when I owned you was to borrow money from me to get drunk with. Now you lend money and sell drink to other people," adding, "Don't deceive yourself, Boozy. You sell drink because you make a bigger profit out of it than you can by selling tea" (*Blanco*, 433, 435–436). When the Sheriff and jury seem ready to convict Blanco based on one witness, Feemy Evans, Blanco states: "I accuse the fair Euphemia of immoral relations with every man in this town, including yourself, Sheriff. I say this is a conspiracy to kill me between Feemy and Strapper because I wouldn't touch Feemy with a pair of tongs" (*Blanco*, 445).

Such a charge of prostitution is more blatant than Pegeen's accusation of the Widow Quin's prostitution in *Playboy*, and certainly more risqué than the mentioning of a woman's shift. But by setting his play in an American western frontier town, there was no Dublin audience outcry against such an attack on womanhood. While many in the Abbey's opening night for *Blanco Posnet* were aristocrats connected to Dublin Castle (McDiarmid, *Controversy*, 110), the likes of Arthur Griffith also attended the premiere and enjoyed the play. Holroyd writes: "The audience took to *Blanco Posnet* enthusiastically, laughing at its humour, passing over the dangerous passages with sympathetic blankness, and at the curtain interrupting their applause with vain calls for the author" (*Bernard Shaw*, 230). The *Freeman's Journal*, which had called *Playboy* a "libel" against Irish men and Irish women, wrote of *Blanco Posnet*, "there is really nothing in the drama played last night that could give offense to any but the most thin-skinned spectator" (as quoted in Hogan and Kilroy, *Abbey Theatre*, 298). Given the pre-performance hype of the Abbey jockeying with Dublin Castle to perform the play, the audience was expecting something as explosive as *Playboy*, but instead many of them failed to understand, again, Shaw's satiric ridicule of themselves in a universal or international context.

Despite the aristocrats on opening night, *Blanco Posnet* delivered extraordinary jabs at the Dublin middle-class respectable audience that had been so incensed by *Playboy*'s direct attack on their bourgeois values presented as Irish, yet they thoroughly enjoyed Shaw's American scoundrel and his words that undermine the "respectable" class. The middle-class Synge detractor Joseph Holloway recorded that *Blanco Posnet* was "an event of a lifetime" (*Joseph Holloway's*, 130). That a Dublin audience could object to or celebrate plays attacking the bourgeois class based solely on whether one directly targets the class as Irish and the other as American (or foreign), suggested, for Shaw, that he was right in *John Bull's Other Island*. The Irish provincial focus could only be negative for Ireland in the modern industrial world of economic classes, not nationalisms. Irish ignorance of themselves as part of international humanity could only lead to "disreputable" and petty outrages like the mob-like detractors of *Playboy*. When he delivered his lecture "The Poor Law and Destitution in Ireland" in Dublin on 3 October 1910, "Shaw deplored the time and energy wasted on the denunciation of Synge's *The Playboy* when it could have been given to some other more useful cause" (Holloway, *Joseph Holloway's*, 142). Clearly, Shaw continued his consistent view that Irish attention on themselves as only Irish, whether from Synge or the Irish response to Synge, was neither "efficient" nor productive. Again, Shaw was more the international socialist, while Synge was the more socialistic nationalist.

For Shaw, Blanco Posnet, like Christy, turns out not to be the scoundrel everyone thinks at play's beginning, since Blanco gave the Sheriff's horse that was in Elder Daniel's possession, in an unselfish Christ-like gesture, to a woman desperately trying to save her ill child.[24] Since the child died, in a sense betraying Blanco, Blanco and Shaw are able to question God while affirming that one do the right thing—not for God but for one's self because it is right. In essence, Blanco is negating the rules that the bourgeois middle class manipulated out of their perception of Christianity to define "respectable." In Dublin, this subtly undermined the respectable who shouted and stamped their feet during *Playboy*'s premier run rather than see and hear the play. They wanted the play, from the playwright who had confronted their non-radical counter-revolutionary pseudo-nationalism in earlier plays, to be an insult to them like Shaw's American townspeople in *Blanco Posnet* want to hang Blanco without knowing what he is about. But, of course, Synge's audience was correct to recognize that *Playboy* was directly attacking them. Yet how many of *Blanco Posnet*'s audience recognized Shaw's negation of them, and all capitalistically respectable people?

Shaw's international socialist undermining of bourgeois respectability in *Blanco Posnet* is consistent with his Fabian philosophy and much of his dramatic canon, believing that people were more apt to change when not being insulted. The Fabian approach of reasoning with audiences rather than antagonizing them is apparent in the play's American setting. For the London audience for which the play was first intended, like the premiere's Dublin audience, the setting among frontier (therefore possibly barbarian) Americans meant that the undermining of respectability was subtle and most would laugh and not feel insulted as the direct targets, whether they got the satire immediately or not.

Like *John Bull's Other Island*, *The Shewing-up of Blanco Posnet* proved quite popular with its early Dublin audiences and delivered biting commentary on that audience that had so disliked *Playboy* nearly two and a half years earlier. This commentary would repeat itself all over again in 1911, as *Blanco Posnet* was included in the Abbey Theatre's 1911 American tour with *The Playboy of the Western World* when the latter was protested against by American Irish who, this time, were too provincial to see themselves as Americans or, as Shaw undoubtedly believed, too provincial to see *Playboy* as a portrayal of humanity.[25] Interestingly, Synge attacked such audiences for being non-radical conservative pseudo-nationalists and Shaw undermined their provincial, Irish nationalist attitudes.

Furthermore, Blanco Posnet's reasoned arguments and objections during his trial, often masked in humor, help to gradually soften the unreasonable townspeople toward Blanco's eventual acquittal: "The devil's gone out of you" (*Blanco* 455). This is interesting testimony from Shaw on the effectiveness of Fabian reasoning over blatant antagonism. But, of course, Shaw's approach offers the opportunity for the bourgeois to be reasoned with. After their reactions to *Playboy*, Synge remarked that his detractors were "not . . . of intellect and honesty with whom we can reason" (*Synge Letters*, I, 289). However, Shaw's audience commentary and testimony for Fabian tactics for Dublin from *Blanco Posnet*, like the premiere in Dublin, was an accident.

Michael Holroyd suggests that *The Shewing-up of Blanco Posnet* was written with the London star actor Herbert Beerbohm Tree in mind (*Bernard Shaw*, 227). This is substantiated by the fact that Tree submitted the play to the Lord Chamberlain for permission to perform. Yet even as the play became a vehicle for the debate against theatre censorship, was it written without Synge and *Playboy* in mind? After all, the protests of performance disruptions against the 1907 Dublin premiere (and the later, 1911 New York and Philadelphia premieres) of *Playboy* were attempts to censor the play. As stated above, Shaw saw *Playboy* performed by the Abbey Theatre in London in June 1907, a revival in which the script had been officially censored by the Lord Chamberlain. Shaw undoubtedly had read about the Dublin protests against *Playboy*, specifically the objections over the play's portrayal of Irish women and Irish men. Still, *The Shewing-up of Blanco Posnet* was not written until nearly two years after Shaw first saw *Playboy* performed. Holroyd maintains that Shaw quickly wrote *Blanco Posnet* "between 16 February and 8 March 1909" (*Bernard Shaw*, 227). This was, coincidentally, the very time Synge was dying. Synge was admitted to hospital on 2 February and died on 24 March. Synge's declining health and final hospitalization were widely known among Dublin theatre and literary people, and it is nearly inconceivable that Shaw did not know. Yeats had informed a number of people about Synge's rapidly failing health, such as in an undated March 1909 letter he wrote to his and Shaw's former lover and continual friend Florence Farr, in which he said Synge was hospitalized and possibly dying (*Collected Yeats Letters*, 526).

In a 7 August 1909 letter to Lady Gregory about the staging of *Blanco Posnet*, which was about to start rehearsals, Shaw gave his opinion about whether the Abbey Theatre actors should attempt an American accent: "I should play it in broad Irish, especially as that language will lead itself very congenially to the blasphemies with which the dialogue bristles" (*Shaw, Lady Gregory*, 11). Given the 1907 *Playboy* disturbances, the Abbey's Dublin audience considered itself well-versed in blasphemies delivered in broad Irish accents. Perhaps this view from Shaw indicates that he saw clear connections between *Blanco* and *Playboy*, with the former obviously being more about its audience (in this case Dublin) than western frontier Americans.[26] *Blanco Posnet* premiered on a day following a revival of *Playboy*. Was this also a coincidence by Yeats and Gregory?[27] Reportedly, the excitement of the coming Shaw premiere led to a full house for *Playboy* (Holloway, *Joseph Holloway's*, 130). So, whether or not Shaw's commentary on the respected bourgeois in *The Shewing-up of Blanco Posnet* was consciously written with Synge and *Playboy* in mind, the socialistic commentary was present on 25 August 1909.[28]

Near the end of *Blanco Posnet*, after Blanco's case is dismissed, the Sheriff tells Blanco he should leave town and, to help him, he will, capitalistically, sell him his (the Sheriff's) questionable horse at what he calls "a reasonable figure" (*Blanco*, 453). The Sheriff asks each person present at the trial to make a contribution to the mother of the deceased child, as if that erases the Sheriff's willingness, and theirs, to hang Blanco without proper evidence. Such subtle undermining in the play with its Dublin premiere reiterated Shaw's approach to advocating socialism among some Irish radicals.

In an effort to articulate the differences between Shaw and Synge while sensing their similarities, Yeats, as *The Shewing-up of Blanco Posnet* was premiering, gave an interview to the *Irish Independent* newspaper, a paper that, with others, had attacked *Playboy* in 1907. Yeats was quoted as saying: "I have said from the very start of our theatre, from the first writing of Mr. Shaw—*John Bull*, for instance—that a Shaw play would not be resented by an Irish audience. He has always a clear argument. One always sees what his satire strikes at." The reporter noted, "And then Mr. Yeats drew a comparison between Shaw and Synge. 'Synge's work, on the other hand is dangerous with an Irish audience. It is very hard to understand, and therefore, the very desire to do so makes them impatient with it. . . . To him everything was capricious and temperamental; and he could not tell his secret quickly'" (as quoted in Hogan and Kilroy, *Abbey Theatre*, 295). Yeats seemingly agrees that the satirical comedy of Shaw could please and entertain, while Synge's direction was obscured by that which it aggressively assaulted; two competing approaches for an increasingly class-divided Ireland. Continuing this contrasting of Shaw and Synge is Synge's last play, *Deirdre of the Sorrows*, which was premiered by the Abbey Theatre on 13 January 1910.

Synge's Deirdre

Deirdre of the Sorrows was unfinished when Synge died. In fact, the task of pulling together a performable script from Synge's extensive drafts mostly fell to Synge's fiancée, Molly Allgood, for whom the title character was written (McCormack, *Fool*, 395). This was appropriate, since Allgood had assisted Synge as he had tried to finish the play during the onslaught of his final illness; she read aloud scenes so he could hear and visualize the play (Synge, *Letters to Molly*, 309). Arguably, Molly Allgood, of a working-class background and the first to play Pegeen in *Playboy*, knew the play.

While *Deirdre of the Sorrows* obviously was not a response to *The Shewing-up of Blanco Posnet* as *Playboy* had responded to *John Bull's* (and the latter to *In the Shadow of the Glen*), the play's socialistic leaning again contrasts to Shaw's approach, given Synge's continual antagonistic direction. As seen above, Synge had written *Deirdre of the Sorrows* in response to Yeats's *Deirdre* (1906) (*Synge Letters*, II, 56). The tale of Deirdre was from pre-Christian Irish mythology. The myth tells the story of Deirdre being born with a prophecy of the destruction of the unified Irish alliance under Conchubar, but was also destined to become an exquisite woman. The High King Conchubar seized the infant Deirdre and raised her in isolation with the intent to marry her when she came of age. Before being forced to marry Conchubar, she falls in love with Naisi, of the legendary Red Band of warriors, who agrees to free her from Conchubar as Naisi and Deirdre, with his brothers, go into exile. On Conchubar's promise not to harm them if they return, the group returns. It was a trap, for Conchubar goes against his word, having Naisi and his brothers killed. As a consequence of Conchubar's treachery, the country sinks into a civil war, the alliance of the Irish kings splinters against the High King. When Deirdre refuses his marriage advances, Conchubar sends her to be the concubine of a lesser king (who has remained loyal) for one year. On learning her fate, Deirdre commits suicide as an act of great defiance against Conchubar.

Yeats's *Deirdre* play downplayed Deirdre's heroine position, perhaps in an effort to humanize the characters. As a result, Yeats's Deirdre is arguably a victim throughout her play. After Naisi is killed, Yeats's Deirdre kneels before Conchubar and begs forgiveness and safe passage to leave (Yeats, *Deirdre*, 196–197). This, of course, was exactly what Nora in *In the Shadow of the Glen* refuses to do. Synge's Deirdre was far more similar to Nora and Pegeen than to Yeats's Deirdre—or to *John Bull's Other Island*'s Nora. Synge interpreted the mythic Deirdre as defiant throughout his play.

As with his earlier plays, Synge's *Deirdre of the Sorrows* presents an Ireland infected by capitalist bourgeois influence, but this time set in mythic Ireland. This setting inadvertently supports Shaw's view that usury (capitalizing) behavior was universal to all times and places, while showing Synge's continual focus only on Ireland, including its past to solve its present. Mythic Ireland for the conservatively and respectable middle-class Dublin nationalists rivaled, if not surpassed, their romantic view of Ireland's west as their ideal of Ireland. As Synge had attacked their idealization of the rural west in *Playboy*, he now assaulted their idealization of mythological Ireland with his Deirdre play. And as *Playboy*'s portrait of Pegeen possessing the peasant-pagan spirit of true Ireland, but entrapped within the bourgeois values infecting 1907 Ireland, Synge's Deirdre also finds herself trapped within bourgeois greedy values infecting mythic Ireland while she (with Naisi and his brothers) possesses the pagan spirit of true Ireland.

Synge expresses his sense of Ireland's spirit in Deirdre and Naisi through their marrying for love, opposing the arranged, convenient, and forced marriages like the one she avoids with Conchubar. Nora, in *In the Shadow of the Glen*, is trapped by either an arranged or convenient marriage, while Pegeen in *Playboy* attempts to avoid the arranged and forced marriage to Shawn Keogh. And as we have seen, *John Bull's* Nora agrees to a marriage of convenience in Shaw's ridiculing jab at such bourgeois values (even by the former gentry). Deirdre and Naisi's marriage ceremony is presented as beautiful, simplified, and dignified as a model of Ireland without a debased and self-serving Church. Naisi's brother Ainnle administers the ceremony: "(joining their hands) by the sun and the moon and the whole earth, I wed Deirdre to Naisi. (He steps back and holds up their hands) May the air bless you, and water and wind, the sea, and all the hours of the sun and moon" (*Deirdre of the Sorrows*, 164). Again Synge presents multiple trinities at play. The trinity of Deirdre, Naisi, and Ainnle, as well as that of the sun, the moon, and the earth, recall Shaw's trinities at the end of *John Bull's* of Keegan, Broadbent, and Larry Doyle and the socialistic trinity Keegan describes as his ideal for Ireland. While both playwrights deconstruct the trinity as practiced and preached by a Catholic Church that both believe serves its capitalist interests rather than the people, they also attempt to re-invest the trinity concept with a holiness of sorts. For Shaw, that holiness is Keegan's socialistic (early Christian) vision where the worshipped and worshipper are one and the same. Synge attempts to re-invest holiness into the trinity by making the real trinity the natural aspects of Ireland that should belong to all, making the trinity about joining lives in love—hence making it about the people. *John Bull's* was still on Synge's mind when writing his last play, and, consistently, Synge presented a socialistic vision focused on Ireland, not Shaw's internationalist focus.

The idealization of Deirdre and Naisi in Synge's play contrasts to the depiction of Conchubar, who is presented as an old, greedy king. When Conchubar questions the character Lavarchan, who has raised Deirdre for Conchubar, she informs the High King: "she [Deirdre] has birds to school her, and the pools in the river where she goes bathing in the sun. I'll tell you if you seen her that time, with her white skin, and her red lips, and the blue water and the ferns about her, you'd know maybe, and you greedy itself, it wasn't for your like she was born at all" (*Deirdre of the Sorrows*, 153). Deirdre is portrayed as coming to age outside the influence of bourgeois values and desires, in spite of Conchubar's obsessive desires to possess her. Deirdre, prior to Conchubar coming for her, is literally bathed in Ireland's untouched, uninfected nature.

W. J. McCormack, who sees Synge's Deirdre play as moving "away from the mythological past towards the contentious present," raises the possibility that the destruction of Conchubar's rule over all Ireland reflected the forces gathering during Synge's time, which would soon explode in Ireland, challenging the then social and political order (*Fool*, 369, 372). If McCormack is correct, then Conchubar's greed, his greed to own Deirdre which consumes and blinds him to the welfare of Ireland, signals or prophesizes Ireland's coming struggles. True to the myth, Synge's vile Conchubar goes back on his word and viciously has Naisi and his brothers slaughtered on their return and seizes Deirdre. Conchubar's former supporter and friend King Fergus (a lesser but still a strong king) responds by labeling the High King "a thief and traitor" (*Deirdre of the Sorrows*, 186). Ireland erupts at this point into a civil war due solely to Conchubar's greed, to which Fergus responds by "setting fire to the world" (*Deirdre of the Sorrows*, 183). Conchubar is reduced to seeing what he has done: "It is I am out of my wits, with Emain [the center of unified Ireland under Conchubar] in flames, and Deirdre raving, and my own heart gone within me" (*Deirdre of the Sorrows*, 186). To this level, Conchubar's greed surpasses that of Synge's Shawn Keogh and Michael James Flaherty, and even Shaw's Broadbent. But the point is the same with all of them, as all could and would destroy their part of Ireland or all of Ireland if allowed the chance. Yet the unrelenting capitalistic-type greed of Conchubar in Synge's play would prove an extraordinary prophesy for the coming Ireland as it played out in contrast to Deirdre.

In his treatment of the myth, Synge emphasizes Deirdre's fierce conviction to be her own person, much in the vein of his Nora and Pegeen. After Naisi has been killed, Synge's Deirdre defiantly states: "I have put away sorrow like a shoe that is worn out and muddy, for it is I have had a life that will be envied by great companies. It was not by a low birth I made kings uneasy" (*Deirdre of the Sorrows*, 186). Synge hints at class while emphasizing and illuminating the clash between Deirdre (who speaks in Pegeen's poetic language) and capitalizing greed as once again, in a Synge play, a loveless marriage being forced on a woman by a man (Conchubar's effort to have Deirdre as his wife) is averted. So while Conchubar's greed ends Deirdre's marriage to Naisi, and he seemingly conquers her, Conchubar underestimates her conviction to stand against his all-encompassing power, for he has not killed her love for Naisi. Rather than let Conchubar have his way with her by sending her as a concubine for a year in order to make her submissive to his will, Synge's Deirdre remains defiant to Conchubar: "It's a pitiful thing to be talking out when your ears are shut to me. It's a pitiful thing, Conchubar, you have done this night in Emain, yet a thing will be a joy and triumph to the ends of life and time" (*Deirdre of the Sorrows*, 187). At this, Deirdre kills herself, robbing Conchubar of possessing her. She creates her own mythic legend of defiance against an all-powerful, greedy king.

Deirdre's stance against Conchubar was Synge's testimony to his nationally warring approach, as Blanco's speeches defending himself in *The Shewing-up of Blanco Posnet* testify to Shaw's reasoned, Fabian approach. It was Deirdre's defiant will, as dangerous as it appeared, that would come into play in Ireland within three years from her play's premiere, when labor clashed with an all-encompassing powerful old king of industry in the Dublin Lockout. That king also would underestimate the commitment and conviction that the warring factions brought to his greed, and underestimate the willingness of some, like Deirdre, to die for that commitment over the next three years.

In 1910 the approaches of Shaw and Synge (Synge via *Deirdre of the Sorrows*) were about to permeate Dublin beyond the theatrical stage, while leading other dramatists to extend their debate of how to achieve a more socially just and liberalizing society that would evolve into a debate on how to advocate socialism in Ireland—all as Shaw increased his provocation in numerous directions. The international gradualist and warring national approaches of Shaw and Synge prophesized and assisted the inroads outside the theatre to the radicalism that was coming to the forefront, beginning in 1907, when *The Playboy of the Western World* premiered and *John Bull's Other Island* first played Dublin. Irish socialism was now stirring.

1907: Toward Labor

As 1907 saw such grand Dublin premieres, it also marked the beginning of the re-awakening of organized socialism in Ireland. There had been little movement in this direction since the 1903 collapse of the Irish Socialist Republican Party (ISRP). There had also been little movement on the front of organized labor, or trade unionism, both suggesting that there was little awareness on the part of labor or socialist leaders of the two approaches to socialism being discussed within some Irish theatre, epitomized by Shaw and Synge. In fact, the theatre discussion of the differing socialist approaches by 1907 was largely limited to Synge's plays and *John Bull's Other Island* (and later in 1909 in *The Shewing-up of Blanco Posnet*). However, in 1907 the theatre discussion was beginning to expand in Dublin. Soon even *Playboy* would reach radicals who would come to echo the Dublin editor for Maunsel's publishing house George Roberts, who stood on his chair following the play's second performance in January 1907 shouting, "The play is the finest ever written if you had only the wit to see it" (as quoted in Holloway, *Joseph Holloway's*, 83). The seedlings for the crucial intellectual connection that would soon develop between the discussions of socialistic approaches in Irish theatre to both organized socialism and trade unionism were planted by the 1907 productions of *Playboy* and *John Bull's*, and extended later by *Blanco Posnet* and *Deirdre of the Sorrows*. Ultimately, Irish theatre, or part of it, would become an important vehicle for Irish socialistic direction.

An indication of the eventual intellectual connection between Irish theatre and organized socialism, as well as trade union leadership, is found in the former ISRP member William O'Brien. O'Brien, it is remembered, had witnessed the 1902 premiere of Frederick Ryan's Shavian play *The Laying of the Foundations*. O'Brien regularly attended the Abbey Theatre, claiming to have witnessed most opening nights, including that of *Playboy*. Unfortunately, O'Brien is ambiguous about his response to the play, but offers an observation of many who saw the play's first performance: "a lot of people who did see it first changed their views" (*Forth*, 19). O'Brien insinuates that many first-nighters who later claimed to dislike the play only did so after the attacks from the conservative Dublin press. O'Brien specifically names Joseph Holloway, the bourgeois playgoer who was outspoken against *Playboy*, as one of those who changed his view once the middle-class papers attacked it. O'Brien recalled: "Take Holloway, for example: he was supposed to write his views of every play he saw on the night he saw it. I have read his version of what happened and I don't think it could have been written on the night of the first performance. I saw his diary . . . [on exhibit] and I doubt what appears there was written on that night" (*Forth*, 19).[29] The notion of Holloway and other audience members changing their opinions in order to conform points directly to the bourgeois conventionality that the play confronts. O'Brien's insinuation also relays contempt for the class. O'Brien noted Synge's death in March 1909 in his diary, which also included an entry on 12 November 1908: "Witnessed fine performance of Shaw's 'Man and Superman' at the [Theatre] Royal [in Dublin]—Grenville [*sic*] Barker as Jack Tanner could not be better[,] first class company all round" (as quoted in Morrissey, *O'Brien*, 27).

An indication of the coming relevancy of the discussion and eventual debate on socialist approaches via Irish theatre is found in the primary belief that existed into 1907 among trade union leaders in Britain and Ireland, that "the strike was an outmoded weapon, that a new age of arbitration and conciliation was dawning" (Gray, "City," 23). Such a belief rings of Fabian philosophy, despite the gulf in 1907 that existed between Fabians and trade unions (Holroyd, *Bernard Shaw*, 117). Nonetheless, the very debates of international and national, and their off-shoot of gradualist persuasion and immediate assault, in *John Bull's* and *Playboy*, would soon intensify, especially when illusions faded in Ireland that capitalist employers were existing in "a new age of arbitration and conciliation."

Six months after witnessing *Playboy*'s premiere, O'Brien, disenchanted with the then non-existent growth of organized socialism in Ireland up to that moment, witnessed the Dublin arrival of James Larkin and Larkin's first Dublin speech: "I was favourably impressed. It struck me that he was the kind of man to rouse up workers in a way that had not been done before" (*Forth*, 37). It appeared to O'Brien that Larkin had the ability not only to effectively organize workers for better working conditions, but also to eliminate the distance between organized socialism and trade unionism in Ireland, even if achieved by turning to blatant antagonistic tactics. Larkin, who had come to Ireland from Liverpool six days before *Playboy* opened, first landed in Belfast as a representative of a British dock union. By the 1907 summer, Belfast dock and coal workers were on strike.

In industrialized Belfast, Larkin was credited for introducing the tactic of sympathy strikes. While the potential for labor success appeared possible in 1907 Belfast, Larkin's efforts were soon undermined by sectarian clashes prompted by the Belfast middle-class press, which supported management, capitalist positions. The press repeatedly labeled union leaders as "extreme and rabid nationalists and Roman Catholics" (as quoted in Gray, "City," 25). Workers turned on each other due to religious hatreds fostered by the capitalist newspapers they read, destroying the solidarity of the strikes (Gray, "City," 28–29). So while Larkin had momentarily invigorated Irish labor in 1907 with aggressive tactics, labor in Belfast would continue to be hindered by bourgeois-provoked sectarianism infecting the working class, just as Synge had believed bourgeois-provoked greed infected most of Ireland. Larkin would soon abandon the British union he had represented upon his arrival and form the Irish Transport and General Workers' Union (ITGWU) in January 1909. The stage was being set for the explosion of Irish socialism and trade unionism as 1910 opened with Synge's *Deirdre of the Sorrows*, followed by Shaw's lecturing Dublin, and the return of James Connolly. Within days of returning to Ireland, Connolly attended the Abbey Theatre (Holloway, *Joseph Holloway's*, 141).

3

Toward 1913 and the "Most Distinguished Irishman" — Shaw

The process of Shaw's provocation into socialism in Ireland after 1909, expanded beyond the confines of theatre spaces, and with Synge dead and James Connolly endeavoring to return to Ireland, we must now pursue multiple avenues as socialistic thought began to develop in Dublin, echoing Shaw-Synge debates. Theatrically expressed ideas were finding their way onto streets as the age of revolution was trickling throughout Europe in the echoes of the crushed 1905 Russian Revolution. Although the main pre-1910 advocate for an Irishized socially liberalizing movement through theatrical expression was dead, a similar approach in Ireland outside theatre was about to be continued and developed by the socialist that Fred Ryan included in his 1902 Shavian play. Shaw's renewed engagement with Ireland was on track toward Connolly.

When Connolly returned to Ireland in 1910, having been in America as a union organizer since the 1903 summer, he found an Ireland much changed. Politically, Dublin, at least, was ready to develop a socialist movement, and trade unionism was poised on the Irish front to take hold, separate from British unions, in the form of the Irish Transport and General Workers' Union (ITGWU). The socialist potential lay among Dubliners, like William O'Brien, Frederick Ryan, Francis Sheehy-Skeffington, P. D. Kenny, W. P. Ryan, among others, who had been engaged with the political, and socialistic, debates presented by the most significant cultural development in Dublin during Connolly's absence—the Abbey Theatre. The Abbey had emerged from the amateur company that had staged Fred Ryan's *The Laying of the Foundations* as Connolly's ISRP was collapsing in

1903. During Connolly's absence, the Abbey's most significant dramatist, Synge, had come, and died. *The Shewing-up of Blanco Posnet* had played on the Abbey stage in the wake of *The Playboy of the Western World*. By showing-up the British censor, it popularized the Abbey with the conservative middle-class audience Synge had confronted and angered, while satirizing that audience's moral hypocrisy.

The Abbey Theatre had emerged as an institution between 1904 and 1910 that reflected, fostered, and continued the political and cultural debates within the Irish city as Dublin's identity began to emerge separately, at least intellectually, from its colonized identity. Synge and Shaw's theatrical discussion on socialistic-leaning issues, including their debate on approaches, epitomized not only the Abbey's emergence as a theatre of ideas, but also the growing importance for other Dublin theatre venues, as when the commercial Theatre Royal hosted Vedrenne-Barker's tours featuring Shaw's plays, including *John Bull's Other Island*.[1] The socialistic discussion that Synge's and Shaw's plays skirted in Dublin reflected and continued debates that were stirring within some intellectual circles, moving now toward radical directions. While Synge portrayed and expressed concern for the Irish proletariat, particularly for the rural peasant as a confrontation to the respectable bourgeois pseudo-nationalists who were romanticizing rural Ireland as an ideal representing the Ireland they desired, Synge was increasingly not alone. Neither were Synge and Shaw alone in their contesting imaging of Ireland that attacked or ridiculed the Catholic Church that reinforced the conservative morality of bourgeois respectability. The aforementioned P. D. Kenny and W. P. Ryan are examples of such attacks on respectability and the Church's role in such.

Kenny, followed by W. P. Ryan, edited the weekly *Irish Peasant*, and both were driven from the paper when they called for laypeople to have a say in determining educational policies in place of the Church's dictatorial control (Glandon, *Arthur Griffith*, 21). The paper ceased publication, with Ryan's removal, when Cardinal Michael Logue (Armagh), called the paper "poisonous and anti-Catholic" (as quoted in Glandon, *Arthur Griffith*, 22). The paper's demise caught the attention of James Connolly in America, who wrote when Logue visited the United States and met John D. Rockefeller: "The time has long since gone by when Irish men and women can be kept from thinking by hurling priestly thunder at their heads. We may still kneel to the Servant of God, but when he speaks as the Servant of our oppressor, he must not wonder if he receives from slaves in revolt, the same measure as his earthly masters. His Eminence cannot act the despot and throttle the press in Ireland, and act the patron of free institutions in America" (as quoted in Nevin, *Connolly*, 675). The fate of the *Irish Peasant* justifies, explains, and reflects the attacks by Synge and the jabs from Shaw against the Church and the conservative morality of bourgeois respectability that stifled social justice in early twentieth-century Ireland.

Kenny and W. P. Ryan in some respects were like Shaw's Peter Keegan, reduced in power by the Church but remaining social visionaries. In 1906, Kenny published his socialistic book *Economics for Irishmen* and became embroiled in the contesting views of *The Playboy of the Western World* following its 1907 premiere.[2] Kenny favorably reviewed the play in which he praised Synge's truthful peasant-class environment which was "more a psychological revelation than a dramatic process, but it is both" (as quoted in Saddlemyer, "Notes," 287).[3] After *The Irish Peasant* collapsed, W. P. Ryan delivered a lecture in 1909 titled "Doctor Socialism and the Irish Hypochondriac." William O'Brien, at the time, recorded that the lecture was the "most inspiring I have ever heard from the standpoint of a socialist in Ireland" it "staggered a good few people" (O'Brien, *Forth*, 22). Two years later, Ryan favorably reviewed the publication of Synge's Collected Works (Levitas, *Theatre*, 193). In 1919, Ryan published his socialistic book *The Irish Labour Movement*. The small struggles that Kenny and W. P. Ryan had encountered on behalf of social reform, against the censorship from "respectable" interests that had been presented and reflected by Synge and Shaw in the theatre, now awaited transformation to the streets as Connolly sought his return to Ireland.

The debates fostered by Synge and Shaw hung in the air of the Abbey Theatre's foyer as Connolly entered it six days after returning to Ireland in 1910. The playgoer Joseph Holloway, the bourgeois architect who made no secret of his dislike for Synge's work, recorded Connolly's presence at the Abbey upon his return (after Connolly was pointed out to him): "Mr. Connolly, a socialist, anarchist. . . . There was a good deal of the Irish-American about him, and he looked a determined bit of goods" (*Joseph Holloway's*, 141).[4]

Connolly most likely attended the Abbey with his old ISRP colleague O'Brien, who, like Holloway, constantly attended Dublin theatre (O'Brien, *Forth*, 19). O'Brien, a working-class tailor by trade, had been instrumental in helping Connolly return to Ireland, eventually securing for him an organizing position within the ITGWU. When the ITGWU formed, James

Larkin, the union organizer who had come to Ireland from Liverpool in 1907, publicly asked if Irish labor was going to continue to depend on English trade unions, surrendering their national identity and national needs in the process. Thomas Morrissey writes that this was the same question Connolly had put to Irish workers in 1897. At that time it was received with little enthusiasm. Twelve years later it was a different case (*O'Brien*, 31). Larkin was by 1909 organizing Irish labor into one union, the ITGWU.

The direction, even formation, of the ITGWU as Larkin defined it early on was moving away from the international socialist ideal. But Larkin was more of a trade unionist than socialist and he, with others, in Ireland had found Irish labor concerns lost within British unions. Emmet O'Connor writes that Larkin "was by no means alone in concluding that British unions would never commit sufficient response to Ireland to build a bargaining power for a small, disparate working class in a backward economy" ("Labour," 33). Irish workers were simply not getting the attention and help needed from English unions. Hence, the ITGWU quickly began pursuing in Ireland the concept of syndicalism, one big union for all or most Irish workers. Given the national, if not nationalistic, aspect of such a union, it seems that in its nature the ITGWU was in opposition to Shaw's Fabian internationalism. But was the philosophy of such a union intellectually distant from Synge's thematic socialistic nationalism? The concept of the ITGWU in 1910 was the socialistic means Connolly was looking for when he left Ireland in 1903.

On the evening of his return to Dublin, 26 July, Connolly, with four other socialists (including O'Brien), called at the home of Frederick Ryan, the Abbey Theatre's treasurer until 1906 (Morrissey, *O'Brien*, 44). O'Brien and Ryan had for weeks been discussing how socialist unity could be created within Ireland, specifically uniting trade unionists with organized socialism (Morrissey, *O'Brien*, 37). While at Ryan's home, Connolly was introduced to the woman's suffrage and labor-sympathetic journalist Francis Sheehy-Skeffington, who would play his role in Irish socialism with both Connolly and Shaw.

Connolly had written to O'Brien almost a year earlier, in September 1909, from the United States inquiring if O'Brien could ask Sheehy-Skeffington to try to find a London publisher for Connolly's book manuscript *Labour in Irish History* (*Between Comrades* 408). Connolly, who had kept a close eye on Ireland during much of his absence, had heard of Sheehy-Skeffington's reputation as a radical journalist. Connolly had maintained the theoretical socialistic writing he had pursued in Ireland prior to his 1903 emigration, and his *Labour in Irish History* was the culmination in 1910 of his socialistic thinking in connection to Ireland.[5] It was such work, along with editing of the *Workers' Republic* (1898–1903), the *Harp* (in New York 1908–1910) and his American union efforts, which made Connolly an ideal person, for O'Brien, to unite socialism with trade unionism (Morrissey, *O'Brien*, 35). Morrissey writes: "O'Brien had been the principal architect of James Connolly's return to Ireland. Whatever his expectations of the effect of the homecoming, he could not have then visualized that in time it would . . . radically change the course . . . of the Transport Union, and even that of Ireland" (Morrissey, *O'Brien*, 44).

Within days of returning to Dublin, Connolly delivered a speech outlining how organized socialism could effectively and efficiently expand. He was followed on the speakers' platform by Sheehy-Skeffington who enthusiastically stated: "what the movement wanted was a *man* and . . . Connolly was *the man*" (as quoted in Morrissey, *O'Brien*, 46). Where such a sentiment left the volatile Jim Larkin, remained to be seen.

While the stage was being set for developing and expanding socialism with Connolly's return and his meeting Sheehy-Skeffington, Shaw had also returned to Ireland in 1910, if only as a visitor, and, was also taking a more active role in Ireland than he had previously. Shaw had also been in Ireland the summer before, 1909, coinciding with the premiere of *The Shewing-up of Blanco Posnet* but remained out of Dublin for the premiere. Again, Shaw had been pulled toward considering Ireland, in one form or another, by Synge. Even before *Blanco Posnet* was scheduled for the Abbey Theatre, Lady Gregory had contacted Shaw about, of all things, how to secure a special printing of Synge's work. By the summer of 1909, Shaw was oddly filling some of the void left by Synge at the Abbey.[6] Shaw turned down an apparent offer to become a director when Conal O'Riordan (who replaced Synge) resigned his directorship after three months. But Shaw provided valuable advice to Gregory as the Theatre neared the end of its stipend from Annie Horniman and would have to financially survive on its own.[7] But Shaw's renewed interest in Ireland now went beyond the Abbey and theatre, as he found himself in Dublin shortly after Connolly's return, just as Connolly was immediately embroiling himself in controversy.

Connolly, a Priest Not Keegan—and Shaw,

Months before Connolly's return to Ireland, the Catholic Church in Ireland took steps to stifle socialism and the radical trade unionism that was emerging since the formation of the ITGWU. A blind Jesuit priest, Father Kane, delivered a series of Lenten sermons that were intended to undermine and erase socialism in Ireland (Nevin, *Connolly*, 332). Kane's sermons were published in the nationally circulated *Irish Catholic*. Donal Nevin points out that Kane's sermons were part of the Church's war on socialism, which had grown from concern with the socialist and labor movements at the time in Italy and France (*Connolly*, 327–328). The Church viewed organized socialism and labor movements as being "an intrinsic part of republican, anti-clerical, anti-capitalist agitation, strongly opposed to the influence of the Catholic Church" (Nevin, *Connolly* 328). Ruth Dudley Edwards suggests that Kane's sermons were not lightly conceived and the Society of Jesus (Jesuits), to which Kane belonged, "was at the time acknowledged to be the foremost intellectual order within the Roman Catholic Church in Ireland; [and] the sermons would have been read in newspaper and pamphlet form by thousands" (quoted in Nevin, *Connolly*, 332). Apparently, Kane was no Father Dempsey from *John Bull's Other Island* with regard to having a theory, or in this case trying to negate socialist theory. Or was he? The Church, through Kane, had drawn on the respectable morality it fostered among the capitalist middle class to denounce the labor and socialist movements that sincerely sought to improve the living and working conditions of the poor. Kane was no Peter Keegan.

Kane's condemnation of socialism and trade unionism was answered by Connolly in a pamphlet published upon his return to Ireland titled *Labour, Nationality, and Religion*. This work established Connolly as a leading theorist on behalf of Irish socialism. Not only did Connolly take an aggressive approach, he also drew on Ireland's past in refuting Kane's and the Church's harsh dismissal of socialism. Connolly's attack on the Kane sermons created a backlash of controversy for its author. A seeming by-product was Shaw's possible attention.

Donal Nevin writes that Connolly's extensive foreword to *Labour, Nationality, and Religion* details many historical examples of laymen in Ireland turning to political action in opposition to the hierarchy of the Catholic Church's staunch positions, including sixteen examples of going against papal and episcopal declarations (Nevin, *Connolly*, 328). The most striking of these examples is the Battle of the Boyne, fought in 1690 in Ireland between the Catholic deposed British king James II with his Catholic Irish army and the Protestant new British king William III with his English army.[8] The battle was for the British crown, and in many ways it signified, then and now, the conflict for Ireland, and specifically Ulster, between Catholic and Protestant. James II was defeated, with the result of William's government imposing the infamous Penal Laws, which prevented Catholics from land ownership, reducing them to and maintaining most of them, at the end of the seventeenth century, as peasants. Connolly writes: "The battle was the result of an alliance formed by Pope Innocent XI with William, Prince of Orange, against Louis, King of France. King James of England joined with King Louis to obtain help to save his own throne, and the Pope joined in the league with William to curb the power of France. When the news of the defeat of the Irish at the Boyne reached Rome the Vatican was illuminated by the order of the new Pope, Alexander VIII, and special masses offered up in thanksgiving" (*Labour*, 61).

Connolly's Boyne example remarkably shines light on the Church's betrayal of Catholic Ireland, which appears quite vile given that Protestant William III was fanatical in his anti-Catholic policies in Ireland, policies which dramatically increased the economic suffering of the Catholic peasantry. In continuing his attempt to bring to light the Church's betrayals of Ireland, Connolly also refers to the 1798 Irish rebellion, particularly the insurrection that occurred in County Wexford, with Irish rebel forces being led by a Catholic priest, Father Murphy. Connolly quotes an Irish Catholic veteran of the Wexford insurrection: "the priests did everything in their power to stop the progress of the Association of United Irishmen" (*Labour*, 62).[9]

Connolly also suggests that the Wexford insurrection's leader, Murphy, as a priest, had persuaded many of his followers to abandon their weapons, hence their defeat. Connolly acknowledges Murphy's heroic battlefield role at Vinegar Hill, but writes: "The soldier-like qualities he showed in the field were rendered nugatory by the fact that as a priest he had been instrumental in disarming many hundreds of men whom he afterwards commanded. As an insurgent officer, he discovered that his greatest hope lay in the men who had disregarded his commands as a priest, and retained the arms with which to fight for freedom" (*Labour*, 62).

More recent examples discussed by Connolly included the Catholic

Bishop of Derry's denouncing the Home Rule movement in 1871, and Archbishop McCabe's 1882 denouncement of the Ladies' Land League, "an association of Irish ladies organized for the patriotic and benevolent purpose of raising funds for the relief of distress, of inquiring into cases of evicted tenants, . . . as 'immodest and wicked'" (*Labour*, 65). Connolly also states that "In all examples covered . . . the reformers and revolutionists have been right, the political theories of the Vatican and the clergy unquestionably wrong. The verdict of history as unquestionable endorses the former as it condemns the latter" (*Labour*, 66). Concluding his pamphlet's foreword, Connolly writes that the capitalist "robber class, conceived in sin and begotten in iniquity, asks the Church to defend it, and from the Vatican downwards the clergy respond to the call" (*Labour*, 67).

Connolly's assault on the Church's policies in Ireland were consistent with the same from Synge and Shaw, particularly as presented in *John Bull's Other Island* and by the attack on Christian middle-class morality in the premiere of *The Shewing-up of Blanco Posnet*. Yet while his attack was aggressive, Connolly carefully fostered a learned and reticent approach.

Donal Nevin writes that in the six chapters of *Labour, Nationality, and Religion*, "Connolly took each objection to Socialism made by Father Kane as it was formulated" (*Connolly*, 329). Connolly includes significant quotation from Kane's published sermons, perhaps to ensure that none could claim he misrepresented Kane's arguments. Kane attempted to negate Marxist theory by undermining the principle that labor "alone is the cause of value, and that labour alone can give any title of ownership," to which Kane states that fruit has value to a hungry person yet no labor is involved. He adds that such Marxist theory is only supported by the belief "that there is no God, no soul, no free will, nothing but mud and the forces of mud" (as quoted in Connolly, *Labour*, 69). Connolly in turn negates Kane's argument here by demonstrating that because of the history of "contending classes in society—one class striving to retain possession . . . of the other class . . . as wage-slaves," the only just ownership must be determined by one's own labor (*Labour*, 70–71).

In his "The Rights of Man" chapter, Connolly quotes Kane's assertion that the "Church of Christ has always approved . . . private and personal property." Connolly replies by quoting historical Church figures who stated otherwise, like St. Clement: "The use of all things that is found in this world ought to be common to all" (*Labour*, 83).

Connolly's third chapter, "Honour of the Home," works to refute Kane's charge that socialism was immoral, namely through socialism's support of divorce. Connolly walks a fine line here, taking up the issue suggested in *In the Shadow of the Glen*. At first, Connolly states that it is the capitalist who benefits from the then divorce courts (outside Ireland). He asserts that no socialist congress had ever imposed divorce on socialists. Then, he specifically quotes Kane: "Divorce in the Socialist sense means that women would be willing to stoop to be the mistress of one man after another" (as quoted in Connolly, *Labour*, 95). Connolly responds by writing that Kane's view of women recalls "the Council of the Church" in the sixth century that "debated the question as to whether woman had or had not a soul" (*Labour*, 95). Connolly continues:

> Many of the early Fathers of the Church were, indeed, so bitter in their denunciation of women and of marriage that their opinions read like the expressions of madmen when examined in the cold light of the twentieth century. Origen said: "Marriage is unholy and unclean—a means of sensual lust." . . . Tertullian, in his hatred of women, thundered forth boldly that which Father Kane dared only insinuate, "Woman," he preaches, "thou oughtest always walk in mourning and rags, thine eyes filled with tears of repentance to make men forget that thou has been the destruction of the race. Woman! Thou art the Gates of Hell." Thus throughout the centuries persists the idea of the Churchmen that women can only be kept virtuous by law. (*Labour*, 95–96)

Connolly carefully turns Kane's blaming socialists for divorce into an argument that the Church has historically debased women, subtly revealing that the Church, and all social conservatives of his time, opposed divorce on the grounds that divorce would lead to amorality among women. While denying that socialists mandated divorce, Connolly supports women as equals of their own identities, which is what was solely behind the socialist and suffragist support for divorce in Connolly's time—a woman was entitled to her own identity and not be a husband's slave, and that could lead to better marriages. Arguably, this is consistent with *In the Shadow of the Glen*'s Nora, who claims her own identity to escape her enslavement to an abusive husband.[10] Connolly was reacting against conservative and Church supported views that subjugated women. Indeed, it was archaic madness when the detractors to *In the Shadow of the Glen* objected to Nora leaving her husband, and the play, of course, had premiered in the twentieth century.

Connolly suggests that the Church does not follow its own socialistic ideals: "The socialist doctrine teaches that all men are brothers, that the same red blood of a common humanity flows in the veins of all races, creeds, colours and nations, that the interests of Labour are everywhere identical . . . Is not this also good Catholic doctrine—the doctrine of a Church which prides itself upon being universal or Catholic? How, then, can that doctrine which is high and holy in theory on the lips of a Catholic become a hissing and blasphemy when practiced by the Socialist? . . . Is it not, then, a joke to see Socialists accused of being unpatriotic, accused by a Jesuit?" (*Labour*, 105–106). Connolly hints that his response to the learned Jesuit represented the work of a self-taught laborer. He accepts, in his pamphlet's last chapter, the belief of most socialists in 1910 that force may be needed to change society, as he concludes the "day has passed for patching up the capitalist system" (*Labour*, 115–117).

While Connolly's own Catholicism was "not all that strong," he is careful throughout *Labour, Nationality, and Religion* not to dismiss the religion, but only to dismiss the way in which the religion is administered, especially through attacks against the aims of socialism in regard to the poor (Lynch, *Radical*, 107).[11] So while being careful not to offend Catholics who may support him, Connolly's attack on Kane's sermons attracted much attention among socialists, trade unionists, and even some of the middle class in Dublin and the British Isles. The socialistic London *Daily Herald* reviewed Connolly's pamphlet (which Nevin believes W. P. Ryan authored) on 25 September 1910, stating that it represented intelligent Irish Catholic layman thinking (Nevin, *Connolly*, 334). Nevertheless, during a socialist speakers' platform, on 3 August, designed to attract Dublin laborers to socialism and addressing Kane's condemnation, the assembly broke up in reaction to public criticism being leveled at a priest. O'Brien noted that "Connolly tried to minimize the effect of it to us [organizing Dublin socialists] afterwards . . . but we all said it was the most unfortunate incident that occurred in our propaganda for years" (as quoted in Morrissey, *O'Brien*, 47).

In October and November, the Catholic Church, through yet another Jesuit priest, Father John MacErlean, published retorts to Connolly's pamphlet against Kane in the paper *Catholic Times*, the same paper which had published Kane's sermons and which was part of the *Irish Independent* newspapers owned by the "respectable" businessman William Martin Murphy. MacErlean's retorts in a capitalist-owned paper led to further public response from Connolly. At this point, O'Brien secured a position for Connolly with recruiting members for the ITGWU in Belfast. While Connolly's response to Kane strengthened his reputation as a socialist theorist and propagandist, his mostly direct and assaulting tactic created an uneasy feeling among some Dublin socialists. Such public controversy between the Church and a self-taught working-class socialist might have had much to attract Shaw had he been in the country at the time—and he was.

While we have no direct evidence that Shaw read Connolly's *Labour, Nationality, and Religion*, or that he knew of the pamphlet and its controversy in Dublin, or even Kane's sermons, there is possible indirect evidence that Shaw responded to the Connolly-Kane debate. While in Ireland for six weeks in 1910, Shaw accepted an invitation near the end of his visit to lecture for the Irish Committee to Promote the Break-up of the Poor-law, a charitable middle-class organization.[12] On the day he delivered his lecture "The Poor Law and Destitution in Ireland," Shaw granted an interview to Dublin's middle-class *Freeman's Journal*. In the interview, Shaw stated that his motto, sounding not quite like the internationalist, is "Ireland for All," and added that the "souls of the writers are sick of Dublin, and of all our stale brags and sentimentalities, our heroic talk, and our horrible squalor and infant mortality and poverty" ("My Motto," 69). Perhaps as a consequence of the interview, the *Freeman's Journal* published much of the speech.

The *Freeman's Journal* noted that Shaw's audience at Dublin's Antient Concert Rooms was large, and specifically named some of the prominent and respectable middle-class attendees.[13] The nationalist Home-Rule MPs John Dillon and Thomas Kettle were present, as were justices, barristers, medical doctors, and churchmen. In fact, the paper noted that the audience "included an exceptionally large number of representatives of the Church" ("Mr. Bernard Shaw," 7). The Church, arguably knowing Shaw's socialist-Fabian reputation, actively wanted to hear his lecture, especially in the wake of Connolly's socialist retort of Kane. Also, the Catholic Church's hierarchy in Ireland officially supported the Poor Law system (Nevin, "Notes, *Between Comrades*, 491). The *Freeman's Journal* also commented on the large number of women in attendance, "considerably in the majority," but chose not to name any ("Mr. Bernard Shaw," 7). Perhaps they were suffragettes, since the women's suffragette movement was, by 1910, forging links in Ireland with socialists, as in England. The audience also included Francis Sheehy-Skeffington. While such prominent middle-class people were listed, the paper made no indication if laborers attended.

Given Connolly's exceptional thirst for everything he could read or listen to on socialism and Irish history, one would have expected that Connolly was present for Shaw's Dublin lecture on 3 October 1910. While he undoubtedly was aware of Shaw, Connolly was in Scotland in early October addressing small socialist meetings. At the time, Connolly's ability to financially avoid starvation in Ireland and to send for his family from New York was still extremely unsettled, hence his brief trip to Scotland, in which he was paid minimally for his talks. However, before he left Dublin in September, Connolly drafted with Sheehy-Skeffington the manifesto for the revitalized Socialist Party of Ireland (SPI), which was issued from the party's office, which happened to be in the Antient Concert Rooms, where Shaw lectured on 3 October (Nevin, *Connolly*, 384). Yet, despite a commonality of place over a three-week span, the structures of Shaw and Connolly's lecturing could not have then been further apart. Shaw addressed a comfortable class in a large hall, while Connolly lectured small working-class socialist groups in Scotland traveling as cheaply as he could manage. The contrast of their lecturing emphasized their differences to approach, economic level, audience size, and so forth, yet they were still socialists, though different types of socialists, and both knew society's ailments very well. So despite their then different spheres, could Shaw have been aware of the Kane-Connolly exchange and the SPI's manifesto on 3 October 1910? While this cannot be answered with certainty, we can assert unequivocally that Connolly's camp knew of Shaw's lecture.

In addition to Sheehy-Skeffington attending Shaw's lecture, one can assume that Connolly's Dublin colleague and SPI member William O'Brien, who was in Dublin on 3 October and was clearly familiar with Shaw through Frederick Ryan and Shaw's plays in Dublin, was also there. In fact, by the time O'Brien was elderly in the 1950s, he was said to have amassed the largest collection of Shavian books, publications, and play and lecture programs in Ireland (Morrissey, *O'Brien*, 394). That the *Freeman's Journal* makes no mention of the working-class O'Brien attending Shaw's lecture (assuming he did) testifies to the paper's thorough bourgeois affiliation.[14]

Undoubtedly, Sheehy-Skeffington and O'Brien listened intently to Shaw and knew there was commonality to Shaw's ideology and abilities.

When Shaw rose to begin his lecture, perhaps still riding the wave of *The Shewing-up of Blanco Posnet*'s jab at the British censor, he was met with "a sustained burst of applause" ("Mr. Bernard Shaw," 7).[15] Shaw commenced by saying that the very kind reception accorded him was rather an embarrassing one because he was not going to be as complimentary to the audience as they had been to him ("Mr. Bernard Shaw," 7). Shaw quickly chastised his audience by saying he "could not acquit them of the most monstrous civic crimes when he thought what destitution and what the Poor Law system was in Ireland at present" ("Mr. Bernard Shaw," 7). Shaw stipulated that he preferred his audience to give up their respectable private virtue in favor of civic virtue ("Mr. Bernard Shaw," 7).

In typical Shavian style, Shaw interwove a comedic tone into his very serious arguments and criticisms of his predominantly middle-class audience. Shaw continued on his desire for the audience to assume a collective civic responsibility, that as "a private person the amount of harm they could do was very small—a few murders, perhaps, or an embezzlement, which would cause a slight amount of inconvenience to people around them," which was reportedly met with "laughter" ("Mr. Bernard Shaw," 7). Shaw quickly turned to the serious by saying he had spent that afternoon visiting a Dublin workhouse. He stated that under no circumstance should children ever be in a workhouse, adding that there were 8,000 children presently in Irish workhouses ("Mr. Bernard Shaw," 7).

Shaw added that "Poverty was a crime—a crime not of the poor, but of the people who allowed them to be poor. Poverty was a crime of society—a preventable crime" ("Mr. Bernard Shaw," 7). Then Shaw turned to religion, not Catholicism specifically as Connolly had done, which would have been too hostile and adverse to the comedic tone the lecture frequently returned to. Shaw quoted Christ: "'The poor ye have always with you.' There were a great many Christians at the present time; instead of understanding that this was a reproach, [they] interpreted it as a warning of something inevitable—'The poor ye have always with you'—as if blasphemy could come out of the mouth of Christ" ("Mr. Bernard Shaw," 7). Shaw stated that Dublin Corporation (the city government) spent thousands of pounds on workhouses to manufacture the poor, and the Corporation then said it "was the pauper's own fault" ("Mr. Bernard Shaw,"

7). He wondered if the audience believed in the judgment day and, if so, it "would require all the mercy of Heaven to prevent them from going to a place which would not be as bad as the ordinary workhouse" ("Mr. Bernard Shaw," 7).

Shaw's allusion to Christianity before respectable Christians, including Catholics and Catholic clergymen, might have been an allusion to Connolly's attack on Kane's sermons. While Connolly exposed the hypocrisy of the Church for not helping the poor by putting the poor first, Shaw suggested that the Church allowed its parishioners to misinterpret the teachings of Christ in regard to the poor, which allowed them to have, as Shaw stated, no sense of civic responsibility toward the poor. While it is impossible to prove Shaw was specifically responding to Connolly and Kane without a direct remark, it seems that given the time frame, Shaw was at the very least reacting to the number of clergymen in his audience, and the great numbers most likely were a result of Connolly's socialist attack on Kane's sermons, which itself grew out of the Church's effort to erase socialism from the Irish scene.[16] Of course, Shaw's allusion to Christianity was consistent with his Fabian approach before his predominantly middle-class audience; to specifically mention Connolly and Kane would have been antagonistic. Being able to speak before such a respectable middle-class audience was something the laborer Connolly was not then able to do, and in a sense, this echoed the differences between *John Bull's Other Island*'s Keegan and *In the Shadow of the Glen*'s Tramp. But Shaw's speech moved on after the Christian allusion, as he charged the audience's workhouse system with spreading diseases, physical and of the "soul" ("Mr. Bernard Shaw," 8).

Shaw also swiped at the middle-class Gaelic Leaguers who were spending so much energy on teaching Gaelic to peasant children but doing nothing to alleviate their economic condition. He asked that while they taught young girls Gaelic, could they admit that clinics should be established to treat the teeth of the children? ("Mr. Bernard Shaw," 8). Shaw charged that instead of promoting people to be paupers, the audience should promote them to decent lives ("Mr. Bernard Shaw," 8). Shaw landed other criticisms, such as against one of his favorite targets, the medical profession: "The abolition of disease in Ireland would simply mean the ruin of the medical profession as it was organized at present" ("Mr. Bernard Shaw," 8). When he had finished, despite his charges against the audience, he was widely applauded.

The *Irish Times*, even more conservative than the *Freeman's Journal*, covered Shaw's lecture with a patronizing tone but did so with two articles. The first, on page four, acknowledged that Shaw called for greater civic responsibility and mentioned Shaw's concern for the poverty-stricken children in Ireland's workhouses. However, the paper's first article did not specify Shaw's arguments, nor his main direction. It did not even elaborate on what type of civic responsibility was needed, though it claimed it was in agreement with Shaw. The paper wrote, "We would prefer to see an ill-informed civic sense making expensive blunders than to have no civic sense at all" ("George Bernard Shaw's Lecture," 4). An ill-informed civic sense could only alleviate middle-class guilt and do nothing for the poor, like most charities in Shaw's view. There was no specific mention that the civic responsibility Shaw called for was a responsibility to the poor.

The *Irish Times*' second article covering Shaw's lecture was on page six and was almost hostile in its attempt to nullify Shaw and his lecture. The article began: "Mr. Shaw on the Poor Law system proved almost as great an attraction last night as Mr. Shaw on Ireland, on the instinctive aim of woman, on Napoleon, on woman suffrage, on the housing question, and various other questions, has been at other times." The article suggested that Shaw, who "has got himself talked about," was a curiosity being in person, insinuating that many attended just to see him:

> It was, no doubt, a disadvantage not to be able to flutter on to the platform in woman's dress, and then commence to disrobe—an incident which helps to popularize his lectures by proxy in "Press Cuttings"; but, on the other hand, it was an advantage to be able to come forward and say—"You now behold the leading jester, the subject of innumerable newspaper paragraphs." The lecture was of the same nature, at all events, and there were a great many people present . . . whom one would equally expect to see at the theatre for Mr. Shaw's lecture in dialogue form. . . . The lecture was distinguished—or spoilt—by the same dogmatising and the same extravagance of simile and illustration that mark his plays. ("Poor-Law System," 6)

The article does acknowledge that Shaw urged his audience "not to pauperise" the poor ("Poor-Law System," 6). The paper also, like the *Freeman's Journal*, published Shaw's speech (inserting "he" for Shaw's "I"), despite its effort to undermine Shaw. Perhaps the *Irish Times* felt its bourgeois readership could only disagree with the speech.

Among the audience for Shaw's lecture was the bourgeois playgoer Holloway. No doubt attending the lecture because Shaw was a playwright, Holloway recorded his response in his theatre journal. His observations and reactions testify to the differences in approach between Shaw and Synge, and now Shaw and Connolly. Certainly, Shaw and Connolly, in Shaw's speech and Connolly's pamphlet, had the proletariat in mind. One attacked a priest who had tried to bury socialism and the other scolded, if comically, a bourgeois audience for failing to significantly alleviate the condition of the poor. Did Holloway, as representative of those who had objected to Synge's plays but enjoyed *John Bull's Other Island* and *The Shewing-up of Blanco Posnet* while missing the satire, now recognize Shaw's indictment of his class?

Holloway recorded:

> Shaw arose clad in a dark suit, with short square-cut double-breasted coat that gave him the appearance of a hardy yachtsman.[17] He went to business at once, and kept at it without pause for over an hour and twenty minutes, stating facts straight in the face and stating them clearly and with stinging humor. It was a wonderfully brilliant talk containing a wonderful amount of food for thought.... Shaw deplored the time and energy wasted on the denunciation of Synge's *The Playboy* when it could have been given to some other more useful cause. He made his uninviting subject extremely interesting, and put his hearers into the dock, as it were, before he concluded his remarks, and they all felt condemned criminals ere he had done with them. (*Joseph Holloway's*, 142)[18]

Holloway, it is remembered, was accused later by the socialist William O'Brien for having changed his view of *Playboy* once the bourgeois press condemned it. It is interesting that while Holloway praises the "brilliant talk containing a wonderful amount of food for thought," he fails to provide the specific arguments and points Shaw made. He does recognize that Shaw's speech took his "hearers" to task, making them feel like "criminals." Perhaps in true bourgeois style, Holloway does not include himself among the criminals, referring to them as "they" rather than "us." Holloway continued his remarks on Shaw's speech by recording: "Everyone felt he had heard an unusually brilliant discourse by an astoundingly clever man, and all said they would not have missed it for anything.... In the course of his remarks, Shaw said he never argued; you could take or leave the statements he made. He saw facts and stated them as plainly as he could. The obvious was always startlingly original.... I felt as I left the hall that I had been through one of those great exciting events of one's life, that came so seldom and stand out so clearly in one's memory" (*Joseph Holloway's*, 142). It is perhaps a testament to Shaw's Fabian approach that Holloway could recognize the condemnation of his class from Shaw, admire the presentation and speaker, but not be outraged by the arguments so he could only rail against the speech. Of course, if William O'Brien was right about Holloway's views, Holloway's praise may have been a reflection of other "hearers." Still, the testament is made to the effectiveness of Shaw's speech and/or the reputation he enjoyed in 1910 Dublin. However, how many of the Dublin "hearers" in 1910 reconsidered their lives and the Irish proletariat due to Shaw's speech? But the internationalist was again on the national stage.

Eleven days following Shaw's lecture, on 14 October, a Father O'Flanagan delivered a lecture in Dublin on the Irish language movement. The lecture included a retort to Shaw's lecture, in light of Shaw's suggestion that Gaelic Leaguers should concern themselves more with the horrid living conditions of the poor, especially the destitute children, rather than merely teaching Gaelic. The priest O'Flanagan, amid his argument that Gaelic will lead Ireland to "her nationality," states: "their friend Mr. George Bernard Shaw, could not let them alone. Mr. Shaw forgot his joking for a little while the other evening, and became serious for at least one sentence, and that sentence was that if he had been educated in the Irish language instead of in the English language he would lose his hold upon the world. Well, perhaps some people, and even Mr. Shaw himself, had an exaggerated idea of the extent of their hold upon the world, and of the great calamity it would be to the world if that hold was lost.... He would tell Mr. Shaw to try and get a hold upon Ireland, and never mind the world" ("Irish Language Movement," 4). O'Flanagan's inept attempts at humor at Shaw's expense could do nothing but support Shaw's indictment of the Irish language movement. While O'Flanagan saw the language as being Ireland's real issue, Shaw saw the real issue as Ireland's people, especially the poor, kept destitute by capitalistic practices—nationality without the enfranchisement of all the Irish was worthless and would change nothing. Surely Shaw was right, and his reasoned arguments made more elaborate retorts from the Church against Shaw impossible on this occasion, lest the Church appear even worse. It is interesting that the *Irish*

Times, which covered O'Flanagan's lecture, noted that the middle-class member of Parliament Thomas Kettle seconded the motion to adjourn the lecture when O'Flanagan had finished. Kettle had also attended Shaw's lecture. Where was his allegiance? It was undoubtedly not with socialism, or was it? During the Great War, the nationalist Kettle fought in the British army, as Shaw called on Irishmen to do, and was killed in action.

Shaw's "Poor Law and Destitution in Ireland" speech and Connolly's *Labour, Nationality, and Religion* pamphlet reflected not only the two philosophical approaches to socialism as pursued by Fred Ryan, Synge, Shaw, and soon St. John Ervine in Irish theatre, but also the growing urgency with socialism in 1910 Ireland. The SPI's manifesto of 1910, authored by Connolly and Sheehy-Skeffington, strove to rally the working class to seize and propel revolutionary change. Yet, like Shaw's lecture, the manifesto argued that poverty was manufactured by the capitalist middle class (Nevin, *Connolly*, 385). But Connolly's nationalized approach continued when his book *Labour in Irish History* was published in Dublin before year's end; it is a militant socialist reading of Irish history. The emerging question was whether or not some shared intellectual ground would move Shaw toward Connolly, beyond their passing one another in the Antient Concert Rooms?

Unfortunately, Connolly's personal library did not survive, so we do not have specific knowledge of the works he read. But being an obsessive reader he undoubtedly read Shaw, and certainly discussed Shaw with O'Brien, Fred Ryan, and Sheehy-Skeffington. And despite their different approaches, and because of their shared concern for the proletariat in Ireland, the paths of Shaw and Connolly would eventually converge, as labor and capitalist interests began to reach a crisis point. But before such convergence occurred, Shaw returned to England, and Connolly to Belfast to organize for the ITGWU. If the process toward convergence had started when Fred Ryan lectured the ISRP in 1899 and continued with the premiere of Ryan's 1902 Shavian-influenced play, that process had been revitalized by Shaw in October 1910, which Fred Ryan verified. Ryan, who also must have attended Shaw's Poor Law speech, given his long admiration for Shaw, wrote to Connolly four days following the speech, on 7 October: "I somehow feel—one senses these things in the air—there is the best opening now in Ireland that I remember for making a real forward move and ripping into the whole fabric of moral and intellectual tyranny in the country. There is no doubt one can get an audience to listen now to things that 5 years ago or even 3 or 4 years ago would have frightened them" (*Between Comrades*, 443). Shaw's participation in the debate was forwarding prospective social change in Dublin.[19]

The most remarkable consequence of Shaw's "The Poor Law and Destitution in Ireland," or Shaw's deliverance of the lecture, was that Shaw had become a visible bridge or link between the emerging socialism and trade unionism of the working class to the consciousness of Dublin's middle class. Shaw's speech, in the wake of Connolly's clash with Kane and the Catholic hierarchy's efforts to stamp out socialism, delivered a hint to the middle class of what was happening to the poor. This is not to suggest that Shaw was consciously serving as a bridge, nor is it to say he was unaware of it. The *Freeman's Journal* and the *Irish Times* made no mention to their bourgeois readership of the SPI's manifesto or of Connolly's retort to Kane. In fact, no capitalist-owned paper mentioned any of it except for the *Irish Catholic*, which published Church responses to Connolly's attack. And, up to the 1910 autumn, the capitalist Dublin press mentioned James Larkin only in passing. The papers neither cared nor yet realized the impact the ITGWU could have on Dublin.[20] But Shaw's lecture raised issues of proletariat suffering in Ireland to some of the middle class— while criticizing that class for their complicity in manufacturing the poor. And as Connolly knew, socialism would need some middle-class allies if it was to make ground in Dublin on behalf of laborers. He noted in 1911 about the involvement of the middle-class "Miss Shannon" in the Socialist Party of Ireland that "we must get that class of people to take an interest in the movement, and leave us plebs to do the rough and tumble work" (*Between Comrades*, 461). Yes, Fred Ryan, P. D. Kenny, W. P. Ryan, and Sheehy-Skeffington were already more than sympathetic, but the capitalist "respectable" forces had so far limited Kenny's impact and were about to economically drive both Ryans from the country—and they worked to belittle Sheehy-Skeffington as a crank, as they would attempt to label Shaw a jester. But Sheehy-Skeffington and Shaw would do much to raise the genuine awareness of socialism within middle-class circles, while Synge's literature was about to permeate to a few. Yet Shaw's intellectual reputation could and would do much.

While not suggesting that Shaw had dramatically propelled socialist issues concerning the poor into the consciousness of the middle class, we might see his lecture as having begun a nudging process that was, at the time, furthered beyond what Kenny, Ryan, and Sheehy-Skeffington had so far managed to do. Besides, when Sheehy-Skeffington stated to a Dublin gathering that Connolly was the man to lead the socialist movement in Ireland, he was addressing a working-class audience. But Shaw's 1910 Dublin lecture, based on his then highly visible reputation, helped to move the socialist appeal in Ireland to those in the middle class who could be reached on a grander scale than what had earlier been accomplished. When Shaw was introduced for his "Poor Law and Destitution in Ireland" lecture, the chair, wearing the chain of deputy Lord Mayor of Dublin, referred to Shaw as "the greatest and most distinguished Irishman" ("Mr. Bernard Shaw," 7). This was a reputation Shaw enjoyed in Ireland which neither Synge in death nor Connolly in his return could have claimed in 1910 Dublin. In light of this, Shaw's speech on behalf of the poor also added further credence to the debate and promotion of socialistic leanings on the Irish stage—and stages.

As 1910 ended, on 27, 28, and 29 December, socialistic leaning on an Irish stage, specifically a Cork stage via the Cork Dramatic Society, was presented in Terence MacSwiney's short, one-act play *The Holocaust*. The play was written in the aftermath of a failed ITGWU strike of Cork dockworkers, and was the first play set in an Irish tenement. The work partially echoes Synge's *Riders to the Sea* in that its mother character, Polly Mahony, is about to lose her fifth and last child to class circumstances, in this case consumption, while Catholicism is questioned by a priest contemplating his faith in the overwhelming bleakness of the Cork proletariat (Levitas, *Theatre*, 176). However, the play does not uncomfortably challenge its middle-class audience, made up mostly of middle-class Corkians, as being directly responsible. Rather, the play attempts to nudge its audience by endeavoring to explain the extreme situation facing the defeated Cork working class. This is evidenced by the commercial newspapers' responses to the play. The Dublin bourgeois paper the *Leader* wrote (in language reflecting its class view of the labor class) that the play was "a poignant little etching of the problem of slum life—of unemployment, underfeeding, joylessness, and unregarded misery" (as quoted in Hogan with Burnham and Poteet, *Abbey Theatre*, 95). The *Cork Constitution* recorded that as the play presented a scene of "humble life," the audience responded with "hearty applause" (as quoted in Hogan with Burnham and Poteet, *Abbey Theatre*, 94). MacSwiney's contemporary the Cork playwright, literary critic, and university professor Daniel Corkery recalled of MacSwiney: "Shaw's dramatic technique he admired very much . . .

Synge he did not like" (as quoted in Hogan with Burnham and Poteet, *Abbey Theatre*, 94). Clearly *The Holocaust*, in its form and philosophy, leaned more toward Shaw's example than Synge's, as it sought to illustrate in order to patiently nudge its audience toward sympathy and its duty to improve society. Would 1911 see similar?

St. John Ervine—A Shaw Disciple

While Connolly headed north to Belfast, a Belfast-born playwright who would become a disciple of Shaw and write a Shaw biography, St. John Ervine, brought his socialistic play *Mixed Marriage* to Dublin, which was premiered at the Abbey Theatre in April 1911. The play spoke of the Belfast bigotry that repeatedly betrayed labor for capitalists.

As a young man during the twentieth century's first decade, Ervine, like Shaw, immigrated to London for employment and like Shaw joined the Fabian Society, at which time he "began to write, first of all for the newspapers and then for the theatre" (Cronin, "Introduction," 7). Ervine, who was clearly opposed to Home Rule for Ireland or any form of Irish political nationalism, was adamantly dismissive of Synge, labeling him "a decadent descendant of the Elizabethans" (as quoted in Cronin, "Introduction," 10). He specifically saw *Playboy*, perhaps in Shaw's universal sense, as presenting the Irish "like the rest of God's creatures" (Cronin, "Introduction," 10). Ervine's 1911 politics and sense of theatre were indeed more in line with Shaw's than not. His *Mixed Marriage* represents a Shavian-inspired, socialistically leaning Irish play.

Mixed Marriage follows the Rainey family, a working-class Belfast household. John Rainey, the patriarchal figure, is an Ulster Protestant and a member of the Orange Order. The play opens with Rainey and his co-workers going on strike. One of Rainey's sons, Hugh, is friendly with a labor leader and socialist named Michael O'Hara, who is Catholic. O'Hara solicits John Rainey to speak to fellow Protestant strikers to offset the employers' agent, who is claiming the strike is a Catholic nationalist plot serving their interests and not the workers'. This employer's tactic echoed the management's tactic during the 1907 Belfast dock strike and is read aloud on stage in the play as a Belfast *Evening Telegraph* editorial: "We feel sure that the loyal peace-abiding Protestants of this, the greatest commercial city in Ireland, will not allow themselves to be led astray by Nationalist agitators from Dublin, and that they will see that their true interests lie in the same direction as those of the employers. We should be the last to encourage religious strife, but we would remind our readers, the loyal Orangemen of Ulster, that the leaders of this strike are Roman Catholic and Home Rulers" (*Mixed*, 25–26). O'Hara is not a nationalist but "a member o' the Independent Labor Party" (*Mixed*, 21).

Rainey, despite being suspicious of O'Hara because of O'Hara's religion, agrees to speak to fellow workers to advocate workers' unity despite religion. Act I ends with Hugh Rainey remarking, "A sometimes think what a fine thing it 'ud be if the workin' men o' Irelan' was to join their han's thegither an' try an' make a great country" (*Mixed*, 28). This possibility ends when John Rainey discovers that Hugh is engaged to Nora Murray, a Catholic. O'Hara had persuaded Hugh and Nora to keep their engagement quiet until after the labor rally, but Rainey overhears the couple and explodes with rage. O'Hara then tries to persuade Hugh and Nora to give up their plans in favor of workers' unity but they refuse. John Rainey exits to denounce the strike's Catholic leaders, playing into the hands of his capitalist, bourgeois employers.

In Act IV, the Raineys, with Nora, are in their house under siege from Protestant rioters demanding the "papist" come out. Throughout the scene, despite the contrary opinions of Mrs. Rainey (John's wife) and his sons, Rainey remains convinced that bigotry toward Catholics is correct. Eventually Catholic rioters approach, with O'Hara trying to turn them back to avoid sectarian violence. British soldiers appear and fire on the crowd as Nora runs into the street saying, "It was my fault" (*Mixed*, 62). She is killed.

The play heavy-handedly exposes the useless capitalist-dictated bigotry of people like John Rainey, which undermines any serious socialist or trade union efforts to improve working-class conditions in Belfast. Not surprisingly, Ervine's approach was not antagonistic to its 1911 Dublin audience, but the play lacks Shaw's comedic and subtle touches. *Mixed Marriage* presents its portrayed events in a straightforward fashion, in a realistic mode, and the audience is comfortably presented with Ervine's message. One Dublin press review noted that the play "drew the biggest audience to the Abbey Theatre to-night that was ever seen there. Why? Well possibly because the subject was one that had a close connection with the Irish politics of the day" (as quoted in Hogan with Burnham and Poteet, *Abbey Theatre*, 121). Rather than believing *Mixed Marriage* was presenting socialistic thought to an appreciative middle-class audience,

Robert Hogan with Richard Burnham and Daniel Poteet write that because Ervine "was criticizing the . . . inhabitants of . . . Belfast, the Dublin audiences took the play to its heart" (*Abbey Theatre*, 121). Given that this most likely was the case, the play, because it attacked Ulster Protestant prejudices, appealed to the prejudices harbored by the Dublin (mostly) Catholic middle-class audience. Still, the play did present labor's plight, even if it failed to specify the type of work of John Rainey and his fellow strikers.

Mixed Marriage reflects the work of Belfast labor and socialist organizer William Walker, in addition to James Larkin's brief 1907 Belfast experience during a dock strike. The working-class Walker had, in 1911, a bigger presence in Belfast than Larkin, having been engaged in expanding the unionization of Belfast workers from the 1890s on. Much of his efforts had been disrupted by capitalist-inspired sectarian hatred and violence that prohibited a true workers' solidarity. It had always been to the advantage of capitalist employers in Belfast to cultivate and promote religious strife among its workforce, keeping workers' minds on religion rather than labor issues. Nevertheless, in June 1911, Walker had grown seemingly optimistic about organizing Belfast labor and came to believe that "it has now become impossible in Belfast to have a religious riot" (as quoted in Patterson, "William Walker," 167). Ervine in his play, which premiered in March 1911, was not so optimistic. Interestingly, when Ervine's character Michael O'Hara persuades John Rainey into addressing Presbyterian Orange workers to support the union's strike in Act I, Rainey suggests that the meeting be held on the steps of Belfast's Custom House (*Mixed*, 27). Walker spoke mostly to Orange loyalist crowds on those very same steps (Patterson, "William Walker," 157).

While Ervine's play does not base the Catholic Michael O'Hara character on the Presbyterian William Walker, as *The Laying of the Foundations*' Nolan character was based on Connolly, Ervine touches on Walker's philosophy and comments on union leaders in Belfast who were Catholic. Walker advocated an international socialism, like Shaw, which therefore presumably made his work attractive to the Fabian Ervine. Arguably, the collapse of the union efforts in *Mixed Marriage* suggested the need for an international socialism and trade union, one that transcended religious and national divisions and borders. Walker, and Larkin in 1907, had promoted British labor unions in Belfast, not Irish unions, which Walker felt only provoked religious confrontations, and as such, Ervine's play reflects

Walker's view of the failure of Irish unions in Belfast. In fact, Walker's views for an international approach extended to the point of his opposing the formation of an independent Irish labor party. In this regard, Ervine's play anticipates the clash between Walker and James Connolly, who would arrive in Belfast a month after *Mixed Marriage* premiered to lead a chapter of the Dublin-based ITGWU. In response to Walker's philosophy, Connolly confrontationally argued that Walker's international socialism "seems scarcely distinguishable from Imperialism, the merging of subjugated peoples in the political system of their conquerors" (as quoted in Patterson, "William Walker," 166).[21] This debate of international and national socialism for Ireland was echoing the international and nationalized considerations broached earlier by Shaw and Synge.

Larkin, the Irish Workers' Dramatic Company, and A. P. Wilson

By the time *Mixed Marriage* was being revived by the Abbey Theatre in 1912, the audience's sense of the play may have been significantly different from the year before during its April premiere. By June 1911, British labor unrest, namely the National Sailors' and Firemen's Union strike in Hull and Liverpool, expanded into sympathy strikes in Ireland. Morrissey argues that as unemployment figures had improved throughout the British Isles in 1911, trade unionists "embarked on a pattern of militancy . . . that was to lead to almost continual unrest until the outbreak of the First World War in August 1914" (*O'Brien*, 57–58). In Ireland this meant Larkin, the ITGWU, and syndicalism.

The concept of one big union fighting to improve workers' conditions quickly led to widespread strikes in Ireland, as the ITGWU established branches in Wexford, Waterford, and Kilkenny (Morrissey, *O'Brien*, 58). However, it is important to note that while the ITGWU began its 1911 strikes in sympathy with British strikers, the ITGWU saw itself as focused on Irish labor and separate from English labor while still observing an international socialist brotherhood. In this vein the ITGWU pressed on.

Morrissey notes that when the Bridge Street Bakers in Dublin went on strike in September 1911, food shortages led to denouncements against the strikers (*O'Brien*, 58). The bakers strike led to transportation strikes that were preventing food being regularly transported into Dublin. It was at this point that Synge's detractor Arthur Griffith, then editor of the conservative middle-class nationalist paper *Sinn Fein*, demanded the British use its army to contain striking Irish laborers to secure food delivery into Dublin (Glandon, *Arthur Griffith*, 100). Larkin, in the ITGWU's newly formed weekly the *Irish Worker*, responded to Griffith's demand: "When the pot boils, the scum comes to the top" (as quoted in Glandon, *Arthur Griffith*, 100).

The *Irish Worker* was originally edited by Larkin, denounced "erring employers and corrupt civil servants by name," and quickly reached a circulation of 20,000 (Morrissey, *O'Brien*, 55). The paper also aggressively attacked all who represented and expressed opposition to Irish labor, such as Griffith and his *Sinn Fein* paper.[22] Larkin's paper particularly attacked the capitalist newspapers, whether the papers claimed to be pro-British or Irish nationalist. Larkin's tactic was hostile aggression.

Attacking the capitalist press in 1911, along with escalating strikes throughout Irish cities, drew hostile retaliation from the *Irish Independent*, owned by William Martin Murphy, who also owned the *Irish Catholic*, which had published Father Kane's sermons and the retort to Connolly's counter to Kane. The developing clash with Murphy's *Independent* resulted in Larkin taking aim at Murphy's Dublin companies, especially the Dublin United Tramways Company (Morrissey, *O'Brien*, 60).

William Martin Murphy was to this point a much respected pillar of Irish society. He was clearly a man of his class and his extensive capitalist means. As a "respectable" Catholic Dubliner, he had worked to rid the Irish Party of Charles Stewart Parnell when Parnell's adulterous affair became public knowledge. As Padraig Yeates points out, in *Lockout Dublin 1913*, Murphy financed the anti-Parnellites in 1890 (*Lockout*, 4). As a result, Murphy wrested the *Irish Daily Independent* away from the Parnell camp. The paper, founded by Parnell, was then used to ruin Parnell's party by calling on Catholic morality (Bennett, *Encyclopaedia*, 136). Yeates writes that Murphy "regarded the [Parnell] divorce case as 'an interposition of divine providence' that released the nationalist movement from bondage to a Protestant landlord and adulterer" (*Lockout*, 4). By turning to his Catholic bourgeois morality, Murphy not only destroyed Parnell, he destroyed Ireland's last hope for peaceful independence and economic reform. While Murphy may have believed in his class's morality and believed that Parnell, despite his long unselfish service, was a blight to Ireland, Murphy profited from Parnell's fall while Ireland remained a British colony. Though supposedly a Home Ruler, Murphy was a capitalist first.

So, it should be no surprise that Synge and Shaw, and others, assaulted bourgeois Catholic morality in Ireland. Of course, Murphy's *Irish Independent* joined Griffith's condemnation in 1907 of *The Playboy of the Western World* "as a slur on the Irish people" (as quoted in Morrissey, *Murphy*, 38). In fact, Murphy's *Irish Independent* was the first Dublin paper to ever attack Synge's work by being the first to condemn *In the Shadow of the Glen*. Writing on the day of the play's premiere, prior to the performance, the paper labeled it as "unwholesome" and insinuated that the play had not grown from Irish peasants but from "the gaiety of Paris" (as quoted in Greene and Stephens, *J. M. Synge*, 156). In 1911, as labor unrest grew, Murphy was ready to fight and harbored no plans to submit to the ITGWU, or any union.

As strikes escalated further in 1911, Larkin became more visible as the ITGWU's leader, and he became the target of personal attacks by Murphy's *Independent*. Morrissey notes that Larkin relished publicity (*O'Brien*, 62). Consequently, some in the ITGWU were beginning to see Larkin as reckless. The explosion of strikes over so short a time prompted employers to contemplate organizing themselves against the ITGWU. By as early as May 1911, Connolly confided to O'Brien that Larkin "is utterly unreliable—and dangerous because unreliable" (*Between Comrades*, 461). Yet despite such reservations, the ITGWU moved forward under Larkin with Connolly following.

Desmond Ryan, a contributor to the *Irish Worker* under Larkin and the son of W. P. Ryan, wrote that James Larkin "aroused the vague, incoherent and almost helpless masses and welded them into harmonious union, articulate, organized and militant." With regard to Larkin's efforts and speeches during the 1911–13 period, Ryan added: "Night after night, this husky roaring giant of labour thunders out the strangest talks that have ever stirred the multitudes: no balanced periods, no favourite whimsicalities, no cleverly prepared surprises. Nay, none of these, nor the recondite philosophy of a Karl Marx, the subtle triflings of a George Bernard Shaw, . . . but rather facts known to the audience, the virtues of temperance, bowelless employers, white-livered curs, adjectived scabs, and other obnoxious individuals" ("Historians on Larkin," 387). Larkin, despite what some of his followers thought of him personally, was uniting Irish workers and strengthening the ITGWU into a formidable trade union movement, giving voice to the proletariat as no one had done before in Ireland.

In promoting his vision for Irish labor, Larkin wanted to improve workers' living conditions beyond merely improving their working conditions. In the 29 July 1911 *Irish Worker*, Larkin wrote: "If it is good for the employers . . . to have clean clothing and good food, and books and music, and pictures, so it is good that the people should have these things also—and that is the claim we are making today" (as quoted in Morrissey, O'Brien, 55). As part of this effort, the ITGWU formed a theatre company in 1912.

In early 1912, the ITGWU acquired Liberty Hall, a building which once had been the Northumberland Hotel. In addition to providing a headquarters for the union, Larkin used the building as a "centre for the social and cultural activities of the union. The 'Hall' soon housed the Irish Workers' Choir, and the Juvenile and Adult Dancers' class, while an Irish language class was formed, followed by the founding of the Irish Workers' Dramatic Company" (E. Larkin, "James Larkin," 5). A young Sean O'Casey worked on the renovations to the interior of Liberty Hall when it was acquired, specifically working on what would become the hall's first stage (Murray, *O'Casey*, 94). The Irish Workers' Dramatic Company was started as a class in June 1912 by Delia Larkin, James Larkin's sister, who led the women's section of the ITGWU, the Irish Women Workers' Union (IWWU). Delia echoed her brother's call for art for the laboring class by stressing the need for theatre; she suggested in November 1912 that workers should regularly attend the Abbey Theatre (Levitas, "Plumbing," 141). On St. Stephen's Night, 26 December 1912, she gave the working class its own theatre, as the Irish Workers' Dramatic Company presented its first performances (Moriarty, "Delia Larkin," 432).

Delia Larkin emerged in the ITGWU when her brother formed the IWWU in 1911 with Delia as its general secretary. Theresa Moriarty writes that "Delia Larkin increasingly became the public face of Liberty Hall" ("Delia Larkin," 433). Christopher Murray suggests that Delia "necessarily had a special interest in involving women" as much as possible to provide them with chances for "bettering themselves" (*O'Casey*, 94). Murray believes Delia's philosophy had much to do with the dramatic classes she organized in 1912, which led to the formation of their company and their first performances.

The Irish Workers' Dramatic Company's first production consisted of four plays: *The Troth* by Rutherford Mayne, *The Bishop's Candlestick* by

Norman McKinnell, *The Matchmaker* by nationalist Seumas O'Kelly, and *Victims* by A. P. Wilson. This performance of *Victims* was a premiere and represented the first play staged in Ireland set in a Dublin tenement. The four plays were all staged by Wilson.

Not a great deal is known about A. P. Wilson, who sometimes went by A. Patrick Wilson in Ireland and later in Scotland was known as Andrew P. Wilson. Christopher Murray suggests that Wilson came to Dublin in 1911 "possibly from Belfast," which was Yeats's opinion, but Lady Gregory in a 1915 letter to Shaw calls Wilson a Scot (Murray, *O'Casey*, 95, Gregory, *Shaw, Lady Gregory*, 97). Close to 1920, Wilson settled in Scotland, where he worked as a playwright, theatre director, and actor, being a co-founder of the Scottish National Players (Burch, "Historical"). But he had emerged into public view in Dublin as early as 1912, writing for the *Irish Worker*; O'Brien remembered Wilson as a "sub-editor" with the paper, signing his articles as "Lucan," "Mac," and "Euchan" (*Forth*, 260; Murray, *O'Casey*, 98). Wilson clearly was heavily involved with the ITGWU by 1912. However, such involvement only partially explains why he emerged as the Irish Workers' Dramatic Company's theatre director with their first production in late 1912.

Christopher Murray believes that after theatre productions temporarily ceased at Liberty Hall in 1913, Wilson joined the Abbey Theatre (*O'Casey*, 95). However, Wilson had joined the Abbey Theatre's acting school in either late 1911 or early 1912, clearly well before the Irish Workers' Dramatic Company's first performance. On 29 February 1912, Wilson performed with the Abbey's acting school in the fifteenth-century morality play *The Worlde and the Chylde* (Hogan with Burnham and Poteet, *Abbey Theatre*, 179).[23] In March 1912, the acting school ended and its students became the Abbey's second company. So presumably, Wilson came to the Liberty Hall Players, as the labor theatre company was informally called, with some experience, ability, and interest in labor and theatre.[24]

Wilson's stage directions for his play *Victims* is vivid: "The whole aspect of the room gives the impression of the most abject poverty. A few huddled rags in a corner denote that the only place available for sleeping is the floor" (*Victims*, 3). The play's action is even more conscious of class and a product of its time. It opens on a young mother, Annie Nolan with her sick baby, who is kept in a box, since there is no cradle. Annie: "Oh God! to think that my little child should be dying with hunger, and his mother powerless to save him . . . But you must not die. You shall not die. God cannot be cruel as to take you from me now. Your father will find a job" (*Victims*, 5). George Purcell, a clerk for Scott and Scott, arrives to collect shirts Annie was sewing for the company, which she has not finished. She pleads with Purcell, saying that Mr. Scott does not understand her circumstances, that if he did, he would give her more time to complete the work. Purcell deflects her pleading with coldness, even after she explains that she only sewed a dozen because she could not work at night, since they have no candles. When she throws the shirts at Purcell, he is outraged that she thinks he, a clerk, would carry shirts: "I'm a clerk, I am, and not a carter. I wouldn't have come here at all only the old boss asked me himself. . . . Scott and Scott don't take notice of dying children; they heard that yarn before. As for your husband being out of work, well, maybe he is, and maybe he isn't. I don't know, and Scott and Scott don't care. (Kicking the shirts out of his way)" (*Victims*, 7). When Jack, Annie's husband, enters, Annie tells him she failed, since she could not work fast enough. Jack: "The blood suckers cannot only sweat women, but they must select what women they will sweat! . . . Surely my very manhood has been sapped and taken away, when I allowed you to attempt such work at all" (*Victims*, 8). Further on, Jack's defeatism sinks more: "Yes, death! It is the only thing for us to do that can cost nothing. . . . They have taken away my right to work; they have taken away our right to live" (*Victims*, 8). Anne explains that she sent for the doctor because their baby is dying, but the doctor sent word that he "wouldn't come unless I sent money first" (*Victims*, 9).

Clearly, Wilson's *Victims* is an agit-prop type play. It is much different from the other three plays it premiered with, and would be different from many of the plays the Liberty Hall Players produced prior to November 1915, which tended to be light comedies. *Victims* often reads as a rallying article from the *Irish Worker*, which did publish it, but the play owes its existence to the use of theatre in Ireland to promote political and, in this case, socialistic ideas. Wilson's *Victims* was, in 1912, consistent with the ITGWU's approach that only one big union can take on employers.

Victims' Jack elaborates to Annie that he learned the employers have labeled him dangerous because he belonged to a small union that had previously gone on strike. That union was broken because no other unions supported its strike: "The masters . . . are going to take no chances. They have all combined together, and they are starting already to nip the next revolt in the bud" (*Victims*, 11). Such comments reflect what Dublin employers were doing in 1912.

The play moves through Jack's continuing sermons, specifying how he has no hope for work and now is penniless so they cannot move. Anne interjects, raising the issue of religion, but like Shaw only names Christians so as to, presumably, avoid the controversy raised when Connolly publicly answered the Catholic Church. Annie states: "These men are not only employers they are Christian men" (*Victims*, 12). Jack: "Christian men! God, how mockingly the Almighty must smile when those profit fiends are called followers of the Prince of Peace. . . . He [their child] is dying of starvation, being slowly murdered by the master gang whom you call Christians" (*Victims*, 12).

The play's dialogue, namely Jack's about how their baby would be better dead, echoes Jonathan Swift's *A Modest Proposal*, which took up the cause of the Irish poor in 1729.[25] Specifically Jack says: "If I thought my child would live, I would take him up in my two hands and save him from such a fate by dashing his brains out!" (*Victims*, 12). *Victims* ends with the rent collector coming for either the three week's owed rent or to evict them. Jack sends the collector away with a threat and the baby dies.

Victims' brutal attack on the Christianity of the employers echoed the socialist assault on the respectable class that rallied around the employers' respectable Christian values, and which Synge, Shaw, Connolly, and others had targeted. But despite the shared religious attack, its agit-prop form distinguished *Victims* from either Shaw or Synge.

The very nature of agit-prop theatre most likely strikes one as pursuing an assaulting and hostile approach. However, a play like *Victims* was presented before, and presumably written for, an audience already likeminded as the playwright and director (who in this instance were the same). The only attempt to persuade in *Victims* is the affirmation of the syndicalist, one-big-union strategy. The play is not attacking or nudging a predominantly middle-class audience which, in the philosophy of socialism then in Ireland, was at least complicit with the capitalist system that was responsible for the abused working class, or, as Shaw charged in his 1910 Dublin lecture, the manufacturers of the poor. So, in this regard, *Victims* was not antagonistic to most of its audience and not in the Syngean vein, except that it concerned itself with the Irish poor. But that *Victims* nudged its original audience toward syndicalism suggests that the play was closer to being in the vein of Shaw, and Fred Ryan and Ervine, but with a different class audience. Yet given the limitations of its agit-prop nature, Wilson's play ultimately had more in common with the lighter plays that the Liberty Hall Players presented in early 1913 and 1914, in that *Victims* was giving its audience strictly what it wanted, giving voice to what it knew and accepted. But what happened when Wilson wrote a labor play for the Abbey Theatre and its audience? By the time that happened, Dublin would be reeling in the wake of 1913.

Shaw, Markievicz, S. Connolly, and Growing Labor Unrest

Wilson was not the only actor with eventual labor connections to join the Abbey Theatre in 1912 through the Abbey's then acting school. Others included Sean Connolly (no relation to James) and Helena Moloney. They would become important actors in the Abbey Theatre and become noted players on the Dublin socialist stage. Sean Connolly made his acting debut, as far as can be determined, in the 1910 production of Seumas O'Kelly's *The Home-Coming* with Cluithcheoiri na hEireann (Theatre of Ireland), a small theatre company that competed with the Abbey Theatre from 1907 to 1912. An additional amateur Dublin theatre in 1910 was the Independent Theatre Company (ITC), founded and led by Count Casimir Markievicz.

Casimir Markievicz was a Polish count who had married Constance Gore-Booth, herself of an aristocratic, Anglo-Irish family in County Sligo. They had met in Paris as artists and eventually settled in Dublin. As Constance Markievicz began to move into nationalist politics in Dublin, her husband moved into Dublin theatre, eventually forming the ITC. In 1910, Casimir Markievicz staged an Irish melodrama he wrote, set during Ireland's 1798 rebellion, titled *The Memory of the Dead*. The production featured Constance in the cast. To this point, of course, the Markieviczes seemed distant from Irish socialist circles, given their aristocratic backgrounds and their participation in then middle-class nationalism and melodramatic theatre. While this perception of the Markieviczes would definitely change in 1913, there were hints of their eventual directions as early as 1907, when Casimir Markievicz was first contemplating the ITC.

In late November 1907, when *John Bull's Other Island* was experiencing its Dublin premier run, Synge and his friend Stephen MacKenna "had a long talk with Count Markiewicz (sp) at the Arts Club." Synge noted in a private letter to his fiancée and actor Molly Allgood that "There seems to be some scheme in the air . . . of buying up the old Queens [Theatre] and starting a sort of municipal theatre to play all the *good* plays of the day on a wide basis . . . If that comes off there will be hope for *us* after the Abbey is buried. I am going to frequent the Arts Club and see what is going on" (*Letters to Molly*, 221–222). Seemingly, the envisioned theatre Markievicz described to Synge and MacKenna must have leaned sufficiently in a direction that piqued Synge's interest as Synge was not an Arts Club regular.

An additional hint of the changes to come to the Markieviczes' political ideology lies in the ITC's 1910 staging of Casimir's comedy *Mary*. While the play was not published and appears to be non-extant, a review of it in the *Irish Times* suggests that the play echoed slightly Synge's *In the Shadow of the Glen*. The play followed the title character, who has left her husband because she is not "inclined to submit to domestic despotism." The respectable paper admitted that "if any justification could be found for desertion of a husband by a wife, such an instance as the present would supply it" (as quoted in Hogan with Burnham and Poteet, *Abbey Theatre*, 82). While the paper could not admit to such with Synge's Nora and her physically abusive husband, perhaps we can infer that Markievicz, by using comedy, was presenting a woman's right to escape her husband's enslavement through reasoning, Shavian tactics. Markievicz's affinity for Shaw would become more apparent in 1913.

In 1911, Markievicz and his ITC staged the comedy *Eleanor's Enterprise*, by George Birmingham, with a cast including Constance Markievicz and the young actors Helena Moloney and Sean Connolly. By 1912, Moloney and Connolly were in the Abbey Theatre's acting school with Wilson, and the Markieviczes were sharpening their politics.

Before James Connolly returned to Dublin in 1910, Moloney wrote him regarding the *Harp*, which he edited in New York, stating that she wished Ireland had such a paper (*Between Comrades*, 399). When Connolly returned to Ireland, he befriended Moloney. She quickly joined the Irish Women's Workers' Union (IWWU) in 1911 on her way to being an important comrade to Connolly's increasing labor successes.

During the 1911 summer, Connolly achieved a number of astonishing ITGWU triumphs in Belfast. In fact, it was Connolly who earned the first major successes in 1911 for the union that set Larkin to call for more strikes throughout many southern Irish cities. It was Connolly who led Belfast dockworkers into a sympathy strike when he discovered that the parent company of the Ulster Steam Ship Company was the owner of a similar company in Liverpool where English dockworkers were on strike. The sympathy strike was settled in late August and had reached significant gains for Belfast ITGWU dockworkers (Nevin, *Connolly*, 396). Connolly had used the sympathy strike tactic while strengthening an Irish union for Irish workers. By the end of August, Connolly was temporarily back in Dublin and was witnessing the numerous strikes Larkin was then calling for on many fronts.

Perhaps the most notable Larkin ITGWU strike in 1911 was that against the Great Southern and Western Railway (GSWR). The GSWR's president was Sir William Goulding, one of the wealthiest men, if not the wealthiest, in Ireland outside of the Guinness family (Yeates, *Lockout*, 2). On the GSWR board was William Martin Murphy. Goulding, with Murphy, took a hard line against the ITGWU, and defeated the union by experimenting with locking out workers (Yeates, *Lockout*, 3). Disturbed—as was the Catholic Church he worshipped—with the growing labor movement throughout 1910 and 1911, Murphy formed the Dublin Employers' Federation, made up of over three hundred Dublin employers of labor, to unite against the union movement. In 1912, Murphy also became president of the Dublin Chamber of Commerce. Shaw's friendly sparring partner G. K. Chesterton described Murphy as being like "some morbid prince of the fifteenth century, full of cold anger and not without a perverted piety" (as quoted in Yeates, *Lockout*, 3). To Murphy, the GSWR's defeat of the ITGWU was paramount, but menacing for the union.

The ITGWU's defeat by the railway, and other defeats in 1911, indicated that the union was not yet strong enough to fulfill Larkin's vision. But in the spring of 1913, much was coming together.[26]

Shaw, Theatre, Larkin, and Impressionists

A strand of this coming together began in October 1912, when an amateur theatre company formed by Evelyn Ashley and his wife Flora MacDonnell (formerly of Herbert Beerbohm Tree's company) rented Dublin's commercial Gaiety Theatre and staged *John Bull's Other Island* ("Gaiety Theatre 'John Bull's,'" 8). While the production received little press, the *Irish Times* reviewed it, noting that it coincided with the play's January 1912 reprinting, which was designed to sell for six pennies, and also coincided with the then Home Rule bill in the British Parliament. It is interesting that such a paper, which was decidedly anti–Home Rule and against socialism, provided space to Shaw's major Irish play, even if buried on page eight. Undoubtedly, such attention was a result of the play's entertainment. The paper noted that because of the play's recent inexpensive printing and its earlier success at London's Royal Court Theatre (and tours), many of the audience knew the play well ("Gaiety Theatre 'John Bull's,'" 8). The bourgeois paper offered no commentary on the play's thematic direction, but noted that Shaw's "abundant 'points' . . . were usually well made, and the audience enjoyed them thoroughly. The celebrated third act, in particular, went down thoroughly well" ("Gaiety Theatre 'John Bull's,'" 8). Perhaps it is telling that the paper was unable to comment on the play's politics in relation to the Home Rule bill and, more importantly, to the growing labor unrest. It is intriguing that the play was presented at such time when Irish employers were united in keeping their fellow Irish economically well beneath them, much like the play's collusionary characters working to deny upward mobility to the likes of Patsy Farrell.

In a similar vein, the Abbey Theatre premiered a new play on 24 April 1912 titled *Broken Faith*, authored jointly by Suzanne R. Day and Geraldine Cummins. Both women were from Cork and were suffragettes, writing a number of works together and separately. The suffragette and socialistic *Irish Citizen* reviewed *Broken Faith*, a play never published:

> Here we have . . . [a] poor interior, where the harassed wife is hard put to it to place even a "dinner" of bread and tea. . . . [The husband] a lazy, wretched, dispirited type . . . without energy to seize a chance of work . . . [and] is at last goaded into crime. Then the despicable man [thinks it] possible to throw the blame on the unhappy wife [who] consents [to confess to the crime] . . . and Michael is exalting in the prospects of a free life in America, when she asks him about the children? Will he take them with him to the states? He callously refused to sling any such burden round his neck, and says the children can go to the workhouse till their mother comes out of jail. (As quoted in Hogan, *Abbey Theatre*, 250)

Such sentiment from the husband Michael that his children "can go to the workhouse" rings of Shaw's pronouncement from his 1910 lecture that Irish children should never be sent to workhouses. Was this Shaw's influence? At least the *Irish Citizen*'s editor could recall Shaw's lecture, as he was Francis Sheehy-Skeffington, who had attended the lecture. It is believed that Sheehy-Skeffington wrote many of his paper's theatre reviews, which were unsigned.

Broken Faith's depiction of poverty-stricken lives was harsh, and before the Abbey's audience it was meant to engage. Without the script, it is difficult to determine whether the authors were attempting to be Syngean or Shavian in approach. We perhaps can say with some certainty that the play was addressing a situation of poverty, since, presumably, it is poverty that drives Michael to his crime and willingness to abandon his family.

The *Irish Citizen*'s review continued: "Instantly Bridget breaks her promise—the father may desert his children, but she will never do so; and the play ends with the arrest of Michael. It is a sordid tragedy, redeemed by the heroic character of the woman, as indeed we should expect to find in the work of a lady who adds no small share of dramatic ability to her well-known feminist and philanthropic activities" (as quoted in Hogan with Burnham and Poteet, *Abbey Theatre*, 250). Sheehy-Skeffington is referring to Day when he alludes to the author's feminism and philanthropy, as she financially supported the *Irish Citizen*, as did Shaw's wife Charlotte (Levenson, *With Wooden*, 170). While the review might not have been the most objective, given Day's assistance, one recognizes further suffragette and possible socialistic explorations of the effects on women of loveless, enslaving marriages that *In the Shadow of the Glen* had explored in 1903. Synge's early play also touched on the Poor Law workhouses for those the capitalist class viewed as economically worthless. When Michael Dara realizes Synge's Nora has no money or wealth, his desire to marry her evaporates immediately and he tells her she can go to the workhouse: "There's a fine Union [workhouse] below in Rathdrum" (*Shadow*, 42). Enslaving marriage and workhouses continued as issues in spring 1913.

Also at that time, Casimir Markievicz had moved from the ITC to join forces with Ashley and MacDonnell, who had staged *John Bull's* the previous October. They called their new company the Dublin Repertory Theatre (DRT), and it would stage a number of compelling productions, including Shaw plays. But at the time the DRT formed, Shaw was in Dublin and the city was engulfed in much public press debate over Hugh Lane's effort to establish a municipal art gallery to house Lane's collection of modern paintings, mostly French Impressionists. Lane, nephew to Lady Gregory, was an art dealer and collector, and was curator of the National Gallery of Ireland, the art gallery that had "become one of Shaw's favorite haunts while growing up in Dublin" (Gibbs, *Bernard Shaw*, 6). Given

Lane's relationship to Gregory and the artistic-cultural cause of Lane's paintings, Gregory, Yeats, and much of literary Dublin advocated for Dublin Corporation to build a municipal gallery for the collection, and Shaw joined in.

Shaw had written to Dublin's Lord Mayor the previous November, urging Dublin Corporation to provide a suitable gallery. In support of his argument for the gallery, Shaw recalled the value of his early visits to the National Gallery: "The taste and knowledge of fine art which I acquired as a boy in the National Gallery of Dublin not only made it possible for me to live by my pen without discrediting my country, but are built into the fabric of the best work I have been able to do since" (*Shaw, Lady Gregory*, 82–83). Shaw had also agreed that the performances of *The Shewing-up of Blanco Posnet* during the Abbey Theatre's second American tour be used as a fund-raiser for the proposed gallery. The condition of Lane's offer to Dublin, the gift of his modern paintings collection, was that Dublin Corporation would build an appropriate gallery. To undertake such a project, the city needed to raise the money and appealed to the city's population, hence the public debate. While Shaw pledged one hundred guineas of his own money, and others made pledges as well, the project needed exceedingly wealthy patrons such as William Martin Murphy. There was, after all, a precedent in Dublin for wealthy art patronage. The nineteenth-century Irish engineer and great railway builder William Dargan had organized and financed the Dublin Industrial Exhibition of 1853 with 20,000 pounds of his own money, an enormous sum in 1853 (Boylan, *Dictionary*, 94). As part of the 1853 effort, Dargan "stipulated that the inclusion of pictures be a feature of the exhibition" (Bennett, *Encyclopaedia*, 177). Stemming from Dargan's effort emerged the National Gallery of Ireland, which opened in 1864 (Bennett, *Encyclopaedia*, 177). Naturally, then, there was expectation that Dublin's commerce leaders would step forward to help fund the gallery.[27]

Perhaps sensing the expectations toward the masters of commerce, Larkin began calling for the gallery to be built, seizing on Lane's notion of a gift to the "people" of Dublin. On 30 November 1912, Shaw wrote in favor of the gallery, which Larkin published in the ITGWU's *Irish Worker*. Shaw's appearance in the paper testifies to his knowledge of radical socialism in Ireland, and his willingness to occasionally stoke its flames. He excitedly wrote to Lady Gregory: "did you see the Irish Worker . . . [with]

my denunciation of Dublin as "a city of derision?" (*Shaw, Lady Gregory*, 85).

The controversy carried into 1913, as William Martin Murphy's *Irish Independent* newspaper became relentless in its opposition to the gallery. On 22 January 1913, Murphy himself wrote in the *Independent* that only a "handful of dilettante [sic]" favored the gallery "for which there is no popular demand and one which will never be of the smallest use to the common people of the city" (as quoted in Morrissey, *Murphy*, 39). All of the players and classes in the growing unrest that was about to explode in Dublin were converging on the issue of Lane's gallery, and Shaw continued to be present.

In response to Murphy's opposition to the gallery from the *Irish Independent*, from Synge's detractor Arthur Griffith in his *Sinn Fein* paper, from the Dublin Chamber of Commerce (of which Murphy was president), and so forth, Shaw granted an interview to the *Irish Times*. The interview was published on 12 April 1913, titled "Municipal Art Gallery, The Bridge Site, Interview with Mr. George Bernard Shaw."[28]

> When asked if he thinks the paintings and gallery are valuable, Shaw responded: "Think it! It is valuable. Is anybody in Dublin so stupendously ignorant as not to know that it will be one of the most precious collections of the kind in Europe?"
> When asked if his proposed location of fashionable Merrion Square was out of reach for those not living near the square, Shaw answered: "Well, do you think the places they [the poor] do live in so nice that they never want to go away from them? Do you think you can popularize art by putting it in dirty places? What the popular quarters of Dublin need is a thorough burning down. When you have done that, and replaced them in a manner worthy of a great city, it will be time enough to talk of putting your art treasures there. A laborer may want a public house at the corner of his slum; but when he has an impulse to look at pictures, he wants them as far away as possible from the squalor in which he is compelled to live. ("Municipal Art," 7)

Appearing to answer Shaw that there were indeed such "stupendously ignorant" individuals in Dublin not knowing the value of art, Murphy responded in the *Irish Independent*: "There has been much eloquence on this subject . . . and all the old platitudes have been trotted out about the 'priceless collection,' the 'envy of Europe' . . . the educational effect on the taste of the citizens, the answer to which may be summed up in the word—Fudge" (as quoted in E. Larkin, "Æ," 215). Murphy and his respectable capitalist class saw no viable profit in a new gallery.

In considering Murphy and his fellow captains of Dublin commerce, the Dublin poet George Russell (Æ) also entered the debate. He wrote that the wealthy men who had refused to support the gallery and opposed it showed themselves to be "the meanest, the most uncultured, the most materialistic and canting crowd which ever made a citizen ashamed of his fellow-countrymen" (as quoted in E. Larkin, "Æ," 214). Lady Gregory, in August 1913, agreed with Æ's assessment of Murphy and his commerce peers, as she saw Murphy as epitomizing vulgarity (E. Larkin, "Æ," 215). As Murphy and his like helped to crush the plans for Lane's gallery, exposing themselves as mean-spirited and excessively selfish, Æ, with others, including Shaw, soon realized that the gallery issue was only scratching the surface. And with this growing, volatile backdrop, the Abbey Theatre named A. P. Wilson, labor journalist and actor-playwright-director, as its new company manager in April, and Casimir Markievicz staged Shaw's *The Devil's Disciple* with the DRT at the Gaiety Theatre for a week-long run starting 12 May 1913.

Markievicz pulled together a large cast. The part of Judith Anderson was given to Casimir's wife, Constance, who had by now forged links through Helena Moloney to James Connolly and Larkin. IWWU member Mary, or Moira, Perolz played Mrs. Williams. The cast also included Ambrose Powers as Lawyer Hawkins, who had played Old Mahon in *The Playboy of the Western World*'s 1907 premiere.[29] The *Irish Times* reviewed the production, praising the actors meticulously and noting that "tribute should be paid to Count de Markievicz for the manner in which he produced the play. It was a distinct success, and it will, doubtless, be enjoyed during the week by Dublin playgoers who appreciate a good play and good acting" ("Gaiety Theatre 'The Devil's Disciple,'" 6).

The play, set in revolutionary America, sets its playboy, Richard Dudgeon, a Blanco Posnet–type scoundrel, against the pious Anthony Anderson. The play's "inversion of conventional ideas about good and evil" was intriguing and timely for 1913 Dublin (Gibbs, *Bernard Shaw*, 193). The play's main character, who is thought evil, therefore to be shunned, turns out to have positive attributes worthy to be admired. He is pitted against Anderson, who was thought pious but ultimately is not quite so good. The shunned becoming admired spoke to a city in which the downtrodden were emerging through the ITGWU as something not to be dismissed, despite efforts by the masters of commerce. Given the Markieviczes' ITGWU sympathies, it is implausible that the play was selected by coincidence.

Markievicz's staging of Shaw's play goes back to the fall of 1911, when Constance Markievicz formed the Fianna, an Irish version of the English Boy Scouts. Larkin provided Constance with an area for the boys to train, presumably in the ITGWU-rented Croyden Park. In return, some Fianna boys joined the ITGWU, since many of them were newsboys who sold various Dublin newspapers. Suddenly, Larkin had some control over Dublin papers (Yeates, *Lockout*, 8). In addition, Larkin, James Connolly, Helena Moloney, and others were frequent guests at the Markievicz home from 1911 through 1913 and on. In staging *The Devil's Disciple,* Casimir used Constance's Fianna boys to play the American male extras (Haverty, *Constance Markievicz*, 103). In other words, the Polish count placed members of the ITGWU on the stage of the capitalist commercial Gaiety Theatre three months before the Dublin Lockout began.

Moving toward lockout, the sixty-nine-year-old William Martin Murphy learned in July that the ITGWU was successfully recruiting workers of the Dublin United Tramways Company, of which Murphy was the chairman (Yeates, *Lockout*, 5). Murphy sacked six known ITGWU agitators in the workforce and told workers that if there was to be a strike, the company's shareholders "will have three meals a day . . . I don't know if the men who go out can count on this" (as quoted in Yeates, *Lockout*, 7). On 9 August the DRT announced it would stage John Galsworthy's labor play *Strife*, set within a protracted industrial strike, in mid-month (with Sean Connolly in the cast). By that time, Murphy had told his *Irish Independent* workers that they had to choose between their jobs or the ITGWU. Larkin responded by calling on the newsboys, who had joined the ITGWU through the Fianna, to stop selling the *Irish Independent*. ITGWU workers at Eason's Stationery, which distributed Dublin papers, then refused to unload or load Murphy's papers. Murphy then escalated events by sacking two hundred tramway workers for ITGWU membership. As events spiraled, Larkin called for all Dublin trams to stop at 9:40 Tuesday morning, 26 August 1913, on the day the annual Dublin Horse Show Week commenced. When the trams stopped, Murphy and the

Dublin Employers' Federation retaliated by locking out ITGWU workers. In turn, Larkin called for sympathy strikes to support the ITGWU from sympathetic unions. Locking out workers and sympathy strikes spread to almost every major Dublin company, including 2,000 workers at Jacob's Biscuit Factory. Over 25,000 workers, and their families, were affected throughout Dublin. The 1913 Lockout was on.

The prophesying of Synge's literature, of *Deirdre of the Sorrows* telling of Ireland erupting into violence through the greed of an old man, was becoming reality, and Shaw was about to share a platform with James Connolly—changing Ireland forever.

4

Lockout—Shaw, Connolly, Synge, and the Red Guard—ICA

The Dublin Lockout was to engage Shaw as no other Irish event had before 1913. In late August 1913 as the Lockout erupted, the Abbey Theatre staged seven plays, including Synge's *In the Shadow of the Glen* and *The Playboy of the Western World*, and William Boyle's popular *The Mineral Workers*. As an actor in the cast of the Boyle revival, Michael Conniffe recalled years later of being on stage the Saturday night of 30 August, with fellow actor and socialist Helena Moloney: "during the play, over the fireside during our pauses what were we discussing but Jim Larkin's coming escapade in the Imperial Hotel" (as quoted in Hogan, *Abbey Theatre*, 437).

Two days previous, on the Thursday, ITGWU strike leaders were arrested for seditious libel, including James Larkin and William O'Brien. The latter was on the strike committee then and associated with the ITGWU but a member of the sympathizing tailors' union. While being arrested at his house, O'Brien managed to tell his mother to telegram James Connolly in Belfast, asking Connolly to come to Dublin to take over in Larkin's absence (Morrissey, *O'Brien*, 73–74). Connolly's chance was coming to hand, but by this time events were spiraling, as more employers locked out workers and more sympathy strikes went into effect.

On the day of their arrest, Larkin and O'Brien were released on bail within hours upon assurances of their future behavior. Immediately Larkin continued to press a mass rally scheduled for the coming Sunday in O'Connell Street, Dublin center's main thoroughfare. On Friday, 29 August, the Dublin Metropolitan Police (DMP) issued a proclamation prohibiting the planned Sunday rally. That evening outside the ITGWU's Liberty Hall, the newly arrived Connolly addressed the thousands of gathered locked-out and striking workers about the police proclamation for Sunday's rally. He vowed that the rally was still on "and there we will come on Sunday, in a peaceful way, to see if the government has sold themselves body and soul to the capitalists" (as quoted in Yeates, *Lockout*, 39). The next day Connolly was arrested. Unlike Larkin and O'Brien, Connolly refused bail and refused to provide assurances for future behavior, telling the police magistrate, "I do not recognize the English government in Ireland" (as quoted in Yeates, *Lockout*, 45).

Larkin went into hiding, as a new warrant was issued for his arrest. He stayed at the Markievicz's home outside Dublin. To avoid a police raid, or by coincidence, Casimir Markievicz hosted a party for his theatre friends (Yeates, *Lockout*, 48), which Helena Moloney undoubtedly attended after the performance at the Abbey.

During the Saturday afternoon and into the evening throughout Dublin, clashes developed between locked-out workers and contingents of the DMP, who called in reinforcements from the Royal Irish Constabulary (RIC). Police command, either on the ground or higher officers, decided to clear the streets. The police baton-charged the hundreds of workers gathering outside Liberty Hall, where two laborers were killed. One such killing was witnessed by playwright Lennox Robinson while he was trying to reach the Abbey Theatre for the evening's performances (Yeates, *Lockout*, 53). As actors Moloney and Conniffe discussed the next day's planned rally on the Abbey's stage, the baton-wielding police drove the workers from outside Liberty Hall up Abbey Street, passing the theatre near the corner of Lower Abbey and Marlborough Streets (Yeates, *Lockout*, 53). The theatre where the audience had rioted against Synge's *Playboy* now, with ITGWU labor journalist A. P. Wilson as its company manager, was itself surrounded by riot. But this time the police had been called out to protect respectable middle-class commerce against the Dublin workers, not to protect a play from the respectable middle-class mob that took offense.

On Sunday, 31 August, Constance and Casimir Markievicz, along with Helena Moloney, disguised Larkin with Casimir's coat and a false beard. They drove him into Dublin to William Martin Murphy's Imperial Hotel on O'Connell Street (Yeates 50).[1] Larkin was then helped into the hotel by the middle-class Nellie Gifford. Gifford, and her three sisters, had abandoned their respectable class values in favor of radical causes like Irish socialism and labor. Her sister Muriel had recently married the radical playwright, poet, and Synge admirer Thomas MacDonagh. MacDonagh had arrived on O'Connell Street just prior to Larkin's appearing on a balcony at the Imperial to address the hundreds gathered outside (Yeates, *Lockout*, 62). Clearly MacDonagh was present to hear Larkin.

When Larkin appeared, the police rushed into the hotel and arrested him. Once Larkin was removed, the massive DMP and RIC units baton-charged the crowd outside on O'Connell Street. Many in the crowd were middle-class people strolling on a summer Sunday afternoon, returning from, of all places, mass, with little connection to Larkin or the Lockout.[2] The police reportedly rushed Constance Markievicz, grabbing her blouse and ripping its buttons (Yeates, *Lockout*, 66). Then the police, from numerous angles in a seeming effort to box in large sections of the crowd, batoned hundreds. If the police efforts of the night before were to clear the streets of workers, their actions on the 31st seemed calculated as a response to what they saw as defiance of their order prohibiting the Sunday gathering in Dublin's center. The violence was staggering.

MacDonagh, having been among the attacked crowd, testified to the Disturbances Commission established afterwards to investigate the police actions: "I saw the police batoning the people and striking them on the head. . . . I saw them attack an old woman with a shawl over her head and baton her brutally. . . . I heard the continual rapping of batons on people's heads" (MacDonagh, Dublin Disturbances Commission, as quoted in Yeates, *Lockout*, 66). Casimir Markievicz reported in the *Irish Times* following the brutality: "No human being could be silent after what I saw. These [police] acts of uncalled for and inhuman cruelty must be punished" (as quoted in Hogan with Burnham and Poteet, *Abbey Theatre*, 298). A liberal member of the British Parliament, Handel Booth, who had not previously been pro-labor, was also a witness, testifying that the DMP were the "most brutal constabulary ever let loose on a peaceful assembly. Up and down the road, backwards and forwards, the police rushed like men possessed. Some drove the crowd into the streets to meet other batches of the government's minions wildly striking with truncheons at every one within reach" (as quoted in Newsinger, *Rebel*, 49).

Padraig Yeates relates that within minutes the police had injured four to six hundred civilians (*Lockout*, 68). Casimir Markievicz, with his Polish-Russian background, compared 31 August 1913 to the January 1905 Bloody Sunday in St. Petersburg, when hundreds of Russian laborers were shot outside the Winter Palace by the tsar's troops (Yeates, *Lockout*, 69).

The police action in Dublin 1913 revealed which side of the Lockout the government was on, "body and soul." When Shaw read the newspaper accounts, he must have remembered London's own Bloody Sunday in 1887, when he witnessed the London Metropolitan Police attack a peaceful working-class demonstration.

"September 1913"—Pennies—and Yeats's Theatre

The police brutality on 30 and 31 August brought the Lockout to everyone's attention in Dublin. Comfortable classes could not ignore the struggle, no matter how individuals viewed developments. The Archbishop of Dublin's secretary, a Father Curran, reported to his superior that the situation was "simply the scum of our slums versus the police" (as quoted in Newsinger, *Rebel*, 50). This was an unfortunate class-influenced response, but no surprise to Larkin or Connolly. On the other hand, Sheehy-Skeffington became the Dublin correspondent for the socialist London *Daily Herald* paper covering the Dublin Lockout.[3] This position would enhance Sheehy-Skeffington's instrumental role in reaching public opinion in London and Britain, a role in which he would prove invaluable to Irish labor and Connolly's agendas. On writing of the police baton-charges, Sheehy-Skeffington reported that the DMP officers "have a look in their eyes I once saw in a dog's" (as quoted in Newsinger, *Rebel*, 52). The dog analogy would soon reappear in Yeatsian and then Shavian contexts.

Sheehy-Skeffington's reporting for the *Daily Herald* quickly coincided with and complemented the ITGWU's effort to enlist assistance for its locked-out and striking workers from British labor. The issue of strike pay and supplies for workers became paramount. The Dublin expectation for support from British labor was not unreasonable. Connolly earlier organized ITGWU sympathy strikes in Belfast for British dock strikers, and there was the bond of international labor solidarity, even if Larkin and Connolly were committed to one large Irish union for Irish labor. Thomas Morrissey writes that William O'Brien was instrumental in arranging the first shipments of food for workers from Britain, which arrived in Dublin by ship on 27 September and 4 October. Morrissey writes that "this initiative changed the nature of the struggle. The employers could no longer count on a speedy end to the dispute" (*O'Brien*, 79).

As the violence of 30–31 August still clung in the air, with no end to the Lockout in sight, W. B. Yeats emerged among those appalled by events.

Yeats remembered those he considered enemies in the past and was aware when they resurfaced on different issues. In the 8 September 1913 issue of the *Irish Times*, Yeats published his poem "September 1913" under its first title "Romance in Ireland." The poem had been composed during the summer in response to the struggle over the efforts to build a Municipal Gallery for Hugh Lane's modern paintings. Yeats was taking aim at William Martin Murphy, the most outspoken gallery opponent. As Murphy led the economic war against the ITGWU and Irish labor in general, the time was right for Yeats's poem, which now took on additional meaning. Yeats accused Murphy of objecting to the gallery as he fumbled "in a greasy till," counting his pennies ("September," 108). Yeats took additional aim at Murphy with further poetry that he wrote in September 1913 (Nevin, *Larkin*, 215). In "To a Friend Whose Work Has Come to Nothing," Yeats addresses Lady Gregory's futile work to establish the gallery which Murphy opposed, and in "To a Shade," Yeats reminded all that Murphy had brought down Parnell, setting "the pack upon him" ("To a Shade," 108). Now Murphy set the police on locked-out workers.

In Yeats's Abbey Theatre, the bourgeois architect and playgoer Joseph Holloway attended the evening of 6 September. He recorded: "I again went down to the Abbey in the evening, and again the house was very slack owing to the strike and the stoppage of tramcars. . . . A fellow of the Labour-leader type, half-seas-over, waited to see the new manager, Wilson" (*Joseph Holloway's*, 159). While having his tea at the theatre that night, Holloway noted he was told by a longstanding staff member, "What a change has come over the theatre of late" (as quoted in Holloway, *Joseph Holloway's*, 159). The gossiper was not impressed with the new manager.

The Abbey Theatre's fall repertoire in 1913 did not reflect a particularly labor, or even employer, venue under Wilson. The theatre's seasonal schedules were usually planned well in advance. However, there was one play, *The Mine Land*, by a Belfast playwright named Joseph Connolly (no relation to James or Sean), that premiered at the Abbey on 2 October with Sean Connolly in the cast. Though the play went unpublished, reviews indicate that the Ulster-set comedy placed a farmer's family against capitalistic speculators posing as geologists wanting to map the land but actually looking for a gold mine. The speculators were foiled in their attempt (Hogan with Burnham and Poteet, *Abbey Theatre*, 258–259). Still, the offering was perhaps not quite what was needed, given the labor war.

Smaller theatre companies had some ability to be more flexible in their offerings. On 6 October, the Irishwomen's Reform League, a suffragette's organization, produced Suzanne Day's *Toilers*. While this play also was not published, Sheehy-Skeffington alludes to it in a 1914 article mentioning that *Toilers*, like Day's earlier *Broken Faith*, was set in a Dublin tenement among the working, toiling class (Hogan with Burnham and Poteet, *Abbey Theatre*, 345). On the same evening, the DRT returned to Shaw.

Starting 6 October, the DRT ran *John Bull's Other Island* for a week at Dublin's Gaiety Theatre. The *Irish Times* reviewed the revival by highly praising the actors, noting: "It is a play which appeals to the tolerance and good nature of every Irishman, and in all the topsy-turvydom of Shavian drama there is nothing which can wound the susceptibilities of any Irishman" ("Gaiety Theatre," 7). Even then, with much of the Dublin working class engaged in a bitter and violent labor war, the *Irish Times'* unnamed reviewer does not comment on the play's depicted greed among the Irish against the Irish, but instead comments on how the play does not offend. The "efficient" capitalist endeavors in the play were exaggeratingly playing on the very Dublin streets outside the Gaiety Theatre. Both Matthew Haffigan's efforts against Patsy Farrell and Broadbent's against all the Irish were illustrating the motivations behind the war Dublin employers were waging on Dublin labor.[4]

Dublin Children and Moral Provocation

As if on cue, events became even grimmer on 2 September, when two tenement buildings, in apparent dilapidated condition in Church Street, collapsed, killing seven people including two young children, and leaving eleven families homeless. Padraig Yeates notes that it took nearly a day to establish the number of residents, suggesting the absence of any real housing regulations, or the lack of enforcement (*Lockout*, 106). Was not the collapse of these two deplorable, decaying buildings foretold in Frederick Ryan's 1902 *The Laying of the Foundations*, and, for that matter, in Shaw's *Widower's Houses*, which had so influenced Ryan's play? Deplorable housing was tolerated by city architects (inspectors), who were bought and owned by the capitalists owning the slum housing. In this increasingly volatile atmosphere, the government soon released Larkin, but not Connolly.

After roughly a week of imprisonment, Connolly opted to provide bail for his own release. The police magistrate denied the request (Nevin,

Connolly, 454). The aggressive Connolly then commenced a hunger strike, the same protest that was being used by imprisoned suffragettes in Britain with dramatic public effect. As Nevin reveals, Connolly's hunger strike was not known outside the prison until Sheehy-Skeffington mentioned it on 16 September while speaking at a strike meeting (*Connolly*, 454). Sheehy-Skeffington's publicizing for Connolly on this occasion may have been the first example of their collaboration in this manner, which would continue as an important tactic for Connolly, especially when seeking to involve Shaw.

Within days of publicizing Connolly's hunger strike, Sheehy-Skeffington and William O'Brien led a group that called on the Lord Lieutenant of Ireland to urge Connolly's release (Nevin, *Connolly*, 454). Morrissey writes that "They impressed on a somewhat apprehensive viceroy the incalculable consequences of Connolly's death, in the wake of recent deaths. That evening Connolly was released" (*O'Brien*, 79). The release of Connolly was a unique move from the government during the Lockout. Had Connolly's protest, along with the collapsed housing in Church Street, swayed public opinion toward labor? Connolly's strike provided favorable propaganda, at least within the labor side. But the next move came from Larkin, who set off to England to raise union funds for strike pay.

While in England, Larkin was approached with a plan to bring the children of locked-out and striking Dublin workers to Britain in order for them to be well cared for. Since the plight of children was a great concern for out-of-work parents, Larkin enthusiastically welcomed the plan and immediately tried to implement it. The plan had its supporters among many freethinkers, like Sheehy-Skeffington. However, the children's plan had detrimental consequences in Ireland. Morrissey argues that Larkin's "support for the idea was given with little reflection on how the sending of children to non-Catholic homes in Britain might be viewed by Catholic authority and Catholic organizations in Dublin" (*O'Brien*, 80). The result was that Dublin newspapers, like the middle-class *Freeman's Journal*, which had started covering the Lockout with a more neutral stance than its competitors, turned hostile to the ITGWU. Immediately, the Archbishop of Dublin, William Walsh, wrote to the commercial Dublin papers warning the suffering mothers to find other means to feed their starving children: "I can only put it to them that they can be no longer held worthy of the name Catholic mothers if they so far forget that duty as to send away their little children to be cared for in a strange land, without security of any kind that those to whom the poor children are to be handed over are Catholics" (as quoted in Nevin, *Larkin*, 224).

The result of Walsh's involvement was a strong uproar from the capitalist press against the children's plan, turning the issue into a religious quagmire. Larkin's support for the children's plan allowed anti-labor supporters to condemn Larkin and the locked-out workers as un-Catholic and ungodly. Now the capitalist class added moral indignation to their side, which played for the undecided opinions among the middle class and undermined some of the solidarity within the labor side. The conservative and respectable middle-class zealots, with their bourgeois morality that Shaw had ridiculed and Synge attacked, and which riotously condemned the latter's plays, now engulfed Dublin in a morality crisis that threatened to obscure the horrors of the Lockout. The respectable capitalist class used a defamatory tactic that was not so respectable. And as Shaw's and Synge's plays followed two separate approaches to socialistic ideas, those very approaches were now being pursued in the street struggles for public middle-class opinion.

The Irish painter William Orpen, who spent much time during the 1913 Lockout at Liberty Hall, working in the soup kitchens with Countess Markievicz and the actors Moloney and Sean Connolly, brought the shameless immorality attacks against Larkin and the ITGWU into perspective: "The anti-Larkin newspapers were full of it. Larkin sends Dublin children to England.... It is an anti-Irish act. And so on. It is strange, but something like this always used to crop up in Ireland, at such times against all who were really trying to do things for the good of the people.... Parnell fell in love. Who can blame him for that? Hugh Lane tried to get rid of pictures he could not sell. An abominable lie. John Synge wrote a criminal play against the morals of his own countrymen and countrywomen. What stupidity!" ("Larkin," 204). Orpen identifies the continuing battles in Dublin and Ireland against the entrenched capitalist respectable class, which was now entering a particularly beastly phase in its Lockout. The continuing battles were, in many ways, of the same struggle which only pulled more into the battle lines as the ITGWU's leadership sought to fight the capitalists for public opinion to persuade those non-laborers who might still join their struggle.

War Words

The poet, playwright, University College Dublin literature professor, and socialist-leaning nationalist Thomas MacDonagh, who was among those gathered on O'Connell Street on 31 August to hear Larkin speak, was editor with another liberally minded nationalist poet, Joseph Mary Plunkett, of the radical but middle-class journal the *Irish Review*. In 1911, MacDonagh had published Yeats's poem "On Those That Hated 'The Playboy of the Western World,' 1907" under the title "On Those Who Dislike the Playboy." The poem strikes at Synge's detractors, labeling them as eunuchs compared to a potent Synge, who himself was likened to Don Juan. Also that year, MacDonagh offered his view of *Playboy*'s depiction of violence and the symbolic hero-savior status of Christy in Act I, with what Christy represents for Ireland at play's beginning: "The fact of the matter is that the son was quite right to strike down the father under the circumstances" (as quoted in Norstedt, *Thomas MacDonagh*, 152). Shortly after Synge's death, MacDonagh wrote in *T.P.'s Weekly* that Synge's "work always remains vivid and firm, of a harsh beauty perhaps, but great with rich power" (as quoted in Hogan and Kilroy, *Abbey Theatre*, 269).[5] MacDonagh in 1913, embracing labor, invited James Connolly to write an article for the October *Irish Review* on Irish "Labour in the present crisis in Dublin" (Connolly, "Labour in Dublin," 385). MacDonagh also published and included in the same issue, immediately following Connolly's essay, "Liberty Under Capitalism," an essay by Shaw's friend James Bertram.

Connolly's "Labour in Dublin" challenged the Dublin middle class and Dublin's writers to turn their attentions to labor. Arguably, Connolly wanted more from Yeats than the attacks on William Martin Murphy's opposition to the Municipal Art Gallery. As Nicholas Allen points out, Connolly placed some of the blame for the plight of Irish labor on the writers who were obsessed with Home Rule (*George Russell*, 57). Connolly writes:

> the literary elements of society, those who might have been, under happier political circumstances, the champions of the down trodden Irish wage labourer, or the painstaking investigators of social conditions, were absorbed in other fields, and the working class left without any means of influencing outside public opinion. As a result, outside public opinion in Dublin gradually came to believe

that poverty and its attendant miseries in a city were things outside of public interest, and not in the remotest degree connected with public duties, or civic patriotism. Poverty and misery were, in short, looked upon as evils which might call for the exercise of private benevolence, but their causes were to be looked for solely in the lapses or weaknesses of individual men and women, and not in the temporary social arrangements of an ever-changing industrial code. ("Labour in Dublin," 387)

Connolly makes no mention of Synge or Shaw, especially the former's public observations of rural peasant living conditions, but part of Connolly's position here is that there had been little focus from writers on the plight of the urban Irish proletariat. Connolly is addressing present writers in hopes of prompting them to take up the cause of Irish urban labor in the important battle for some middle-class support.

However, Connolly's above take on the middle class's view of Irish poverty as being the result of "lapses or weaknesses of individual men and women" echoes in part the sentiment of Shaw's 1910 "Poor Law and Destitution in Ireland" lecture. Shaw argued that poverty was not the fault of the poor, but the crime "of the people who allowed them to be poor" ("Mr. Bernard Shaw," 7). This reverberates in Connolly's argument in "Labour in Dublin," that poverty was not due to those who were poor but was, in fact, very much the public's duty to rectify. In fact, Connolly's article and Shaw's lecture both work toward, as Connolly states, the development of "a social conscience" which will "lay the foundation for an orderly transformation of society in the future into a more perfect and juster social order" ("Labour in Dublin," 391). In this appeal, Connolly was following more or less a Shavian-gradualist approach, one of the few times he ever did so.

Connolly's goal with his article was to nudge Irish writers toward labor in both the long run and in the immediate to help with the Lockout. He believed there were still some middle-class people who could be made to see the Lockout's injustice. He wanted those people to see the continuing brutality of the police who supported the employers and the cruelty of the employers who refused to negotiate with labor, or with any of the numerous commissions that had been established to help mediate a resolution. In his goal to enlist Irish writers, Connolly was quickly successful. Of course, the employers' entrenchment and the violence of Bloody Sunday also must have helped influence certain writers toward labor. The enlisted writers included Shaw, but the poet George Russell and a few others preceded Shaw's involvement.

Russell, highly respected among his peers, was a mystic poet and painter who worked closely with Shaw's friend Sir Horace Plunkett in the Irish Agricultural Organization Society (IAOS), which Plunkett headed. The IAOS was a cooperative movement that sought to restructure society throughout rural Ireland and especially in the congested districts in the west, which Synge had reported on in 1905. The restructuring that the IAOS sought to implement was the creation of co-ops among small farmers to help them survive in the emerging economic conditions. To this end, the IAOS supervised "the setting up of co-operative banks" in areas of rural poverty with the hope of helping the small farmers instead of draining them with high-interest mortgages (Welch, *Irish*, 503). Gibbs writes that Horace Plunkett's IAOS work was "strongly supported" by Shaw, who "greatly admired" Plunkett, appropriately so, since the IAOS cooperatives appeared to rectify some of the capitalist traps for rural Ireland, like those depicted in *John Bull's Other Island* (Gibbs, *Bernard Shaw*, 360–361). Similarly, Connolly also valued cooperatives, believing that they could bring rural and urban laborers together for a more just society (*Re-Conquest*, 53). The Shaws—G. B. and wife Charlotte—regularly stayed with Plunkett when visiting Ireland. The IAOS cooperatives supplied much food to locked-out and striking workers through the ITGWU's Liberty Hall during the Lockout (Allen, *George Russell*, 62). The IAOS journal, the *Irish Homestead*, was edited by Russell starting in 1905. Robert Welch writes that Russell, as a social reformer, sought to move society to a greater social destiny than had been previously achieved (*Irish*, 503).

While neither Gibbs nor Shaw's biographer Holroyd mentions Russell beyond his early involvement with helping to organize the INTS in 1902, Nicholas Allen maintains that Shaw and Russell were friends, and the 1913 events were pulling them together. In 1910, following the industrial socialist congress that advocated socialists "to join co-operative movements in their home countries to unite them in federations," Russell was skeptical in that he believed the capitalist influence supported by the Catholic Church was much too strong in Ireland (Allen, *George Russell*, 45). He wrote in the *Irish Homestead*: "Karl Marx himself, if born in Ireland, could not advance socialism one inch here. . . . Our most furious Irish Socialist, Bernard Shaw, showed what a quick intelligence he has by using Ireland simply as a pleasure ground on his holidays without attempting the vain task of trying to spread Fabian ideas" ("NOTW," 752, as quoted in Allen, *George Russell*, 45). While the above most likely was an attempt to prompt Shaw to take more direct interest in Ireland, as many others would attempt, by the next year Russell optimistically wrote that "the last move of Socialism in Europe is to seek to make the co-operative organizations a kind of basis for a Fabian party of social expansion and reconstruction of society" ("Co-operation and the Problem of Rural Labor," 646, as quoted in Allen, *George Russell*, 45). Seemingly, Russell was aligned with Fabian socialist methods. But did Russell remain Fabianish through the Lockout?

Outraged by the early events of the Lockout, Russell answered Connolly's appeal to literary Dublin. On 7 October, the *Irish Times* published Russell's letter, which he addressed as an "Open Letter to the Masters of Dublin."[6] Russell accusingly stated:

> That you are an uncultivated class was obvious from recent utterances of some of you upon art. . . . You have allowed the poor to be herded so that one thinks of certain places in Dublin as of a pestilence. There are twenty thousand rooms, in each of which live entire families, and sometimes more, where no functions of the body can be concealed and delicacy and modesty are creatures that are stifled ere they are born. . . . Your insolence and ignorance of the rights conceded to workers universally in the modern world were incredible, and as great as your inhumanity. If you had between you collectively a portion of human soul as large as a threepenny bit, you would have sat night and day with representatives of labour, trying this or that solution of the trouble, mindful of the women and children, who at least were innocent of wrong to you. But no! You reminded labour you could always have your three square meals a day while it went hungry. ("Open Letter," 62–63)

Russell's letter, designed to nudge public favor toward labor, still echoed Fabian philosophy. An additional Dublin literary voice to emerge for labor was Padraic Pearse.

Pearse in 1913 was a poet, playwright, Gaelic language enthusiast, and educator, as well as a friend and comrade of Thomas MacDonagh.[7] As editor of the Gaelic League's bilingual newspaper *An Claidheamh Solius* from 1903 to 1909, Pearse was among the conservative bourgeois nationalists who had attacked *The Playboy of the Western World* in 1907, which Pearse had labeled at the time a "gospel of animalism" (as quoted in McCormack, *Fool*, 319). But as the 1913 Lockout played out, Pearse turned to labor in his regular column in the militantly nationalist paper *Irish Freedom*, edited by radical nationalists Tom Clarke and Sean MacDiarmuid. In October 1913, Pearse wrote: "My instinct is with the landless man against the master of millions. I may be wrong, but I do hold it a most terrible sin that there be landless men in this island of waste yet fertile valleys, and that there should be breadless men in this city where great fortunes are made and enjoyed" (as quoted in Ellis, *History of the Irish Working-Class*, 223–224). Pearse went further in his labor writing, suggesting that the employers should live up to their claim that one pound per week was sufficient "to sustain a Dublin family in honest hunger." He proposed employers should step into the "shoes of our hungry citizens."

> I am quite certain they will enjoy their poverty and hunger. They will go about with beaming faces. . . . When their children cry for more food they will smile; when their landlord calls for rent they will embrace him; when their house falls upon them they will thank God; when policemen smash in their skulls they will kiss the chastening baton. They will do all these things—perhaps; in the alternative they may see there is something to be said for the hungry man's hazy idea that there is something wrong somewhere. . . . If I were as hungry at this moment as many equally good men of Ireland undoubtedly are, it it probable that I should not be here wielding this pen; possibly I should be in the streets wielding a paving stone. (As quoted in Yeates, *Lockout*, 220)

Pearse in the above was not wielding a Shavian approach, despite the satire, as he was quite focused on the national. In fact, Pearse was now beginning his personal movement toward militant commitment. As Synge's plays had divided Irish nationalists into two camps, those who were radical enough to lean toward socialistic liberalism and therefore advocate for a real revolution, and those conservative enough to support capitalist respectable values and therefore advocate for an Irish state that mimicked Britain and harbored its capitalist social order, so too did the Lockout divide nationalists. And intriguingly, as Pearse leaned toward labor in 1913, he simultaneously re-evaluated Synge.

Pearse's re-evaluation of Synge may have been facilitated by Francis Bickley's 1912 *J. M. Synge and the Irish Dramatic Movement*. Bickley relates that W. B. Yeats told him that while Synge was writing *Deirdre of the Sorrows*, Synge told Yeats that he was "contemplating" his next play to portray "Dublin slum life" (*J. M. Synge*, 48).[8] Synge's interest in urban labor undoubtedly came from labor issues arising during his last years. A labor play from Synge would have dramatically anticipated Connolly's call to literary Dublin.

In 1913, Pearse publicly praised *The Playboy of the Western World* as "a thing of beauty" (as quoted in Edwards, *Patrick Pearse*, 169). This was part of Pearse's repentance for "his part in the attacks" on the play in 1907 (Kiberd, *Synge* 258). At this time, Pearse wrote: "When a man like Synge, a man in whose sad heart there glowed a true love of Ireland, one of the two or three men who have in our time made Ireland considerable in the eyes of the world, uses strange symbols which we do not understand, we cry out that he has blasphemed and we proceed to crucify him" ("Hermitage," 145–146). Then, in November 1913, as the Dublin crisis continued, Pearse made a most extraordinary and insightful observation, in writing of the employers behind the Lockout: "an employer who accepts the aid of foreign bayonets to enforce a lock-out of his workmen and accuses the workmen of national dereliction because they accept foreign alms for their starving wives and children . . . [is] matter for a play by Synge" ("Hermitage," 183). Pearse had come, interestingly, over time to see the hypocrisy of Irish employers destroying fellow Irish while playing the nationalist card, just as the respectable capitalist class had condemned Synge on nationalist terms when his plays had exposed the hypocrisy of their respectability as they sought to enslave the peasant-spirited Irish, from Nora to Pegeen to Deirdre. Pearse had now come to understand Synge's voiced radical concern for the Irish poor against the infection of capitalism and saw the Ireland for which Synge was advocating. In regard to Pearse, Synge's antagonistic national approach had worked, not immediately, but gradually over time, as Shaw's work was meant to do. Now Pearse was free to understand *Playboy*'s thematic portrayal of relevant and non-relevant violence. In the 1913 autumn, liberal-minded writers were finally seeing labor.

On 27 October 1913, a meeting of the newly formed Dublin Industrial Peace Committee met in the Mansion House on Dawson Street in Dublin, the Lord Mayor's residence. The meeting was to promote an impartial recommendation to both the ITGWU and the Dublin Employers' Federation for a way to reach a settlement. While the ITGWU's nightly speaker outside Liberty Hall, this time William Partridge, attacked the Catholic Church, which now seemed partnered to the employers, W. B. Yeats addressed the Mansion House meeting, saying that no man could walk through the Dublin poor neighborhoods and remain apathetic to the locked-out and striking workers (Yeates, *Lockout*, 294; 297). However, Yeats's full address that he intended to deliver was suppressed by the Lord Mayor. As Larkin was again in prison and Connolly left in charge, Connolly published Yeats's full address in the *Irish Worker*.

In his speech, published as "Dublin Fanaticism," Yeats railed against the conservative Dublin nationalist papers, from *Sinn Fein* to the *Irish Independent*: "I charge the Dublin Nationalist newspapers with deliberately arousing religious passion to break up the organization of the workingman, with appealing to [bourgeois] mob law day after day, with publishing the names of workingmen and their wives for purposes of intimidation. . . . Intriguers have met together somewhere behind the scenes that they might turn the religion of Him who thought it hard for a rich man to enter the Kingdom of Heaven into an oppression of the poor" ("Dublin Fanaticism," as quoted in Nevin, *Larkin*, 224–225). Yeats had seen his former and continuous enemies in the 1913 press. They were in the bourgeois mob that had condemned Synge's work, they blocked the Municipal Art Gallery of Lane's paintings, and they now used their respectable morality, out of the children-to-England plan, to attack locked-out labor. Literary Dublin was responding. Now it was time for Shaw.

On 1 November, a rally organized by London's *Daily Herald* was scheduled in London's Royal Albert Hall to advocate Larkin's release from prison and support for locked-out Dublin labor. The speakers' platform featured elite British socialists and suffrage activists, as well George Russell, James Connolly, and Shaw.[9]

"Mad Dogs" and Three Irishmen

The three most provocative speeches delivered on 1 November in the Royal Albert Hall were from the three Irishmen: Russell, Connolly, and Shaw. All three speeches were published, naturally, in Sheehy-Skeffington's report in the *Daily Herald*. With the goal of enlisting British public opinion, socialists, and labor to support Dublin workers, Russell went on the attack. He angrily criticized the respectable opposition in Dublin against the children-to-England plan, including Archbishop Walsh's and the Church's opposition. Arguably, Russell was trying to reveal the forces that were collaborating with the Dublin employers. He stated with Swiftian biting satire: "You see, if these children were even for a little out of the slums, they would get discontented with their poor homes, so a very holy man has said. Once getting full meals, they might be so inconsiderate as to ask for them all their lives" (as quoted in Nevin, *Larkin*, 216–217).

Russell's biographer, Nicholas Allen, writes that Russell's speech "was explicit in his criticism of Dublin employers, mocking a race of capitalists who imagined they were 'superhuman beings.' . . . Russell's speech is remarkable in its consistent connection of the apparatus of civil government to the interests of industry and its placement of both in opposition to the democratic rights of organized labor. He damned the attitudes of those [against labor], including . . . [the] Archbishop of Dublin" (*George Russell*, 58). Russell attacked the courts that imprisoned Larkin but not the "masters of Dublin" who conspired to maintain thousands in extreme poverty. He also attacked the Dublin police, who are like "wild beasts that kill in the name of the state" ("A Plea for the Workers," as quoted in Allen, *George Russell*, 59).

Russell's speech was heavily attacked in the capitalist Dublin press, which attempted to undermine him by claiming he was "anti-Irish" and in favor of the plan to send Irish children to English Protestant homes, ringing with the air of morality, or lack thereof (Allen, *George Russell*, 59). Murphy's *Irish Independent* reported on the rally under the headline "Anti-Clerical Campaign." It obviously played on the morality point, as it insinuated the "Socialist Meeting in London" was only a British anti-Catholic rally. In the paper's coverage of Russell's speech, it focused on what it identified as Russell's attack on "the action of the priests" ("Anti-Clerical Campaign," 5). The article made no mention of Russell's condemning comments on Murphy and the other Dublin employers. Following Russell was Connolly.

Connolly must have felt buoyed by the presence on the speakers' platform of such culturally Irish elite as Russell and Shaw, and perhaps indeed believed Irish labor had a chance with such assistance.[10] Of course, Connolly's own position was buoyed as well, as he found himself in the presence of not only important British socialists, but also, by reputation, the most persistent of Irish socialists outside of himself. The two perceived strongest socialist minds connected to Ireland, Shaw and Connolly, were together on the platform, and they had been as similar and as different up to this moment as Shaw and Synge had been in theatre. Connolly addressed the crowd, swinging both fists for Irish labor.

Connolly began by highlighting the extremely high death rate in Dublin's tenements, arguing that the poor were being killed by the conditions in which they were forced to live. He urged or demanded all supporters in Britain to vote against the ruling Labour Party in all upcoming elections until Larkin was released from prison. Then Connolly expanded his agenda: "You cannot build a free nation on the basis of slavery. We are against the domination of nation over nation, class over class, sex over sex. But if we are to make Ireland the Ireland of their dreams and aspirations we must have a free and self-respecting and independent people. You can never have freedom or self-respect whilst you have starvation, whether it is the green flag or the Union Jack that is flying over our head. If there is nothing in your stomach it matters mighty little what flag is flying" (Sheehy-Skeffington, "London's Magnificent Rally to the Dublin Rebels," *Daily Herald*, 1). The *Irish Independent* included in its comments on Connolly's speech his conclusion, insinuating the depth of Connolly's danger to Dublin: "He declared that they would not be defeated, and that they meant to continue the fight, and concluded by appealing to the meeting for financial support" ("Anti-Clerical Campaign," 5). The subtitle for the *Independent*'s coverage included: "Priests Attacked/Socialist Meeting in London: 'G.B.S.' Speaks" ("Anti-Clerical Campaign," 5). Shaw spoke.

While Shaw struck a comedic tone in his speech titled "Mad Dogs in Uniform," he responded to laughter early on by directing those present not to laugh. Like Russell, Shaw took early aim at the Catholic Church's blockage of the children-to-England scheme. After remarking that those who objected to the scheme had done so because they said morality in Dublin would suffer with the children away, that the parents would "misbehave themselves," Shaw asked: "Ponder over that a little. Let your imagination add to that state of things the horror of a strike, the cessation of the weekly wage, and all that it means. Imagine what kind of men they must be who, seeing all this, thrust the children back into that starvation and misery. . . . Imagine something more horrible: a Christian priest doing that. *[Hisses]* No! I don't ask you to hiss. I am here as a Dublin man to apologize to you for the priests of Dublin. . . . There is something even more terrible than the horror of their individual action, and that is the horror of the great Christian Church to which they belong being made the catspaw of gentlemen like Mr. Murphy" ("Mad Dogs," 95–96).

Shaw then moved onto the Dublin employers: "Even an Englishman can employ people at decent Trade Union wages and make it pay" ("Mad Dogs," 96). On the recent charging and imprisonment of Larkin, Shaw commented: "Any government which will countenance such a thing as the Crown Prosecutor in Dublin charging Larkin with sedition on the grounds that he said the employing class lived on profits has reached a cynical depth of absence of all shame which it is hardly possible to characterize without using improper language" ("Mad Dogs," 96). Shaw then became even more provocative in his speech.

Shaw declared there must be law and order in "working class and industrial questions." Then he alluded to the police brutality, echoing Sheehy-Skeffington's above *Daily Herald* description likening the police to dogs and Yeats's "pack" on Parnell:

> I mean this, that when it comes—as it is inevitable in all civilized communities that it must come—to the employment of physical force, that physical force shall only be applied by responsible men under the direct guidance of an officer responsible to a Minister in Parliament.
>
> If you once let loose your physical force without careful supervision and order you may as well let loose in the streets a parcel of mad dogs as a parcel of policemen. It has been the practice, ever since the modern police were established, in difficulties with the working class to let loose the police and tell them to go and do their worst to the people. Now, if you put the policeman on the footing of a mad dog, it can end in one way—that all respectable men will have to arm themselves. ("Mad Dogs," 97)

Shaw's call for the arming of men to defend themselves against the police was extraordinary. While it may have been in a satirical tone, in the light that Edward Carson and Ulster Unionists at this time were threatening armed revolt against the British government if Home Rule for Ireland was ever implemented while not being arrested for sedition, the arming call was a potent statement. When a voice in the crowd asked with what should they arm themselves, Shaw responded: "I should suggest you should arm yourself with something that would put a decisive stop to the proceedings of the police." Then, as if taunting the British Labour government and its police detectives who were present and recording the proceedings, he concluded: "I hope that observation [about arming] will be carefully reported. I should rather like to be prosecuted for sedition and have an opportunity of explaining to the public exactly what I mean" ("Mad Dogs," 97).

The British press that sided against labor and socialism, like the *Daily Sketch*, reacted strongly to Shaw's speech by calling for his arrest for "inciting to armed revolt" (Laurence and Grene, "Introduction and Notes," 96). The reaction from the capitalist press in Dublin was much different. Rather than give credence to Shaw in Ireland by calling for the British to arrest him, the Dublin papers sought to undermine and dismiss Shaw as a crank. The *Irish Times*: "[Shaw] boasts that he left Ireland at the age of twenty, and has not lived here since. As a licensed buffoon and consecrated prophet of the patently absurd, he has to support his reputation by insisting that what is obviously wrong is quite clearly right" ("Mr. Bernard Shaw on the Strike," 6). The *Irish Independent*'s Sunday edition, *Sunday Independent*, echoed the buffoon label for Shaw, as it published a cartoon depicting Shaw as "G.B.S., the Buffoon," next to a caricature of Yeats labeled "W.B., the Spook." The cartoon also dismissively portrays Russell as the friend of "spirits" and Sheehy-Skeffington with a sash for women's suffrage (as quoted in Yeates, *Lockout*, 348). Connolly responded to the cartoon in the *Irish Worker* with a cartoon of Murphy depicted as a vulture, captioned "William Murder Murphy" (Glandon, *Arthur Griffith*, 107).

The *Irish Independent*'s reporting on the rally in its Monday, 3 November, edition focused more on Shaw's comments than anyone else's, including Connolly's. The paper's Shaw focus was under the subheading "G.B.S. Attacks Priests." The paper quoted a section of the speech that was not included in the *Daily Herald*'s reporting, and, consequently, not in the anthology of Shaw's Irish articles, *The Matter with Ireland*. After relating Shaw's comments against the Catholic priests' efforts to stop the children plan, the paper quoted the two paragraphs not included in the *Daily Herald*.

> Just consider . . . the glorious position we are in at the present time in England with reference to the great traditions of English liberty. Mr. Asquith [then British prime minister] may go from one end of

Europe to another and say look at free England; a man may not only stand up and denounce the Government, but take arms against it and collect money to make war upon it, and yet he may stand a free man with no fear of prison.

I am extremely glad that our Prime Minister is in the position to say that in regard to Sir Edward Carson. I entirely approve of Sir Edward Carson's plea for liberty to raise the standard of rebellion; but why is it Mr. Asquith does not go about making that proud boast? It is because somebody in the crowd might cry out—What price Tom Mann and Jim Larkin? ("Anti-Clerical Campaign," 5)[11]

Tom Mann was a charismatic British Marxist who, at the time, advocated social revolution through industrial syndicalist action. In other words, Mann saw the use of one big union, or a league of united unions, using sympathy strikes for revolutionary purposes. This made him, in 1913, ideologically in tune with Connolly. In fact, in Mann's *Memoirs*, he noted that he read Connolly's theoretical writings and found that they "were identical to those he had expressed" (Nevin, *Connolly*, 414). Both Mann and Connolly were socialist theorists who were turning to syndicalism for social revolutionary purposes, while Larkin tended to be primarily a trade unionist using syndicalism to break the employers for the betterment of workers. But Shaw's allusion to both Mann and Larkin in his above speech suggests that he fully understood the sympathy strike strategy, even the socialistic theory someone like Connolly harbored. Yet it is interesting that the *Daily Herald*, or Sheehy-Skeffington in particular, left out the above section of Shaw's speech while the *Irish Independent* included it.

Sheehy-Skeffington probably left the passage out due to sensitivity in both Ireland and Britain to Edward Carson's seditious proclamations of arming Ulster to resist Irish Home Rule if ever granted by the British government. The reverse explains the *Irish Independent*'s inclusion, insinuating that Shaw's mentioning of Carson meant that Shaw and the laborers he spoke for were against Home Rule for Ireland, which, in the same mindset, would suggest they were all anti-Irish as well as anti-Catholic. The Catholic William Martin Murphy, and his newspapers, publicly supported Irish Home Rule but obviously not a revolutionalizing of Irish society. Shaw's comments in the above-quoted two paragraphs, alluding to Carson intellectually, reinforced the rest of Shaw's speech that exposure of the absurdity of the government's arrest of Larkin, and added to Shaw's taunting the government to arrest him for sedition. The two paragraphs also brought legitimacy to the arming of Irish locked-out workers in that Carson was arming Ulstermen against the government without government reprisals. After all, how could one be disarmed and not the other? The reasoning and fullness of Shaw's argument was brilliant.

While many historians look to Carson's threats of forming and arming the Ulster Volunteer Force (UVF) as the start of the militarizing of Ireland, the real ideological arming of Ireland begins with Shaw's speech. It was Shaw's drawing on Carson's democratic right to arm, on behalf of Irish labor arming itself that began Ireland's arming. Of course, Shaw's argument plays on the government's lack of initiative to stop Carson's arming efforts, which insinuated that the British government was not really serious about Irish Home Rule, even though Asquith's Labour government continued to contemplate such, and would eventually pass a severely limited Home Rule bill in 1914 only to immediately suspend it for the duration of the Great War. Shaw's argument exposed the would-be hypocrisy of the government if it stopped Irish laborers from arming but not middle-class Ulstermen, whose rhetoric rang of archaic religious hatreds. The real moral right in a "civilized" community "to the employment of physical force" was not with Ulster bigots, nor with the police protecting the rights of capitalist masters who refused to pay "decent Trade Union wages," but with the Dublin workers who asked for those wages in order to alleviate the horrid living conditions of the slums in which they were forced to inhabit ("Mad Dogs," 97, 96).

In light of 30 and 31 August 1913, workers arming to protect themselves was a necessity; a necessity voiced by Shaw. Such a move subtly revealed that Shaw was intellectually aligning himself more with the social revolutionist Connolly than the practical trade unionist Larkin. The *Irish Independent* ended its coverage of Shaw's speech, which also was not included in the *Daily Herald*'s version of the speech, by paraphrasing or quoting Shaw's last sentence, which concludes his taunt of the government to arrest him. The statement echoed Connolly's speech made during the same rally in which he (Connolly) called on the British public to vote against the Labour Party then in power in Britain, Shaw stated: "Any Government that instituted a prosecution for sedition ought never be returned to power" ("Anti-Clerical Campaign," 5). The question, of course, is how in tune to each other were Shaw and Connolly while together on the platform? Had Connolly, or possibly Russell, told Shaw, before Shaw's speech, that Irish labor was going to arm itself?

Two weeks after Shaw's "Mad Dogs in Uniform" speech, the government released Larkin months short of his seven-month sentence, attesting, perhaps, to the effectiveness of the 1 November rally. To mark the occasion, Connolly, not Larkin, addressed a crowd of locked-out workers outside the ITGWU's Liberty Hall: "I am going to talk sedition. The next time we are out for a march, I want to be accompanied by four battalions of trained men. I want them to come with their corporals, sergeants and people who will be able to form fours. Why should we not drill and train our men in Dublin as they are doing in Ulster? . . . I have been promised the assistance of competent chief officers, who will lead us anywhere. . . . See if the police will clear us off the street [now] as they [have] threatened" (as quoted in Nevin, *Connolly*, 463). The Irish Citizen Army (ICA), labeled by historian D. R. O'Connor Lysaght as Europe's first "Red Guard," had been born two weeks after Shaw proclaimed "that all respectable men will have to arm themselves . . . [to] put a decisive stop to the proceedings of the police" (O'Connor Lysaght, 21, Shaw, "Mad Dogs," 97). While Larkin may have earlier alluded to arming but did nothing to this end, it was the militant theorist Connolly who seized the initiative. If nothing else, Shaw had articulated legitimacy for forming the ICA.

Donal Nevin writes that while on the eve of Larkin's release from prison on 13 November, a retired British army captain turned radical, an Ulsterman and Presbyterian named Jack White, met with Connolly about forming an army and offered to drill the force.[12] As if answering Shaw's suggestion to arm themselves with something to stop the police, early ICA recruits were armed with Irish hurling sticks and axe handles that were longer than police batons.

On 30 November 1913, the ICA met formally for a drilling session in the ITGWU-rented Croydon Park in northeast Dublin. The *Irish Times* reported that, "Outside the members of the Citizen Army and the Transport Union [i.e., the ITGWU], no persons were allowed admission." Despite this, the reporter gained admission in some fashion. It was noted that viewing the session were "Messrs. George Russell, James Connolly, Bill Haywood [a United States labor leader observing in Dublin], Sheehy-Skeffington, and others associated with the labour movement" ("In Croydon Park," 6).

While waiting for the drilling to commence, many of the ICA members present were playing football. Captain White asked the members "if they realised what they were doing in asking him to drill them at such an epoch-making crisis. If they did they should give up disorder, and be obedient to others." Once he had everyone's attention, White extraordinarily invoked Shaw and Connolly: "He [White] had a conversation with a Jesuit priest, and they discussed George Bernard Shaw, when the priest said 'he wrote Socialism.' He (Captain White) asked him if the democracy of Ireland was not fit for the socialistic life, and the priest replied that they were not. He [White] had received an invitation to address an anti-Carson meeting in London, but he had replied stating that he looked forward to the day when his force [the ICA] would join that of Sir Edward Carson in the fight for democracy. The result of their drilling would be to bring out the strength, will, and determination of all the men. (Cheers)" ("In Croydon Park," 6).

By relating a conversation, or argument, with a Jesuit priest, White recalled Connolly's 1910 debate with Father Kane, and the allusions to democracy and Carson obviously recalled Shaw's "Mad Dogs in Uniform" speech. White's story of mildly clashing with a priest over Shaw and socialism even subtly suggested Shaw's comic touch. Yet it is very telling that Shaw could be directly mentioned to the laborers making up the early recruits of the ICA with recognition, a testament to Shaw's reputation among the Dublin working class, the class that did not make up any measurable section of the commercial Dublin theatres that almost regularly hosted productions of Shaw plays. White's mentioning Shaw testifies to the fact that the workers present knew in some form Shaw's "Mad Dogs in Uniform" speech and knew of Shaw's role or participation in their ICA formation.

In a 13 December 1913 article in the *Irish Worker*, Connolly described how the ICA was already having an effect, as the DMP were now backing away from confrontations with Dublin labor. The article title was "Arms and the Man," of which William O'Brien recalled years later as "the title of Shaw's play," suggesting that Connolly's borrowing of the title was consciously made (*Forth*, 121). Shaw's presence was advancing Irish socialism, separating somewhat from his international socialism, since he knew that the 1913 labor situation in Ireland was unique to Ireland.[13] Shaw's 1913 participation would be remembered by Connolly.

Shaw's participation in the advancement of Irish socialism through the

ICA raises the question of whether Shaw was flirting with the aggressive, national, liberalizing ideology of Synge and its more volatile developed embodiment in Connolly. Certainly Shaw, like early ICA member Sean O'Casey, believed the arming of Irish labor was a defensive move, a strategy desperately needed in order to stop the police from brutalizing laborers (O'Casey, "Citizen Army" 254–255). Even Captain White may have originally believed in the ICA as a defensive army. But Padraig Yeates writes that "Only a figure as politically naïve as White could have failed to realise the direction in which men such as Connolly would take his project [the ICA]" (*Lockout*, 424). Soon after the ICA's formation, Connolly addressed ITGWU members, making very clear the direction he would lead the ICA: "We mean to defend our rights as citizens, and any man who means in the future to become a member of the Transport Workers' Union must be prepared to enroll himself in the Citizen Army; so that we will not have the whole of that work to . . . the Orangemen [Edward Carson's UVF] who, I hear, have ordered a supply of rifles. We have not done so yet . . . but we want our men to be trained and drilled, so that when it comes to the pinch they will be able to handle a rifle; and when King Carson comes along here we will be able to line our own ditches" ("Meeting in Beresford," 11).[14]

The implication of Connolly's remarks about the ICA being ready to "line our own ditches" when "King Carson" marches south, suggests that Connolly saw the ICA also fighting for Irish independence, a socialistic independence, no doubt, that included freedom for all classes. So while Shaw, White, and Connolly made use of Carson's arming Ulster to arm labor, they saw the conservative-establishment Carson as ultimately a threat to Ireland and Irish labor.[15] But clearly, Shaw was not "politically naïve," as Yeates suggests that White was, meaning that Shaw must have at least had some inkling as to where the arming of laborers might go under a syndicalist socialist revolutionary like a James Connolly.

The significance of arming political factions in Ireland in 1913 could not have been underappreciated by Shaw. Furthermore, his statement in "Mad Dogs," whether in response to an earlier remark by Connolly or not, that physical force was inevitable, made Shaw's speech one of his most aggressive Irish efforts. It was probably made more so by others, like Connolly, than by Shaw's satirical style. Still, Shaw's call to arms rings of *The Playboy of the Western World*'s theme of relevant violence, the celebration of violence symbolizing physical force from the oppressed against the oppressor while violence for personal gain (in the context of 1913), the police violence committed for the selfish employers, is condemned. It was at this Synge-echoing moment of "Mad Dogs in Uniform" that legitimacy was offered by Ireland's most famous London man of letters and most publicly accepted socialist to the arming of Irish labor. It was in this that Shaw had come the closest, so far, to Connolly, just as he had come close to Synge in 1909 when battle lines with the bourgeois were still (in Ireland) within the confines of a theatre.

November 1913 indeed marked the arming of Ireland. The Irish Volunteers were founded within weeks of "Mad Dogs in Uniform," with one of its founding members being Padraic Pearse, who stated at the time: "I should like to see the Transport Workers armed" ("The Coming Revolution," 99). It was also in November 1913, as Ireland was arming, that Pearse made his statement about the Lockout being "matter for a play by Synge" ("Hermitage," 183). The foretold epic struggle for Ireland had begun, and Synge, Shaw, and Connolly were thematically present—an ideological trinity indeed.

Lockout's Dissipation: "Dublin Is Isolated"

As Connolly harbored specific ideas about how the ICA might be used in the future, before November 1913 was over, he and Larkin gambled on British labor support. Such support had been in place to a certain extent since the Lockout began, namely food and money supplies for locked-out and striking workers. British labor leaders also actively sought to force resolutions to the crisis. But now Larkin and Connolly, with events becoming more extreme in Dublin, called for widespread sympathy strikes in Britain. If British labor leaders agreed, the potential existed for breaking the capitalist hold throughout the British Isles, restructuring society. A phenomenal moment was at hand.

To this end, Larkin embarked to England and Connolly wrote in the *Irish Worker*: "We are only concerned now with the fact . . . that the English workers, who have reached the moral stature of rebels, are now willing to assist the working class rebels in Ireland, and that those Irish rebels will, in their turn, help the rebels of England to break their chains and attain the dignity of freedom. . . . For us and ours the path is clear. The first duty of the working class of the world is to settle accounts with the master class of the world—that of their own country at the head of the list. To that point this struggle is converging" (as quoted in Yeates, *Lockout*, 499).

But by the end of December, some ITGWU workers who were engaged in sympathy strikes returned to work, receiving the same pay as when they commenced their strikes. In Britain, the labor leaders were nearing the end of their support of Irish labor. A leader of the Durham Miners' Federation (union), which had been contributing weekly money to the ITGWU, told members that the call for widespread sympathy strikes in England was due to Larkin's ego, which had only grown after his release from prison in mid-November (Yeates, *Lockout*, 496). Money from British labor began to end as their leaders grew weary of the Dublin Lockout and resented Larkin and Connolly's call for British sympathy strikes. This had to do with the fact that British unions had depleted their own strike funds supporting locked-out Irish workers, and now could not have supported their own members in a prolonged strike. Additionally, British labor leaders resented Irish labor dictating to them policy and direction. The end of the dispute in Dublin was near and the capitalist masters were intact.

By mid-January, the ITGWU held a mass meeting in which workers were told to return to work as there was no more money in the strike fund. Larkin then addressed the crowd saying they could fight on for another year, or two, but "was received in silence" (Morrissey, *O'Brien*, 84). Workers attempted to return to work but not all were accepted back. Many who were accepted were done so only if they renounced their ITGWU membership. In March 1914, Connolly reported that at the Quaker-owned Jacob's Biscuit Factory only 100 ITGWU men out of nearly 700 had been rehired, and those rehired received cuts in their wages (Newsinger, *Rebel*, 105). Women union workers at Jacob's suffered more, as they "were the last large group of workers still locked out in the city" after others were let back or blacklisted by employers (O'Maitiu, *W & R Jacob*, 38–39). When individual women were accepted back to Jacob's, they were forced to submit to humiliating physical examinations by their male managers (Newsinger, *Rebel*, 105).[16]

As workers tried to regain their employment, Connolly emerged as the continuing activist writing in the ITGWU's *Irish Worker*. In the immediate aftermath of the Lockout, Larkin took defeat hard and personally, growing increasingly lethargic and withdrawn (Morrissey, *O'Brien*, 85).

The propaganda and struggle was left to the theorist Connolly, who in February 1914 described defeat in aggressive, nationalized terms:

> We asked our friends of the Transport Unions to isolate the capitalist class of Dublin and we asked the other Unions to back them up. We appealed to the collective soul of the workers against the collective hatred to the capitalist. We asked for no more than the logical development of that idea of working class unity that the Working Class of Britain should help us to prevent the Dublin capitalists carrying on their business without us. We asked for the isolation of the capitalists in Dublin, and for answer the leaders of the British Labour movement proceed calmly to isolate the Working Class of Ireland. . . . And so we Irish workers must again go down into Hell, bow our backs to the lash of the slave drivers, let our hearts be seared by the iron of his hatred, and instead of the Sacramental wafer of brotherhood and common sacrifice, eat the dust of defeat and betrayal. Dublin is isolated. ("Isolation," 4)[17]

By the summer of 1914, Larkin became embroiled in quarrels with some ITGWU officials and eventually accepted an invitation to lecture from the American Industrial Workers of the World and left Ireland in October. After maneuvering, Connolly was made the ITGWU's acting general secretary and the official editor of the *Irish Worker* in Larkin's absence. The appointment placed Connolly in sole control of the ICA, as well as, eventually, the Irish Workers' Dramatic Company.[18] This all led to Connolly's "taking and keeping the lead in the movement towards revolution" (Morrissey, *O'Brien*, 88).

Labor Theatre: Wilson and Shaw's McNulty

By the spring of 1914, as the ruins of the Lockout continued to smolder, A. P. Wilson began scheduling a handful of new plays at the Abbey Theatre that thematically served Irish labor, even socialistic directions. One of the first was authored by Shaw's lifelong friend Edward McNulty.

Gibbs describes McNulty and Shaw, as boys, sharing "mature artistic and intellectual interests" (*Bernard Shaw*, 49). Gibbs relates that McNulty throughout his life maintained his literary interests while pursuing a banking career, writing various novels and three plays on Irish life (*Bernard Shaw*, 48). In June 1908, Shaw wrote to McNulty urging him to continue his writing, even relating how he had praised his (McNulty's) work to Yeats (*Shaw Letters*, 790). McNulty finally placed a play with the Abbey Theatre that arguably bore Shavian influence, as well that of Fred Ryan's Shavian *The Laying of the Foundations*, all while also being mindful of the recent Lockout. McNulty's *The Lord Mayor* premiered on 13 March 1914.

The subtitle of *The Lord Mayor* is, in perhaps a conscious Shavian-like move, "A Dublin Comedy in Three Acts." Like Ryan's *The Laying of the Foundations*, McNulty's play sets its sights on the corruption of municipal government as fueled by capitalist greed. The negative portrayal of the capitalist class in March 1914 obviously carried the relevance of the Lockout as it attempted to expose the class's greed. *The Lord Mayor* had much to offer a Dublin fresh from witnessing coldhearted capitalists starving a significant portion of the city's population.

Set in Dublin, McNulty's play centers on James O'Brien, a bankrupt ironmonger at play's start. Prior to the action, O'Brien's socially ambitious wife persuaded him to run for a seat on Dublin's Corporation, which stretched O'Brien's finances and led to his bankruptcy. Act I opens in the office of O'Brien's solicitor, named Gaffney. The O'Briens are present to meet with their creditors to work out a settlement. As the creditors want fifteen shillings on the pound and O'Brien can only pay two, Gaffney suggests a scheme to earn the creditors twenty pounds while significantly increasing their business opportunities. The plan is to run the meek O'Brien as Lord Mayor, with his speeches written by Gaffney's clerk Kelly. Like many of Dublin's then capitalists who claimed to be nationalists, such as William Martin Murphy, O'Brien's campaign issue, determined by Gaffney, is a nationalist refusal to welcome the British king to Dublin during the royal visit.[19] Similar to *The Laying of the Foundations*, a powerful capitalist, Gaffney, plans to profit enormously through a city official, namely the Lord Mayor, as O'Brien is a man Gaffney believes he owns due to the scheme to financially save him.

In Act II, set in the Lord Mayor's mansion house after O'Brien's election victory, it becomes clear that Gaffney also wants O'Brien's daughter Moira as his wife. Moira, horrified at the idea, is in love with Kelly. In a different scene, Mrs. O'Brien meets with a Major Butterfield of Dublin Castle, who asks her to persuade her husband to welcome the visiting king in return for a baronet and the lucrative job of insurance commissioner after leaving office.

Later in Act II, McNulty includes a highly comical scene in which O'Brien delivers a speech from a landing with Kelly prompting every phrase. O'Brien becomes confused, reciting words not intended for the speech. Alone with Moira, Kelly confesses his dislike for his involvement with Gaffney.

Act III opens with O'Brien trying to memorize a speech with Kelly. A deputation appears to see O'Brien about building new public baths. The deputation is composed of O'Brien's creditors, who now want a significant payback from the mayor they created with Gaffney. Reminiscent of Sartorius in *Widower's Houses*, the creditors own a number of tenement houses they wish the city to purchase at an inflated price under the guise of building public baths in their place. Interestingly, one of the creditors–slum landlords is a woman. This specifically recalled the landlord of the two tenement houses that had collapsed on Church Street in September 1913, who was a Mrs. Ryan (Yeates, *Lockout*, 106). And drawing on the capitalist class's use of respectability, another creditor repeatedly states "with the help of God" and "please God" (*Lord*, 42–43). Was such reminiscent of *Playboy*'s hypocritical Shawn Keogh and Christy Mahon?

Armed with such pious phrases, the creditors argue that their plan for the baths is to benefit "our poorer fellow citizens," to which O'Brien begins to awaken, "I think it's their rents you want to raise" (*Lord*, 42). When he realizes the creditors own the buildings, he also realizes the extent of their plan, which will include evicting the tenants. O'Brien states: "I'm not going to help you sell out your rotten holdings at the expense of tax payers" (*Lord*, 42). O'Brien stands up to the slum landlords as Michael O'Loskin did in *The Laying of the Foundations*. Butterfield enters, to which O'Brien refuses to welcome the king, refusing to go against his campaign promise. Gaffney enters, telling O'Brien to welcome the king, revealing an arrangement between Butterfield and Gaffney. Gaffney reminds O'Brien how he saved him from financial ruin and made him Lord Mayor and now wants Moira in marriage. O'Brien refuses to force Moira into an unwanted, arranged marriage, echoing the earlier plays that took issue with forced and arranged marriages. Mrs. O'Brien interjects, urging her husband not to throw away the chance for Moira to make a "respectable match" (*Lord*, 49). As if on cue for all the socialist-leaning Irish plays that had earlier battled the "respectable," O'Brien states: "Respectable, is it? If that's your idea of respectability I'm done with it. Respectability drove me into the Corporation. It was respectability nearly drove me into bankruptcy; but it won't drive me into making my daughter marry a dirty wire-puller like that. No more respectability for me" (*Lord*, 49).

As O'Brien turns against Gaffney, the charwoman Mrs. Murphy, whom O'Brien befriended regardless of their class differences, enters to witness O'Brien's stance against the capitalists. She starts, "Give us a speech, Jimmy." Gaffney states that O'Brien "better get Kelly to write it first. This is an outrage." O'Brien then closes the play: "I don't see any outrage. Kelly's a decent young fellow. I've nothing against him . . . so far. He'll marry my daughter, right enough, and he'll be my secretary. But, for the future, I'll make my own speeches in my own way. I'll neither be run by clique or Castle. I'll be the independent champion of the people's rights. I'll be the citizen's Lord Mayor" (*Lord*, 50).

For the most part, *The Lord Mayor* tries to function as a Shavian comedy but, as with *The Laying of the Foundation*, its author does not possess Shaw's subtle and brilliant gift for satire. The influence of Shaw can be seen in elements borrowed from *Widower's Houses*, in the attempt to use comedy (not without success) to portray its serious message (an indictment of the Dublin master class), and in the Fabian notion that a middle-class man like O'Brien can awaken to social justice if prompted. McNulty also seemingly attempts to provide a Shavian hero in O'Brien. While not a playboy like Richard Dudgeon or Blanco Posnet, O'Brien is an unlikely hero. However, O'Brien's closing lines of being the "champion of the people's rights" and being "the citizen's Lord Mayor" ring of socialist defiance in the wake of the Lockout's collapse. Such closing lines may seem to have been more influenced by the closing remarks from "Mad Dogs in Uniform" than from a Shavian play—unlike most of McNulty's play. Certainly given Shaw's encouragement of McNulty's writing, *The Lord Mayor* was written in a Shavian vein touching on Dublin's 1914 class context. Ben Levitas suggests that the class context of the play received "appropriate emphasis" from the "sympathetic direction" of Wilson, especially in the line "where is the use of patriotism if we can't get our wages raised?" (*National*, 211, and as quoted in Levitas, *National*, 211). Again, Shaw's presence is felt in Dublin, this time before the Abbey Theatre's middle-class audience in an effort to nudge that audience into understanding the vile greed of Dublin capitalist masters, like the play's Gaffney and men like William Martin Murphy.[20]

Dublin's *Evening Mail*, of the capitalist press, expressed in its review of *The Lord Mayor* that it could make no sense of the charwomen characters:

"They form no essential feature in the story of the comedy, and yet they obtrude themselves at the most unexpected moments" (H.R.W., "New Abbey Plays," 2). The significance of the charwomen characters lies in the friendship O'Brien forms with them, signaling his sympathetic stance with Dublin's poor—a point lost on the pro-employer press.

The Lord Mayor, which Wilson directed, featured Sean Connolly as James O'Brien. It was Connolly's first leading role. He had worked in the Liberty Hall soup kitchen during the Lockout and had joined the ICA upon its formation ("Sean Connolly").

A month later, on 13 April 1914, Sean Connolly was again acting in a socialistic play at the Abbey Theatre. This time it was in Wilson's one-act play *The Cobbler*, which Wilson also directed and played the leading role.[21] The play, set in Antrim, Ulster, was unpublished, but one review provides some idea of at least the plot. A cobbler's apprentice, a young boy, wins a learning prize at school, a Bible. The cobbler tries to support the boy, thinking his apprentice is destined for the clergy. But the boy, uninterested, tosses the Bible into a river, bringing much disappointment to his sponsor, the cobbler (Hogan with Burnham and Poteet, *Abbey Theatre*, 330). While it is difficult to get a full sense of the play, perhaps one can suggest that the labor journalist Wilson was commenting on the working class's antiquated reliance on religion, as the cobbler naturally assumes that a bright young boy should become a clergyman. Touching on religion echoes problems associated with labor during the Lockout. But, from what can be construed without the script, it seems that *Cobbler* was not as zealous an agit-prop work as Wilson's earlier *Victims* in 1912. But Wilson was seemingly more mature as both a theatre artist by 1914 in his position as manager of the Abbey Theatre and as a socialist following the Lockout. He would make a more developed impact with his full-length play *The Slough*, which premiered on 3 November 1914 at the Abbey.

Wilson was twenty-six years old when *The Slough* premiered in 1914, and he directed and acted in the production. It was the first full-length straight labor play produced in Dublin since the DRT staged Galsworthy's *Strife* in August 1913 and the first full-length Irish labor play since Ervine's *Mixed Marriage* in 1911, which it shares some similarities in plot via the portrayed family, similar love interest, and so forth. The action of Wilson's play begins after and prior to major syndicalist strikes, with the second strike crumbling after a number of months.[22] A family named Hanlon is the main focus. The head of the family, Peter Hanlon, is a drunkard who is suspected of having been a scab in the earlier strike. One of Peter's daughters, Peg, leaves in Act I for Liverpool in hope of securing shop work. The youngest daughter, Anne, is a factory worker in frail health who contracts consumption. She is in love with Tom Robinson, a union member.

The play's second act is set within a committee room of a union, meant to suggest the ITGWU. Presiding in the meeting is Jake Allen, the union's leader, who is based on James Larkin. Allen and his meeting discuss strike strategies, namely the sympathetic strike. In this fashion, Wilson provides for the Abbey Theatre's middle-class audience a discussion, an explanation, of the reasoning behind sympathy strikes. He even attempts to justify the tactic in light of the demise of the Lockout and the failure of the sympathy strikes in Dublin to force the employers into negotiations. Without sympathy strikes expanding to Britain, Dublin labor was of course defeated in the 1913–14 Lockout.

The play's Act II committee scene also concerns the Hanlons, as one of their neighbors, Edward Kelly, steps forward to defend Peter. He suggests that Peter was reduced in the previous strike to a scab due to his wife's illness. Jake Allen and the committee are not moved, and they expel Peter from the union.

Act III is set with the backdrop of the new strike's failure and collapse. As part of the backlash within the play, many suspected of being scabs are attacked by defeated union workers offstage, including Peter Hanlon. Peg Hanlon returns from Liverpool, as her shop employment failed and she turned to prostitution. To enhance her misfortune, she darkly glories "in freedom from her former shop life" (as quoted in Hogan with Burnham and Poteet, *Abbey Theatre*, 343). Her sister Anne, dying now of consumption, hears that Tom Robinson had attempted to stop the beating of her father, but when police baton-charged the street crowd, Tom was brutally beaten, then arrested. On such news, Anne dies.[23]

Wilson's *The Slough* portrays the Hanlon family, and Tom Robinson, as victims of their class and their class's struggle against capitalism. This is even apparent with the drunken father, who is not sympathetic due to his actions as a scab and his devastating alcoholism. Stephen Dedalus Burch writes that the fates of these characters are "pre-determined . . . by their class, and, in the end, all are crushed by their seemingly inescapable poverty" ("Historical Invisibility"). It appears that Wilson, as he attempts to explain the sympathy strike strategy in Act II, also attempts, through the Hanlons, to explain the reality for working-class families in Dublin.

If Wilson was using his play to explain a situation to its middle-class audience, which appears the case, rather than antagonizingly assault them, then it would seem Wilson's play was more in a Shavian manner than not. Part of his nudging approach is through the play's second act; more specifically, through the Jake Allen character based on Larkin, which Wilson played himself.

While Allen, or Larkin, is portrayed as having little patience with the meeting's procedures, he is presented as being steady to his principles. However, the character and performance may have lent themselves too much to the Dublin middle-class audience's perception of Larkin, which exclusively had come to them via the capitalist press during the Lockout. Burch writes that "Wilson presents a recognizable composite of the general public's perception of 'Larkin': bellicose, highhanded, megalomaniac" ("Historical Invisibility"). While such characteristics were apparently present in Larkin, which made him difficult to work with, the inclusion of such did not instill admiration for Larkin in the middle-class audience. Of course, Wilson, who knew Larkin firsthand from inside the *Irish Worker* and ITGWU movement, may have wanted the Larkin character to be extremely recognizable in order to be clear that the play was commenting on the recent situation. But the portrayal gave the middle-class audience what it wanted. The *Irish Times* noted in its review that the Act II scene, "that of the committee room of the General Union, is extremely humorous, and terminates in an uproar as Peter Hanlon is fired out as a defaulter" (i.e., a scab). As a consequence, the paper thought the play "is not used to point a moral" (as quoted in Hogan with Burnham and Poteet, *Abbey Theatre*, 343). This view is at odds with that of Ben Levitas, who sees the Allen-Larkin character as a sympathetic note of radical optimism in the play ("Plumbing," 14). But the original audience clearly laughed. William O'Brien, who obviously knew the above characteristics to be in Larkin more than Wilson did, and had grown to dislike Larkin by 1914 due to such characteristics, recalled that *The Slough* "was a play about Larkin and the strike. It was very true to life but it showed Jim [Larkin] up rather badly. He was seen at a meeting of the men's executive bossing the show for all he was worth, opposed by just one member and slavishly supported by the rest. 'Twas a sight for the gods when his one opponent told him he couldn't do so and so 'because it was agin the standin orders,' to hear Jim's double rise and say with dramatic emphasis 'Oh, I can't can't I? Well, then I move the suspension of the standing orders'! All the same I didn't relish outsiders laughing at it. I wouldn't mind if it was confined to ourselves" (*Forth*, 260).

O'Brien clearly felt Wilson's textual and performance portrayal of Larkin damaged and demeaned the labor position, perhaps even playing into the capitalist charges that the Lockout was only a result of Larkin's arrogant belief that he could "boss" Dublin, suggesting further to the play's first audience that the Hanlons are victims not of capitalists, but of Larkin. O'Brien was not inaccurate in this assessment, as the bourgeois Holloway, who recorded in his journal with class snobbery that Wilson "never could be a gentleman," noted of Wilson's play, which he called Wilson's "slum play," "the 'Jake Allen' of the play, forcibly enacted by the author, is in very truth drawn from Jim Larkin, and the realistic committee room scene in Act II[,] I have little doubt is very like the real thing too" (*Joseph Holloway's*, 163, 167). Holloway, it seems, enjoyed seeing the culprit behind the previous year's tramcar stoppage portrayed as a comedic, arrogant megalomaniac.

Perhaps in an effort at some damage control, Sheehy-Skeffington reviewed Wilson's play in the *Irish Citizen*, where he tried to brush aside the committee room scene. Sheehy-Skeffington praised the play's first and third acts, which provided "a vivid and realistic picture of Dublin's industrial warfare, and of the suffering" (as quoted in Hogan with Burnham and Poteet, *Abbey Theatre*, 344). Still, the question arises as to Wilson's intent with Act II. Was he trying to present a positive image of Larkin in order to explain Larkin as well as the sympathy strike strategy, and the middle-class audience got it wrong? Or was he sacrificing the defeated and absent Larkin to laughing ridicule in hopes that some in that audience would come to understand syndicalism and see that it was a program that should have worked had British unions struck in sympathy? If it was the latter—and it most likely was, given Wilson's apparent theatrical abilities—then the comedy of Act II was meant to work in a perceived Shavian manner, providing its intended audience with humor to slide in the play's messages and agenda. But the danger of the laughing at Wilson's play was similar to Shaw's playing in Dublin when those in the bourgeois audience missed the satirical confrontation to their values and just laughed at the physical comedy. And since *The Slough* is void of brilliant Shavian-type satire, there was less chance that any of its Dublin middle-class audience could have seen the play's explanation of the sympathy strike, even gradually over time, as they laughed at whom they saw as the Lockout's culprit.

It is worth remembering that Wilson's earlier *Victims*, at the Irish Workers' Dramatic Company, presented its working-class audience with what it had wanted. Wilson had done the same with *The Slough* at the Abbey.

Wilson's consistent approach of playing to his audiences was reflected throughout his management of the Abbey Theatre during 1913–15, as he heavily focused on producing many new plays, presumably to cater to his audience. In fact, this approach led to the end of his position at the Abbey in spring 1915. According to Holloway, Wilson told him that in April, while planning the Abbey's summer London engagement, Gregory and Yeats stipulated that *In the Shadow of the Glen*, *Riders to the Sea*, *The Playboy of the Western World*, and *Deirdre of the Sorrows* were to be done (*Joseph Holloway's*, 170). In mid-May, Yeats asked Wilson during another play's rehearsal why *Deirdre of the Sorrows* was not being rehearsed for London, to which Wilson replied by saying audiences did not like the play, implying they did not like any of Synge's plays. Yeats supposedly exploded with "Synge has left us a glorious heritage, and I have worked to make the theatre a Synge theatre" (as quoted in Holloway, *Joseph Holloway's*, 171–172). Wilson asserted that he then told Yeats that it was unfair to the actors to produce unpopular plays, "robbing them of their livelihood; Yeats and Gregory had their homes and didn't mind, but it was different with the players." Yeats allegedly responded, again as related to Holloway by Wilson: "I was never spoken to so before in my life!" (as quoted in *Joseph Holloway's*, 172). Due to the row over his refusal to stage, interestingly, an antagonistic leftist-leaning national Synge play, Wilson promptly resigned from the theatre.

Again, Wilson's sense of playing to rather than against the audience arguably bears some connection to Shaw, in the context of socialistic theatre then in Ireland. One can assuredly assume that given his interest in the labor cause in Dublin, Wilson knew of Shaw's "Mad Dogs in Uniform" and may well have also heard Captain White discuss Shaw when addressing the ICA at the end of November 1913. While not echoing Shaw's 1913 speech in *The Slough*, Wilson had anticipated a later Irish Shaw play in his one-act *A Call to Arms*, which was staged at the Abbey as a benefit for the Soldiers' and Sailors' Family Association in October 1914. It was an Irish recruiting play for British military service in the Great War. The unpublished play was viewed by the capitalist press as being "amusing," leaving one to conclude that it too had not assaulted its audience's sensibilities (as quoted in Hogan with Burnham and Poteet, *Abbey Theatre*,

356). Presumably, a recruiting effort on behalf of the British army placed Wilson also at odds with James Connolly.

War

There is no record of Connolly's having seen *The Slough*, or *A Call to Arms*, and no record of his view of Wilson. But by the time these two Wilson plays premiered, Connolly was sharpening the focus of his energies as the working-class situation in Dublin, and the world, had been plummeted into further nightmare. In August 1914, the Great War in Europe commenced between Britain, with its allies, and Germany, with its allies. In the *Irish Worker*'s first issue published after war was declared, Connolly wrote:

> What should be the attitude of the working-class democracy of Ireland in the face of the present crisis? . . . Should the working class of Europe, rather than slaughter each other for the benefit of kings and financiers, proceed tomorrow to erect barricades all over Europe, to break up bridges and destroy the transport services that war might be abolished, we should be perfectly justified in following such a glorious example and contributing our aid to the final dethronement of the vulture classes that rule and rob the world. . . . This may mean more than a transport strike, it may mean armed battling in the streets to keep in this country the food for our people. . . .
> Starting thus, Ireland may yet set the torch to a European conflagration that will not burn out until the last throne and the last capitalist bond and debenture will be shriveled on the funeral pyre of the last war lord. ("Our Duty," 4)

As most of the laboring classes in Europe, including Ireland, enlisted in the armies to fight the war, a few socialist theorists in Russia and the British Isles saw in war an opportunity. Shaw and Connolly were among them. Immediately after war was declared, Connolly told William O'Brien: "I will not miss this chance" (as quoted in O'Brien, *Forth*, 269).

5

War and Revolution

The Convergence

Within weeks of war being declared, Shaw began writing "Common Sense about the War." As if in response to Connolly's call for European laborers to unite against the forces of war, "that war might be abolished . . . [to dethrone] the vulture class" ("Our Duty," 4), Shaw wrote: "No doubt the heroic remedy . . . is that both armies should shoot their officers and go home to gather in their harvests . . . and make a revolution in the towns . . . [but] this is not at present a practicable solution" ("Common," 17). Immediately Shaw and Connolly were seeing the opportunity war provided in differing terms, with Shaw suggesting Connolly's early visions of revolution in August 1914 were impractical, if not dangerous. Yet the war was to facilitate Shaw's and Connolly's further interactions, as Irish socialism reached for revolution.

As Shaw wrote "Common Sense," Connolly published "A Continental Revolution," in the Scottish Socialist *Forward*, recalling the significant advances made by socialists throughout Europe during the previous years. He blended socialism and trade unionism, as such had occurred in Ireland with the ITGWU: "The whole working-class movement stands committed to war upon war—stands so committed at the very height of its strength and influence" ("Continental," 240). But Connolly then lamented that war declared by the capitalist and imperialist classes was among the very countries that had the strongest capitalism and the strongest socialist movements, which now rendered socialists "helpless." The war, to Connolly, was emerging to erase the socialist movement(s), as laborers enlisted in the armies of war: "What then becomes of all our resolutions, all our carefully built machinery of internationalism, all our hopes for the future? Were they all as sound and fury, signifying nothing? . . . Civilization is being destroyed before our eyes; the results of generations of propaganda and patient heroic plodding and self-sacrifice are being blown into annihilation . . . this war appears to me as the most fearful crime of the centuries. In it the working classes are to be sacrificed that a small clique of rulers and armament makers may state their lust for power and their greed for wealth.[1] Nations are to be obliterated, progress stopped, and international hatreds erected into deities to be worshipped" ("Continental," 240–242).

Connolly was witnessing the collapse of international socialism, as he understood it, as many socialists also joined war efforts. Even the English militant socialist Thomas Mann, who had advocated the syndicalist approach on behalf of labor against capitalist interests and had been mentioned by Shaw in "Mad Dogs in Uniform," now supported Britain's war. As Connolly had seen Mann as ideologically aligned to his own socialism and recognized Mann as "the greatest of internationalists" before the war, he now publicly condemned Mann's war support, labeling him "a raving jingo, howling for the blood of every rival of the British capitalist class" (as quoted in Nevin, *Connolly*, 625). Connolly now began sharpening his anti-war propaganda.

Connolly, Shaw, and the Dublin Propaganda Press

By the end of the war's first month, Connolly attacked in the *Irish Worker* the "political tricksters who lured" Ireland's young men into the European killing trenches. He argued in "The War Upon the German Nation" that "this war is not a war upon German militarism, but upon the industrial activity of the German nation" ("War Upon," 243–244). In response to British propaganda that the war as being fought by Britain for small nations, like Belgium, Connolly wrote: "the cry of 'Belgium' was a mere subterfuge. . . . The British capitalist class have planned this colossal crime in order to ensure its uninterrupted domination of the commerce of the world" ("War Upon," 247–248). Connolly's anti-war, class-driven propaganda continued into fall 1914, as the war's intensity grew, its armies grew, and more prominent socialists publicly supported the war, and, closer to home, supported Britain's call for military enlistment. Most prominent among the socialist war-supporters was Shaw.

While his early anti-war articles lamented the abandonment of international socialism, Connolly was moving his propaganda to the socialist debate on Ireland and the war. The Great War had broken out less than eight months following British labor leaders' failure to heed Larkin and Connolly's call for sympathy strikes in Britain to support Irish labor during the Dublin Lockout. As such, Connolly was suspicious of British socialistic trade union leaders. Even Connolly's first anti-war article called on Irish labor to lead the socialist fight against the war by freezing the transport system and preventing food from leaving Ireland. It was within this debate in Ireland, on the surface an anti-war debate but ultimately a socialist debate on what opportunity the war presented to Ireland, that Connolly and Shaw (who in the year before collaborated in the arming of Irish labor) were now in opposition. Their polar war positions in the 1914 autumn stemmed from the differences between their philosophical approaches to socialistic change, and their differing on the war brought this debate, which had been anticipated on the Dublin stage between Synge and Shaw a decade earlier, to a new stage with heightened consequences.

Shaw's entrance into the 1914 socialist war debate in Ireland was not as direct as his foray into Irish socialism in 1904, in reaction to Synge's 1903 antagonizing national approach revealed in *In the Shadow of the Glen*. Shaw entered the War-Ireland debate by being prompted by the anti-war propaganda of Dublin's nationalist press, along with the ITGWU's *Irish Worker*, which contained many Connolly anti-war articles. On 30 November 1914, following the *London Times*' call for the suppression of Dublin's anti-British and anti-war newspapers, the Dublin commercial pro-British *Freeman's Journal* published a letter from Shaw. Shaw chose not to send his letter to William Martin Murphy's *Irish Independent*. His letter was printed under the heading "Ireland and the War—the Erratic View of Mr. Bernard Shaw."[2] The paper's title revealed surprise at Shaw's war view. Perhaps Shaw was expected to agree with Connolly, as he had in 1913, and the paper undoubtedly monitored the *Irish Worker* since the Lockout. But the *Freeman's Journal* also knew that Shaw was embroiled in controversy in Britain for the publication of "Common Sense about the War." That essay appeared in London's *New Statesman* on 14 November and immediately "earned him [Shaw] the brand of traitor" (Zorn, "Cosmopolitan," 192).[3] Shaw had criticized aspects of the British war-government, including its foreign policy, its promoted patriotism, and the rampart jingoism that fostered irrational war fever. So expecting Shaw to be pro-German and agreeing with Connolly, Shaw instead reminded the *Freeman's Journal*'s readers that France had long been Ireland's ally and a world symbol for republicanism. He called on the Irish to fight with France: "If they will not join the French army as volunteers, or the British army as regulars, they can, nonetheless, understand that the one thing they must not do if they are good Irishmen is to join the Germans or help the Germans against the French" ("Ireland and the First," 103).

Shaw addressed the Dublin anti-war press editors: "You cannot consistently fill your paper with the old injuries from England, and refuse to remember the old championship, hospitality, and armed support we have received from France" ("Ireland and the First," 101). Shaw, consistent with his gradualist internationalism, but with greater urgency in regard to time, called on the Catholicism of most Irish. Rather than jab at the Church, as in his past Irish works, Shaw now evoked Catholic commitment to nudge his readers to his desired direction: "The holiest shrines and most glorious monuments of the Catholic Church are in the charge of France, and make her cities places of pilgrimages. Is Catholic Ireland going to exalt in seeing them battered with Prussian cannon?" ("Ireland and the First," 102). Such argument echoed British recruitment efforts that appealed for Ireland to help Catholic Belgium, overrun by German troops.[4]

The Catholic angle had been repeatedly used in early British war propaganda in Ireland, particularly as it labeled the war as a "democratic crusade, and its suggestion that Belgium had suffered due to its Catholicism" (Horne, *Our War*, 8). As Belgium was drifting out of British propaganda by November 1914, Shaw still echoed the Catholic rallying point as he called for support for republican and Catholic France. While some contemporaries in Ireland might have viewed Shaw as blatantly echoing British war jingoism, he nonetheless urged British authorities in Ireland not to suppress the anti-war press, recognizing the non-democratic move such suppression would represent. He warned the British that they must not drive "sedition underground, the only place where it can do any real harm" ("Ireland and the First," 103). On this point Shaw was dead-on. If his pro-war stance was confusing to some Irish in late November 1914, or "erratic" as the *Freeman's Journal* editors thought, his position was not an abandonment of his socialism but merely a tack.

Shaw clarified his early Irish war position in a private correspondence that started two days before his *Freeman's Journal* letter appeared. On 28 November, Mabel Fitzgerald wrote to Shaw seeking help in trying to block Britain's suppression of the Irish anti-war papers. Fitzgerald sent Shaw samples of the threatened papers: "I think the result will be that no matter what your opinion as to the part Ireland should take in this war, you will raise your very forcible voice in defense of a free press for Ireland" ("Mabel Fitzgerald," 185).

Being a Fabian and suffragette, Fitzgerald was confident about enlisting Shaw's help. She saw him as a significant Irish voice among the English and an advocate of free speech—especially given his theatre battle against the censorship of the Lord Chamberlain in 1909, when Fitzgerald, then unmarried, had filled in for a few months as Shaw's secretary. She also knew of his support of Irish labor during the Lockout. Among the seditious papers she sent Shaw was the *Irish Worker*, whose editor, James Connolly, she noted, was "a straight thinker and a good writer" ("Mabel Fitzgerald," 185). Shaw's response to Fitzgerald was consistent with his *Freeman's Journal* letter.

Shaw wrote, "You are just a day after the fair: I have already taken action. I do not want Prussia to win this game" ("Mabel Fitzgerald Correspondence," 189). Shaw also explained: "I want to establish the assumption that Ireland is on the Republican side, and on the democratic side: which in this war means the side of France against Prussia" ("Mabel Fitzgerald Correspondence," 189). Shaw did admit that Britain's ally Tsarist Russia was an "unlucky complication," which Connolly had criticized ("Mabel Fitzgerald Correspondence," 189, Connolly, "War Upon," 248). Shaw's pro-democratic position in regard to the war and Ireland was, despite Connolly's view, an internationalist socialistic view. Shaw wrote in "Common Sense about the War" that "Plutocracy makes for war because it offers prizes to Plutocrats: Socialism makes for peace because the interests it serves are international. So, as the Socialist side is the democratic side, we had better democratize our diplomacy if we desire peace" ("Common," 61). But Connolly had argued that because war was being fought, socialists throughout Europe had abandoned their commitment to peace. Shaw, on his side, maintained his desire for peace in what he believed was a consistent socialist stance. With regard to Ireland, Shaw desired the establishment of enlightened democratic government before the old, and, in his view, archaic national animosities expanded. He was advocating democracy as the future, and the triumph of democracy in the war would lead Fabianly toward a more just social order in world society. Ideally, democracy would promise a voice for all, including laborers. So, for Shaw, the war presented the possibility of change through the gradual alteration of society, and the right to vote offered that gradual Fabian-like change. Shaw's war position in autumn 1914, in general and Irish terms, was consistent with his socialism. While Shaw and Synge had shared common socialistic beliefs but differed in international and national-leaning approaches, did Shaw and Connolly now share socialistic beliefs in regard to war and Ireland in 1914?

As Connolly lamented the collapse of international socialism at war's start, Shaw was also troubled by the collapse. Christa Zorn suggests that Shaw was a cosmopolitan in "the desire for an international order" ("Cosmopolitan," 188–189). In "Common Sense about the War," Shaw suggests that in the future there will be no national boundaries, "only two flags, the red of socialists and the black of capitalists" (Davis, *George Bernard Shaw*, 104). Holroyd relates that within days of Germany's invasion of Belgium, Shaw saw the warring parties as "committing a crime against civilization" (*Bernard Shaw*, 347); Connolly also saw the warring as "the most fearful crime of centuries" and saw civilization as the victim ("Continental," 240). While Connolly viewed the war as capitalist masters vying for "domination" of the world's commerce ("War Upon," 248), Daniel O'Leary writes that Shaw similarly held "the German and the British aristocratic capitalists and industrialists responsible for the carnage" ("Censored," 171). Still, Connolly and Shaw appeared as polar opposites in their public considerations of the war and Ireland in November 1914.

Shaw had clearly indicated in his *Freeman's Journal* letter, and in his letter to Fitzgerald, that he wanted Germany to lose the war in favor of the democracy France represented. While Shaw was accused in Britain of being pro-German following the appearance of "Common Sense about the War," he maintained that he desired Britain's victory. O'Leary writes that Shaw's "war-time essays explicitly outline his commitment to European and British civilization, and he was willing to contribute what he could to do his duty in supporting the war effort once the war had come" ("Censored," 181). Part of his duty included the *Freeman's Journal* letter, hence Shaw's war and Ireland position, where his hope for democracy's triumph could lead to social re-order. This was not Connolly's choice.

Within days of the war's start, Connolly approached William O'Brien seeking introductions to important nationalists extreme enough for an Irish insurrection. The result was a meeting on 9 September that included Connolly and O'Brien. The nationalists present included Synge and pro-labor advocates Thomas MacDonagh and Padraic Pearse. Tom Clarke,

Sean MacDiarmuid, Joseph Plunkett, and Eamonn Ceannt were also present, and they, too, in 1913 supported labor, a radical strain running through each.[5] According to O'Brien, Connolly pressed for organizing an insurrection and, for such purpose, approach Germany for support (*Forth*, 269–270). Many historians, and some contemporaries, have viewed such action on Connolly's part as a move away from socialism. This was not the case. It did differ from Shaw's position, but Connolly had reached the point where he saw war as the opportunity for socialist reform in Ireland, not through an expanding democracy that might emerge afterwards, but through insurrection for tangible democracy now.[6] Essentially, Connolly saw revolution as his direction. Connolly and Shaw were now diametrically opposed—or were they?

At this time, Russian Vladimir Lenin wrote in *The Socialist Revolution and the Right of Nations to Self Determination*: "Victorious Socialism must achieve complete democracy and, consequently, not only bring about complete equality of nations, but also give effect to the right of oppressed nations to self-determination, i.e. the right of free political secession. Socialist Parties which fail to prove by all their activities now, as well as during the revolution and after its victory, that they will free the enslaved nations or establish relations with them on the basis of free union—and a free union is a lying phrase without right to secession—such parties would be committing treachery to Socialism" (as quoted in Ellis, "Introduction," 34). Simply, Shaw and Connolly were consistent with Lenin's above socialist theory. Shaw was committed in his war stance for democracy, which should eventually lead to the freeing of nations with their individual rights to secession in hand. Connolly was committed to using war as the chance to attain democracy for all classes and freedom of secession in Ireland—which, he had envisioned, would "set the torch to a European conflagration" that will destroy capitalism's hold on the world (as quoted in O'Brien, *Forth*, 269).[7] Again, Shaw and Connolly shared socialistic goals, but their philosophies and approaches differed. It was the difference between the mostly international Shaw and the more national Connolly, characterized by one to patiently work over time and the other to war with opponents in the immediate.

Connolly's chance to immediately counter Shaw's position on the war as expressed in the *Freeman's Journal* was lost when the *Irish Worker* was suppressed by British authorities in early December 1914. The very final issue appeared as a leaflet including the announcement that the Irish

Citizen Army was continuing its drilling, and women wishing to join the Red Cross nurses of the ICA should contact Connolly, ICA commander (Nevin, *Connolly*, 520). To further clarify its position, the ITGWU hung a banner across the front of Liberty Hall: "We Serve Neither King Nor Kaiser, But Ireland" (O'Connor Lysaght, "Irish Citizen," 18). Connolly's process of antagonizing Britain, for a socially just Ireland, had commenced. While Shaw urged British and French victory in the war for democracy's triumph, Connolly took up the business of the reconquest of Ireland. Of course, Connolly could have responded to Shaw's pro-war *Freeman's Journal* letter in the Scottish *Forward*, but chose not to. Perhaps he had an eye to the future, or past.

Connolly and the Reconquest—Shavian and Syngean

After Connolly's first effort to restart a labor paper was also suppressed, he acquired an antiquated printing press for Liberty Hall and started the second series of the *Workers' Republic* in May 1915. Now with his own press, Connolly printed his sixty-four-page pamphlet-book *The Re-Conquest of Ireland*. In some respects, the work was a continuation of his 1910 book *Labour in Irish History*. While much of *Re-Conquest* had appeared as articles in the *Irish Worker* in 1912, the work was heavily expanded during the 1913 experience (Nevin, *Connolly*, 538). This was the last major theoretical work that Connolly wrote, and it carried influences distinctly Shavian and some Syngean. The flyleaf within the front cover contained a quote from the pamphlet: "the re-conquest of Ireland must mean the social as well as the political independence from servitude of every man, woman and child in Ireland" (*Re-Conquest*, i).

Connolly's first two chapters explore the historical background of the conquest of Ireland by capitalizing Britain. Chapter 3 is titled "Dublin in the Twentieth Century," and in this chapter Connolly chastises the Dublin municipal government for the city's high death-rate—in 1911 it was worse than that in Moscow or Calcutta. Connolly places blame on the Dublin Corporation, with its majority of corrupt self-serving capitalists, as found in the Shavian-inspired plays *The Laying of the Foundations* and *The Lord Mayor*.

In the next chapter, "Labour in Dublin," Connolly echoed Shaw's 1910 Poor Law speech, as he explained dominant Irish views of laboring classes: "Poverty and misery were, in short, looked upon as evils which might call for exercise of private benevolence, but that their causes were to be looked for solely in the lapses or weaknesses of individual men and women" (*Re-Conquest*, 26). Connolly then explained the rise of "the working class agitator" in Ireland who investigated relations between labor and employers, exposing unfair salaries and conditions. Connolly next described the ITGWU, which had battled for Irish labor (*Re-Conquest*, 27). Connolly finished the chapter by explaining the sympathy strike, without the debasing bourgeois humor A. P. Wilson had used to frame his explanation of the tactic in *The Slough*.

Connolly also addressed women within Irish society, especially rural women, aggressively clashing with those who disagreed:

> The worker is the slave of capitalist society, the female is the slave of that slave. . . . She has toiled in the farms from her earliest childhood, attaining usually to the age of ripe womanhood without ever being vouchsafed the right to claim as her own a single penny of the money earned by her labour, and knowing that all her toil and privation would not earn her that right to the farm which would go without question to the most worthless member of the family if that member chanced to be the eldest male.
> The daughters of the Irish peasantry have been the cheapest slaves in existence—slaves to their own family who were in turn slaves to all the social parasites of a landlord and gombeen-ridden community. (*Re-Conquest*, 38)

Connolly added that the enslavement of Irish women was "fiercely insisted upon by the clergymen of all denominations" (*Re-Conquest*, 38). Even marriage, Connolly argued, "does not mean for her a rest from . . . labour, it usually means that . . . she has added the duty of a double domestic toil . . . her whole life runs—a dreary pilgrimage from one drudgery to another" (*Re-Conquest*, 40–41). The enslavement of peasant-class Irish women reverberates with the confronting sentiments of Synge's *In the Shadow of the Glen*, where a young poor Irish woman finds herself in an isolating drudgery of enslavement to an abusive husband, where she owns nothing. Connolly: "So down from the landlord to the tenant or peasant proprietor, from monopolist, and from all above to all below filtered the beliefs, customs, ideas establishing a slave morality which enforces the subjection of women as the standard morality of the country" (*Re-Conquest*, 41). Connolly's description of the usury and capitalistic-like creation and enforcement of the morality of Irish woman enslavement was the very morality Synge attacked in his plays, and which the conservative, paternalized, and respectable middle-class Dublin society attacked in response. The theatrically expressed and debated Irish socialistic ideas were surfacing in Connolly, echoing Synge and Shaw.

In *Re-Conquest*, Connolly ideologically also saw value, in a Shavian vein, of the cooperative movement of Horace Plunkett and George Russell, the IAOS. Connolly notes the opposition the IAOS encountered was from the petty middle-class capitalists who infected rural Ireland, the very type attacked and ridiculed by Synge and Shaw, respectively. As if echoing both, particularly as expressed in *John Bull's Other Island*, Connolly wrote: "the gombeen men and their kind from their position in the country towns, their ostentatious parade of religion and their loud-mouthed assertions of patriotism, were usually the dominant influences in the council of the local Home Rule or other constitutional national organization" (*Re-Conquest*, 50). Perhaps knowing of the shared consistencies between himself and those like Shaw, Connolly wrote in his pamphlet's summation: "Not the least of the many encouraging signs given to the world during the great Dublin Labour dispute . . . was the keen and sympathetic interest shown by the intellectuals in the fortunes of the workers" (*Re-Conquest*, 56).

By the time *The Re-Conquest of Ireland* appeared, events were moving quickly, as war entrenched itself in Europe, and Connolly was again about to enjoy assistance from intellectuals, namely Sheehy-Skeffington and Shaw.

Recruitment's Emergence: Sheehy-Skeffington, Shaw, and a Fenian Funeral

When the war commenced, socialist and suffrage journalist Francis Sheehy-Skeffington immediately sent a note to William O'Brien: "This war means the end of the British Empire. [. . .] I am hoping . . . for a German victory" (*Between Comrades*, 518). Agreeing with his friend Connolly (rather than Shaw, whom he greatly admired) about Ireland's role in the war, Sheehy-Skeffington found his suffragette paper, *Irish Citizen*, in fierce financial difficulty.[8] The paper's feminist-pacifist stance on the war cost it much revenue, as many suffragettes, like socialists, supported Britain's war. In an effort to save the paper, Sheehy-Skeffington wrote to potential donors, including Shaw's wife Charlotte. Sheehy-Skeffington's letters to Charlotte coincided with the correspondence between Shaw and Mabel Fitzgerald. The call for Ireland's free press was made to the Shaws on at least two fronts in November 1914.[9]

While still an ITGWU elected vice-chairman of the ICA, Sheehy-Skeffington organized anti-recruitment meetings every Sunday outside Liberty Hall. These rallies were conducted in association with the ITGWU and were held for forty consecutive Sundays in an effort to dissuade ITGWU members and others from enlisting in the British military. Sheehy-Skeffington delivered speeches each Sunday. He explained privately that he felt compelled to wage his anti-recruitment drive to offset for the "ignorant people" the pro-enlistment propaganda delivered by Dublin's popular press, politicians, and clergy (as quoted in Levenson, *With Wooden*, 175). On 29 May 1915, Sheehy-Skeffington was arrested by the British army under the Defense of the Realm Act for making "statements likely to be prejudicial to recruiting" ("Speech," 11).

Sheehy-Skeffington was tried by a police magistrate and was sentenced to six months hard labor. In response, he commenced a hunger strike (O'Brien 251). During his brief trial, Sheehy-Skeffington stipulated that his efforts against recruitment were "necessary" to expose the "infamous cascade of lies poured forth in the papers of so-called German atrocities in Belgium and elsewhere" ("Speech," 7–8).

On her husband's sentencing, incarceration, and hunger strike, Hanna Sheehy-Skeffington wrote to Shaw seeking assistance, despite knowing Shaw's position on the war and Ireland. Shaw responded with a letter in which he stated: "I have naturally been interested in your husband's case, and have carefully read not only the newspaper accounts of the proceeding before the magistrates, but the transcript of the speech which you have sent me" ("Letter From," i).[10] He added: "There is nothing to be done. The Defense of the Realm Act abolishes all liberty in Great Britain and Ireland, except such as the authorities may and have to leave us. Even if the powers given by the Act were insufficient, the Government could act arbitrarily without the least risk, as there is no remedy for such arbitrariness except a revolution. . . . Unfortunately this confidence of mine sends the British alarmists into ecstasies of fright. They commonly allude to me as Pro-German; and if they knew that I sympathized with your husband they would declare that nothing but his imprisonment for life could save England. I can fight stupidity; but nobody can fight cowardice" ("Letter

From," ii–iv). Shaw not only allowed Hanna Sheehy-Skeffington to publish his letter in the *Freeman's Journal*, he also allowed her to publish it in a pamphlet, with her husband's speech, that was edited and published by James Connolly at Liberty Hall.

Connolly's Sheehy-Skeffington and Shaw pamphlet, which cost one penny, was titled "F. Sheehy-Skeffington's Speech from the Dock. With Letter from George Bernard Shaw. Eloquent Defense of the Rights of Free Speech." Again Shaw and Connolly were together on an issue, with Shaw lending his name and words. While Shaw's support of Sheehy-Skeffington, as support for free speech, and the publication of Shaw's letter in the *Freeman's Journal* were not surprising, was the publication of his letter in a Connolly–Liberty Hall labor pamphlet unexpected in 1915? As with the ICA's formation, it is doubtful Shaw was totally oblivious to Connolly's agenda(s). In Connolly's printing of Shaw's Sheehy-Skeffington letter, Connolly typeset the letter with occasional full capitalization that heavily emphasized certain phrases. For example, Connolly's pamphlet transformed an above-quoted section as: "there is no remedy for such arbitrariness EXCEPT A REVOLUTION" ("Letter From," ii). There was no full capitalization in the *Freeman's Journal* printing. Connolly was using Shaw's letter to forward the national revolution he now advocated.[11] Shaw most likely did not know how Connolly would print his letter, but he certainly knew of Connolly's stance against the war and his militancy, especially if Shaw read the *Irish Worker* Mabel Fitzgerald sent him in November 1914.

Connolly's Sheehy-Skeffington and Shaw pamphlet was indicative of the acceleration of Connolly's agenda and actions in the summer of 1915.[12] Following the death in New York of an Irish rebel named Jeremiah O'Donovan Rossa, who had been exiled for participating in Fenian rebellions during the nineteenth century, his body was transported for an August burial in Dublin's Glasnevin Cemetery. Marching in the funeral procession was a contingent of the ICA.

The O'Donovan Rossa Funeral Committee planned the largest public Dublin funeral since Parnell's in 1891, and the committee included militant nationalist leaders as well as trade union leaders such as Connolly, William O'Brien, and the Bricklayers' leader Richard O'Carroll. Connolly was also on the subcommittee "Guards and Procession" as ICA commandant. The inclusion of trade unionists, and particularly the ICA, was indicative of the connections Connolly had fostered with extreme nationalist leaders. Connolly furthered the ICA by contributing an article to the Funeral Souvenir booklet. Connolly committed the ICA to his agenda while issuing a warning to the middle-class nationalist leaders; if they balked, the ICA would fight alone: "In honouring O'Donovan Rossa the workers of Ireland are doing more than merely paying homage to an unconquerable fighter. They are signifying . . . that there is no outside force capable of enforcing slavery upon a people really resolved to be free, and valuing freedom more than life. . . . The Irish Citizen Army in its Constitution pledges its members to fight for a Republican Freedom for Ireland. . . . by right of our faith in the separate destiny of our country, and our faith in the ability of the Irish Workers to achieve that destiny" (Connolly, "Honours Rossa").

O'Donovan Rossa's funeral procession was a dramatic display in spite of increasing British military enlistment efforts in Ireland, which were bolstered by the spring torpedoing of the *Lusitania* off Cork. Padraic Pearse, in Volunteer uniform, delivered the funeral oration in which he mentioned women in an effort to appease Connolly: "Life springs from death; and from the graves of patriot men and women spring living nations. The Defenders of this Realm have worked well in secret and in the open. They think that they have pacified Ireland. They think that they have for seen everything, think that they have provided against everything; but the fools, the fools, the fools!—they have left us our Fenian dead, and while Ireland holds these graves, Ireland unfree shall never be at peace" (as quoted in Ruth Dudley Edwards, *Patrick Pearse*, 236–237).[13] Following Pearse's seditious words, six uniformed members, not of Pearse's Volunteers, but of the ICA, which Shaw had helped form, fired a volley over Rossa's grave.[14] ICA bugler William Oman "played the Last Post" (Connell, *Where's Where*, 51). Revolution was now less than a year away and Irish theatre would again facilitate events in a Shaw-Synge dynamic.

Recruitment and Shaw's Irish Theatre

Since the outbreak of war, Dublin theatres struggled to survive. German U-boats significantly decreased touring companies and curtailed the Abbey Theatre's American tours. To compound matters, London theatres were also suffering due to zeppelin raids and the general effects of war, which made the Abbey's June 1915 London tour, when Wilson resigned as company manager, disastrous. Touring was a major revenue source for the Abbey, since Horniman withdrew her support in 1910.[15]

Dan Laurence and Nicholas Grene suggest that the financial woes of the Abbey Theatre in 1915 prompted Shaw to write *O'Flaherty V.C.* ("Introduction and Notes," xviii). Shaw was privy to the Abbey's problems, since Lady Gregory wrote to him on 19 September relating that the theatre's financial situation was demoralizing their actors (*Shaw, Gregory*, 97). Holroyd suggests further that a second reason for writing the play was having been asked for recruiting help by Sir Matthew Nathan, British undersecretary for Ireland (*Bernard Shaw*, 379–380). Murray Biggs concurs, writing that the play "had been called for in 1915 by . . . Nathan" ("Shaw's Recruiting," 107). The opportunity to write another play for Ireland was appealing to Shaw, especially within the context of the war. He may have viewed the process, fulfilling Nathan's request, as a means to counter the British public's view that he was pro-German. And there was consideration by Gregory, Yeats, and Shaw for the Abbey to run the play in a music hall venue starting at London's Coliseum, in addition to a Dublin premier (Laurence and Grene, "Introduction and Notes," 103).[16]

By mid-October 1915, the Abbey was in position to begin rehearsals, as a new company stage director was finally hired to replace Wilson, St. John Ervine, of the 1911 *Mixed Marriage*. On 21 October, the *Manchester Guardian* announced Ervine's appointment and the imminent premiere of Shaw's new play (Laurence and Grene, "Introduction and Notes," 104–105). On 30 October, Ervine was quoted in Dublin's *Weekly Freeman*: "We are hoping that the Shaw play will draw very well" (as quoted in Hogan with Burnham and Poteet, *Abbey Theatre*, 382). By at least around the second week of November, *O'Flaherty V.C.* was in rehearsals and scheduled to premiere on 23 November (Laurence and Grene, "Introduction and Notes," 106). Yet before the play could open, and before controversy emerged, Shaw's play was superseded by Connolly and the Irish Workers' Dramatic Company.

The Irish Workers' Dramatic Company performed little of importance since its manager Delia Larkin took the company on a small tour of England's west in the 1914 spring. Discontented with her brother in America, Delia Larkin resigned from the IWWU in summer 1915. Within weeks, Connolly appointed the Abbey actor Helena Moloney general secretary of IWWU (of the ITGWU), which included managing the Irish Workers' Dramatic Company. As news of *O'Flaherty V.C.* reached Liberty Hall, a play that presents an Irishman in the British army involved in recruiting other Irishmen for war, Moloney scheduled and produced a play advertised in the *Workers' Republic* as *The Recruiting Office*. It was performed on 7 November. While a play with that title is unknown, it is probable that it was George Farquhar's 1706 *The Recruiting Officer*, which was appropriate, as it prominently features a recruiting sergeant who seduces and tricks laborers to enlist in the British army. In the 16 October *Workers' Republic*, Connolly attacked Irishmen seduced to enlist by "the recruiting sergeant" ("Notes on the Front," 4). While it is impossible to say *The Recruiting Office(r)* was scheduled due to *O'Flaherty V.C.*, there is evidence that Liberty Hall knew much about Shaw's play.

Moloney was an important Abbey Theatre actor by the time *O'Flaherty* was scheduled, as was ICA captain Sean Connolly. Both Moloney and Sean Connolly would either have had access to Shaw's script or knew actors, like J. M. Kerrigan or Arthur Sinclair, who did.[17] Moloney and Connolly at least knew *O'Flaherty's* story-line and, without doubt, reported it to James Connolly, who would eventually respond directly and dramatically. But what could Moloney and Sean Connolly have reported to James Connolly about Shaw's play beyond its mere plot to provoke Connolly's response, which would play a major role toward revolution?

Laurence and Grene note that to *O'Flaherty V.C.* Shaw added the subtitle "A Recruiting Pamphlet" in 1930, yet suggest: "it is hard to tell just how seriously he may have intended it as such" in 1915 ("Introduction and Notes," xviii). Murray Biggs believes the play becomes a "different kind of 'recruiting pamphlet' . . . one that preaches turning swords into plowshares" ("Shaw's Recruiting," 11). Certainly in mid-play the title character proclaims, "No war is right" (*O'Flaherty*, 264). But the play was written nearly a year after Shaw's November 1914 letters to Dublin's *Freeman's Journal* and Mabel Fitzgerald, in which he adamantly voiced his view that Irishmen should fight against Germany for democracy, a view that Shaw reiterated in his "War Issues for Irishmen" in 1918. In addition, one month after *O'Flaherty V.C.*'s scheduled 1915 Abbey premiere, Shaw prepared a "poster text" for Dublin Castle, at their request, outlining how Britain should recruit Irishman (Laurence and Grene, "Introduction and Notes," 184). So while Shaw was against war in general, abhorring its glorification, he preferred a victory of democracy over Imperial Germany and appeared prepared to help recruit Irishmen for the purpose. Given *O'Flaherty V.C.*'s Shavian context when written, the play was consistent with Shaw's 1914–15 stance on war and Ireland, and it certainly was perceived as such in 1915 Dublin.

Completed in September 1915, four months after Sheehy-Skeffington had been arrested for making and organizing anti-recruiting speeches, *O'Flaherty V.C.* ultimately presents a young Irishman in the British army who does not regret enlisting and desires to return to war. In the preface written for the play's 1930 publication, Shaw criticizes Britain's recruiting efforts during the Great War for trying to rally the Irish with British patriotism, which Shaw asserts was of little use to Irishmen (*O'Flaherty* Preface, 255). Instead, Shaw relates that in his efforts to recruit Irishmen for the British army, he drew on "personal experience . . . that all an Irishman's hopes and ambitions turn on his opportunities of getting out of Ireland" (*O'Flaherty* Preface, 256) and the war provided such opportunity. Laurence and Grene remind us that escaping Ireland "made a man" of Shaw and Larry Doyle in *John Bull's Other Island* ("Introduction and Notes," xviii). The same can be said of Peter Keegan from the same play. Getting out of Ireland also, from Shaw's perspective, benefited Connolly, given Connolly's years as an American union organizer—Synge, too, perhaps, benefited from his Paris years prior to writing plays.

Shaw's play draws on Sergeant Michael O'Leary's receiving the Victoria Cross, Britain's highest military decoration, in early 1915 for combat heroism. O'Leary was used heavily in Ireland for recruitment in summer 1915, much as Dennis O'Flaherty is in Shaw's play.[18] When O'Flaherty enters, he is worn out from the day's recruiting speeches and appearances. Socialistically, or seemingly so, Shaw makes O'Flaherty a lowly private rather than of O'Leary's sergeant rank. The action opens with O'Flaherty sitting and talking with General Sir Pearce Madigan before the front door of Madigan's "big house" in Ireland's west, based on Lady Gregory's Coole Park (Shaw, *Shaw, Lady Gregory*, 94). Not only has war provided O'Flaherty some escape, it has elevated him in numerous ways, allowing him to speak openly with his general and his landlord, as O'Flaherty is a tenant on Madigan's estate. From the play's beginning, O'Flaherty is seen in his elevated status. On Madigan's statement to O'Flaherty that the V.C. he wears gives O'Flaherty "a higher rank in the roll of glory than I can pretend to," O'Flaherty utters: "I'm thankful to you, Sir Pearce; but I wouldn't have anyone think that the baronet of my native place would let a common soldier like me sit down in his presence" (*O'Flaherty*, 258).

O'Flaherty's achieved liberties continue, as he is able to counter Madigan's claim that their recruiting effort is for king and country, while simultaneously satirizing all recruitment jingoism. Madigan states: "it's our own country," to which O'Flaherty replies: "Well, sir, to you that have an estate in it, it would feel like your country. But the devil a perch of it ever I owned" (*O'Flaherty*, 259). O'Flaherty's freedom to break class restrictions in this moment allows him to reveal his mother's true nature as an irrational, fire-breathing patriot to Madigan, who had thought her a "most loyal woman" (*O'Flaherty*, 259). There is always in the play the reality that Mrs. O'Flaherty is a self-serving sham, closer to Tim Haffigan in Act I of *John Bull's Other Island* than anyone really interested in Ireland beyond cheap sentiment. Madigan relates that "whenever there is an illness in the Royal Family, she asks me every time we meet about the health of the patient as anxiously as if it were yourself, her only son" (*O'Flaherty*, 259). The hollowness of Mrs. O'Flaherty is emphasized later, when she is more interested in her old-age pension and the separation allowance the army pays her while O'Flaherty is at the front, than her nationalism or patriotism. Most consistent with Shaw's "Common Sense about the War" and *John Bull's Other Island*, the play attacks all fervent patriotisms and nationalisms, British and Irish. O'Flaherty states: "They never thought of being patriotic until the war broke out" (*O'Flaherty*, 265).

The religious justification for the war as preached by pro-British clergy is, as Biggs argues, undermined when O'Flaherty relates Father Quinlan's telling him to love his enemies and to "have a mass said for the souls of the hundreds of Germans you say you killed" (*O'Flaherty*, 262). The enlightened O'Flaherty asks indignantly, "Is it me that must pay for masses for the souls of the Boshes? . . . Let the King of England pay for them" (*O'Flaherty*, 262). One of O'Flaherty's insinuations, in a Syngean and Shavian vein, is that the Church's real interest is in receiving payment for the masses rather than prayers for souls.

O'Flaherty also can see into the fallacy of celebrated heroism, namely his own: "I kilt them [German soldiers] because I was afeared that, if I didn't theyd kill me" (*O'Flaherty*, 262). In the same manner, O'Flaherty reveals to Madigan that the reasons for the war are to him "and the like of me" unknown: "how the devil do I know what the war is about?" (*O'Flaherty*, 262). This, Biggs suggests, is quite different from Madigan's sense of the war as redefining "his" world ("Shaw's Recruiting," 109). O'Flaherty voices the common soldier's perception of the war, devoid of the grandiose patriotism of enlistment jingoism.

When Mrs. O'Flaherty appears, she is as unsavory as O'Flaherty had foretold. When she scolds him for shaking hands with the British king, "a tyrant red with the blood of Ireland," O'Flaherty retorts: "he's not half the tyrant you are, God help him. His hand was cleaner than mine that had the blood of his own relations on it, may be" (*O'Flaherty*, 268).[19] Most importantly, the war experience has provided O'Flaherty with the knowledge to see his mother for what she is, as well as to see Teresa Driscoll, his romantic interest, as she is. When he gives Teresa a gold chain he removed from a German POW, she asks before thanking him: "Do you think its real gold, Denny?" (*O'Flaherty*, 271). She further asks if she can take it to the jeweler. O'Flaherty recognizes her real interest, which is emphasized by her questions regarding his V.C. pension, if the pension would increase should he be wounded. When he answers affirmatively, she asks if he will be returning to the front, clearly hoping he does so he might be wounded. O'Flaherty angrily notes: "And if I do get a pension itself, the devil a penny of it will youll ever have the spending of" (*O'Flaherty*, 272). Shaw presents in Teresa the crass materialism he illustrated as infecting *John Bull's'* Rosscullen characters. However, Teresa and Mrs. O'Flaherty seem to be, if possible, pettier and greedier in the national portrait, as demonstrated by their row near play's end over the gold chain.

When his mother asks what has happened to him, O'Flaherty states: "Whats happened to everybody? That's what I want to know. Whats happened to you that I thought all the world of and was afeared of? Whats happened to Sir Pearce, that I thought was a great general, and that I now see to be no more fit to command an army than an old hen? Whats happened to Tessie, that I was mad to marry a year ago, and that I wouldn't take now with all Ireland for her fortune? I tell you the world's creation is crumbling in ruins about me; and then you come and ask whats happened to me?" (*O'Flaherty*, 273). The war has changed O'Flaherty, enlightening him into being able to see his mother, Teresa, Madigan, and Ireland for what they are. At play's end, O'Flaherty tells Madigan that he will return to war in order to find peace. O'Flaherty's greed-infected rural domesticity is seen as far too quarrelsome and leads him back to the trenches, affirming Shaw's public position on the war and Ireland's role in it.

As a recruiting play, *O'Flaherty V.C.* affirms the Irish fighting in the war for Britain but at the expense of indicting national Ireland and the Irish who made life unbearable, so much so O'Flaherty prefers the horrors of international war to home. The indictment is made all the more powerful in that Shaw, as he did in *John Bull's*, turns to rural Ireland, the Ireland idealized by many Irish nationalists. O'Flaherty's rural Irish life was far from ideal. The play's recruiting role for the war was not through patriotism, but instead for the escape and world knowledge that war provided. This to Shaw, on one level, was what should have inspired common Irishmen, particularly the uneducated like O'Flaherty, to enlist. After all, the war provided the labor class a cheap means to learn of the outside world, to learn that their living conditions could and should be better. In fact, the learning opportunity actually paid them. In this regard, Shaw most likely believed that if many of the ignorant enlisted and survived the war, they would return with the knowledge to change their conditions—whether it be working conditions or social situations. They would, as O'Flaherty, see the uselessness of the petty greed of his mother and Teresa, the greed, in the context of Ireland's then socialist debate, that infected the laboring class from the bourgeois class—directing any possible labeling of it as social Darwinism into capitalism-inspired greed, universal to all peoples and times. On such a level, the play works socialistically in Fabian fashion; a socialistic goal furthered while supporting the government's need for more Irish soldiers on behalf of the democratic cause.

O'Flaherty V.C. also undermines the rigid class order in Ireland near play's end, when Teresa ignores her duties in serving tea, as she and Mrs. O'Flaherty argue. The landlord Madigan has no control over them. The suggestion is that the class system is but a thin veil which can be brushed aside by worldly education, as in O'Flaherty, who sees that Madigan is no better. Together, landlord and peasant restore order.

A criticism of the play might be that while presenting the war as an educating opportunity, some might have thought that Shaw was underplaying the war's horrors. But such, of course, was the price for a recruiting play from Shaw serving the war that, if won by the Allies, should bring about world change. That change, which is presented on the individual level through O'Flaherty, is democratic. Democracy is what O'Flaherty gains by achieving his own voice while at war, hence Shaw's reason for Irishmen to fight Britain's war which he had expressed in November 1914.

As *O'Flaherty V.C.*'s recruiting role was true to Shaw's wartime socialist philosophy, it was written specifically as an Irish play, as was *John Bull's*

Other Island. But unlike *John Bull's*, Shaw wrote *O'Flaherty* as an Irish play in the form and structure of most early one-act Abbey Theatre plays, and was not meant to counter the Abbey play form as he had in 1904. In fact, Shaw explained to Gregory in a 14 September 1915 letter that *O'Flaherty* "ought to take from forty minutes to forty-five to get through—longer than [Gregory's] *The Workhouse Ward*, but on that scale generally" (*Shaw, Gregory*, 94). Still, to write the Irish *O'Flaherty V.C.*, Shaw, as he had in 1904, looked to Synge as he (Shaw) un-Syngean-like promoted Irishmen to serve in the British army. The audience(s) Shaw hoped to reach with an Abbey production were key to his thinking. By conceiving the production as making a music hall tour in Britain, which the Abbey needed for revenue, Shaw was almost taking a page from the Irish Workers' Dramatic Company, in that music hall performances would reach Irish laboring classes, namely those in Britain's industrial cities.[20] The press coverage of such a tour could dispel the British public's belief that Shaw was pro-German. But the Abbey's Dublin, mostly middle-class audience was much different. In one direction, *O'Flaherty* could reach recruiters, government or press, who could then redirect their efforts as Shaw prescribed. But the various types of nationalists in the Abbey's audience, conservatives to radicals, differed further. While the international Shaw disliked nationalisms and patriotisms, he did not always seem to appreciate the differing types of nationalists in the Abbey audience. To him, they had rioted at Synge's *Playboy*, but in reality only the conservatives rioted (which he had to have suspected), and all of them, for Shaw, were dangerously provincial in their narrow views. To explore how *O'Flaherty* was designed to play, and perhaps satirize, its audiences, we must explore Shaw's use of Synge in composing the play. Shaw sought to again counter Synge's national approach (not his structure), which, in turn, countered Synge's idealism for a socialistic Irish existence as represented by a pagan-like commune with nature. In so doing, Shaw was able to address the nationalists as he saw them, the obstructionists to Irish enlistment in the war and to his international socialistic vision. The result was a role for Shaw in Connolly's revolution.

Shaw's Quasi-Syngean *O'Flaherty*

By writing *O'Flaherty V.C.* as an Abbey Theatre play, Shaw created a play that conflicted in form with the British recruiting plays then regularly playing Dublin. These were commercial plays relying on either spectacle, like *Secret Order*, which included a naval battle and the downing of a German zeppelin, or British jingoism, like *It's a Long Way to Tipperary* (Hogan with Burnham and Poteet, *Abbey Theatre*, 403, 406). Shaw clearly dismissed such mindless forms in *O'Flaherty*, as he included no spectacle and O'Flaherty states he "never heard the tune of Tipperary in my life until I came back from Flanders" (*O'Flaherty*, 259). So while he writes a recruiting play, Shaw challenges the recruiting formulas that appealed to working-class audiences. Since one of Shaw's intended audiences was the Irish working class through music halls, Shaw wanted to appeal to their potential intelligence, and, for his middle-class Dublin audience he (again) wanted to alter how they attempted to deal with the poor in connection to the war, and present, through Synge, a supreme Shavian joke. The key is *O'Flaherty*'s form.

In Shaw's 14 September letter to Lady Gregory announcing the completion of *O'Flaherty*, he wrote that the play's "picture of the Irish character will make the Playboy seem a patriotic rhapsody by comparison. The ending is cynical to the last possible degree. The idea is that O'Flaherty's experience in the trenches has induced in him a terrible realism and an unbearable candor. He sees Ireland as it is, his mother as she is, his sweetheart as she is; and he goes back to the dreaded trenches for the sake of peace and quietness" (*Shaw, Gregory*, 95). Shaw's allusion to Synge's *The Playboy of the Western World* was not slight. Of course, Shaw makes the allusion as indicating the controversy the play might provoke among nationalists, especially for a Dublin audience. But consideration of Shaw's play with *Playboy* reveals that Shaw consciously drew on Synge's play; not to rework a Synge play as he did with *John Bull's*, but rather to borrow Syngean devices and conventions to enwrap his Irish war message. The last name of *Playboy*'s pagan ideal, Pegeen, is Flaherty. O'Flaherty is the more Irish, even more pagan version of the name, allowing Shaw to playfully portray his rural Irishman in an international cause as "truer" than Synge's national ideal. Then there is *O'Flaherty V.C.*'s rural language, which is much closer to Synge's play language than in *John Bull's*, which purposely uses non-Syngean language.

Specifically, Mrs. O'Flaherty's language, and bullying character, recalls *Playboy*'s Old Mahon. In Synge's Act II, when the Widow Quin says, "It's a sacred wonder the way that wickedness will spoil a man," Old Mahon replies: "My wickedness, is it?" (*Playboy*, 98). Similarly, O'Flaherty tells his mother that "I went where I could get the biggest allowance for you," to which she says: "Allowance, is it!" (*O'Flaherty*, 269). Synge's Old Mahon uses coarse language, indicating his character, as he employs words such as "blackguard," which Mrs. O'Flaherty repeatedly uses in her coarse language and persona (*Playboy*, 99, *O'Flaherty*, 269). The similarities between the characters Old Mahon and Mrs. O'Flaherty are highly suggestive, as both are bullying and abusive parents, and both drove their offspring, prior to the action of their respective plays, away from their homes.

There are additional convention-language phrases from *Playboy* that reappear in *O'Flaherty*. Pegeen's remark "Doesn't the world know you reared a black ram," is recalled in O'Flaherty's "all the world knows I never saw in my life" (*Playboy*, 86, *O'Flaherty*, 263). The word "whilst" is also abundant in both plays. At one point, Shaw's Mrs. O'Flaherty states: "It's mad he is with the roaring of the cannons," which echoes *Playboy*'s Widow Quin, "they fearing this time he was maybe roaring, romping on your hands with drink" (*O'Flaherty*, 273, *Playboy*, 85). Of course, some of these words and phrases may have been common among the rural west Irish, as Synge maintained, but so many similarities suggest more than coincidence, especially as Shaw never enjoyed Synge's familiarity with western peasants (*Playboy*, "Preface," 96).

In addition, Shaw's borrowing of Syngean language was more than mere borrowing. The continuation of Mrs. O'Flaherty's above quote states: "and he killing the Germans and the Germans killing him, bad cess to them!" is a direct reconfiguration of Pegeen's Act I statement in *Playboy*, "Isn't there the harvest boys with their tongues red for drink, and the ten tinkers is camped in the east, and the thousand militia—bad cess to them!" (*O'Flaherty*, 273, *Playboy*, 76). Shaw used language from Synge's national vision to project his international stance on the war and Ireland, changing the target of Pegeen's "bad cess to them!" from British soldiers, and other elements to be feared in her Ireland, to German soldiers. In a sense, Shaw used Synge's nationalized language, familiar to Abbey audiences due to the many Synge revivals by 1915, to project his argument that it was natural, right, and even "Irish" to take the international road during the first modern world war. Yet there are more Syngean conventions borrowed for *O'Flaherty V.C.*

In Shaw's play, as in Synge's *Playboy* and *Riders to the Sea*, the priest, who speaks through another character, therefore becoming a character himself, does not appear onstage. This is seen in *Playboy*'s Father Reilly, who delivers conservative bourgeois morality through Shawn Keogh. In *O'Flaherty*, Father Quinlan's words of pious conservatism and capitalist-like greed are repeated by O'Flaherty. And Mrs. O'Flaherty's threat to "clout" her son's ears repeats Pegeen's boxing Shawn's ears at the end of her play, which itself mirrors a difference between the two dramatists in that one's character commits the act and the Fabian's character only threatens it. Also, O'Flaherty tells his heroism story in grander, boasting terms each time he repeats it during recruiting rallies, which Madigan notices: "I think that story about you fighting the Kaiser and the twelve giants of the Prussian guard singlehanded would be the better for a little toning down" (*O'Flaherty*, 261). The same boasting, of course, is practiced by Christy Mahon as he retells his heroic tale of killing his brutish father. In fact, Shaw probably saw O'Flaherty the way he saw Christy, especially in that Christy in getting away from his home gains confidence, for a while, from Pegeen, which Christy even identifies as "knowledge" (*Playboy*, 100). Also, as Christy turns the tables on his father and bullies him at play's end, O'Flaherty pushes his mother away into the house at his play's end, essentially bullying her who had bullied him. In fact, the argument between O'Flaherty's mother and Teresa, as well as O'Flaherty's echoing Christy, recalls Pegeen's speech near *Playboy*'s end: "I'll say a strange man is a marvel with his mighty talk; but what's a squabble in your backyard and the blow of a loy, have taught me that there's a great gap between a gallous story and a dirty deed" (*Playboy*, 144). Shaw turned the backyard squabble behind the shebeen into a vocal squabble before the landlord's front door, democracy for peasant and landlord, and subtly connected O'Flaherty's gallous story of killing German soldiers at recruiting rallies to Christy's false tale of killing his father. Shaw was not undermining the heroism of killing in war, but rather the bragging about killing for recruitment. But *Playboy* was not the only Synge play Shaw used in 1915.

The most significant Syngean elements that Shaw employs in *O'Flaherty V.C.* are from *In the Shadow of the Glen*, the play that first engaged Shaw in Irish theatre. And by 1912, not only was *Shadow* frequently in the Abbey's repertoire, it was often performed by the Abbey in its music hall bookings in the London Coliseum. When Teresa questions O'Flaherty about the gold chain he gave her and about his pension, she appears much the same as *Shadow*'s Michael Dara, who, thinking Nora's husband dead, counts the money he thinks is now hers and states his intent to marry her. The petty greed is the same, and as in *Shadow* (as well as in *Playboy*, between Pegeen and the capitalistic Shawn) the loveless marriage to Teresa is avoided by O'Flaherty, a marriage that would have abusively enslaved him as much as Nora's marriage enslaved her, and as much as she'd likewise have been enslaved to Michael. Escaping and avoiding the enslaving, loveless marriage was repeatedly explored by Synge, and by Shaw too, differently in *John Bull's* but not so in *O'Flaherty*. Shaw still, though, presents a dim view of Irish women, as he had in *John Bull's*, unlike Synge's strong and admirable women protagonists.[21] But by replicating the Syngean-portrayed escape from the loveless marriage, Shaw was using Synge to "Irishize" his play to further envelop his international recruitment statement within an Irish nationalized setting. There was no room in *O'Flaherty* for audience cries that the play was not Irish. The joke in this was that Shaw was using Synge, who had been attacked a decade earlier for writing supposedly un-Irish work, starting with *Shadow*.

Shaw's use of *Shadow*'s structure for *O'Flaherty* is seen in the denouements of both plays, which are reached following chaotic scenes. In *Shadow*, it comes after Dan leaps from his bed with stick in hand, threatening all. In Shaw's play, the denouement arrives after the "tempest of wordy wrath" row between Mrs. O'Flaherty and Teresa. Both scenes lead their respective protagonists toward realizing what they must do and where they must go to free themselves.

In reaching the end of Synge's *Shadow*, the Tramp relates an ideal existence and haven to Nora, offering her a life of freedom from the bourgeois values and morality that enslaved her in Dan's cottage: "Come with me now, lady of the house, and its not my blather you'll be hearing only, but you'll be hearing the grouse and the owls with them, and the larks and the big thrushes when the days are warm" (*Shadow*, 43). The idealism of this speech leads Nora to leave her husband and her drudgery. Similarly, at the end of *O'Flaherty*, O'Flaherty tells Madigan of the ideal which he craves and hence will go to in order to escape his abusive home: "Only month ago, I was in the quiet of the country out at the front, with not a sound except the birds and the bellow of a cow in the distance as it might be, and the shrapnel making little clouds in the heavens, and the shells whistling, and may be a yell or two when one of us was hit" (*O'Flaherty*, 276). O'Flaherty's speech expresses its idealism by touching on the images and sounds of nature and war at the front, just like the Tramp's speech touches on images and sounds of nature in Synge's communal idealism within Ireland's landscape. Since O'Flaherty's idealism is ironic, Shaw was satirizing

Synge's nationalized idealism as he playfully offered international war as O'Flaherty's escape from the unpeaceful domestic rural west Ireland—arguably made unpeaceful by the limited national outlook of the domestic characters. Shaw used Synge's conventions to recreate a rural Ireland, then recognized by Abbey audiences, in order to pull the audience in and then portray that Ireland as outdated folly for 1915 in favor of Shaw's prescribed international role in the war.

Shaw, of course, saw Synge's overall projection of reaching a utopian free Irish existence as excessively provincial during the Great War. To further his internationalist take on Ireland and the war, Shaw continued his satire in *O'Flaherty* of Synge's Tramp and *Shadow*'s Irish nature-national idealism through the Tramp's above inspirational speech mentioning the "big thrushes." Perhaps in Shaw's view, Shaw outdoes Synge by having a thrush sing during his play, whereas in Synge's play the audience is only told of thrushes singing (oddly contrasting Pegeen's actual boxing of ears to Mrs. O'Flaherty's threat). In his 14 September letter to Gregory about *O'Flaherty*, Shaw writes that there is an important part "played by a thrush" (*Shaw, Gregory*, 94). *O'Flaherty* opens with a thrush singing until it "utters a note of alarm and flies away" (*O'Flaherty*, 258), deliciously satirizing Synge's thematic idealism. After Mrs. O'Flaherty and Teresa are pushed into the house near play's end and O'Flaherty knows his path, Shaw's stage direction announces "the thrush begins to sing melodiously" (*O'Flaherty*, 276). The bird sings again at the very end, ironically signaling that all is well with O'Flaherty returning to war.

By drawing on *In the Shadow of the Glen* to deliver his play's ironic idealism that subtly bespeaks of the overwhelming horror of the war, but which can educate the working class, Shaw replaces Synge's message of a socialistic-leaning Irish idealism with an internationalist goal. That goal is twofold: it recruits Irishmen for the world's war, particularly laborers, while playing its satiric joke on Synge's national audience, the Dublin conservative audience that had objected to Synge's plays on nationalist terms and inhibited the development of social liberalism in Dublin. The conservative nationalists, if they missed Shaw's satire on Synge's Ireland, and on the national focus, but enjoyed the play, as they had *John Bull's Other Island* in 1907 Dublin, then the joke would have been on them. If the 1915 Dublin audience of *O'Flaherty V.C.*, which had rioted *Playboy* in 1907 for its supposed insult to Irish morality, did not riot over the Irishman O'Flaherty in the British army who does not regret his enlistment, recruits more Irishmen, and then wants to return to Britain's killing trenches rather than remain in rural Ireland, then they would not have rioted because there is no threat to Irish morality in *O'Flaherty V.C.*—echoing their pleasure on seeing *John Bull's* English Broadbent acquire Rosscullen in 1907. Therefore, *O'Flaherty V.C.* would have proven that Dublin bourgeois nationalists were bourgeoisie before political nationalists. The danger in this for Shaw, and Ireland in 1915, was that the satirical joke was in an Irish recruiting play for Britain, which was to prove extremely provocative for militant Irish socialists like James Connolly, whether the play was performed or not.

O'Flaherty V.C.'s scheduled Dublin premiere did not occur. On 12 November W. B. Yeats received a telegram from the Abbey Theatre's financial advisor, W. F. Bailey, stating that the play must not be performed. Yeats related to Shaw that Bailey indicated that the reasoning was because the British military in Ireland objected (Hogan with Burnham and Poteet, *Abbey Theatre*, 385). While Yeats was against pressing the issue with the military, Shaw wrote to Matthew Nathan, the Castle official who had asked for recruiting help from Shaw, and to Horace Plunkett for help in pressing Dublin Castle (Hogan with Burnham and Poteet, *Abbey Theatre*, 385).[22] Bailey wrote again to Yeats saying that there was danger that some might consider the play an insult to Michael O'Leary V.C.: "The title . . . raises . . . suspicion in the city which is placarded with pictures etc. of 'O'Leary V.C.'" (as quoted in *Shaw, Gregory*, 108). Fearing numerous types of disturbances against the play, Nathan wrote to Shaw on 16 November that he and General Friend, then British military commander in Ireland, believed "that the production of the play should be postponed till a time when it will be recording some of the humour and pathos of a past rather than of a present national crisis" (as quoted in Hogan with Burnham and Poteet, *Abbey Theatre*, 387).[23] As a consequence, the play was removed from the Abbey's schedule.

But while *O'Flaherty V.C.* was removed from its planned premiere, as various people involved in pressuring Shaw to pull the play failed to see its potential and the likelihood that the audience would not riot, Shaw's play was to have its dramatic effect. Most importantly, Connolly responded. Did the internationalist Shaw believe Connolly would not?

Connolly: Response and Preparation

The Dublin press coverage of *O'Flaherty V.C.*'s suppression undoubtedly maintained the play in Connolly's mind while the issue of recruitment became even more extreme for him in the following weeks. When Matthew Nathan asked Shaw for help in recruiting Irishmen for the war, he also asked Dublin employers for help. By the end of November, William Martin Murphy called on the Dublin Employers Federation to pressure military-age male employees to enlist in the British army. If workers refused, they were to be sacked. The employers met to finalize their plan, which included officials from Dublin Castle; Nathan was most likely present. Connolly wrote of the meeting in the *Workers' Republic*, "Enlist or Starve": "All the employers who locked out their workers in 1913 were there. . . . [including] Mr. Wm. Martin Murphy, ever prominent in anything that savours of an attack upon popular rights" ("Enlist or Starve," 1). Such efforts from the employers only strengthened Connolly's views that the war only served imperialist and capitalist interests. At the same time, Connolly moved on the opportunity the war provided.

By November 1915, Connolly was becoming engulfed in preparing for and propagating revolution. O'Brien recalled that during late 1915, Connolly stepped up his efforts toward insurrection and spoke to each member of the Irish Citizen Army individually. He informed them that they would soon be called to fight, and wanted no one who was not prepared to do so (*Forth*, 276). On 27 November, Connolly wrote in the *Workers' Republic*: "Should the day ever come when revolutionary leaders are prepared to sacrifice the lives of those under them as recklessly as the ruling class do in every war, there will not be a throne or despotic government left in the world" ("Conscription," 1). The comment was directed toward the middle-class nationalist leaders of the Irish Volunteers (IV), who Connolly felt at the time would never lead their followers into revolt, despite their talk of Irish independence, or needed provocation to act.

As Padraic Pearse, who with others was wrestling for control of the middle-class nationalist IV from its conservative leader Eoin MacNeill, had voiced his public sympathy with locked-out Dublin labor in 1913 while re-evaluating Synge, Ben Levitas suggests that Pearse's new admiration for *The Playboy of the Western World* led him to see it "as an assertion of the artist as visionary and a conduit of revolt that lent politics the possibility of being equally creative" (*Nation*, 242). Indeed, as Pearse saw the

Lockout as "matter for a play by Synge," he recognized Synge's concern for the poor and translated that, via his view of Synge having been crucified for "strange symbols which we . . . [do] not understand," into a Christ-like figure leading the Irish people—in all classes ("Hermitage," 146, 183). In that vein, and in Levitas's notion that *Playboy* gave Pearse the "conduit" to move from poet-playwright (and teacher) into leader of revolt, while embracing *Playboy*'s theme of relevant violence, Pearse, like Connolly, increased his insurrection propaganda. Levitas suggests that Pearse's last play, *The Singer* (not performed until after Pearse's death), presents its protagonist, the poet-teacher MacDara, as Synge: "misunderstood, crucified, redeemed" (*Nation*, 224).[24] Pearse carried this in MacDara's final speech: "One man can free a people as one Man redeemed the world . . . I will stand up/ Before the Gall as Christ hung naked before men on the tree!" (as quoted in Levitas, *Nation*, 224). Embracing *Playboy*'s relevant political violence and Synge's affinity for the Irish poor, Pearse turned his essays toward provocation and toward Connolly.

In December 1915, Pearse wrote in "Peace and the Gael" that "war is a terrible thing, and this is the most terrible of wars." While this might appear first to echo Shaw's O'Flaherty in stating "No war is right," Pearse was attempting to draw Connolly toward himself.[25] Pearse, like Connolly and Shaw, saw the Great War as an opportunity to end or lessen Europe's evils: "What if the war kindles in the slow breasts of English toilers a wrath like the wrath of the French in 1789? . . . What if the war sets Poland and Ireland free? . . . When war comes to Ireland, she must welcome it" ("Peace and the Gael," 216–217). The opportunity was emerging for Pearse and Connolly, with Shaw and Synge close by.

In January 1916, Connolly met secretly with Pearse and other radical nationalist middle-class leaders who were all members of the Irish Republican Brotherhood's military council. They included Joseph Plunkett, Thomas Clarke, Sean MacDiarmuid, and Eamonn Ceannt. Plunkett's sister Geraldine recalled years later that her brother "had been an admirer of James Connolly since the strike of 1913" (as quoted in O'Brien, *Forth*, 289). Geraldine Plunkett also recalled that the IRB Dublin leaders had initiated the meeting with Connolly because they feared he would start an insurrection before they were ready (O'Brien, *Forth*, 289). Connolly and Pearse, and the others, were now together in the commitment to relevant political violence, of the oppressed against the oppressor. This was solidified in Pearse's poem "The Rebel," written after the January meeting.

Roisin Ni Ghairbhi explains that "The Rebel" "rehearses the oppression of servile masses by 'tyrants' [as it serves as] a warning in declamatory rhetoric that . . . oppression can no longer endure and that the people themselves must act to free themselves" ("A People," 164). In fact, the poem is much in line with Connolly: "I am flesh of the flesh of these lowly" ("The Rebel," 337). Ghairbhi writes that "'The Rebel' . . . has Pearse offer witness of, and empathy with, ordinary working people who have suffered historic disadvantage" and suggests that the poem, as it does not specify Ireland, connects to Connolly's "international socialism," which was now feeding Connolly's nationalized socialism ("A People," 166, 183). The ideological coming together of Connolly and Pearse would be provocative.

The result of the two-day IRB meeting with Connolly was a planned insurrection at Easter in the coming April. Due perhaps to their admiration for Connolly, or his persuasiveness, Connolly was made an IRB member and placed on the military council, and it was decided that Connolly would be commandant of all insurgent forces in Dublin, the ICA and the IV. Connolly had established a voice for labor and socialism within the insurrection's leadership, believing that if the insurrection was victorious and a socialistically just republic established, then socialism would arise throughout Europe (Metscher, "James Connolly," 141). Connolly and Shaw were distantly apart in their use of the Great War, as the former now consorted with Synge-inspired Pearse.

Shortly after conservative, non-revolutionary nationalists rioted against *The Playboy of the Western World*'s premiere, Synge wrote an essay that remained unpublished for decades: "Can We Go Back into Our Mother's Womb?" As Connolly had publicly criticized middle-class nationalists prior to his January meeting with IRB leaders for being hesitant to lead and act, Synge had done similar in 1907: "A hundred years ago Irishmen could face a dark existence in Kilmainham Jail, or lurch on a halter before a grinning mob, but now they fear any gleam of truth. How the mighty have fallen!" ("Can We," 213).[26] Continuing, Synge longed for someone to lead the Irish to move beyond voiced bourgeois and self-serving morality as expressed by those like by Arthur Griffith, who had led the protests against Synge's plays and later called on British soldiers to act against striking Irish workers. Synge wrote, prophesying, willing: "It will not be long—we will make it our first hope—till some young man with blood in his veins, logic in his wits and courage in his heart, will sweep over the backside of the world. . . . [He] will teach Ireland again that she is part of Europe, and teach Irishmen that they have wits to think, imaginations to work miracles, and souls to possess with sanity. He will teach them there is more in heaven and earth than the weekly bellow of the Brazen Bull-calf and all his sweaty gobs" ("Can We," 213). Was the proletarian Connolly fulfilling Synge's call? Was it Pearse in joining with Connolly—or both? Significantly, Griffith, the "brazen bull-calf," was not, despite his supposedly nationalist stance, among those in alliance with Connolly and Pearse. Griffith was decidedly against any revolt in 1916. But as the Connolly-Pearse alliance was formed, was Shaw's use of Synge in *O'Flaherty V.C.* dangerously provoking?

On 5 February 1916, two weeks after his IRB meeting, Connolly's article "The Ties That Bind" appeared in the *Workers' Republic*. While moving toward an Irish revolt to establish a true republic that would foster the rights of all classes and genders in an embracement of *Playboy*'s defined political violence, Connolly struck again at Irish enlistment, as thousands of Irishmen had enlisted and continued to enlist in the British army, especially working-class Irish. Perhaps they were discovering what Shaw's O'Flaherty had discovered, or perhaps Shaw's play was on Connolly's mind: "It is with shame and sorrow we say it, but the evil influence upon large sections of the Irish working class of the bribes and promises of the enemy cannot be denied. . . . For the sake of a few paltry shillings per week thousands of Irish workers have sold their country in the hour of their country's greatest need and hope. For the sake of a few paltry shillings Separation Allowance thousands of Irish women have made life miserable for their husbands with entreaties to join the British Army" ("Ties," 1).

Connolly's disgust with Irish laborers joining the British Army included the misery of their home life, miserable, in agreement with Shaw, as petty greed infected their class due to economic oppression. Connolly's last sentence in the above echoes Shaw's O'Flaherty when responding to his mother's greed over the separation allowance: "That's all you care about. It's nothing but milch cows we men are for the women with their separation allowances, ever since the war began, bad luck to them that made it!" (*O'Flaherty*, 274). Shared views but different solutions and approaches. Connolly's advanced response to *O'Flaherty V.C.* was on the horizon.

While Connolly was increasing his propaganda for insurrection, Helena Moloney was also building the Irish Workers' Dramatic Company, resulting in its most prolific period. Since *The Recruiting Office(r)* in early November 1915, the company was offering a production on Sunday evenings roughly every two weeks. According to ICA historian R. M. Fox, most of the plays presented by the company prior to Connolly and Moloney were non-Irish plays, presented with English "music hall songs" (as quoted in Murray, *O'Casey*, 96). However, following *The Recruiting Office(r)*, the company's plays were Irish but generally not overtly political. These plays tended to be contemporary works by popular Abbey Theatre playwrights, such as Lady Gregory, William Boyle, Rutherford Mayne, and T. C. Murray. Since Moloney and Sean Connolly acted in some of their plays, with Moloney directing, while still acting at the Abbey Theatre, one can assume the quality of productions was being elevated. Raising the level of the productions was to become a crucial part of James Connolly's efforts to implement his significant plans for the workers' theatre. Having two rising Abbey actors at hand, who were also ICA officers, Connolly was seeing his plans take shape.

In the 19 February 1916 *Workers' Republic*, Connolly ran an advertisement announcing not only the workers' theatre's production for the next night, but also announcing that the hall in Liberty Hall had been "fitted up as a Theatre to Accommodate the Huge Crowds for which the Front Room is insufficient." A "Workers' Orchestra" was now to accompany every performance under the direction of Michael Mallin, ICA chief of staff under Connolly. The heading for the advert read: "Next to the Revolution/The Greatest Event of 1916" ("Next To," 4). Connolly was readying Liberty Hall for revolution, including more prominence for the Irish Worker's Dramatic Company. Provocatively, the new theatre-space was designed as an integral part of preparations, and Connolly's advert made it quite clear that what was coming in Easter was not merely a rebellion, but revolution in which the ICA, Europe's first Red Guard that capitalists made possible and Shaw legitimized, was to play a leading role. As events began to spiral, Connolly's play *Under Which Flag?* was produced in the new Liberty Hall theatre, a reconfiguration of *O'Flaherty V.C.*, Shaw, Synge, and all.

Within days of Connolly's above advert announcing the Liberty Hall renovation and Irish revolution, the British army printed a recruiting pamphlet that used a unique call to Dublin laborers: "the Dublin slums were more unhealthy than the trenches in Flanders" (Nevin, *Connolly*, 615). This sentiment, or recruiting tactic, was repeated in Shaw's 1918 *War Issues for Irishmen*, "A Trench is a safer place than a Dublin slum" (*War*

Issues, 198). Since *War Issues* reiterated many of Shaw's recruiting strategies and ideas expressed in *O'Flaherty V.C.*, like war providing opportunity, one can argue that the February 1916 British army pamphlet got the "slum" tactic from the "poster-text" Shaw provided Dublin Castle shortly after *O'Flaherty V.C.* was withdrawn in November 1915. Clearly, Shaw did not derive the tactic for *War Issues* from the army pamphlet, and prior to the pamphlet, British army recruitment in Ireland was limited to British patriotism or avenging Catholic Belgium. While Connolly most likely could not have known that the "slum" tactic may have come from Shaw, he wrote a response to the army pamphlet in the *Workers' Republic* on 26 February that warred against British recruiting, from the army pamphlet to O'Leary V.C. and *O'Flaherty V.C.*: "You can die honourably in a Dublin slum, . . . if you die of fever or even of want, rather than sell your soul to the enemies of your class and country, such death is a thousand times more honourable than if you won a VC committing murder at the bidding of your country's enemies" (as quoted in Nevin, *Connolly*, 616). A month later, the *Workers' Republic* included the advert for the next evening's performance of the Irish Workers' Dramatic Company: "UNDER WHICH FLAG,/A New Play dealing with the '67 Movement in Three Acts, BY JAMES CONNOLLY" ("*Under Which Flag* Advert," 4). Connolly also could write a recruiting play.

In his biography of Sean O'Casey, Christopher Murray, from O'Casey's perspective of years later, writes that the Liberty Hall production of Connolly's play suggests that "the labour movement was flying under false colours" (*O'Casey*, 97). While O'Casey would himself be influenced by Shaw's work, he chose not to remember Connolly's agenda of March-April 1916.[27] Nevertheless, as *Under Which Flag?* points toward a nationalist revolt, and is not a great literary play, a close reading reveals that Connolly's socialism was intact. To appreciate this is to see the play as a response to *O'Flaherty V.C.*

In the introduction to the first publication of *Under Which Flag?*, James Moran writes that the play was "designed to counterbalance the British recruiting shows" ("Introduction," 20). Moran probably concludes this based on the play's one review, which states that the country has had a wave of "what the foreign garrison calls 'patriotic' plays designed to seduce the Irish . . . to the Pirate Empire," and suggests that Connolly's play is "of a different sort" (Sheehy-Skeffington, "Under," 4). Francis Sheehy-Skeffington, who wrote the review, was in America during *O'Flaherty*

V.C.'s rehearsals and suppression so was not as familiar with Shaw's play as Connolly. Of course, *Under Which Flag?* was different from the usual spectacle and jingoistic recruiting plays, but it was different as *O'Flaherty* was different. Connolly wrote his play, like Shaw, in the Abbey Theatre form without replacing British jingoism with Irish. The question is, was *Under Which Flag?* written with *O'Flaherty V.C.* in mind?[28] As Shaw and Synge had responded to each other, now Connolly attempted the same.

James Moran suggests that Connolly's play was influenced by Dion Boucicault's 1876 *The Shaughraun* (16). Certainly some of Connolly's attempts at humor, especially in the domestic conversations in the O'Donnell cottage, appear borrowed from Boucicault.[29] Interestingly, Synge reviewed a 1904 revival of *The Shaughraun* in which he noted: "It is unfortunate for Dion Boucicault's fame that the absurdity of his plots and pathos has gradually driven people of taste away from his plays" ("Boucicault," 398). Connolly, as Moran argues, borrows *Shaughraun*'s portrayed vehemence toward the political informer and a song from Boucicault's 1860 *The Colleen Bawn* ("Introduction," 16–17), but Connolly does not mimic the "absurdity" of Boucicaultian plots. In fact, Connolly abhorred such melodramatic plots. On 27 November 1915, Connolly published an unsigned review (which he probably wrote) of P. J. Bourke's Boucicault-type patriotic melodrama *For the Land She Loved*, damning its plot: "The play is such a terrible mixture of duels, 'jades of the devil,' climax and anti-climax, that it would be, indeed, very difficult to . . . give an idea of what it was all about" ("The Land She Loved," 3).

Moran also cites Yeats-Gregory's 1902 *Kathleen Ni Houlihan*, as I did in 1998, as an influence for Connolly's play.[30] Connolly certainly is aiming at some of the propaganda value of *Kathleen*, but excludes the allegorical aspects of Kathleen, the Poor Old Woman of the play. This was in line with Pearse, who recalled that as a child believed in the allegorical figure, "and had Mr. Yeats' 'Kathleen Ni Houlihan' been then written and I had seen it, I should have taken it not as an allegory, but as a representation of a thing that might happen any day in my house" (as quoted in Grene, *Politics*, 70). The implication is that an adult Pearse did not believe in fantasies, and neither did Connolly.

Under Which Flag? is set during the Fenian Rebellion of 1867 and opens in a rural peasant cottage. Briefly, Frank O'Donnell, one of the young men born to the cottage, opts to join the British army, as employment options are few and his brother intends emigration to America. Eventually, Frank is persuaded by the character Mary O'Neill, with help from Dan McMahon, to join the Fenians instead and fight for Ireland in a fashion true to Connolly's wartime socialism.

Connolly was a socialist theorist and trade-union organizer, and had only once before written a play, *The Agitator's Wife*, dating to his American years (Nevin, *Connolly*, 728).[31] So, as might be expected, *Under Which Flag?* is not tremendously subtle and not on a par with Shaw or Synge, but such did not daunt Connolly's attempt.[32] Setting his play in rural, peasant Ireland might not have been what one would have expected from the urbanely inclined Connolly, who had criticized writers for not focusing on the urban poor. But Connolly knew the peasant scene was one his Liberty Hall audience would recognize, as all the plays presented to them since November 1915 were rurally set. Connolly's humble kitchen opening contrasted with Madigan's door-porch in *O'Flaherty V.C.*, but the same can be said for all the non-commercial rural plays from the period, whether they played in Liberty Hall or not. The class of Connolly's O'Donnell characters is the same as Shaw's O'Flahertys. Connolly quickly establishes a scene of quiet, calm, and peaceful domesticity among the O'Donnells, the opposite of Shaw's play. It is in these moments that Connolly borrows Boucicault-like humor in the gentle teasing among characters.[33]

The opening sees Ellen O'Donnell, the mother, speaking with Mary O'Neill, the young woman who has lived with the O'Donnells since being orphaned as a child. Mary praises Ellen, "who reared me all these years when they had enough to do to rear their own" (*Under*, 106). Not only do Mary and Ellen establish the domestic tranquillity, Mary's above line establishes the generosity of the peasant O'Donnells. This is quite the opposite of the greed of Shaw's Mrs. O'Flaherty's over her old-age pension, her separation allowance, and the gold chain O'Flaherty gave to Teresa and not her. In fact, Connolly's Ellen and Mary, mother of the play's main young man and his potential wife, while not as literarily developed as Synge's Nora, Maurya, Pegeen, or Deirdre, are clearly the opposite of Shaw's petty capitalistic Mrs. O'Flaherty and Teresa. But as with Synge, there are some Irish not infected with bourgeois (and Darwinian) greed.

The domestic peace of the O'Donnell household is not threatened until Mary questions why McMahon is blind; he explains that in a previous rebellion he was imprisoned and was blinded while incarcerated. To ease Mary's fright, McMahon states: "what good does your crying, or their crying, or their cursing do? 'Tis the way of Ireland. We are always worked up over the wrongs of a man or a woman, here an' there, never thinking that the whole country is being wronged, and that until the country has its rights we will all of us suffer wrong" (*Under*, 112). Under the *Workers' Republic* subscription information, Connolly published: "An injury to one is the concern of all" ("An Injury," 4). Such a sentiment grew from Connolly's socialist theory and the play's disruption of domestic peace comes not from within the home as in Shaw, but from outside, like political and economic oppression.

Following McMahon's above comments, John O'Donnell further disrupts the domestic calm by announcing: "I'm for America, . . . Ireland is only fit for slaves. America is the place where a man is a man, a free man" (*Under*, 112). Ellen responds with the benefit of Connolly's America experience: "Always slaving for other people, . . . And do you think you will get out of that by going to America? . . . The poor of the world are always slaving for other people, always going hungry that others may be clothed, badly housed that others may live in palaces. 'Tis the way of the world in America as well as in Ireland" (*Under*, 112). Connolly's international socialism rings through, even in the socialistic New Testament reference in the above from Matthew 25:35–36, which Moran observes: "Naked, and ye clothed me" (as quoted in Moran, "Introduction," 131). Connolly's socialistic aspects of his play work to counter the socialistic approach Shaw presents in *O'Flaherty V.C.* while affirming his own. John's desire to leave Ireland, as countered by Ellen's speech, undermines and attempts to negate Shaw's portrayal of leaving Ireland as a means to educate and elevate O'Flaherty's class. Ellen's further response to John's emigration plans recall Maurya in Synge's *Riders to the Sea;* and Synge's *Aran Islands*' observation of mothers losing their children to economic realities of emigration and death from dangerous labor: "Their sons grow up to be banished as soon as they are of age, or to live here in continual danger on the sea; their daughters go away also, or are worn out in their youth with bearing children" (*Aran*, 77). Ellen states: "Leaving us, an' never to see your father and mother again. . . . 'Tis a hard cruel thing to say and do" (*Under*, 113). This nearly echoes Synge's Maurya to her last departing son: "Isn't it a hard and cruel man won't hear a word" (*Riders*, 66).

Connolly's undermining of Shaw's call for leaving Ireland to gain worldly knowledge is furthered by the son Frank, who follows John's announcement by saying he intends to enlist in the British army, in the vein of Shaw's O'Flaherty, which further breaks the domestic harmony, as Pat and Ellen O'Donnell are horrified: "I will see the world, be well taken care of, and after my time is done, retire on a pension, and come home and spend my days in Ireland" (*Under*, 113). Frank's speech envisions retiring to Ireland after the army, whereas Shaw's O'Flaherty also envisions retiring after service, but to France rather than Ireland, preferring Shaw's perceived home of republicanism: "And would you ask me to live in Ireland where Ive been imposed on and kept in ignorance" (*O'Flaherty*, 274). But as Ellen's above-quoted speech from Connolly's play suggests, conditions are the same everywhere under capitalism. At this moment, Connolly may have seen his socialism as more international than Shaw's.

As Shaw's Mrs. O'Flaherty is appalled that her son wishes to live in France after the war, Frank's father Pat is similarly horrified in Connolly's play over Frank's enlistment intentions. Mrs. O'Flaherty is presented as "only a silly ignorant old country-woman" (*O'Flaherty*, 273), and her objection to O'Flaherty grows out of her horror that he, if he marries, will marry a Frenchwoman. The objection rings of conservative nationalists' objections to anything perceived from risqué France, recalling the morality attacks on Synge's plays. Contrastingly, Connolly's Pat objects to his son's intentions mostly over the pension: "A pension is blood money got from the British government, and every bit of food that's bought with a soldier's money has blood on it, the blood of the people murdered to keep the bloody empire going!" (*Under*, 114). As some might view this as indicating pure nationalism, one must keep in mind Connolly's view that the empire was a capitalist venture solely generating capitalist wealth on a global basis by enslaving native populations. But the further contrast between Mrs. O'Flaherty wanting the separation allowance and Pat O'Donnell is clear.

While Shaw's recruiting play presents O'Flaherty's motivation for returning to the trenches, Connolly initially presents Frank's motive for enlisting, and Frank enlists prior to Scene III. Frank states in Scene I, in response to his father's objection to the army pension: "I don't see any difference in the money. It will buy as much as any other money. I notice too that the women are very fond of the men that have the soldier's money" (*Under*, 114). While Connolly had attacked in his propaganda articles such petty greed among the Irish, and admitted its existence among many Irish men and women, he touches on it in his play through Frank but not in either Ellen or Mary—the opposite of *O'Flaherty*'s Mrs. O'Flaherty and Teresa, but the same as Synge's Nora and Pegeen. But by portraying monetary greed in Frank, Connolly intellectually agrees with both Synge and Shaw, who had expressed such bourgeois greed as infecting even peasant levels. In 1919, labor (and Syngean) journalist W. P. Ryan quoted Connolly, Syngean-like, on the issue, placing blame on capitalists: "I regard the capitalist class of each nation as being the logical and natural enemy of the national culture.... Therefore the stronger I am in my affection for national tradition, literature, language, and sympathies, the more firmly rooted am I in my opposition to that capitalist class which in its soulless lust for power and gold would bronze the nations as in a mortar" (as quoted in W. P. Ryan, *Irish Labour*, 240). This was the full expression of Connolly's nationalized or nationalistic socialism, explaining not only his play in opposition to *O'Flaherty V.C.*, but also his movement toward revolution in 1916.

Strengthening Connolly's countering of *O'Flaherty V.C.*'s position, McMahon states at play's end that the Irishman in the British army is a traitor and the emigrant a deserter (*Under*, 115). The latter, of course, jabbed both Shaw and the 1903 Connolly.[34] As McMahon says: "'tis the poor foolish race that we are. Fighting for every country but our own. Ireland has many curses, but the worse curse of all is the poor amadams who takes the blood money of the enemy, and imagines that they could eat and drink at England's expense without being corrupted" (*Under*, 115).[35] While McMahon's view of British military service contrasts Shaw's in *O'Flaherty*, that Britain's money corrupts, such is partially agreed to by O'Flaherty when he condemns the separation allowance that has fed his mother's greed: "bad luck to them that made it" (*O'Flaherty*, 274). The difference is that O'Flaherty is made complete by military service, while Connolly's McMahon advocates that such service can only corrupt those like Frank.

Connolly's Scene II opens with Mary on a country road contemplating Frank but not blaming "him for wanting to see the world" (*Under*, 116). Such acknowledges *O'Flaherty V.C.*'s theme that British military service brings "knowledge and wisdom" to O'Flaherty (*O'Flaherty*, 272), while proceeding to counter such a direction. Following Mary's thoughts on Frank is her comment that she wishes she were a man "so that I could do something to see the world" (*Under*, 116). Knowledge comes to Mary as she stumbles across numerous people she recognizes, from town merchants to her neighbors, all of various classes, drilling with rifles in the woods as Fenian rebels planning for insurrection. Her observations speak of class: "I saw Matt Hegarty of the shop beyant in the town, him that has his hair plasterd down the middle, and talks polite to the gentry when they come in and keeps the poor people standing" (*Under*, 118). Mary's comments of seeing rural laborers (her neighbors) together with merchants as Fenian rebels reflect the mixed-class makeup of the coming together of Pearse's IV to Connolly's ICA in the coming rebellion. But Mary's comments also match the interclass makeup of landlords with rural laborers seen in Shaw's class-playing between Madigan and O'Flaherty in *O'Flaherty V.C.* While the British army brings representatives of two classes together, a planned Irish insurrection does the same but on a community level, according to Connolly. All of which connects in Connolly's play in its promotion of women's societal rights as Mary gains the knowledge by scene's end, through McMahon, of the consequences of informing and vows to remain silent about the Fenians she witnessed. She now possesses the means to alter Frank's enlistment.[36] Mary is a significant counter to O'Flaherty's self-serving Teresa; Mary's contrast to Teresa was as dramatic in 1916 as Synge's Nora was to Shaw's Nora in 1904. In Connolly's play, Irish insurrection, revolution, brings not only classes to an equal level, it empowers women, as knowledge makes a woman of Mary. This was Connolly's revolution.[37]

Under Which Flag?'s Scene III opens again in the O'Donnell cottage, with further testament to domestic tranquillity as the room receives neighbors for a dance. Frank enters and asks Mary to dance; she repeatedly declines. He eventually admits: "I met the recruiting sergeant today and took the shilling" (*Under*, 127).[38] At this point, all of the young men present go to McMahon, who whispers to each and they exit, except for Frank. McMahon then delivers a recruiting speech near play's end, not for the British but for revolution: "They are gone where countless thousands of the Irish race went before them, where it may be countless more will go after them" (*Under*, 128). Mary then asserts that Frank remains. Frank asks her what he should do, and Mary tells him to join the rebels, and he does. Frank goes into war for Connolly's Ireland, being sent by Mary who loves him, which is Connolly's portrayed opposite of what sends Shaw's O'Flaherty back to Britain's trenches. Irish insurrection, not a British uniform, makes a man of Frank.

The very title *Under Which Flag?* obviously poses the question of allegiance to Liberty Hall's March 1916 audience. It is a title that speaks of the dilemma facing most of Dublin's laborers at the time, as it offered class and gender equality in opposition to the individual elevation of *O'Flaherty*

V.C. And Shaw's argument, which *Under Which Flag?* challenges, namely, the argument of educating the laboring class by encouraging them to enlist in the British army and go abroad, was not featured in mainstream recruiting plays that sought to appeal to British patriotism, but was the point of *O'Flaherty V.C.* Connolly, who had some access to Shaw's play through actors Helena Moloney and Sean Connolly, knew Shaw's play enough to attempt his countering. While we know James Connolly read much and attended the Abbey Theatre, we cannot know for certain he was aware of the connection between the works of Shaw and Synge. But intriguingly, as Shaw had borrowed O'Flaherty's last name from Synge's *Playboy* and made the name more Irish and pagan by changing Flaherty to O'Flaherty, Connolly, for his character McMahon, also borrowed a prominent last name from *Playboy*, Mahon, and similarly made it more Irish-pagan as McMahon. Further indication that Connolly wrote his play in response to Shaw's is found in a 29 December 1915 letter, only weeks after *O'Flaherty* had been suppressed, from Connolly to Winifred Carney, his ITGWU secretary who typed most of his work asking: "Have you heard yet from McMahon?" (*Between Comrades*, 539). Seemingly, Carney was either awaiting a handwritten draft *Under Which Flag?* or was in the process of typing it.[39] But the question now is whether Connolly's play was antagonistic to the majority of its audience when premiered?

While Connolly pursued an aggressive nationalized approach throughout his role as socialist revolutionary agitator, it would seem unlikely he would change tactics with *Under Which Flag?*, staged a month before the revolution he was now planning. In February, when the refurbished hall in Liberty Hall was opened as the workers' theatre, Connolly reportedly addressed the audience from the stage.[40] It was an audience that had, prior to November 1915, been accustomed to non-Irish plays, and after November, been offered Irish plays, but not radical plays. When Connolly addressed the February audience in an "uncompromising mood," he told them from then on, "they could either join in with the dramatic and social activities that suited the rebellious aims of the Citizen Army or get out" (Moran, "Introduction," 21). Yet based on the *Under Which Flag?*'s only review when premiered, it was noted that "the play had struck the right note to appeal to their [the audience's] tastes and sympathies" (Sheehy-Skeffington, "Under," 3). While the review was propaganda in its own right, it appears that Connolly may have attracted the audience he wanted in the seats of Liberty Hall, through his usual tactic, therefore his immediate audience received what it wanted. This suggests that we must consider *Under Which Flag?* as we had Wilson's 1912 *Victims*: that, despite its revolutionary rhetoric, Connolly's play was not antagonistic to its audience. But if we contextualize *Under Which Flag?*, which we must given its circumstances, we have to begin with its scheduling, roughly two months after Connolly and radical IV leaders set a date for insurrection. Connolly and Pearse had a pre-insurrection strategy of provoking the British into attempting a limited suppression of rebellious activities, believing that such a British move would mobilize great sympathetic support from the Irish populace in Ireland and beyond.

The beginning of the pre-insurrection strategy was most likely the *Workers' Republic*'s February announcement of the new Liberty Hall Theatre, as the "most exciting event of 1916 except for revolution." Not only was such blatant, it was outrageous, in that Connolly and his co–insurrection leaders knew they were being heavily watched by police detectives. Their movements and all their writing were scrutinized. And February 1916 was less than a year since Sheehy-Skeffington had been arrested for words the government found seditious. When the nationalist paper *The Gael* printed an inflaming article in March 1916, the British decided to act, ordering the paper seized by sending DMP officers raiding newsagent shops. The ITGWU's cooperative society, adjacent to Liberty Hall, was raided. When Connolly discovered the police were without a warrant, he produced a pistol and ordered them out (Nevin, *Connolly*, 619). Connolly then provokingly called the ICA to mobilize, which it did, with members leaving work to protect Irish labor's voice, the *Workers' Republic*'s press (A. Matthews, "Vanguard," 30). The next *Workers' Republic* printed an account of the raid on and defense of Liberty Hall, citing a Belfast paper's report that the British military were planning an attack on Liberty Hall, but decided against it in consideration of the ICA's show of force (Nevin, *Connolly*, 620). Most likely the British military realized such a raid would have made them the aggressors and the ICA legitimate defenders of free speech. The fallout would have been great, significantly harming their recruitment efforts in Ireland, which their war effort now desperately needed for its survival. In the same *Workers' Republic* issue appeared the advert for Connolly's play, naming him as the author, which went against the paper's tradition of not naming playwrights. That too was provocative, given Connolly's high profile with British authorities. Undoubtedly, DMP detectives attended the performance and reported to Dublin Castle.

A few days later on 31 March, following *Under Which Flag?*'s premiere, Pearse published his last pamphlet, *The Sovereign People*. Pearse boldly defined his ideal free Irish nation: "Every man and every woman within the nation has normally equal rights. . . . No class in the nation has rights superior to those of any other class. No class in the nation is entitled to privileges beyond any other class" (*Sovereign*, 338). In thoroughly aligning himself to Connolly, Pearse directly wrote of the coming rising: "This destruction *is* creation . . . whenever you see a greedy tyranny (constitutional or other) grinding the faces of the poor, join the battle. . . . But the day . . . is here, and you and I have lived to see it" (*Sovereign*, 368, 372). Pearse's pamphlet, like Connolly's increasingly seditious *Workers' Republic* articles, the defense of Liberty Hall, the premier performance of Connolly's play, made very clear that the coming insurrection was to be a political and social revolution. This was not lost on W. P. Ryan, who noted in 1919 that *The Sovereign People* proves "that Pearse was Connolly's comrade" and their revolution was "the social and mental gospel of the workers who advance, and of those who help them advance, towards the sovereign and co-operative nation" (*Irish Labor*, 247). And the publication of Pearse's pamphlet was also part of the provocation aimed at the British system in Ireland.

This provocation was Connolly's aggressive, antagonistic national approach in *Under Which Flag?* as the play functioned in the theatre of grand propaganda and, as such, its real or full audience was the British government's Irish administration, its army in Ireland, its recruitment efforts, its police, and its capitalist system—all of which warred against Irish labor. As *Under Which Flag?* called on Frank O'Donnell's class to fight in Ireland's revolution rather than in Britain's army, it directly confronted British authorities in order to provoke their response, just as Synge had provoked his audience nine years earlier, but this time all had been magnified, as Synge's definition of relevant violence and his prophesy of erupting Ireland was at hand. The grand propaganda theatre that the premiere of *Under Which Flag?* played for, was 1916 Ireland, and the socialistically free Irish Nation awaiting its birth.

In considering Connolly's strategy we must consider the consequences had the British raided Liberty Hall and seized the *Workers' Republic*'s printing press while the ICA was out in force, or, more to the point, had raided Liberty Hall during the performance of *Under Which Flag?*[41] The revolution would have started, far surpassing Yeats's call for police during

The Playboy of the Western World's premiere, and justice would have automatically been on Connolly's side, as the raid would have been a magnification of DMP officers batonning hundreds in 1913. Since the British, perhaps, wisely refrained from raiding Liberty Hall in March 1916, Connolly increased the pre-insurrection efforts—and now turned to Shaw.

Shaw and Final Preparations

Contributing to the expanding of propaganda performance in which *Under Which Flag?* participated was Sean Connolly in the role of McMahon. Connolly, a rising Abbey Theatre actor, had emerged as an important ICA captain who was also known to police. The play's review noted that Sean "devoted particular loving care to the characterisation of . . . [McMahon], who stands out as the unforgettable figure of the piece. . . . in the hands of Sean Connolly it produced a profound impression on the audience" (Sheehy-Skeffington, "Under," 2).[42] Sean's sister, Katie Barrett, played Ellen O'Donnell and was also in the ICA. If the production's ICA presence was not blatant enough for the police detectives who paid their one-penny admission to see the play and watch the audience, the evening also included music by the Workers' Orchestra under ICA chief of staff (second-in-command) Michael Mallin, and a solo performance by ICA bugler William Oman.[43] In addition, Liberty Hall was still guarded by armed and uniformed ICA soldiers whom audience members had to pass when entering. Adding to such provocation was Sheehy-Skeffington's review of *Under Which Flag?* in the 8 April *Workers' Republic*.

While known as a pacifist, Sheehy-Skeffington, in writing his review, played his part in the propaganda provocation-theatre: "[the play] breathes the true spirit of patriotism and at the present time nothing could be healthier for the youth of Ireland than the lesson it teaches" (Sheehy-Skeffington, "Under," 2). The review played more toward Connolly's provocation agenda than its author's pacifism. After all, Sheehy-Skeffington was decidedly committed to Connolly's revolution, and may have been for months if not years. While lecturing in America in late 1915, he had raised funds used for arming Irish rebel forces (Levenson, *With Wooden*, 197). Sometime in April 1916, Connolly assigned Sheehy-Skeffington to "establish a Citizen's committee that might form the basis for a civilian government in the event of the revolution's victory" (Yeates, *Lockout*, 572).[44] In this capacity, Sheehy-Skeffington wrote a letter to Shaw on 7 April, two and half weeks prior to Irish revolution and one day before his review of Connolly's play appeared.

Despite Shaw's public position on the war and Ireland, Sheehy-Skeffington and Connolly knew Shaw as a socialist, perhaps not their type, but still a socialist. While speaking in Boston in November 1915, Sheehy-Skeffington remarked that he considered Shaw "perhaps the most distinguished living Irishman" (as quoted in Levenson, *With Wooden*, 199). Sheehy-Skeffington and Connolly remembered Shaw's public support of Irish labor in 1913 and his legitimizing the ICA's formation; they remembered his 1915 letter supporting Sheehy-Skeffington which he allowed Connolly to publish. Now they sought Shaw's help in London. Specifically, Sheehy-Skeffington wrote Shaw about a letter he had written and failed to publish in the London press. He enclosed this letter and asked Shaw to get it published. The letter reported that rebel leadership in Dublin believed that the British military was about "to disarm them and seize their quarters" (Shaw, "Neglected," 122). The letter anticipated a British document, known as the "Castle Document," which contained British plans to disarm rebel forces, arrest leaders, and occupy buildings such as Liberty Hall. This document was leaked by rebel leaders in Dublin on Wednesday, 19 April, almost two weeks after Sheehy-Skeffington wrote to Shaw. The Castle Document, long believed by many a forgery, was possibly instead, as Charles Townshend argues, based on a genuine British plan but "sexed up" by rebel leaders for greater effect (*Easter*, 133). Undoubtedly, Sheehy-Skeffington was privy to the pre-insurrection strategy, which in April included the leaking of the "document" to the London and Dublin press. In fact, this leaking was crucial to the strategy, which was designed to justify insurrection *and* generate advanced support and sympathy among the Irish in Ireland and Britain in advance of the actual fighting. The IV's official leader, the conservative Eoin MacNeill, issued orders to the IV once he heard of the document: "be prepared for defensive measures" (as quoted in Townshend, *Easter*, 132). The rebels needed to prevent MacNeill, who opposed starting an insurrection but not defending themselves, from interfering with their plans. Additionally, the Castle Document, or more to the point, Sheehy-Skeffington's letter anticipating it, was part of the provoking strategy.

If Shaw had published Sheehy-Skeffington's letter in mid-April, he would have once again legitimized the ICA and its allies. The leaking of the document would have simultaneously further provoked the government and prevented it from acting, all while portraying the government as the aggressor against civil liberties. All the government could have done was to deny its accuracy, which it did when the document was released on 19 April. But the earlier leaking would have been a major development in the propaganda theatre and presumably would have attracted more Irish in Britain to actively support the revolution. But Shaw, doubting the document was real, elected not to act when he received Sheehy-Skeffington's request. The bid for Shaw's direct involvement in Irish revolution was unsuccessful, at least in part.

In the 8 April 1916 *Workers' Republic*, a day after Sheehy-Skeffington's letter to Shaw, Connolly's article "The Irish Flag" appeared. Connolly announced that the "ICA had resolved . . . to hoist the green flag of Ireland over Liberty Hall" ("Irish Flag," 1). Connolly lamented how Irishmen in the present, and for centuries, had fought in the British army for Britain's gains at the cost of Irish and native oppression within the empire. He asked, "Where better could that flag fly than over the unconquered citadel of the Irish working class?" ("Irish Flag," 1). Then Connolly attempted to redefine Ireland away from the petty Irish users Synge had attacked and Shaw ridiculed for oppressing their fellow Irish: "We are out for Ireland for the Irish. But who are the Irish? Not the rack-renting, slum-owning landlord; not the sweating, profit-grinding capitalist; not the sleek and oily lawyer; not the prostitute pressman—the hired liars of the enemy. Not these are the Irish upon whom the future depends. Not these, but the Irish working class, the only secure foundation upon which a free nation can be reared. . . . The cause of labour is the cause of Ireland, the cause of Ireland is the cause of labour" ("Irish Flag," 1). Provocation was nearly complete.

On 16 April, the flag of Irish revolution was raised on Liberty Hall as the ICA stood in formation. The reportedly large crowd assembled where locked-out workers had been addressed nightly by ITGWU leaders in 1913. The actual hoisting of the flag on Liberty Hall's roof was by a teenage union and ICA member, Molly Reilly, who was depicted in the *Workers' Republic* as standing against the prevailing rumors, "Field guns were to level the Hall with the ground, all avenues of approach were to be occupied by masses of [British] troops" (Connolly, "Labour in Ireland," 2). The ceremony was obviously a continuation of *Under Which Flag?*, solidifying the play's crucial role in the overall grand theatre of the pre-insurrection strategy.[45] Yet by this time, the British administration, essentially in the hands of Shaw's acquaintance, Undersecretary Sir Matthew Nathan, had had enough.

Following the delayed leak of the Castle Document, Nathan began to conclude, based on police and military intelligence reports, that action was necessary. The Lord Lieutenant of Ireland, Lord Wimborne, agreed and insisted on 20 April that one hundred rebel leaders be arrested and Liberty Hall raided. Nathan awaited the chief secretary's approval, who was in London (Nevin, *Connolly*, 637). However, while Nathan waited, the damage was done by Eoin MacNeill, once he learned of the planned insurrection for Easter Sunday, which was to occur throughout the country. He ordered that the scheduled IV maneuvers be canceled.[46] In the confusion over conflicting orders, the radical IV leaders and Connolly met on Sunday. They decided they had no choice but to go ahead, even while knowing that MacNeill's intervention would cost them most of their numbers. They hoped that once the fighting commenced, the majority would join in. The revolution would start on Easter Monday. But once conservative bourgeois Ireland intervened at the crucial moment, rather than the British, all that remained for revolution leaders was the relevant symbolic violence of the oppressed against the oppressor, as depicted in *The Playboy of the Western World*, written in response to Shaw's *John Bull's Other Island*. Shaw's direct and indirect provocation in Irish socialistic revolution was at hand.

"Revolution de Luxe"

On the morning of the revolution, Connolly told William O'Brien, who had assisted in final preparations, "We are going out to be slaughtered." O'Brien asked, "Is there no chance of success?" The reply: "None whatever" (as quoted in Morrissey, *O'Brien*, 103). Similarly, as Captain Sean Connolly led his ICA unit of fourteen men and nine women to pin down Dublin Castle, Connolly told the actor, "Good luck, Sean. We won't meet again" (as quoted in Nevin, *Connolly*, 638). The defeatism was due to MacNeill's interference, which seriously reduced the rebel ranks in Dublin and all but negated the insurrection outside Dublin. Connolly had studied, written of, and lectured on street fighting, which he mainly deduced from the 1905 Russian Revolution. Being without machine guns and artillery, the the rebels planned to impede British advances with barricades and dominate streets with rifle fire from multiple positions. With limited people, Connolly now knew there was little hope for success. Still, Connolly's revolution was under way and Irish labor had a real voice. When the revolution began, not only did Connolly command Dublin forces, he was also vice-president of the provisional government of the Irish Republic proclaimed on 24 April 1916.

The republic's proclamation carried Connolly's imprint: "We declare the right of the people of Ireland to the ownership of Ireland. . . . The Republic guarantees religious and civil liberty, equal rights and equal opportunities to all its citizens, . . . cherishing all the children of the nation equally, and oblivious of the differences carefully fostered by an alien government" ("Easter Proclamation," 99). The proclamation was printed in Liberty Hall by the ITGWU (DeBurca, *Irish Struggle*, 98). Connolly, like Shaw, saw real democracy as the goal.

Once news spread of the revolution's start on Easter Monday, Synge's radical friend Stephen MacKenna rushed to Dublin's General Post Office (GPO), the rebel headquarters. MacKenna was seen staring at the rebels with admiration and uttered "at last" (as quoted in Dodds, "Memoirs," 51).[47] MacKenna, then nearly crippled with arthritis, returned the next day to offer his services to the revolution (Dodds, "Memoirs," 51–52). Perhaps MacKenna recognized the continuing process against stifling bourgeois values that went back to Parnell's 1890 ruin as he faced the GPO with the Imperial Hotel, the crowning business of William Martin Murphy, looming behind him on O'Connell Street. If MacKenna understood the socialistic stamp on the revolution, or Easter Rising as it is known, he was not alone. More and more historians are recognizing this as well, from Peter Berresford Ellis in 1972 to Ann Matthews in 2008. The latter writes: "In Dublin on Easter Monday 1916 . . . the Irish Citizen Army were a major force" ("Vanguard," 35).

Sean Connolly's ICA unit commenced the combat by attacking Dublin Castle.[48] While the Castle was the center of British rule in Ireland, attacking it was intensely symbolic, but Connolly's unit was too minuscule to capture and hold it. When the DMP officer at the Castle gate tried to block the unit's advancement, Sean Connolly shot him dead, the revolution's first casualty.[49] Europe's first Red Guard was in action, as the unit then occupied buildings, like Dublin's City Hall, across from the Castle in order to control movements in or out. But while on the City Hall's roof, Sean Connolly was killed by a British sniper, the first rebel casualty. He died with Helena Moloney beside him. While this was the first instance of women in modern combat, the words of *Under Which Flag?* had reached a chilling reality that is not directly considered in the play, nor is it in *O'Flaherty V.C.* James Connolly and his fellow rebel leaders had reached the point of being as reckless with their followers as British generals were with their ranks. The difference was that Connolly was as reckless with himself as he was with his ranks; while checking barricades late in the week, he was severely wounded. The Easter Irish theatre was under way.

Under Connolly's directive, Thomas MacDonagh's command occupied Jacob's Biscuit Factory, where owners were especially vicious toward labor during the 1913 Lockout. MacDonagh had stood on O'Connell Street to see Larkin defy a police ban on 31 August 1913 and witnessed the police baton attack that followed. Eason's Stationery, another site of bitter dispute in 1913, was occupied by rebels on Easter Monday. The large ICA unit under Michael Mallin and Constance Markievicz seized St. Stephen's Green, a park that epitomized bourgeois Dublin. William Martin Murphy's *Irish Independent* newspaper office was occupied, as was his grand Imperial Hotel. While the new Irish Republic's flags flew over most of the occupied buildings, Connolly flew the ICA flag, the Plough and the Stars, over Murphy's Hotel: "Connolly plainly derived intense satisfaction from seeing the socialist banner atop this palace of capitalism" (Townshend, *Easter*, 160). That the British understood the socialist element in the rising lies in their response. One of their first objectives was to shell Liberty Hall.

Many leading Irish socialists were killed during the Rising, like Peadar O'Maicin of the Painters' Society (union). So, too, were many middle-class militant nationalists. However, a British Army patrol continues to draw attention. Under the command of an Irish officer in the British army of fifteen years' service, Captain Bowen Colthurst, the patrol consisted of forty soldiers. It was formed after Francis Sheehy-Skeffington was arrested at a British military checkpoint on Easter Tuesday evening and ordered to be held by the British army command, who well knew of him (Caulfield, *Easter*, 153). While in custody, Colthurst interrogated him. Then Colthurst led his patrol to search the premises of Alderman James Kelly's tobacco shop, taking Sheehy-Skeffington along as a "hostage." Townshend suggests that Kelly's shop was a mistake, that the patrol's real objective was pro-labor Alderman Tom Kelly, who had released the Castle Document on the preceding Wednesday (*Easter*, 193). However, in the shop two journalists with labor ties were seized.[50] During the next morning, Colthurst ordered Sheehy-Skeffington and the two journalists executed by a firing squad. British command at first affirmed that Colthurst's execution decision was "carried out with discretion" (Foy and Barton, *Easter*, 190). Colthurst then took his patrol back onto the streets, where they located Richard O'Carroll, head of the Bricklayers Union that had supported the ITGWU in 1913. Once identified, Colthurst shot O'Carroll and had his body dragged into the street. He died ten days later.

As Sheehy-Skeffington was such a public figure and his wife Hannah argued relentlessly for an inquiry into her husband's death, which was granted, the British army began a cover-up and sacrificed Bowen Colthurst (Foy and Barton, *Easter*, 191). He was court-martialed and found guilty but insane. Released after one year, he emigrated to Vancouver, where he enjoyed a banking career without insanity (Henry, *Supreme*, 133). It appears that Shaw also believed in a British cover-up, that the shooting of Sheehy-Skeffington was perhaps actual army policy. On 22 August 1916, Shaw wrote to Lady Gregory: "I refuse flatly to put foot in Ireland without a safe conduct from the present Terrorist Government. If I do not fear the fate of Skeffington, at least I can pretend to" (*Shaw, Gregory*, 122).

The British military's first releases to the London press indicated belief that the rising was socialistic. The *Illustrated London News* on 6 May 1916, with a photograph of the ruins of Liberty Hall, reported that James Connolly was "the chief rebel leader, and a Syndicalist Labour Agitator" ("Sinn Fein," 581, 584). By the end of the rising, on Saturday, 29 April, the Irish socialist and radical leaders who agreed with Connolly's direction were either dead or awaiting death, like Connolly.

On 28 April, the intense artillery shelling of the GPO and O'Connell Street forced the rebel leadership to evacuate, but streets were covered by machine guns and efforts to escape the area became impossible. Still, Connolly managed high spirits for his troops while lying on a bed after his ankle was shattered by a British bullet, trying to direct the fighting: "A morning in bed, a good book to read, and an insurrection, all at the same time. It's revolution de luxe" (as quoted in Nevin, *Connolly*, 655).[51] The white flag of surrender was carried from the last rebel headquarters by ICA nurse Elizabeth O'Farrell. Following military courts-martial, the radical leaders were condemned to death. The symbolic relevant violence of *Playboy* had been emulated during Easter Week, and Shaw again looked to Dublin and Connolly.

Epilogue

Shaw and Execution

When the weeklong Irish revolution collapsed and the details of street fighting poured into London's papers, Shaw published Sheehy-Skeffington's 7 April letter in the *New Statesman* on 6 May, with his own letter, "Neglected Morals of the Irish Rising." Sheehy-Skeffington's letter indeed anticipated the Castle Document, warning of British militarism set on disarming Pearse's IV and the ICA: "military authorities are pursuing their Prussian plans in Ireland unobserved by the British public" (as quoted in Redmond-Howard, *Six Days*, 94). Sheehy-Skeffington claimed the militarists wished to "slaughter" the radical nationalists and labor militias, "that their crime may be overlooked in a world of criminals" (as quoted in Redmond-Howard, *Six Days*, 95). While Shaw believed the supposed British military plan before the Rising was untrue, he now used the letter and his own letter in an effort to counter the British military's reprisals he believed could become unrestrained.

In "Neglected Morals," Shaw pondered: "Will Punch give us a cartoon of Mr. Connolly, in the pose of the King of the Belgians, telling his conqueror that at least he has not lost his soul by his desperate fight for the independence of his country against a foe ten times his size? Probably not; and yet the parallel is curiously close in everything but the scale of the devastation and the number of deaths" ("Neglected," 120). Shaw noted that the death toll may rise if "the Government gives way to any clamor" for excessive punishments from those "who were so shocked by" such when German occupiers did the like in Belgium ("Neglected," 120). Shaw had turned the hypocrisy of British patriotic war fever to the present Irish scene.[1] Now Belgium had a new relevancy for Ireland.

Shaw furthered his call for British leniency by calling attention to the fact that "these men were patriotic according to their own lights, brave according to our own lights, public in their aims, and honorable in their Republican political ideal" ("Neglected," 123). Shaw even alluded to his own efforts for Irishmen to fight the war in Britain's army on the side of republican France: the rebels' "ideal cannot be insulted without insulting our ally France" ("Neglected," 121).[2] Having been a reasoned voice against nationalist-patriotic fever for decades, Shaw was careful to depict the rebels as republicans in trying to counterbalance British patriotic fever that was being loosed in Dublin.

Unbeknownst to Shaw when "Neglected Morals" was published, but anticipated, eight rebel leaders had already been executed by British firing squads. The British reprisals Shaw sought to forestall were under way with ferocity. After the first three executions, Pearse, MacDonagh, and Clarke on 3 May, even Prime Minister Asquith was "surprised" at his military's speed (as quoted in Townshend, *Easter*, 279). The militarism that had killed Sheehy-Skeffington and now concerned Shaw sought to continue the fearsomeness started by its artillery barrage during the rising by now executing rebel leaders.

On 10 May, Shaw's letter "The Easter Week Executions" appeared in London's *Daily News*. At this point, twelve rebel leaders had been shot. Shaw began, exasperated by the paper's claim that "no voice has been raised" against the executions (as quoted in Shaw, "Easter," 124). Shaw wrote: "As the Government shot the prisoners first and told the public about it afterwards, there was no opportunity for effective protest" ("Easter," 124). In presenting his protest, Shaw argued: "the men who were shot in cold blood after their capture or surrender were prisoners of war, and that it was, therefore, entirely incorrect to slaughter them . . . an Irishman resorting to arms to achieve the independence of his country is doing only what Englishmen will do if it be their misfortune to be invaded and conquered by Germans in the course of the present war" ("Easter," 124).[3]

Shaw continued to chastise the British military and government, explaining that in executing the rebel leaders, those leaders have become martyrs ("Easter," 125): "The military authorities and the British Government must have known they were canonizing their prisoners. But they said in their anger: 'We don't care: we will shoot them'" ("Easter," 125). Shaw knew this was the same government that let loose the baton-charging police in 1913 Dublin, "the party which openly aims at" destroying

"Trade Unionism" ("Easter," 120). He further stated that he could not "regard as a traitor any Irishman taken in a fight for Irish independence" ("Easter," 125). But Shaw's protest against the executions was more than a protest of what had already transpired.

When Shaw wrote "Easter Week Executions" he knew twelve rebel leaders had been shot, as their names had been reported in the daily press. But he also saw that James Connolly was not among them. Shaw's protest that the rebels were POWs and not criminals to be shot as traitors was an effort to spare Connolly's life, and the lives of remaining imprisoned rebels.[4] Shaw probably knew Connolly had been wounded and may have surmised that the injury delayed execution. He did not know the details of how Connolly's attending surgeon in Dublin Castle's Hospital Ward insisted on stabilization before court-martial.[5] Shaw knew that the London daily papers had named Connolly as the main rebel leader and most likely believed that by mentioning Connolly's name in his letter, Shaw would have provoked the capitalist press into clamoring for Connolly's execution. But not all capitalist papers needed reminding of Connolly.

In Dublin, on the same day Shaw's "Easter Week" letter appeared, William Martin Murphy's *Irish Independent* editorialized: "Let the worst of the ringleaders be singled out and dealt with" (as quoted in Yeates, *Lockout*, 574). Like Shaw, the editorial did not mention Connolly's name, but did publish Connolly's photograph with the sarcastic caption: "Still lies in Dublin Castle, slowly recovering from his wound" (as quoted in Connell, *Where's Where*, 5). Murphy's paper for the next two days repeatedly demanded Connolly's execution. The general commanding the British military in Ireland, John Maxwell, agreed, viewing Connolly: "very poisonous" and "the worst of the lot" (as quoted in Foy and Barton, *Easter*, 190). As Dublin's capitalist press had crucified Synge's plays, it now sought Connolly's execution. On 12 May, with Murphy again as victor but his Imperial Hotel destroyed, Connolly was transported to Dublin's Kilmainham Prison at dawn wearing only pajamas. He was tied to a chair, as his leg wound prevented standing, and faced the firing squad, only ten paces away (Foy and Barton, *Easter*, 233).

A number of writers after the executions tried to eulogize the fallen, or sought to make sense of what had transpired in works longer than letters to the press. These ranged from Synge's friend Stephen MacKenna to Lenin. Sensitive to socialist criticisms leveled on Connolly for involving the ICA with middle-class nationalists (ignorant of the radical steps toward Connolly's socialism by Pearse and others), Lenin wrote in 1916 that such involvement was necessary for socialist revolution within colonies: "Whoever expects a 'pure' social revolution will never live to see it. Such a person pays lip service to revolution without understanding what revolution is" (as quoted in Ellis, *Irish Working Class*, 234). MacKenna, in *Memories of the Dead* under the pseudonym Martin Daly, recalled the high-mindedness of the dead rebels he personally knew. Others, such as Yeats and George Russell, eulogized the rebels in "Easter 1916" and in "To the Memory of Some I Knew Who Are Dead and Who Loved Ireland." Russell's poem included a tribute to Connolly, "Who cast the last torch on the pile" (as quoted in Nevin, *Connolly*. 704). Yet a remarkable effort of understanding the rising was compiled by a witness, L. G. Redmond-Howard.

Redmond-Howard's *Six Days of the Irish Republic* recounts events experienced during the fighting and explores some reasons for revolution. Redmond-Howard was a nephew of John Redmond, leader of the constitutional Irish Party, Home Rule advocates. Redmond had remained silent during 1913, hence he was indicted by socialists and trade unionists as colluding with capitalists. Redmond also led the recruiting efforts in Ireland for the British military, believing Home Rule would be the reward. Being of the wealthy class, Redmond-Howard was an unlikely chronicler of Irish revolution to understand its nature and some causes. After relating personal experiences, such as dining in the Imperial Hotel when it was seized by rebels (*Six Days*, 43), Redmond-Howard revealed why he was a unique commentator as he reread "during the height of rebellion" Connolly's *The Re-Conquest of Ireland* (*Six Days*, 85). Redmond-Howard asked why had the "general policy of Fabianism" not served Connolly's goals (*Six Days*, 85). He found the answer and revolution causes in *Re-Conquest*, which he saw as the testament of the basic right "to be able to live freely, that is, no longer the property of a class" (*Six Days*, 85).[6] In the work Redmond-Howard "discovered the key not only to the man but to the movement as well, in his [Connolly's] definition of prophesy: 'The only true prophets are they who carve out the future which they announce.... Every dreamer should also be a man of action" (*Six Days*, 85). Perhaps this indeed explains Connolly's and Pearse's directions, echoing Synge's words.

Synge's Christy Mahon is denounced at *The Playboy of the Western World*'s end when he is revealed not to be a man of relevant action-violence. Pegeen's rejection of him portrayed what was not desirable by the national Synge, complementing the play's portrayal of relevant violence. The violence of the rising was that which *Playboy* celebrates, and Connolly and Pearse had become the figures of action Synge had called for in "Can We Go Back into Our Mother's Womb?" But as the counterpoint radical Shaw pointed out in "Common Sense about the War," open and immediate revolution was impractical. Perhaps so, given that by 13 May 1916, militant radical Irish ideology within Ireland was in a quick-lime trench in a British army barracks yard, leaving no volatile buffers to check the growing conservatism that would dominate Ireland, leading to the advent of the counter-revolutionary Free State in 1922—with Synge's detractor Arthur Griffith as first president.[7]

Yet the battle for Irish revolution in 1916 was the very battle begun when bourgeois values ruined Parnell, erasing Ireland's last chance for peaceful independence and social reform. It was carried into socialist directions by Fred Ryan's 1899 Shaw lectures, the debate over liberalizing Irish society between Shaw and Synge as they attacked or ridiculed conservative middle-class Ireland, into the ITGWU's battles with Parnell's adversary William Martin Murphy, to Shaw's and Connolly's recruiting plays, to Connolly's revolution. As Yeats asked late in his life if his conservative *Kathleen Ni Houlihan* had sent out men in 1916 who died in revolution, we must look elsewhere for the words of radical provocation. It was Connolly's ICA that fired the first shots of the 1916 revolution, a force Shaw helped form as Synge helped Pearse to Connolly.

Shaw's thoughts and actions toward Connolly after revolution's collapse speak of understanding and perhaps admiration for Connolly and his efforts, despite differences. Shaw had imagined that Connolly and his like had "contempt for pro-British pacifists like myself" ("Neglected," 121). After execution, the surgeon, Richard Tobin, who had tended Connolly's wound, and George Russell organized financial relief for Connolly's widow and young children (Nevin, *Connolly*, 778). Among those who significantly contributed were Horace Plunkett and Shaw, with Shaw contributing the most at fifty pounds—half the amount he donated in 1912 for Hugh Lane's proposed art gallery (Gahan, "Bernard Shaw," 237).[8] All were endeavoring to assist Lillie Connolly to emigrate with her young children to America.[9]

In his *War Issues for Irishmen* (1918), Shaw once again endeavored to encourage Irishmen to enlist in Britain's war effort. He drew on Connolly, asserting the militant socialist had been no isolationist and was one who saw the common cause for human decency for all regardless of class (*War Issues*, 196). Gahan writes that "Shaw points out he had shared a platform with Connolly in London in 1913" in support of Irish labor during the Lockout ("Bernard Shaw," 215). As Gahan notes, Shaw writes that "We cannot now with any decency forget Connolly . . . I am an Irishman; and I have not forgotten" (Shaw, *War Issues*, 197). But Shaw was trying to support his effort by calling on the memory of Connolly as a socialist to do what Connolly had worked so hard against. Did Shaw think that because of Connolly's execution, his anti-recruitment efforts would be forgotten in 1918?

Yet Shaw was trying to appeal, in *War Issues*, to Irish labor-socialists— even his title recalls P. D. Kenny's socialistic appeal to Irish labor that was largely ignored in 1905 but valued by 1913, *Economics for Irishmen*. So drawing on Connolly made perfect sense for Shaw, who still extraordinarily, in *War Issues*, reconnects himself to Connolly, or Connolly to himself, through Shaw's understanding of Connolly's socialism. In a way, this mirrored Shaw's connection to Synge in *O'Flaherty V.C.*, using Synge for a cause Synge would have rejected had he been alive. But in effect, Shaw recognizes that Connolly's revolution was serving a socialist agenda, even internationally, in that had Irish revolution succeeded, Connolly believed it would have spread to other countries. Shaw wrote: "it is only through Connolly and the international solidarity that Connolly stood for that the Irish worker can be made to feel that his cause and that of the English worker is a common cause" (*War Issues*, 197). As Gahan notes, Shaw added that only in union with European and American labor can Irish labor defeat empires ("Bernard Shaw," 215). Of course, this is what Connolly had written when war began in 1914, but then lamented in that rather than unify, European labor ignored the brotherhood of workers and enlisted in the war efforts of their respective imperial and capitalist masters. It was the same equation Connolly had witnessed in 1913, when British labor leaders failed to "internationally" stand fully with locked-out Irish labor. In Shaw's 1918 effort to appeal to Irish laborers who admired Connolly, Shaw and Connolly were again together and still apart.

Shaw's gestures toward Connolly's memory had a more practical application in 1920, when ICA and revolution veteran George Spain wrote Shaw asking for socialist books (Spainneach, "Irish Socialist," 16). Gahan reports that Charlotte Shaw donated a box of books, presumably those requested, for the James Connolly Labour College in Dublin ("Bernard

Shaw," 237). Spain claimed the books remained until raiding British soldiers destroyed them in 1920–21 (Spainneach, "Irish Socialist," 16). British militarism still feared socialism in Ireland.

Shaw would continue socialistic efforts on behalf of Ireland, as in "The Children of the Dublin Slums" (1918), in which he condemned respectable middle-class charity as "only a poisoned dressing for a malignant sore" ("Children," 182). In some ways, Shaw's "Children" article complemented Joseph O'Connor and Oliver St. John Gogarty's 1917 Abbey play *Blight: The Tragedy of Dublin*. Elizabeth Mannion describes *Blight* as directly attacking the Dublin "middle-class leadership of the medical community, the Church, and Church-related charities" as part of "the social and governmental order of the city . . . complicit in perpetuating . . . [and] maintaining a ghettoized class" ("Beyond" 75). But such interaction between Shaw and Ireland dwindled, as most of Shaw's Dublin counterparts who might react into militant or confronting socialistic directions were gone and the Free State forces worked to erase radicalism from Ireland, from its history and literature.[10] Even the trade union movement splintered apart in Connolly's absence, and Larkin's return to Ireland did not reinvigorate it. Yet in the intellectual development toward 1916 militant socialist revolution that had been debated theatrically and moved into trade unionism, that had collectively helped form the radicalism of some bourgeois nationalists, was indisputably shaped, directly and indirectly, by Shaw and his provocations with Synge and Connolly.

Notes

Chapter 1. A Dublin Socialist and an Irish Theatre

1. Shaw's concern for the living conditions of the proletariat in London slums went back to at least 1888, during the frenzy over the Jack the Ripper murders. After the fourth murder, Shaw wrote to the London *Star* noting that the killer, "by simply murdering and disemboweling four women," had outdone the social radicals by raising the British middle and upper classes' attention to living conditions in East London slums (as quoted in Cullen, *When London*, 236).

2. William O'Brien noted that the ISRP's meetings only drew about fifteen out of possibly fifty members (Anderson, *James Connolly*, 51).

3. The ISRP did not admire all aspects of the Fabian Society, such as decorating their rooms for Queen Victoria's 1897 Diamond Jubilee. During the Jubilee in Ireland, James Connolly publicly staged "a mock funeral of John Bull" (McCormack, *Fool*, 151).

4. Yeats labeled *The Laying of the Foundations* a socialist play (*Yeats Letters*, III, 341).

5. No contemporary published version of Ryan's play exists, and the manuscript is presumed lost. The play's Scene II exists in Frank Fay's surviving prompt book for the play's premier. It was published in the 1970 *Lost Plays of the Irish Renaissance*, and a detailed synopsis of the entire play exists in the 8 November 1902 *United Irishman*. The synopsis and Scene II provide a sense of the whole play. Frank Fay, William Fay's brother, was an acting theorist who trained INTS actors in an Irish style he created by combining French acting with native Irish performance traditions. He was also one of the society's leading actors.

6. Given the Independent Theatre Society's 1892 production of *Widowers' Houses*, Shaw possibly wrote *Mrs Warren's Profession* in 1893 believing the society would produce it.

7. James Connolly had been born in 1868 in Edinburgh, Scotland, of Irish parents. Being from acute poverty, Connolly became a self-taught socialist theorist and editor, working much of his life as a laborer. He emigrated from Scotland to Ireland with his family in 1896 and immediately founded the Irish Socialist Republican Party. He is described as arriving in Ireland with "his library of books on socialism and Irish history"

(Morrissey, *O'Brien*, 8). Unfortunately, it is not known if the 1889 *Fabian Essays* was among Connolly's socialist books. Once in Dublin, Connolly was a constant reader at the National Library in Dublin, where he read all he could find on socialism and Ireland's past (Long, "National Library," 56).

8. Yeats notes that Shaw's fellow Fabian and friend Harley Granville-Barker attended the private reading in London on 4 May of an early version of what would become Yeats's play *The King's Threshold* (*Yeats Letters*, III, 357). It is probable that Granville-Barker also attended the INTS's 2 May performances. Even if he did not, his attendance at Yeats's reading gave him a sense of the INTS, which he undoubtedly related to Shaw. Granville-Barker acted in and staged a number of Shaw's plays for the Stage Society (1899–1904) and later at the Royal Court Theatre, which he managed with J. E. Vedrenne (1904–1907).

9. The other two plays Shaw offered, according to Yeats, were *Arms and the Man* and *The Devil's Disciple* (*Yeats Letters*, III, 302). Shaw's offer was in response to Yeats's December 1903 request to perform *Man of Destiny* (*Yeats Letters*, III, 288). Arguably, both *Arms and the Man* and *The Devil's Disciple* had foundations in Irish images. Declan Kiberd asserts that Shaw's "usual technique of substitution . . . may have reflected something of his experience as an Irishman 'set down' in England" in the character Bluntschli "set down" in Serbia/Bulgaria (*Irish Classics*, 345). There has been a long history of Irishmen fighting in the armies of other countries. *The Devil's Disciple*, on the other hand, utilized the formula of Irish patriotic melodramas so popular among the Irish in Ireland and abroad during the late nineteenth century.

Yeats's request for *Man of Destiny* was due to much Dublin interest in Napoleon regarding his connection to the United Irishmen in 1798 and with Robert Emmet in 1803. The INTS staged *Emmet and Napoleon*, "a dialogue in costume" for the Cumann na nGaedheal Celtic Literary Society Branch's Emmet Centenary Commemoration on 9 March 1903 (Ritschel, *Productions*, 16).

10. My own publications on Synge, from 1999 on, argue the liberal socialistic leaning of Synge's work, most notably in *Synge and Irish Nationalism: The Precursor to Revolution* (2002) and *Performative and Textual Imaging of Women on the Irish Stage, 1820–1920: M. A. Kelly to J. M. Synge and the Allgoods* (2007).

Interestingly, like Shaw, Synge witnessed police baton-charging a crowd. When Connolly in 1897 led a mock funeral of British imperialism, Synge coincidently, or not, traveled into Dublin on the very afternoon. He recorded in his diary: "To town—evening" (as quoted in McCormack, *Fool*, 151). Synge witnessed another baton-charge in the same year in Paris. He was struck on his head when he and Stephen MacKenna were caught in an outside café as street protestors were attacked by police (Dodds, "Memoirs," 13).

11. Land on Inishmaan during Synge's visits was owned by an absentee landlord, but given the remoteness and harshness of the land, landlord agents rarely lived on the island. When unpaid rent ran up, the landlord sent an agent with an armed escort of Royal Irish Constabulary officers to evict tenants and/or collect livestock in lieu of rent. However, the islanders collectively harassed the constables' efforts to round up livestock, and ultimately the agent would determine that since the livestock was so emaciated they were not worth taking (*Aran*, 33–40). The infrequent interference from the landlord and lack of bosses, in Synge's view, provided some of the islanders with the opportunity for

maintaining a richness to their lives of poverty that no longer existed on the mainland in the modern age. Hence, Synge could imagine that on Inishmaan were a people relatively untouched by modern capitalism.

12. Additional attacks against *In the Shadow of the Glen*, along the lines of Griffith's objection, appeared throughout the Dublin press, as in the popular pro-British *Irish Times*, which condemned the play's depiction that an Irish wife would leave her husband (Hogan and Kilroy, *Foundations*, 74).

13. Arthur Griffith, as editor of the *United Irishman* (1899–1906) and *Sinn Fein* (1906–1914), did publish numerous defenses of Synge's plays by admirers like J. B. Yeats.

14. It should be noted, however, that some recent research, as Frank A. Biletz points out, questions the long-standing perception during Shaw's and Synge's time that women indeed enjoyed a higher social and legal status in Gaelic Ireland ("Women," 63).

15. Raftery's "Killeaden, or County Mayo" also provided Synge with a native Irish precedent for a literature with socialistic-type leanings. "Killeaden," like all of Raftery's work, was written for the rural western Irish peasantry. The poem relates a utopian ideal vision of County Mayo, symbolizing ideal Ireland, as a place rich in nature, where there is plenty of work and food for all ("Killeaden," 725–26). The poem's socialistic-like utopian ideal is directly stated in its closing stanza, which speaks of land without a rent and where food and help is offered to widows and orphans ("Killeaden," 726).

16. Synge signed many love letters to Molly Allgood, his fiancée at the time of his death, as Tramp (*Letters to Molly*, 47).

17. During *In the Shadow of the Glen*'s premier, a number of audience members walked out when the performance began. They were led by the nationalist Maud Gonne MacBride. Karen Steele writes that Gonne "professed shock at Synge's Nora walking out of a bad marriage precisely when she was preparing to do the very same thing herself" ("Literary," 187). Gonne sought a divorce in France from her abusive husband John MacBride shortly after *Shadow*'s premier.

18. John Quinn was a wealthy Irish-American attorney who took an interest in Irish theatre, literature, and art. Quinn proved a great, if difficult, sponsor for Yeats, Gregory, and Synge by purchasing some of their manuscripts and securing U.S. copyrights. Quinn was also helpful to the Abbey Theatre during its first American tour in 1911–12.

19. *On Baile's Strand* opened the Abbey Theatre with Gregory's *Spreading the News*. The run also included, but not on opening night, *Kathleen Ni Houlihan* and *In the Shadow of the Glen*. Synge's full-length *The Well of Saints* was held until February 1905, even though it was ready and could have easily opened in December.

20. Yeats had his problems with many nationalists in Dublin, often clashing with them over Synge's plays staged by the INTS, and National Theatre Society Ltd., after 1905.

21. Round towers in Ireland, built by monastic settlements during the ninth to eleventh centuries, became romantic symbols of Ireland during the nineteenth century. The towers, which were tourist icons when Shaw wrote *John Bull's*, were popularized by patriotic Irish melodramas in the Dion Boucicault style. Boucicault was an actor-manager-playwright who wrote numerous Irish melodramas that were popular in England, Ireland, and America from roughly 1860–90. Such plays presented various Irish

stereotypical images which the early modern Irish theatre movement sought to counter. Shaw's use of a round tower was a loaded issue for those opening the Abbey Theatre.

22. John Bertolini's argument that Shaw wrote in rivalry with Wilde and Shakespeare was a phenomenon shared by many of Shaw's contemporary writers. Arguably, Yeats's *On Baile's Strand* was written against Shakespeare's *Hamlet*. Yeats turned to Irish mythology and wrote not of a son avenging his father's murder, but of a father who kills his son for his country.

23. The allusion to South Africa is to the Boer War of 1899–1901.

24. The Gillane family in *Kathleen Ni Houlihan* all have material goals in the play's opening moments. Michael wants the wife his father has arranged for him, the father wants the hundred-pound dowry the wife-to-be will bring, Michael's mother wants the wife who will help her, and Michael's young brother wants the pup the wife has promised. Michael turns his back on all of this when he leaves with the Old Woman to fight and die for Ireland.

25. Professors Mahaffy and Atkinson were staunch loyalists in 1899 Ireland, as was Trinity College at the time, despite the fact that notable figures in Ireland's cultural and political revolution attended the university, including Synge.

26. *Kathleen Ni Houlihan* was little more than a middle-class respectable fantasy of rural west Ireland. The Gillane family is presented in a peasant cottage yet are receiving a dowry from the family of Michael's bride-to-be in the amount of one hundred pounds. Such a sum was enormous in 1902, let alone for the Gillanes, who are set in 1798. A hundred pounds was an amount a 1902 middle-class Dubliner could understand. The hundred pounds, like Kathleen's chastity, played directly to the conservative middle-class Dubliners who fancied themselves nationalists. In comparison, the amount Michael counts in *In the Shadow of the Glen* is "five pounds and ten notes" (41).

Another aspect of *Kathleen Ni Houlihan* is the play's portrait of Kathleen as a Mother Ireland figure, calling her sons to fight and die for her. Synge's *Riders to the Sea* (1904) counters this image by presenting an Irish peasant mother who loses all of her sons to the dangerous life they must pursue. This undoubtedly was a more truthful image of Ireland in 1902–04.

27. Shaw's Nora Reilly has a per annum income of forty pounds. While the amount was minuscule for Londoners, it was a more appropriate amount for rural Ireland than the hundred-pound dowry in *Kathleen Ni Houlihan*; a further jab at Yeats's play.

28. The extended dialogues and discussions of Act I, between Broadbent and Tim Haffigan then Broadbent and Larry, also counter the INTS's 1904 plays. The society's early plays largely focused on character actions, not long conversations revealing ideas and opinions. *In the Shadow of the Glen*, for example, focuses on Nora's leaving her husband. The only early INTS play with extended discussions was *The Laying of the Foundations*.

29. When Farrell questions how he can carry three men's luggage simultaneously, Dempsey tells him he should leave something behind and get it later. Farrell astutely asks, "An whose things was I to lave behind? Hwat would your reverence think if I left your hamper behind in the wet grass; n hwat would the master say if I left the sammin

and goose be the side o the road for anywan to pick up?" (*John Bull's*, 98). Farrell is clearly playing at being the foolish stereotypical laborer his "betters" want him to be.

The dropping luggage scene was also objected to by Synge, according to Yeats's letter to Shaw (*Yeats Letters*, III, 662). Synge's objection was to the apparent stage-Irishness of the scene. While Synge most likely recognized that Farrell was playing at being a stereotype to survive, Synge probably did not think Dubliners would get the ruse. The INTS had been founded on ridding Ireland of the Irish stereotype, whether a ruse or not.

30. The Hindu's "clear-eyed" resigned acceptance of death almost echoes Maurya's acceptance of the death of her last son at the end of Synge's *Riders to the Sea*: "No man at all can be living for ever, and we must be satisfied" (*Riders*, 72). Maurya's acceptance is void of the Christian belief in an afterlife. In fact, her play's closing moments reveal Maurya turning away from Christianity, as she turns the holy water cup upside down and ends her Catholic prayers to join the traditional Gaelic keening song. Were Shaw and Synge suggesting that Catholicism, as dictated by the Church in Ireland, had no relevance as a comfort?

31. Of course, Keegan's realization of his life vision and socialistic dream coming in his moment with the dying Hindu might place him on the level of paganism in the eyes of the Church. If this is one of Shaw's conscious textures of Keegan, then it represents a subtle altering of Synge's pagan-representing Tramp.

32. Caitriona Clear writes that the "male vagrant provoked contempt [for the middle class in early twentieth-century Ireland] not only because he was a 'masterless man' but because he was not master of his own house" (*Social Change*, 138). Most middle-class Dubliners did not share Synge's affinity for the itinerant bardic tradition of Antoine Raftery that *Shadow*'s Tramp represents. In fact, the very socialistic ideals that such a wanderer as the Tramp thematically symbolize for Synge condemns the Tramp in the eyes of the conservative audience members.

33. Synge's Tramp is invited into a home in *Shadow*, but done so by Nora, who was considered non-respectable by much of the play's 1903 Dublin audience.

Chapter 2. Answering *John Bull's* Provocation—Synge

1. Molly Allgood was a leading actor with the Abbey Theatre whose stage name was Maire O'Neill. Her sister Sara was another leading Abbey actor. Molly performed Pegeen in the premiere of *The Playboy of the Western World* and, in 1906, took over the role of Nora in *Shadow*. The concert's conductor was Michele Esposito, who frequently conducted traditional Irish concerts.

2. Owen Dudley Edwards points out that Patsy Farrell's supposed fear of Keegan during the grasshopper scene reveals the then beliefs of rural Irish peasants that defrocked Catholic priests, like Keegan, possessed "neo-druidic powers" ("Shaw," 105). If so, this is further evidence of Shaw's comedic jab at Synge's portrayed thematic affinity for pagan nature-rich Ireland in *In the Shadow of the Glen*.

3. Synge's temper was corroborated by his friends and companions. Stephen MacKenna, recalled that Synge became "very angry when I disliked something he liked" (as

quoted in Dodds, "Memoirs," 12). Also, in an 18 March 1907 letter to Molly Allgood, when Synge learned that Yeats and Gregory were negotiating for an Abbey tour of America, he wrote: "I hear that they are showing... *one* [Synge's emphasis] play of mine *Riders*, five or six of LG's [Lady Gregory's] and several of Yeats. I am raging about it... if I am not getting fair play I'll withdraw my plays from both tours English and American altogether. It is getting past a joke the way they are treating me" (*Letters to Molly*, 113). An American Abbey tour in 1907 never materialized. The Theatre's first American tour was in 1911, two years after Synge's early death, and it heavily featured Synge's plays while including only one by Yeats.

4. In addition to John MacBride, there was the Irish-Australian Arthur Lynch, who also led an Irish brigade for the Boers against the British. In 1901, Lynch was elected to the British Parliament for Galway. While arriving in London he was arrested for treason, and sentenced to be hanged. His sentence was reduced to life in prison, then he was released in 1907. So while the allusion to the pro-Boer Irish veteran might have been a composite of MacBride and Lynch, MacBride's Mayo background and connection to Gonne and Yeats make him the main figure of "the man beyond."

5. Even though Holloway disliked Synge's plays, he saw them repeatedly. In 1908, Holloway attended an Abbey Theatre revival of *The Well of Saints* and recorded in his journal: "Yeats came to me after Act I with, 'Here you are again! You never miss one of Synge's plays!' in a tone of voice as if he meant, 'You hypocrite, although you rail against them!'" (*Joseph Holloway's*, 111).

6. This perception of the father is supported in the play once Old Mahon appears. He is brutish, coarse, and authoritarian. He symbolizes the Irish who mimicked British bullying military authority. This is borne out when Christy becomes like his father at play's end, stating: "Go with you is it? I will then, like a gallant captain with his heathen slave. Go on now and I'll see you from this day stewing my oatmeal and washing my spuds, for I'm master of all fights now." Christy's becoming like his father is welcomed by Old Mahon, like most fathers who relish seeing their sons follow them: "Glory be to God!" (*Playboy*, 117). Synge's characterization of Old Mahon through his coarse language, tying him to British army officers, had a direct precedent. When Synge was completing the play in November 1906, Arthur Griffith ran an editorial complaining about the proclivity of British army officers in Ireland to use foul language. Interestingly, the connections between this and Old Mahon's characterization through his language was lost on Griffith, whose attacks on *Playboy* charged that Old Mahon spoke "the language of the gutter ... certainly no man, unless an utterly degraded one, would use [such]" ("The Abbey Theatre," 4).

Also while Synge was awaking from one of his surgeries, Lady Gregory recorded his stating, "those damned English can't even swear without vulgarity" ("Synge," 86).

7. This quotation is from a letter published in Griffith's *Sinn Fein* signed only as P.M.E.K. Her or his identity remains elusive.

8. In Act II, Sara Tansey is called "the one yoked an ass cart and drove ten miles to set your eyes on the man bit the yellow lady's nostril on the northern shore" (*Playboy*, 89). Such violence has no symbolic relevance, revealing that Sara likes all violence.

9. Synge did not have a positive view of most rural Irish priests. In a letter explaining his negative portrait of the priest in *The Well of Saints*, Synge maintained that certain rural priests physically abused their parishioners (Greene and Stephens, *J. M. Synge*, 187).

10. Jimmy Farrell is an interesting balance to Shaw's Patsy Farrell.

11. Of course, Christy retains his desire for Pegeen through most of the action until she expels him from the play, even though other women desire him, like the Widow Quin and Sara Tansey. Is it possible that some or most of Christy's desire for Pegeen is because she is the publican's daughter and her father's only heir?

12. Kiberd reaches his conclusion because he contends that Christy exits the play in triumph. However, given that Christy becomes like his bullying father at play's end, to return to their grubby home and miserable existence, Christy hardly exits in triumph (*Playboy*, 117). See chapter 2, note 6.

13. Ben Levitas also sees *Playboy* assaulting the conventional, conservative middle-class audience but likens Christy to Synge (*Theatre*, 123). In actuality, Synge aligns Ireland, and perhaps himself, to Pegeen as the countering point to the infectious capitalist class embodied in Christy and most others in the play. Levitas does not see the ties between Christy and the original audience that the play deliberately attacks, nor does he see the failures of Christy that reverberate for Pegeen and Ireland.

14. While Griffith's *United Irishman* was radical when it began in March 1899, the nationalist paper became increasingly more conservative after the 1901 death of Griffith's co-editor, the working-class William Rooney. The radical Rooney did not share the conservative middle-class respectable values that Griffith fostered after Rooney's death. See Matthew Kelly's article " . . . And William Rooney Spoke in Irish" in *History Ireland*, January-February 2007.

15. When Pegeen in early Act I states that she does not want to be left alone in the pub when her father exits for an all-night wake, she is not being docile but rather is emphasizing the failings of Shawn, the man whom her father wants her to marry. Jimmy Farrell sees through Pegeen's pretense of being afraid: "What is there to hurt you, and you a fine hardy girl would knock the heads of any two men in the place?" (*Playboy*, 76).

16. Reportedly, William Fay, who played Christy Mahon in the premier run, substituted "Mayo" for "chosen" (Saddlemyer, "Stormy," 273). There is evidence that Fay consciously flubbed the line. At the time of *Playboy*'s premiere, the Abbey Theatre was hiring a company manager and stage director to share some of the duties that had been exclusively Fay's, against Fay's wishes. Synge wrote to Yeats asking that the new person, Ben Iden Payne, not be introduced to the company until after *Playboy*'s premier run owing to Fay's temper: (*Synge Letters*, I, 281). Despite Synge's request, Payne was introduced to the company during the premier run. Unbeknownst to Fay, Synge opposed hiring anyone, especially an English person, to infringe on Fay's responsibilities.

17. W. B. Yeats noted that part of the detractors' objections to *Playboy*'s portrayal of Irish women was that "Irish women would never sleep under the same roof with a young man without a chaperon," even if in separate rooms ("J. M. Synge and the Ireland," 55). This echoes Shawn Keogh in Act I, when he refuses to stay with Pegeen alone in the pub.

18. There was a precedent when Synge wrote *Playboy* with County Mayo thematically

representing Ireland, namely Antoine Raftery's early nineteenth-century poem "Killeaden, or County Mayo." This precedent was perhaps strengthened by the fact that Mayo was hard hit during the 1840s Famine.

19. Since Synge's family frequently enjoyed Kingstown, perhaps Synge numbered them among the bourgeois hypocrites. None of Synge's relatives saw his plays during his life.

20. Following *Playboy*'s premier run, W. B. Yeats opened the Abbey Theatre for a one-night debate on the play. Synge, who was ill, did not attend. He thought the debate was unwise (McCormack, *Fool*, 318).

21. Shaw would reiterate his view that *Playboy* was not an Irish play in his 1918 lecture "Literature in Ireland" ("Literature," 177). Oddly, this was a contention of some of Synge's detractors.

22. Maire Nic Shiubhlaigh had been with the Abbey Theatre Company from its inception until the end of 1905. She rejoined in 1910. She had been the first to perform Nora in Synge's *In the Shadow of the Glen*. She saw *Playboy*'s premiere as an informed spectator.

23. A battle over theatre censorship in Britain expanded in 1907. The London *Times* published a letter condemning censorship on 29 October 1907 that was signed by seventy-one authors—including Shaw and Synge. Lucy McDiarmid provides a full account of the censorship of *Blanco Posnet* and its Dublin premiere in *The Irish Art of Controversy*.

24. The belief of the townspeople at the beginning of *Blanco Posnet*, that Blanco is a scoundrel, is exactly what the people want to believe, as they want the excitement of a hanging. Synge's Christy is celebrated at the beginning of his play for being the hero the Belmullet-area characters want. On a nationalistic level, which Shaw routinely dismisses, there was much reason for wanting a hero in Synge's play. Of course, *Blanco Posnet* is more subtle internationally, suggesting that the respectable middle-class wants a scoundrel so they can enjoy, in a not-so-respectable manner, bringing him down.

25. *The Shewing-up of Blanco Posnet* did not disturb American audiences during the Abbey's 1911 United States tour, as most attention was on Synge's plays. The 1911 tour only played northeastern cities and Chicago, not the American frontier West.

26. *The Shewing-up of Blanco Posnet* was played by the Abbey with attempted American accents. Would the Dublin audience have reacted differently if played in "broad Irish"?

27. Owen Dudley Edwards writes, "It must have been a terrific moment in the Abbey" when *Blanco Posnet* premiered, as the character "Feemy was played by Sara Allgood and the Woman by Maire O'Neill, the great sisters who had created Synge's *Playboy*," Widow Quin and Pegeen, respectively ("Shaw," 111–112). Both had acted their original roles in the revival of *Playboy* the day before *Blanco* premiered. Interestingly, the role of Blanco Posnet was acted by Fred O'Donovan, who played Christy Mahon in the 1909 *Playboy* revival. O'Donovan had taken over Christy after William Fay, the first Christy, left the Abbey in 1908.

28. Any argument about whether Shaw had Synge and *Playboy* in mind when writing *The Shewing-up of Blanco Posnet* has to acknowledge that Posnet had forerunners in the Shaw canon, like Dick Dudgeon of *The Devil's Disciple* (Gibbs, *Bernard Shaw*, 260). Perhaps Synge had more in mind than *John Bull's* when writing *Playboy*. In addition to

Christy Mahon's name implying Christ, it may also recall *The Devil's Disciple*'s Christy Dudgeon, Dick's simpleton brother—signaling further Christy Mahon as a false playboy.

29. Holloway recorded, supposedly within hours of *Playboy*'s first performance, "Blackguardism" (81).

Chapter 3. Toward 1913 and the "Most Distinguished Irishman"—Shaw

1. Additional theatrical fallout from the Abbey Theatre's emergence as a theatre of ideas came in the form of numerous splinter theatres, such as the Cluithcheoiri na hEireann (Theatre of Ireland). Commercial theatres like the Theatre Royal occasionally hosted serious drama companies like Vedrenne-Barker, breaking from their usual fare of mostly light, popular entertainment. But in commercial theatres, Shaw's plays were able to cross the line into popular status while being of ideas.

2. The Scottish artist James Patterson wrote to Synge in March 1907, thanking Synge for sending him copies of the play and Kenny's *Economics for Irishmen*. Synge replied saying that he had not sent the books, but intended to send *Playboy* (*Synge Letters*, I, 312). Had Patterson associated *Playboy* with Kenny's socialistically flavored book?

3. Kenny's review of *Playboy* reflected his understanding of Synge's presentation of the rural poor and the infection of capitalist bourgeois values. Kenny also chaired the debate at the Abbey Theatre on *Playboy* that Yeats organized after the play's premier run.

4. Connolly probably attended the Abbey, so soon after returning, because he had heard much of the theatre while in America. Performing on 1 August was extremely unusual for the Abbey. Usually the theatre was off for much of the summer, reopening at the end of August during Horse Show Week. In 1910, the 1 August performance was a one-evening run, also unusual for the Abbey. The bill consisted of *Kathleen Ni Houlihan* and William Boyle's *The Eloquent Dempsey*, two decidedly non-socialistic plays.

5. *Labour in Irish History* is a socialistic reading of Irish history in which Connolly argues that Ireland's political rebellions, up to the time of his writing, failed due to their dependence on the capitalist class. He suggests that informants who betrayed rebellions had done so out of capitalist greed. Most notably, the book undermines some iconic Irish historical figures, including Daniel O'Connell. O'Connell had been a constitutional nationalist who was instrumental in achieving Catholic Emancipation in 1828. Connolly exposes O'Connell for being self-serving and capitalistic, citing O'Connell's role in suppressing Robert Emmet's 1803 rebellion. On the other hand, Connolly categorizes Emmet as a socialistically leaning revolutionary. *Labour in Irish History* was published in 1910 by the Dublin publishing house Maunsell. Maunsell was the first to publish Synge's work in book form in Ireland, starting in 1907. In 1918 it published Shaw's *War Issue for Irishmen*. Maunsell's editor was George Roberts, a friend of Synge's who had worked for a while as an actor. He was the first to play Dan Burke in *In the Shadow of the Glen*.

6. Synge had been a director of the National Theatre Society (Abbey Theatre) with Yeats and Gregory from 1905 to his death.

7. After Synge's March 1909 death, Yeats and Gregory named O'Riordan as a director. O'Riordan was an Irish-born writer, writing as Norreys Connell, who had worked as an actor and stage-director in Britain. He was also a friend of Shaw's and was a Fabian-styled

socialist. He clashed with Annie Horniman, the wealthy middle-class English tea heiress who had subsidized the Abbey from 1904 to 1910, when she objected to an Abbey actor reading a short work at a private suffragette meeting. O'Riordan promptly resigned from the Abbey. Interestingly, James Connolly wrote to O'Riordan in 1914 for help in finding a publisher for *The Re-Conquest of Ireland*. Based on O'Riordan's 8 May 1914 letter to Connolly (Connolly's letters to O'Riordan are not extant), Connolly apparently chastised O'Riordan for the idea of having Shaw write a preface for one of O'Riordan's books (*Between Comrades* 513). Connolly's reasoning is not explained.

8. William III, formerly of Orange, was a Dutch prince who married James II's daughter Mary. William and Mary dethroned James, who fled to Ireland, where he raised a Catholic Irish army to re-win the throne. William defeated James largely at the Boyne.

9. The United Irishmen was the organization behind much of the struggle for Irish freedom in 1798. Many of the United Irishmen were Protestants, hence the Church's dislike.

10. This sentiment is also consistent with Ibsen's *A Doll's House*, which helped lead a young Shaw to see Ibsen as undermining middle-class conservative respectability.

11. In 1908, Connolly admitted privately, "though I have usually posed as a Catholic I have not gone to my duty for 15 years, and have not the slightest tincture of faith left. I only assumed the Catholic pose" (as quoted in Anderson, *James Connolly*, 26).

12. Specifically, the Poor Law dealt with the poor by placing them in municipal- or county-maintained workhouses. By 1900, the living conditions for their "inmates" were horrid. It was a system that was perceived, by some, as clearly punishing the poor for being poor.

13. The Antient Concert Rooms was the site of the start of the early modern Irish theatre movement in 1899 when W. B. Yeats's *The Countess Cathleen* premiered. The building was often used for lectures and concerts. James Joyce competed for a tenor award at the Rooms in 1902, where he set his story "The Mother." Even Shaw and Synge had personal connections to the building. Shaw's mother sang there with the Amateur Musical Society ("My Motto," 70), and in 1890, Synge, aged nineteen, gave his first concert there with the Royal Irish Academy (where he studied music) (Saddlemyer, "Chronology," xix).

14. O'Brien was certainly not as well known in October 1910 as were some of the "respectable" middle-class people mentioned by the *Freeman's Journal*. Also the admission price, 1 to 4 shillings, for Shaw's lecture prevented many working-class socialists from attending. But O'Brien, being a regular attendee at theatres and concerts in Dublin from 1902 onwards, presumably could have (or would have) afforded the admission, and most definitely had to have been in attendance for Shaw's 1910 Dublin lecture. The admission charge testifies to the intended middle-class audience.

15. The Dublin press coverage of Shaw's "Poor Law and Destitution in Ireland" lecture offered commentary and paraphrasing. At best, the *Freeman's Journal* and the *Irish Times* transcribed Shaw's words in the third person, presumably from Shaw's delivery.

16. Throughout his career, Shaw jabbed religion-promoted respectability, so his jabs at Christianity in his Dublin 1910 lecture may have had no relation to Connolly's public clash with Father Kane, other than the fact that as socialists, Shaw and Connolly had the

same type of adversaries. Again, Connolly's clash with Kane probably added to the large presence of clergy attending Shaw's lecture.

17. Holloway's physical description of Shaw is reminiscent of Jack Tanner from *Man and Superman*, whom Gibbs describes as "the amiable revolutionary gentleman-Socialist" (*Bernard Shaw*, 232). Gibbs also notes the similarities, at the time *Man and Superman* was written, between Shaw and Tanner: "a revolutionary socialist who had recently married a rich heiress; and a gentleman who at this time was largely living on the unearned income from skillful investments in nineteenth-century capitalist enterprises made by his bride's father, Horace Payne-Townshend" (*Bernard Shaw*, 232). This is interesting in relation to above discussions of Shaw and Synge. Synge, in contrast to Shaw, was engaged when he died to the actress Molly Allgood, of a working-class background. Shaw fashioned himself as Tanner, made possible by the wealth of Shaw's wife Charlotte, and enjoyed a public persona, while the reticent Synge fashioned himself as a figure close to the penniless Tramp from his play *Shadow*.

18. Neither the *Freeman's Journal* nor the *Irish Times* included Shaw's remark about *The Playboy of the Western World* in their transcripts of Shaw's speech.

19. Frederick Ryan blended elements of Shaw with Connolly in an article in the January 1912 issue of the *Irish Review* titled "The Latest Crusade," in which he criticized the Catholic Church's efforts to censor the Dublin socialist and labor press for trying to better conditions for the working class ("Last," 524).

20. However, the bourgeois nationalist paper *The Leader* warned its readers in the fall of 1910 about "the danger of a socialist movement growing in Ireland" (as quoted in Nevin, *Connolly*, 384). Additionally, the Church continued to be concerned with socialism in the country, as it held a conference in October 1910 on the danger of socialist development (Nevin, *Connolly*, 384). The Church knew how socialism was growing in Europe, and neither *The Leader* nor the Church could have been eased by Shaw's lecture.

21. Along the lines of the debate between international and national socialism is *Mixed Marriage*'s character Nora. As Synge and Shaw had presented differing Noras in *Shadow* and *John Bull's*, representing social liberalizing nationalism and internationalism, respectively, Ervine's Nora is meant to echo Shaw's philosophy. When asked by O'Hara to give up Hugh for the sake of workers' unity, Nora refuses, yet she dies claiming all is her fault. This is telling on Ervine's part, if his Nora is intended to represent Ireland, as Synge's and Shaw's Noras. If so, Ervine may be placing some of the blame for the play's developments on Nora as Ireland, in the sense of selfishly wanting her men, in addition to Ulster Orange bigotry. Unfortunately, Ervine's play is not on a par with those of Shaw and Synge.

22. Griffith was vehemently anti-labor. In October 1911, Griffith attacked the labor movement under Larkin in *Sinn Fein*: "In Dublin the wives of some men that Larkin has led out on strike are begging in the streets. The consequences of Larkinism are workless fathers, mourning mothers, hungry children and broken homes. Not the capitalist but the policy of Larkin raised the price of food until the poorest in Dublin are in a state of semi-famine" (as quoted in Ellis, *History*, 191).

23. The Abbey Theatre established an acting school during its 1911–12 American tour

in order to create a second company that could play Dublin while the main company toured.

24. Wilson probably had prior theatre experience before joining the Abbey's acting school, given that his rise in Dublin theatre, if brief, was significant and swift. Wilson's simultaneous involvement in the Abbey Theatre and the Irish Workers' Dramatic Company set a precedent for later Abbey actors, who also participated in both.

25. In *A Modest Proposal*, Swift satirically suggests that the wealthy classes in Ireland should eat the one-year-old children of the poor. The pamphlet thoroughly anticipates Shaw's contention that the poor are manufactured by the middle and upper classes.

26. As much was converging in Dublin in the socialist context at this time, it was to do so without Frederick Ryan, who died in April 1913 at age thirty-nine. O'Brien noted to Connolly that Sheehy-Skeffington had authored a strong tribute to Ryan in the middle-class but radical *Irish Review* and sent Connolly a copy (*Between Comrades*, 491). Sheehy-Skeffington praised Ryan's many public contributions to Ireland, including his socialist propaganda ("Frederick Ryan," 118).

27. Given Dargan's railway background, there was definite expectation from the Dublin public for transportation leaders, like Goulding and Murphy, to fund the gallery.

28. Hugh Lane was in favor of a proposed municipal gallery being built over Dublin's River Liffey. In his 12 April interview, Shaw opposed the river location in favor of Merrion Square, on the grounds of the National Gallery of Ireland.

29. In September 1916, Ambrose Powers played Barney Doran in *John Bull's Other Island* when it was finally staged by the Abbey Theatre.

Chapter 4. Lockout—Shaw, Connolly, Synge, and the Red Guard—ICA

1. Murphy was not the only recognizable figure on the employers' side. George Jacob, chairman of Jacob's Biscuit Factory, was also a force in the Employers' Federation. Despite being a Quaker, Jacob took an extremely hard line with workers.

2. Many locked-out workers had assembled at Liberty Hall to march to Croyden Park for a day of speeches. The Croydon rally had been planned while Larkin was in hiding and Connolly in jail, by strike leaders who adhered to the police ban on the O'Connell Street rally. At least a few hundred workers still assembled in O'Connell Street to hear Larkin, as there had been confusion as to the two rallies.

3. Shaw's friend G. K. Chesterton also wrote for London's *Daily Herald*, joining the paper in February 1913.

4. Coinciding with the DRT's October 1913 revival of *John Bull's Other Island*, Casimir Markievicz resigned his co-directorship of the DRT. By late September, the Gaiety Theatre's manager, David Telford, voiced his objection to the DRT's planned revival of *Eleanor's Enterprise* with Constance Markievicz in its cast and Casimir directing. The DRT rented the commercial Gaiety Theatre for its 1913 offerings. Casimir's co-director, A. E. Ashley, sided with Telford in October. Telford cited Constance's activities on behalf of locked-out workers as being objectionable to the Gaiety's audience (Hogan with Burnham and Poteet, *Abbey Theatre*, 299). Angry with Telford's attempt to censor his production, and the disappointment of his co-director's capitulation to the capitalist

position, Markievicz resigned and publicly explained that he was driven out by capitalist pressure. Telford's sense of the Gaiety's middle-class audience testifies to Shaw's general Dublin audience, but it was this audience that now needed Shaw's insights.

5. MacDonagh's admiration for Synge's work was enhanced by their brief working relationship on MacDonagh's first play, *When the Dawn Is Come*, set in the future, with a poet leading a militant rebellion for Irish freedom. Synge accepted the play for the Abbey Theatre in March 1908, and made suggestions to MacDonagh for improving it. Originally scheduled for May 1908, with Synge directing, the play and directing duties had to be rescheduled for October, as Synge went into hospital for his last operation.

6. Russell's "Open Letter to the Masters of Dublin" was reprinted in the 1915 publication of Connolly's book-pamphlet, *The Re-Conquest of Ireland*, published at Liberty Hall.

7. Pearse ran a school for boys, St. Enda's, which offered an Irish education as an alternative to the parochial schools controlled by the Catholic Church. A sister school, St. Ita's, was later offered for girls. Larkin's son attended St. Enda's during the Lockout.

8. The use of "slum" was most likely Yeats's or Bickley's choice.

9. The other speakers during the 1 November 1913 Irish labor rally included Ben Tillett, Delia Larkin, Dora Montefiore, Charlotte Despard, Robert Williams, George Lansbury, and Sylvia Pankhurst.

10. On 4 February 1914, Connolly wrote to George Russell about getting the Dublin publisher Maunsell to re-issue *Labour in Irish History* in an inexpensive edition, but related that Maunsell agreed to do so provided he raised 37 pounds. He asked Russell for help, saying that the money had to be paid the following week, and stated that he only asked because it was for propaganda, not personal. He pledged to repay any sum within the year (*Between Comrades*, 508). The inexpensive reprint appeared in late 1914.

11. Based on the *Irish Independent*'s coverage of "Mad Dogs in Uniform," I believe the above-quoted paragraphs of Shaw's speech originally came after the speech's comments on Dublin priests and their Church's role in blocking the children-to-England plan, and right before the section on Dublin employers.

12. Captain Jack White had served in South Africa during the Boer War with distinction. His father was a retired British army general who also served in the Boer War. White's past suggested that he was from the respectable-class establishment. However, offering his services to Connolly to train the ICA was the beginning of non-conformist directions that White pursued for the rest of his life.

13. Shaw knew that the 1913 labor dispute had a national character, evidenced by his comment in "Mad Dogs in Uniform" that Irish employers were not paying workers what British employers paid their laborers. He also most likely knew that British labor unions, in the past, were not effective in Ireland. Plus, the priest dimension of the 1913 Lockout was unique to Ireland. While there were other socialists working in Britain who delivered speeches on 1 November 1913, only Shaw called for the arming of Irish labor.

14. Carson had threatened to march his Ulster army through Ireland to demonstrate and fight against Home Rule (Yeates, *Lockout*, 425).

15. Prior to engaging in Ulster Unionist politics, Carson was a successful barrister. His most famous case was his prosecution of Oscar Wilde. Indeed, the battles between the

more enlightened and the heavily conservative elements of Irish society, from Parnell to Wilde to Synge to labor to radical Irish independence, were much of the same war.

16. ITGWU workers who had been involved with organizing before the Lockout were blacklisted by employers. One such member was Rosie Hackett, who had worked at Jacob's factory. The union did what it could, which often was limited, but in this case Hackett became a union clerk in Liberty Hall. She soon enlisted in the ICA.

17. The isolation of Irish labor in early 1914 reverberated of the socialistic leaning of Synge's work. Synge's confidant Stephen MacKenna noted shortly after the 1 November 1913 rally for Irish labor, that while he did not fully approve of the rally due to a "general dislike of English fingers in Irish pies," and wanted "Ireland Irish," he nevertheless preferred it "to be just . . . therefore am . . . with the workers" (*Journal*, 137–138).

18. The Irish Workers' Dramatic Company was dormant during the Lockout, but in its aftermath, in March 1914, Delia Larkin organized a small tour to British industrial cities, such as Liverpool and Manchester. It was an effort to offer relief to women workers who were not taken back by employers (Murray, *O'Casey*, 94).

While there is little evidence of Lady Gregory's specific views toward labor and the Lockout, Gregory made some of her Abbey plays available to the Irish Workers' Dramatic Company. When the company visited Britain in 1914, Gregory's *The Workhouse Ward* was in the limited repertoire.

19. The nationalist campaign issue of refusing to welcome the British monarch in Dublin rang of recent relevance. In 1907, during the public debate on *The Playboy of the Western World* that the Abbey Theatre sponsored following the premier run, W. B. Yeats insinuated that *Playboy*'s objectors were only "so-called nationalists [since they] had their heads bowed in the dust at the time of the Royal visit." Yeats further added that during the visit he "spoke out against [the visit] when their patriots [the detractors' leaders] were silent" (as quoted in Hogan and Kilroy, *Abbey Theatre*, 152). Objections, or not, to British royal visits during the early twentieth century had revealed the hypocrisy of some middle-class respectable nationalists, which McNulty is no doubt alluding to.

20. In the famous 1928 caricature of W. B. Yeats rejecting Sean O'Casey's *The Silver Tassie*, in which Yeats is depicted as kicking O'Casey and his play manuscript out the Abbey Theatre's front door, the advert board in the background announcing the current play being performed is McNulty's *The Lord Mayor*. Curiously, the cartoon portrays a working-class playwright being booted out while an older Irish socialistic play from a middle-class writer is still in the repertoire after fourteen years. Perhaps the longevity of the latter was due to its comedy and Irish focus, while the newer play had a far more international focus.

21. *The Cobbler* also included in its premier cast a new Abbey actor named Arthur Shields, who had a socialist background. His father was Irish socialist Adolphus Shields, who was active in the 1880s and early '90s, and had invited James Connolly to Ireland in 1896 (Nevin, *Connolly*, 59). Arthur Shields enjoyed a long Abbey career, and later appeared in many Hollywood films, mostly directed by John Ford. Shields's brother was Barry Fitzgerald, who had a longer film career. Shields fought in the 1916 Rising.

22. Wilson's *The Slough* is unpublished. However, since the play was performed in Liverpool (Larkin's native city) in 1914, the Lord Chamberlain's Office has a copy of the

script used in England. Ben Levitas, in both *The Theatre of Nation* and "Plumbing the Depths: Irish Realism and the Working Class from Shaw to O'Casey," as well as Stephen Dedalus Burch, in "Historical Invisibility: The Vexatious A. P. Wilson and the Abbey Theatre," have written extensively on the play.

23. The character Anne, as well as the debased character of the father, Peter, anticipate Sean O'Casey's Dublin plays of the 1920s. Anne seems recalled in the character Mosher in *The Plough and the Stars*, while the type Peter represents is recalled in *Juno and the Paycock*. Levitas writes that *The Slough*'s "Hanlons are evidently drawing-board precursors of O'Casian invention: as riven as the Boyles; and just as are the Clitheroes, a hub of tenement activity" ("Plumbing," 143). The anticipation of O'Casey by Wilson is interesting, as there was intense animosity between O'Casey and Wilson. The two publicly clashed prior to the Lockout over the value of Gaelic to the labor movement. O'Casey objected to Wilson's expressed view that Gaelic had no practical value to labor in Ireland, ignoring Wilson's perception of the Gaelic League's bourgeois concerns, which Shaw expressed in his 1910 Poor Law speech. O'Casey's position on Gaelic decidedly placed him in the national labor and socialism camp (if not entirely among conservative nationalists), rather than the internationalist camp he later tried to covet.

Chapter 5. War and Revolution

1. Connolly's view of "armament makers" recalls Shaw's *Major Barbara* (1905).
2. Laurence and Grene included Shaw's *Freeman's Journal* letter in *The Matter with Ireland* under "Ireland and the First World War," which is the title that is cited.
3. The *New Statesman* was founded by Beatrice and Sidney Webb, with Shaw, in 1913.
4. An early British army recruiting poster in Ireland asked, with an image of a romanticized Irish Colleen, "Have you any women-folk worth defending? Remember the women of Belgium—JOIN TO-DAY" (Clear, "Fewer Ladies," 177).
5. The 9 September meeting of Connolly and radical nationalists was held the day after a limited Home Rule bill for Ireland was given "the royal assent," then postponed for the war's duration (Morrissey, *O'Brien*, 91).
6. While democracy in theory existed in Ireland in 1914 under Britain, labor politicians had difficulty breaking into rural areas dominated by capitalist-friendly political parties.
7. In January 1918, months after the 1917 October Revolution in which Bolsheviks seized control of St. Petersburg and much of eastern Russia, William O'Brien met Maxim Litvinoff, the representative of Russia's Bolshevik government to Britain. He reportedly told O'Brien that Lenin and Bolshevik leaders admired Connolly before and after 1916 (Morrissey, *O'Brien*, 157).
8. Sheehy-Skeffington wrote one play of his own, *The Prodigal Daughter*, that was performed in Dublin in April 1914 by the Women's Franchise League, and again in 1915. The play was predominantly a suffragist work, depicting a young middle-class woman rejecting conventional views that she should live a stifling life. She joins a suffragist demonstration and is arrested for breaking a store window. The review of the play in Sheehy-Skeffington's *Irish Citizen*, which he probably wrote, noted: "The author adopted

the Shavian method of argument. The weak characters present the wrong views only to be successively bowled over like ninepins by the strong character, who shares the outlook of the author. The result is very good propaganda" (as quoted in Hogan with Burnham and Poteet, *Abbey Theatre*, 355).

9. The Shaws' involvement with Sheehy-Skeffington's *Irish Citizen* did not end with Charlotte's contribution. In November 1915, while Sheehy-Skeffington was in the United States on a lecture and fund-raising tour, he wrote to his wife Hannah in Dublin, who was editing the paper in his absence, suggesting she reprint G. B. Shaw's article from the *New Statesman* on Edith Cavell. Cavell was an English nurse working in Brussels who was executed by the German military after helping allied POWs escape (Levenson, *With Wooden*, 197).

10. Laurence and Grene include Shaw's letter on behalf of Sheehy-Skeffington's 1915 conviction in *The Matter with Ireland* under "On Behalf of an Irish Pacifist." The version of the letter that I am quoting and citing appears in the Sheehy-Skeffington pamphlet, published in 1915 by Connolly.

11. One might theorize that Connolly's capitalization of inflammatory phrases in Shaw's letter was done to help uneducated working-class readers to understand Shaw's points. However, since there is no such capitalization in Sheehy-Skeffington's speech in the pamphlet, we can conclude that Connolly's capitalization was intended to emphasize Shaw's points, or the points he wanted emphasized in Shaw's letter.

12. Sheehy-Skeffington was released from prison in a state of collapse on the seventh day of his hunger strike. He was released under the Cat and Mouse Act, meaning that once his health improved he could be returned to prison to finish serving his term.

13. Pearse's speech at Rossa's burial is the speech that Sean O'Casey transports to Act II in his 1926 *The Plough and the Stars*. It serves as the speech of the war-monger-speaker outside the act's pub-setting. O'Casey moved Pearse's speech from Glasnevin Cemetery to the outside of a Dublin pub as a backdrop for drunkenness. The result ties Pearse's insurrection rhetoric to excessive drinking. Such a tie was unfair, given that Pearse and other nationalist leaders, and socialist leaders like Connolly, called for abstinence from their followers. ICA captain and actor Sean Connolly was, for example, a member of the Pioneer Total Abstinence Association (*1916*, 272), and a participant in revolution.

14. A photograph exists of O'Donovan Rossa's burial taken as Pearse is tucking his speech back into his uniform pocket and six men in ICA uniforms are taking their place beside the grave to fire a rifle salute (http://file024b.bebo.com/9/original/2006/12/29/09/3000137772a3000390038b8624595190). ICA uniforms were dark green with a hat that had one side pinned up with a badge signifying the ITGWU.

15. See Lauren Arrington's "The Censorship of *O'Flaherty V.C.*" for the financial difficulties of the Abbey Theatre in 1914–15.

16. Since 1912, the Abbey Theatre performed one-act plays from their repertoire in London's Coliseum, a large music hall, during the summer months following June engagements in London's theatres, like the Royal Court. The Abbey's Coliseum appearances, booked among one-act plays by other companies and usual music hall acts, were profitable for the Abbey during months when the theatre had previously been dark.

17. Shaw wanted Sinclair to play O'Flaherty, but the actor had left the Abbey before the 1915 autumn. At Shaw's insistence, Sinclair was rehired (Laurence and Grene, "Introduction," 105–106). While the rest of the casting for *O'Flaherty* is unknown, it is probable that Moloney was to play Mrs. O'Flaherty. She usually played older characters and Shaw's choice of Sara Allgood was unavailable.

18. A 1915 recruiting poster with Michael O'Leary, V.C., reads: "An Irish Hero/ 1 Irishman Defeats 10 Germans . . . / Have you no wish to emulate the splendid bravery of your fellow countryman" (Horne, *Our War*, ii).

19. O'Flaherty's quoted remark about the British king played on the German heritage of Britain's royal family, another jab at the war's patriotism.

20. Shaw was not sure the Lord Chamberlain would allow *O'Flaherty V.C.* to be performed in England, but thought a premier run in Dublin would help the play with the British censor. He wrote on 12 October 1915: "It is by no means sure that it will be licensed in England; and a few preliminary trials in Dublin might do no harm" (*Shaw, Gregory*, 104). In November, Yeats sent a copy of the play to the Abbey's agent who booked their music hall appearances. Yeats reported to Shaw that the agent said no English theatre would object to the script (as quoted in *Shaw, Gregory*, 107).

21. Of course, Shaw's focus was on Irish men, like O'Flaherty, for recruiting. But focusing on the male had a secondary aspect in that it undermined Synge's portrait of Ireland through Nora in *Shadow*.

22. Lady Gregory was at this time on a lecture tour in America. Shaw believed that had she been in Dublin, she would have pressed the issue to perform *O'Flaherty* (Hogan with Burnham and Poteet, *Abbey Theatre*, 385).

23. Nathan closed his 16 November 1915 letter to Shaw, in which he expressed the desire for the play's cancellation with: "I feel strongly that the main idea . . . [of the play] is entirely right, that this war does give to the most thinking of all peasantries the chance of contact with the wider world . . . [to] enable them to rise above . . . hopelessness" (as quoted in Hogan with Burnham and Poteet, *Abbey Theatre*, 387).

24. Redemption was present for Synge after his death, evidenced by W. P. Ryan's praising review of Synge's *Collected Works* (1910), noting that *Playboy* was "now fairly appreciated" (as quoted in Levitas, *Theatre*, 193).

25. Connolly had been trying to forge solid relations between the ICA and the IV, but the latter's leader, MacNeill, repeatedly blocked it (O'Brien, *Forth*, 275–276). Connolly, in late 1915, did not yet appreciate Pearse's efforts to mobilize the IV without MacNeill.

26. Pearse also criticized Ireland's would-be rebellion leaders of the years leading to 1916: "the failure of the last generation has been mean and shameful. . . . The whole episode is squalid" ("Ghosts," 223).

27. O'Casey had been ICA secretary but resigned in August 1914 after he had filed a motion calling on Constance Markievicz to resign from the ICA, since she was also in the IV. The motion was defeated, as Markievicz had established herself with Connolly and others in the ITGWU during the Lockout. When called to apologize, O'Casey resigned (Murray, *O'Casey*, 89, O'Brien, *Forth*, 122). Christopher Murray notes that after Larkin's departure, O'Casey often stood on the steps of Liberty Hall, "no longer welcome

inside," criticizing Connolly (*O'Casey*, 92). However, Murray records that as late as January 1916, O'Casey was still being published in Connolly's *Workers' Republic* (*O'Casey*, 106). Such, of course, raises doubt about O'Casey's voicing opposition to Connolly at the time, and was probably fabricated decades later. In his introduction to the recent publication of *Under Which Flag?*, James Moran demonstrates that O'Casey "adapted" much of Connolly's play into *The Plough and the Stars* (1926) ("Introduction," 23–25). Writing in response to earlier plays continued in Irish theatre.

28. Again, it is unfortunate Wilson's October 1914 recruiting play *A Call to Arms* is non-extant. A contrast of it to *Under Which Flag?* and *O'Flaherty V.C.* would be interesting.

29. The borrowed phrases from Boucicault by Connolly are not excessively stereotypical-type phrases, like those Shaw dismisses in Act I of *John Bull's Other Island*.

30. The 1998 article "James Connolly's *Under Which Flag?*, 1916" re-introduced interest in Connolly's play, which many erroneously had considered non-extant. I rediscovered the manuscript amongst William O'Brien's collection of Connolly's papers in Ireland's National Library. Many of my views of Connolly's play have changed since the article, the first critical discussion of the play, which appeared in the *New Hibernia Review*.

31. *The Agitator's Wife* appears to be non-extant.

32. Connolly's new colleagues in insurrection, Pearse and MacDonagh, were playwrights using theatre for radical purposes. In addition, Plunkett acted in some Dublin productions and was, with MacDonagh and Edward Martyn, a director of the Irish Theatre Company. Arguably, Connolly may well have expanded his labor theatre along the lines of the Irish Theatre Company's Hardwicke Street Theatre, a space MacDonagh and Plunkett used for IV meetings. The enlarged Liberty Hall theatre would similarly be used by the ICA.

33. One of these exchanges, between Ellen and Pat, recalls the joking from *Kathleen Ni Houlihan* between father and mother, with both fathers teasingly recalling their courting, but as Moran observes, "Connolly detested the capitalist ethos of the Gillane family" in Yeats-Gregory's play, and removes such from his O'Donnell family ("Introduction," 17). It is remembered that Shaw and Synge also disliked *Kathleen ni Houlihan*.

34. Connolly was doubly jabbed, as he was briefly a British soldier during the 1880s.

35. .*Amadam* is Gaelic for "idiot" (Moran, "Introduction," 131).

36. Moran argues that Mary's pro-active role was to counter Michael's would-be bride Delia, in *Kathleen Ni Houlihan* ("Introduction," 17–18). While Connolly's Mary does this, she also counters, yet again, Shaw's Teresa.

37. Connolly's class concern is found throughout his play, as in Scene II, when Mary recalls the charity offered her when she was very ill, "from them that had little to spare for themselves" (*Under*, 120).

38. Taking the "shilling" also recalls Padraic Colum's 1903 play *The Saxon Shillin'.*

39. Donal Nevin, editor of *Between Comrades: James Connolly*, provides notes on people mentioned in Connolly's letters, but provides nothing for the McMahon reference.

40. Addressing audiences from the stage was frequently practiced by W. B. Yeats prior

to 1910. Thomas MacDonagh revived the practice with the Irish Theatre Company in 1914.

41. No other Dublin theatre dared to stage a work like *Under Which Flag?* at the time, especially as the Abbey had backed away from *O'Flaherty V.C.*

42. The review of Connolly's play mistakenly referred to Dan McMahon as Brian McMahon.

43. Usual admission price to Liberty Hall plays was three pence. The price cut was undoubtedly an effort to attract a full house to maximize the provocation effect.

44. In the 1960s, William O'Brien recalled that the Citizen's Committee Connolly formed included Hannah Sheehy-Skeffington, rather than her husband. Padraig Yeates argues that Francis Sheehy-Skeffington's anti-looting efforts during the revolution were on behalf of the Citizen's Committee. Judging from the aligned political activism the Sheehy-Skeffingtons enjoyed in their marriage, they probably were both committee members, in that if one was on it, both were on it. Unquestionably, both were in and out of the rebel's headquarters consulting with Connolly and Pearse during the revolution's first two days. The other members of the committee were pro-labor Alderman Tom Kelly, O'Brien, and the nationalist Sean O'Kelly (Townshend, *Easter*, 161).

45. Connolly claimed the flag raising was part of the plan (O'Brien, *Forth*, 282).

46. Due to secrecy, only the rebel leaders actually knew when and if the insurrection was to occur.

47. During the 1905 failed Russian Revolution, MacKenna was a reporter for the *New York World* covering the revolution and the Russo-Japan War. In July 1905, he wrote: "Russia's awakening is the great interesting fact of our day.... There will be in the universal intelligence an answering change" (as quoted in Dodds, "Memoirs," 25).

48. Sean Connolly's ICA unit was curiously composed, but its small size epitomized the depleted rebel ranks. While James Connolly was set on the ICA attacking Dublin Castle, the depleted IV numbers meant that the roughly 210 ICA members had to be stretched thin across numerous garrisons. However, the near equal number of men and women in Sean's main unit reflected the ICA's equal gender opportunities. Sean's sister Katie Barrett, who also acted in *Under Which Flag?*, was in the unit, as were three of their brothers. The family makeup was replicated by George Norgrove, who was in the unit following his wife and two daughters. After Sean was killed, and his succeeding officer was killed, the ICA medical officer, Dr. Kathleen Lynn, surrendered their position after massive British assaults involving floor-to-floor combat. Despite the symbolic nature of the attack on Dublin Castle, James Connolly sent no IV members to bolster Sean's command. It was entirely an ICA action—the seat of power attacked by the proletariat's army.

49. While the DMP officer at the Castle gate was unarmed when shot, it must be understood that ICA members remembered DMP officers batoning unarmed locked-out workers in 1913. There was little sympathy for the DMP.

50. Most have believed that the two journalists seized at Kelly's Tobacco shop, P. J. MacIntyre and Thomas Dickson, were loyalist editors. However, Virginia Glandon demonstrates that this was not the case. MacIntyre was a labor proponent who waged a war of words with Connolly in the press. He resented Connolly becoming acting secretary of

the ITGWU when Larkin left. Dickson edited the *Eye Opener*, a scandal paper targeting working-class readers with a masthead that claimed it was "published by Irishmen and trade unionists" (Glandon, *Arthur Griffith*, 12–13; 113).

51. Reportedly, Connolly's book was a detective story (Caulfield, *Easter*, 245).

Epilogue

1. In "Neglected Morals," Shaw chastised any who lamented the destruction of buildings like Dublin's GPO, regretting that British artillery had not leveled Dublin's slums: ("Neglected," 121).

2. Shaw's friend Edward McNulty, who had authored *The Lord Mayor*, for which Sean Connolly played the lead in 1914, had joined the Dublin Reserve Guards of the Volunteer Training Corps. This was a reservist unit of the British army composed mostly of older professional-class Dubliners. When the rising began, the unit was on maneuvers outside Dublin. On hearing that a rising was on, they returned to Dublin to assist regular British army troops. They had British uniforms and rifles, but no ammunition. One column marched directly into a position held by rebels under orders to stop British troops from advancing into the city. A number of reservists were killed or wounded. Those who survived did so by entering houses and discarding their uniforms for civilian dress (Foy and Barton, *Easter*, 76). McNulty wrote to Shaw relating the experience, to which Shaw wrote to his sister Lucy about the absurdity of McNulty and others condemning the rebels as murderers for doing what they themselves were training to do (*Shaw Letters*, 400–401).

3. On 1 April 1916, the *New Statesman* published Robert Lynd's article, "If the Germans Conquered England." The article described Germany's occupation of Britain, if England was to lose, in terms of Ireland's colonization under Britain. During the insurrection, Pearse and Connolly published one issue of a four-page paper, *Irish War News*. The cover feature was on Lynd's article. While Shaw probably did not know of *Irish War News* on 10 May, he did know of Lynd's article. The unsigned *Irish War News* feature reveals Connolly's familiarity with the *New Statesman* and Shaw's articles therein.

4. A side goal of Shaw's "Easter Week" letter was an attempt to prevent the undersecretary to Ireland, Shaw's acquaintance Matthew Nathan, from being made a British scapegoat for the revolt. Shaw suggested that Nathan and the chief secretary "did what they could with their hands tied by the Army commands" and the government's failure to disarm Carson's UVF ("Easter," 125).

5. The British military held quick and secretive court-martial trials for the rebel leaders that denied legal representation, guaranteeing guilty verdicts.

6. Even the British General Maxwell regarded the "poverty and squalor of the Dublin slums . . . as a primary source of Irish disaffection" (Foy and Barton, *Easter*, 224). William Martin Murphy "believed the seeds of rebellion had been sown in 1913," not in the poverty, but in socialists like Connolly (Yeates, *Lockout*, 574).

7. Even socialist revolution in 1917 Russia proved, in the long run, impractical in Shavian terms, as it gave way to numerous twentieth-century horrors.

8. Peter Gahan relates correspondence between Russell and Shaw over the latter's

contribution to the fund for Connolly's widow and children in "Bernard Shaw and the Anglo-Irish War" ("Bernard," 237).

9. On writing to Lillie Connolly regarding her husband's personal effects, British commanding General Maxwell mentioned that he was being pressed to grant her permission to move to America by Horace Plunkett, and hoped to grant her the permission. However, Donal Nevin relates that when Lillie met Maxwell to collect her husband's effects, Maxwell, who had upheld the execution order, offered his hand to Lillie and she refused it (*Connolly*, 670). Her request to emigrate was denied.

10. Sean O'Casey's Dublin trilogy plays, which thematically indicted the nationalist direction of 1916 in light of its effect on the working class, as O'Casey saw it, was favored by the conservative Free State government during the 1920s. The plays served the Free State's counter-revolutionary aims of erasing radicalism from the Easter revolution, rather than the author's desire to focus attention on the laboring class. But as indicated above, in *The Plough and the Stars* O'Casey made rather unfair portrayals of Connolly and the goals of his ICA, beginning the revisionist efforts to remove socialistic leanings from Connolly, 1916, and Synge.

Bibliography

"Abbey Theatre Scene." In *J. M. Synge: Interviews and Recollections*, edited by E. H. Mikhail, 36–37. London: Macmillan, 1979.
Allen, Nicholas. *George Russell (Æ) and the New Ireland, 1905–30*. Dublin: Four Courts Press, 2003.
Anderson, W. K. *James Connolly and the Irish Left*. Dublin: Irish Academic Press, 1994.
"Anti-Clerical Campaign." *Irish Independent*, 3 November 1913, 5.
Arnold, Bruce. *Jack Yeats*. New Haven: Yale University Press, 1998.
Arrington, Lauren. "The Censorship of *O'Flaherty V.C.*" In *Shaw: The Annual of Bernard Shaw Studies*, vol. 28, *Shaw and War*, edited by Lagretta Tallent Lenker, 85–106. University Park, Pa.: Pennsylvania State University Press, 2008.
Bennett, Douglas. *The Encyclopaedia of Dublin, Revised and Expanded*. Dublin: Gill and Macmillan, 2005.
Bertolini, John A. "Wilde and Shakespeare in Shaw's *You Never Can Tell*." In *Shaw: The Annual of Bernard Shaw Studies*, vol. 27, edited by MaryAnn K. Crawford and Michel W. Pharand, 156–64. University Park, Pa.: Pennsylvania State University Press, 2007.
Bickley, Francis. *J. M. Synge and the Irish Dramatic Movement*. Boston: Houghton Mifflin, 1912.
Biggs, Murray. "Shaw's Recruiting Pamphlet." In *Shaw: The Annual of Bernard Shaw Studies*, vol. 28, *Shaw and War*, edited by Lagretta Tallent Lenker, 107–11. University Park, Pa.: Pennsylvania State University Press, 2008.
Biletz, Frank. "Women and Irish-Ireland: The Domestic Nationalism of Mary Butler." *New Hibernia Review* (Spring 2002): 63–75.
Bourgeois, Maurice. *John Millington Synge and the Irish Theatre*. London: Constable, 1913.
Boylan, Henry. *A Dictionary of Irish Biography*. Dublin: Gill and Macmillan, 1998.
Brown, Terence. "Notes." In *Dubliners* by James Joyce, 237–317. New York: Penguin, 1992.
Burch, Steven Dedalus. "Historical Invisibility: The Vexatious A. P. Wilson and the Abbey Theatre." http://goliath.ecnext.com (accessed 27 August 2007).
Caulfield, Max. *The Easter Rebellion*. 1966. Dublin: Gill and Macmillan, 1995.
Clear, Caitriona. "Fewer Ladies, More Women." In *Our War: Ireland and the Great War*, edited by John Horne, 157–80. Dublin: Royal Irish Academy, 2008.

———. *Social Change and Everyday Life in Ireland, 1850–1922*. Manchester: Manchester University Press, 2007.

Connell, Joseph E. A., Jr. *Where's Where in Dublin: A Directory of Historic Locations, 1913–1923*. Dublin: Dublin City Council, 2006.

Connolly, James (different from the subsequent). "Some Plays and a Critic." *United Irishman*, 7 May 1904, 6.

Connolly, James (1868–1916). *Between Comrades: James Connolly, Letters and Correspondence 1889–1916*, edited by Donal Nevin. Dublin: Gill and Macmillan, 2007.

———. "Conscription." *Workers' Republic*, 27 November 1915, 1.

———. "A Continental Revolution." In *James Connolly: Selected Writings*, edited by P. Berresford Ellis, 239–42. London: Pluto Press, 1973.

———. "Correspondents." *Workers' Republic*, 25 December 1915, 4.

———. "Enlist or Starve." *Workers' Republic*, 27 November 1915, 1.

———. "An Injury to One Is a Concern of All." Slogan. *Workers' Republic*, 8 January 1916, 4.

———. "The Irish Flag." *Workers' Republic*, 8 April 1916, 1.

———. "The Isolation of Dublin." *Forward*, 9 February 1914, 4.

———. "Labour in Dublin." *Irish Review*, October 1913, 385–91.

———. "Labour in Ireland." *Workers' Republic*, 22 April 1916, 2.

———. *Labour, Nationality, and Religion*. In *James Connolly Selected Writing*, edited by P. Berresford Ellis, 57–118. London: Pluto Press, 1973.

———." Next to the Revolution" Advert. *Workers' Republic*, 19 February 1916, 4.

———. "Notes on the Front." *Workers' Republic*, 16 October 1915, 4.

———. "Our Duty in the Crisis." *Irish Worker*, 8 August 1914, 4.

———. *The Re-Conquest of Ireland*. Dublin: Liberty Hall, 1915.

———. "The Ties That Bind." *Workers' Republic*, 5 February 1916, 1.

———. "Under Which Flag?" Advert. *Workers' Republic*, 25 March 1916, 4.

———. *Under Which Flag?* In *Four Irish Rebel Plays*, edited by James Moran, 105–32. Dublin: Irish Academic Press, 2007.

———. "The War Upon the German Nation." In *James Connolly: Selected Writings*, edited by P. Berresford Ellis, 242–48. London: Pluto Press, 1973.

———. "Why the Citizen Army Honours Rossa." www.marxist.org/archive/Connolly/1915/07/whyrossa.htm. (accessed 22 May 2009).

Connolly, S. J., and Bronagh Ni Chonaill. "Divorce." In *The Oxford Companion to Irish History*, edited by S. J. Connolly, 151. Oxford: Oxford University Press, 1998.

Cronin, John. "Introduction." In *Selected Plays of St. John Ervine*, as edited by John Cronin, 7–16. Gerrards Cross: Colin Smythe, 1988.

Cullen, Tom A. *When London Walked in Terror*. Boston: Houghton Mifflin, 1965.

Cummins, R. Dublin Metropolitan Police Report, 20 January 1908, *Sinn Fein and Republican Suspects, 1899–1921*. Vol. I. Dublin Castle Special Branch Files CO 904 (193–16), Eneclann, 2006.

Daly, Mary E. *Dublin, The Deposed Capital: A Social and Economic History, 1860–1914*. Cork: Cork University Press, 1985.

Davis, Tracy C. *George Bernard Shaw and the Socialist Theatre*. Westport, Conn.: Praeger, 1994.
De Burca, Eamonn. *The Irish Struggle: De Burca Rare Books*. Dublin: Summer 2008.
Dodds, E. R. "Memoirs." *Journal and Letters of Stephen MacKenna*, edited by E. R. Dodds, 1–90. New York: William Morrow, n.d. [1937].
Easter Proclamation of the Irish Republic. In *The Irish Struggle: De Burca Rare Books*. Dublin: Summer 2008.
Edwards, Owen Dudley. "Shaw and Christianity: Towards 1916." In *Librarians, Poets, and Scholars*, edited by Felix M. Larkin, 95–119. Dublin: Four Courts Press, 2007.
Edwards, Ruth Dudley. *Patrick Pearse: The Triumph of Failure*. London: Poolbeg, 1979.
Ellis, Peter Berresford. *A History of the Irish Working Class*. London: Pluto Press, 1972.
———. "Introduction." In *James Connolly: Selected Writings*, edited by P. Berresford Ellis, 7–54. London: Pluto Press, 1973.
Ellman, Richard. *Yeats: The Man and the Masks*. London: Penguin, 1989.
Ervine, St. John. *Mixed Marriage*. In *Selected Plays of St. John Ervine*, edited by John Cronin, 17–64. Gerrards Cross: Colin Smythe, 1988.
"The Favorite Sounds of Finn." In *The Field Day Anthology of Irish Writing*, vol. I, edited by Seamus Deane, 305. Derry, Ireland: Field Day, 1992.
Fay, Frank. Frank Fay Papers, MS 10,950, National Library of Ireland.
Fitzgerald, Mabel. "Mabel Fitzgerald's Correspondence with George Bernard Shaw." In *Desmond's Rising: Memoirs, 1913 to Easter 1916*. 1968, 185–204. Dublin: Liberties Press, 2006.
Foy, Michael, and Brian Barton. *The Easter Rising*. Gloucestershire, England: Sutton, 1999.
Frazier, Adrian. *Behind the Scenes: Yeats, Horniman, and the Struggle for the Abbey Theatre*. Los Angeles: University of California Press, 1990.
Gahan, Peter. "John Bull's Other War: Bernard Shaw and the Anglo-Irish War, 1918." In *Shaw: The Annual of Bernard Shaw Studies*, vol. 28, *Shaw and War*, edited by Lagretta Tallent Lanker, 209–38. University Park, Pa.: Pennsylvania State University Press, 2008.
———. *Shaw Shadows: Rereading the Texts of Bernard Shaw*. Gainesville, Fla.: University Press of Florida, 2004.
"Gaiety Theatre, 'John Bull's Other Island.'" *Irish Times*, 29 October 1912, 8.
"Gaiety Theatre, 'John Bull's Other Island.'" *Irish Times*, 7 October 1913, 7.
"Gaiety Theatre, 'The Devil's Disciple.'" *Irish Times*, 13 May 1913, 6.
"George Bernard Shaw Lecture." *Irish Times*, 4 October 1910, 4.
Ghairbhi, Roisin Ni. "A People That Did Not Exist? Reflections on Some Sources and Contexts for Patrick Pearse's Militant Nationalism." In *The Impact of the 1916 Rising*, edited by Ruan O'Donnell, 161–86. Dublin: Irish Academic Press, 2008.
Gibbs, A. M. *Bernard Shaw: A Life*. Gainesville, Fla: University Press of Florida, 2005.
Glandon, Virginia. *Arthur Griffith and the Advanced Nationalist Press Ireland, 1900–1922*. New York: Peter Lang, 1985.
Gogarty, Oliver St. John. "A Word on Criticism and 'Broken Soil.'" *United Irishman*, 19 December 1903, 6.

Gonne MacBride, Maud. "A National Theatre." *United Irishman*, 24 October 1903, 2–3.
Gray, John. "City in Revolt: Belfast, 1907." In *James Larkin: Lion of the Fold*, edited by Donal Nevin, 23–29. Dublin: Gill and Macmillan, 1998.
Greene, David H., and Edward M. Stephens. *J. M. Synge, 1871–1909*. Rev. ed. New York: New York University Press, 1989.
Gregory, Lady Augusta. *Seventy Years*. Gerrards Cross: Colin Smythe, 1973.
———. "Synge." In *J. M. Synge: Interviews and Recollections*, edited by E. H. Mikhail, 86–95. London: Macmillan, 1977.
Grene, Nicholas. *The Politics of Irish Drama: Plays in Context from Boucicault to Friel*. Cambridge: Cambridge University Press, 1999.
Griffith, Arthur. "The Abbey Theatre." *Sinn Fein*, 2 February 1907, 4.
———. "All Ireland." *Sinn Fein*, 2 February 1907, 1.
———. "All Ireland." *United Irishman*, 17 October 1903, 1.
———. "All Ireland." *United Irishman*, 11 February 1905, 1.
———. "Editorial." *Sinn Fein*, 17 November 1906, 6.
———. "Editorial." *Sinn Fein*, 9 February 1907, 2.
———. "Editorial." *United Irishman*, 12 April 1902, 3.
———. "Editorial." *United Irishman*, 24 October 1903, 2.
———. "Editorial." *United Irishman*, 14 May 1904, 5.
———. "J. M. Synge's *The Shadow of the Glen*." *United Irishman*, 28 January 1905, 1.
———. "Municipal Art Gallery." *Sinn Fein*, 8 February 1913, 1.
———. "Shaw at Home." *Sinn Fein*, 30 November 1907, 3.
———. "The Theatre of Ireland." *Sinn Fein*, 25 February 1911, 1.
Haverty, Ann. *Constance Markievicz: An Independent Life*. London: Pandora, 1988.
Hogan, Robert, with Richard Burnham and Daniel P. Poteet. *The Abbey Theatre: The Rise of the Realists, 1910–1915*. Dublin: Dolmen, 1979.
Hogan, Robert, and James Kilroy. *The Abbey Theatre: The Years of Synge, 1905–1909*. Dublin: Dolmen, 1978.
———. *The Irish Literary Theatre, 1899–1901*. Dublin: Dolmen, 1976.
———. *The Laying of the Foundations, 1902–1904*. Dublin: Dolmen, 1976.
Holloway, Joseph. *Joseph Holloway's Abbey Theatre: A Selection from His Unpublished Journal "Impressions of a Dublin Playgoer,"* as edited by Robert Hogan and Michael J. O'Neill. Carbondale: Southern Illinois University Press, 1967.
Holroyd, Michael. *Bernard Shaw*. Vol. 2, *1898–1918: The Pursuit of Power*. New York: Random House, 1989.
Horne, John. "Our War, Our History." In *Our War: Ireland and the Great War*, edited by John Horne, 1–14. Dublin: Royal Irish Academy, 2008.
H.R.W. "New Abbey Plays by New Players." *Evening Mail*, 14 March 1914, 2.
"In Croyden Park." *Irish Times*, 1 December 1913, 6.
Innes, C. L. *The Devil's Own Mirror: The Irishman and the African in Modern Literature*. Washington, D.C.: Three Continents, 1990.
"Irish Language Movement." *Irish Times*, 14 October 1910, 4.
Jenckes, Norma. "*John Bull's Other Island*: A Critical Study of Shaw's Irish Play in Its

Theatrical and Socio-Political Context." Ph.D. diss., University of Illinois at Urbana-Champaign, 1974.

Kelly, John. "Notes." In *The Collected Letters of W. B. Yeats*, vol. III, *1901–1904*, edited by John Kelly and Ronald Schuchard. Oxford: Clarendon Press, 1994.

Kelly, Matthew. " . . . And William Rooney Spoke in Irish." *History Ireland* (January-February 2007): 30–34.

Kiberd, Declan. *Inventing Ireland*. London: Jonathan Cape, 1995.

———. *Irish Classics*. London: Granta Books, 2000.

———. *Synge and the Irish Language*. 2nd ed. Dublin: Gill and Macmillan, 1993.

"The Land She Loved." *Workers' Republic*, 27 November 1915, 3.

Larkin, Emmet. "Æ and the Dublin Lock-out." In *James Larkin: Lion of the Fold*, edited by Donal Nevin, 211–29. Dublin: Gill and Macmillan, 1998.

———. "The *Irish Worker*, 1911–1914." In *James Larkin: Lion of the Fold*, edited by Donal Nevin, 152–58. Dublin: Gill and Macmillan, 1998.

———. "James Larkin: Labour Leader." In *James Larkin: Lion of the Fold*, edited by Donal Nevin, 1–7. Dublin: Gill and Macmillan, 1998.

Laurence, Dan H., and Nicholas Grene. "Introduction and Notes." In *Shaw, Lady Gregory, and the Abbey: A Correspondence and a Record*, edited by Dan H. Laurence and Nicholas Grene. Gerrards Cross, Buckinghamshire: Colin Smythe, 1993.

Levenson, Leah. *With Wooden Sword: A Portrait of Francis Sheehy-Skeffington, Militant Pacifist*. Dublin: Gill and Macmillan, 1983.

Levitas, Ben. "Plumbing the Depths: Irish Realism and the Working Class from Shaw to O'Casey." *Irish University Review* (Spring/Summer 2003): 133–49.

———. *The Theatre of Nation: Irish Drama and Cultural Nationalism, 1890–1916*. Oxford: Clarendon Press, 2002.

Long, Gerard. "The National Library of Ireland, 1890–1983: Informal Perspectives." In *Librarians, Poets, and Scholars*, edited by Felix M. Larkin, 51–70. Dublin: Four Courts Press, 2007.

Luddy, Maria. "Working Women, Trade Unionism, and Politics in Ireland, 1830–1945." In *Politics and the Irish Working Class, 1830–1945*, edited by Fintan Lane and Donal O Drisceoil, 44–61. New York: Palgrave Macmillan, 2005.

Lynch, David. *Radical Politics in Modern Ireland: The Irish Socialist Republican Party, 1896–1904*. Dublin: Irish Academic Press, 2005.

MacDonagh, Thomas. *Literature in Ireland*. London: T. Fischer Unwin, 1916.

MacKenna, Stephen. *Journal and Letters of Stephen MacKenna*, edited by E. R. Dodds. New York: William Morrow, n.d. [1937].

———. "Synge." In *J. M. Synge: Interviews and Recollections*, edited by E. H. Mikhail, 14–15. London: Macmillan, 1977.

Mannion, Elizabeth. "The Dublin Tenement Plays of the Early Abbey Theatre." *New Hibernia Review* (Summer 2010): 69–83.

Mathews, P. J. *Revival: The Abbey Theatre, Sinn Fein, the Gaelic League, and the Co-operative Movement*. Cork: Critical Conditions Series, Field Day Monographs, Cork University Press, 2003.

Matthews, Ann. "Vanguard of the Revolution? The Irish Citizen Army, 1916." In *The*

Impact of the 1916 Rising, edited by Ruan O'Donnell, 24–36. Dublin: Irish Academic Press, 2008.

McCormack, W. J. *Fool of the Family: A Life of J. M. Synge*. London: Weidenfeld and Nicolson, 2000.

McDiarmid, Lucy. *The Irish Art of Controversy*. Dublin: Lilliput Press, 2005.

McNulty, Edward. *The Lord Mayor*. Dublin: Talbot Press, c1915.

"Meeting in Beresford Park." *Irish Times*, 19 November 1913, 11.

Metscher, Priscilla. "James Connolly, the Easter Rising, and the First World War." In *The Impact of the 1916 Rising*, edited by Ruan O'Donnell, 141–60. Dublin: Irish Academic Press, 2008.

Mikhail, E. H. "Notes." In *J. M. Synge: Interviews and Recollections*, edited by E. H. Mikhail, 41. London: Macmillan, 1997.

Moran, James. "Introduction." In *Four Irish Rebel Plays*, edited by James Moran, 1–42. Dublin: Irish Academic Press, 2007.

Moriarty, Theresa. "Delia Larkin: Relative Obscurity." In *James Larkin: Lion of the Fold*, edited by Donal Nevin, 428–38. Dublin: Gill and Macmillan, 1998.

Morrissey, Thomas J., S.J. *William O'Brien, 1881–1968: Socialist, Republican, Dail Deputy, Editor, and Trade Union Leader*. Dublin: Four Courts Press, 2007.

———. *William Martin Murphy*. Dundalk: Dundalgan Press, 1997.

"Mr. Bernard Shaw in Dublin." *Freeman's Journal*, 4 October 1910, 7.

"Mr. Bernard Shaw in Dublin: 'Poor Law and Destitution in Ireland.'" *Freeman's Journal*, 4 October 1910, 7.

"Mr. Bernard Shaw on the Strike." *Irish Times*, 3 November 1913, 6.

"Municipal Art Gallery: The Bridge Site, Interview with Mr. George Bernard Shaw." *Irish Times*, 12 April 1913, 7.

Murray, Christopher. *Sean O'Casey: Writer at Work*. Dublin: Gill and Macmillan, 2004.

Nevin, Donal. *James Connolly: "A Full Life."* Dublin: Gill and Macmillan, 2005.

———. "Notes." In *Between Comrades: James Connolly, Letters and Correspondence, 1889–1916*, edited by Donal Nevin. Dublin: Gill and Macmillan, 2007.

———. "Notes." In *James Larkin: Lion of the Fold*, edited by Donal Nevin. Dublin: Gill and Macmillan, 1998.

Newsinger, John. *Rebel City: Larkin, Connolly, and the Dublin Labour Movement*. London: Merlin Press, 2004.

Nic Shiubhlaigh, Maire. *The Splendid Years: Recollections of Maire Nic Shiubhlaigh as Told to Edward Kenny*. Dublin: James Duffy, 1955.

1916 Rebellion Handbook. 1916. Dublin: Mourne River Press, 1998.

Norman, Diana. *Terrible Beauty: A Life of Constance Markievicz*. Dublin: Poolbeg, 1988.

Norstedt, Johann A. *Thomas MacDonagh: A Critical Biography*. Charlottesville: University of Virginia Press, 1980.

O'Brien, William. *Forth the Banners Go: Reminiscences of William O'Brien as Told to Edward MacLysaght*. Dublin: Three Candles Press, 1969.

O'Casey, Sean. "The Citizen Army Is Born." In *James Larkin: Lion of the Fold*, edited by Donal Nevin, 253–56. Dublin: Gill and Macmillan, 1998.

———. *The Plough and the Stars.* In *Sean O'Casey: Plays 2.* London: Faber and Faber, 1998: 63–161.
O'Connor, Emmet. "Labour and Politics, 1830–1945: Colonisation and Mental Colinisation." In *Politics and the Irish Working Class, 1830–1945,* edited by Fintan Land and Donal O Drisceoil, 27–43. New York: Palgrave Macmillan, 2005.
O'Connor Lysaght, D. R. "The Irish Citizen Army, 1913–1916: White, Larkin, and Connolly." *History Ireland* (March-April 2006): 19–23.
O'D., D. (O'Dwyer, Delia). "The Irish National Theatre Company." *United Irishman,* 9 April 1904, 6.
O'Donovan Rossa Funeral Photograph, 1 August 1915. http://file024b.bebo.com/9/original/2006/12/29/09/3000137772a3000390038b8624595190 (accessed 2 February 2009).
O'Leary, Daniel. "Censored and Embedded Shaw: Print Culture and Shavian Analysis of Wartime Media." In *Shaw: The Annual of Bernard Shaw Studies,* vol. 28: *Shaw and War,* edited by Lagretta Tallent Lenker, 168–87. University Park, Pa.: Pennsylvania State University Press, 2008.
O Maitiu, Seamas. *W & R Jacob: Celebrating 150 Years of Irish Biscuit Making.* Dublin: Woodfield Press, 2001.
O'Neill, Maire (Molly Allgood). "Synge and the Early Days of the Abbey." In *The Abbey Theatre: Interviews and Recollections,* edited by E. H. Mikhail, 81–83. London: Macmillan, 1988.
Orpen, William. "Larkin at Liberty Hall." In *James Larkin: Lion of the Fold,* edited by Donal Nevin, 203–5. Dublin: Gill and Macmillan, 1998.
Patterson, Henry. "William Walker, Labour, Sectarianism, and the Union, 1894–1912." In *Politics and the Irish Working Class, 1830–1945,* edited by Fintan Land and Donal O Drisceoil, 154–71. New York: Palgrave Macmillan, 2005.
Pearse, Padraic. "The Coming Revolution." In *Political Writings and Speeches,* 89–100. Dublin: Talbot Press, 1952.
———. "From a Hermitage." In *Political Writings and Speeches,* 139–212. Dublin: Talbot Press, 1952.
———. "Ghosts." In *Political Writings and Speeches,* 219–50. Dublin: Talbot Press, 1952.
———. *The Letters of P. H. Pearse.* Edited by Seamus O'Buachalla. Gerrards Cross, Buckinghamshire: Colin Smythe, 1980.
———. *The Master.* In *Plays, Stories, Poems,* 69–110. Dublin: Helicon, 1980.
———. "Peace and the Gael." In *Political Writings and Speeches,* 213–18. Dublin: Talbot Press, 1952.
———. "The Rebel." In *Plays, Stories, Poems,* 337–39. Dublin: Helicon, 1980.
———. "The Sovereign People." In *Political Writings and Speeches,* 331–72. Dublin: Talbot, 1924.
P.M.E.K. "A Plea for 'The Playboy.'" *Sinn Fein,* 9 February 1907, 3.
"Poor-Law System." *Irish Times,* 4 October 1910, 6.
Quin, James, Eilis Ni Dhuibhne, and Ciara McDonnell. *W. B. Yeats: Works and Days.* Dublin: National Library of Ireland, 2006.
Raftery, Antoine. "Killeaden, *or* County Mayo." Translated by Douglas Hyde (1899), ed-

ited by Seamus Deane, 724–26. In *The Field Day Anthology of Irish Writing*, vol. II. Derry: Field Day, Ireland, 1992.
Redmond-Howard, L. G. *Six Days of the Irish Republic*. Cork: Aubane Historical Society, 2006.
Roberts, George. "J. M. Synge." In *J. M. Synge: Interviews and Recollections*, edited by E. H. Mikhal, 111–30. London: Macmillan, 1977.
———. "A National Dramatist." *The Shanachie* (1907): 160.
Ritschel, Nelson O'Ceallaigh. "James Connolly's *Under Which Flag?*, 1916." *New Hibernia Review* (Winter 1998): 54–68.
———. *Performative and Textual Imaging of Women on the Irish Stage, 1820–1920: M. A. Kelly to J. M. Synge and the Allgoods*. Lewiston, N.Y.: Edwin Mellen Press, 2006.
———. *Productions of the Irish Theatre Movement, 1899–1916*. Westport, Conn.: Greenwood Press, 2001.
———. *Synge and Irish Nationalism: The Precursor to Revolution*. Westport, Conn.: Greenwood Press, 2002.
Russell, George. "Co-operation and the Problem of Rural Labour." *Irish Homestead*, 19 August 1911, 646.
———. "NOTW." *Irish Homestead*, 10 September 1910, 752.
———. "To the Masters of Dublin." In *The Re-Conquest of Ireland*, edited by James Connolly, 62–63. Dublin: Liberty Hall, 1915.
Ryan, Desmond. "Historians on Larkin." In *James Larkin: Lion of the Fold*, edited by Donal Nevin, 387–88. Dublin: Gill and Macmillan, 1998.
Ryan, Frederick. "Censorship and Independence." *United Irishman*, 23 November 1901, 3.
———. "The Latest Crusade." *Irish Review*, January 1912, 521–26.
———. *The Laying of the Foundations*. In *Lost Plays of the Irish Renaissance*, edited by Robert Hogan and James Kilroy, 23–38. Newark, Del.: Proscenium, 1970.
Ryan, W. P. *The Irish Labour Movement*. Dublin: Talbot Press, 1919.
Saddlemyer, Ann. "Appendix B." In *J. M. Synge: Collected Works IV, Plays Book 2*, edited by Ann Saddlemyer, 293–365. Gerrards Cross, Buckinghamshire: Colin Smythe.
———. "Chronology." In *The Collected Letters of John Millington Synge*, vol. I, *1871–1907*, edited by Ann Saddlemyer, xix–xxvi. Oxford: Clarendon, 1985.
———. "The Creation of *The Playboy* and a Love Returned." In *The Collected Letters of John Millington Synge*, vol. I, *1871–1907*, edited by Ann Saddlemyer, 146–47. Oxford: Clarendon, 1985.
———. "Introduction." In *The Playboy of the Western World and Other Plays*, edited by Ann Saddlemyer, vii–xxi. Oxford: Oxford University Press, 1995.
———. "Notes." In *The Collected Letters of John Millington Synge*, vol. I, *1871–1907*, edited by Ann Saddlemyer. Oxford: Clarendon, 1985.
———. "Return from Exile." In *The Collected Letters of John Millington Synge*, vol. I, *1871–1907*, edited by Ann Saddlemyer, 41–46. Oxford: Clarendon, 1985.
———. "A Stormy Aftermath." In *The Collected Letters of John Millington Synge*, vol. I, *1971–1907*, edited by Ann Saddlemyer, 273–75. Oxford: Clarendon, 1985.
"Sean Connolly." http://republican-news.org/archive/1999/April01/01 (accessed 27 August 2007).

Seumar. "Irish Drama at the Antient Concert Rooms: 'The Laying of the Foundations.'" *United Irishman*, 8 November 1902, 1.

Shaw, George Bernard. *Bernard Shaw: Collected Letters, 1911–1925*, edited by Dan H. Laurence. New York: Viking, 1985.

———. "Children of the Dublin Slums." In *The Matter with Ireland*, 2nd ed., edited by Dan H. Laurence and David H. Greene, 180–83. Gainesville, Fla.: University Press of Florida, 2001.

———. "Common Sense about the War." In *What Shaw Really Wrote about the War*, edited by J. L. Wisenthal and Daniel O'Leary, 16–84. Gainesville, Fla.: University Press of Florida, 2006.

———. "The Easter Week Executions." *The Matter with Ireland*, 2nd ed., edited by Dan H. Laurence and David H. Greene, 124–26. Gainesville, Fla.: University Press of Florida, 2001.

———. "Economic." In *Fabian Essays*, 35–61. London: George Allen & Unwin, 1962.

———. "Ireland and the First World War." In *The Matter with Ireland*, 2nd ed., edited by Dan H. Laurence and David H. Greene, 101–4. Gainesville, Fla.: University Press of Florida, 2001.

———. "The Irish Players." In *The Matter with Ireland*, 2nd ed., edited by Dan H. Laurence and David H. Greene, 71–77. Gainesville, Fla.: University Press of Florida, 2001.

———. *John Bull's Other Island*. Definitive Text, edited by Dan H. Laurence. London: Penguin Books, 1984.

———. "Letter from George Bernard Shaw on Sheehy-Skeffington's Sentence." In *F. Sheehy-Skeffington's Speech from the Dock with Letter from George Bernard Shaw*, edited by James Connolly, i–iv. Dublin: Liberty Hall, 1915.

———. "Literature in Ireland." In *The Matter with Ireland*, 2nd ed., edited by Dan H. Laurence and David H. Greene, 176–79. Gainesville, Fla.: University Press of Florida, 2001.

———. "Mabel Fitzgerald's Correspondence with George Bernard Shaw." In *Desmond's Rising: Memoirs, 1913 to Easter 1916*. 185–204. 1968. Dublin: Liberties Press, 2006.

———. "Mad Dogs in Uniform." In *The Matter with Ireland*, 2nd ed., edited by Dan H. Laurence and David H. Greene, 95–97. Gainesville, Fla.: University Press of Florida, 2001.

———. "My Motto Is Ireland for All." In *The Matter with Ireland*, 2nd ed., edited by Dan H. Laurence and David H. Greene, 69–70. Gainesville, Fla.: University Press of Florida, 2001.

———. "Neglected Morals of the Irish Rising." In *The Matter with Ireland*, 2nd ed., edited by Dan H. Laurence and David H. Greene, 120–23. Gainesville, Fla.: University Press of Florida, 2001.

———. *O'Flaherty, V.C.* In *Selected Short Plays*, 253–78. New York: Penguin, 1988.

———. "Preface for Politicians" (Preface to *John Bull's Other Island*). In *The Field Day Anthology of Irish Writing*, vol. II, edited by Seamus Deane, 472–93. Derry, Ireland: Field Day, 1992.

———. *The Quintessence of Ibsenism: Now Completed to the Death of Ibsen*. New York: Hill And Wang, 1958.

———. *Shaw, Lady Gregory, and the Abbey: A Correspondence and a Record*. Edited by Dan H. Laurence and Nicholas Grene. Gerrards Cross: Colin Smythe, 1993.

———. *The Shewing-up of Blanco Posnet*. In *The Doctor's Dilemma, Getting Married, and The Shewing-up of Blanco Posnet*, 427–57. London: Constable, 1937.

———. *War Issues for Irishmen*. In *The Matter with Ireland*, 2nd ed., edited by Dan H. Laurence and David H. Greene, 184–201. Gainesville, Fla.: University Press of Florida, 2001.

———. *Widowers' Houses*. In *Plays Pleasant and Unpleasant*, vol. I, 3–65. London: Constable, 1947.

"Sinn Fein Rebellion and Suppression: The Personalities." *Illustrated London News*, 6 May 1916, 581–84.

Sheehy-Skeffington, Francis. "Frederick Ryan." *Irish Review*, May 1913, 113–19.

———. "London's Magnificent Rally to the Dublin Rebels." *Daily Herald*, 3 November 1913, 1.

———. "Reviews of New Books: More Shavian Prefaces." *Irish Review*, May 1911, 152–56.

———. "Speech from the Dock." In *F. Sheehy-Skeffington's Speech from the Dock with Letter from George Bernard Shaw*, edited by James Connolly, 5–12. Dublin: Liberty Hall, 1915.

———. "Under Which Flag?" *Workers' Republic*, 8 April 1916, 2.

Spainneach, Liam. "Irish Socialist Party." *History Ireland* (November-December 2005): 16.

Steele, Karen. "The Literary Revival." In *Maud Gonne's Irish Nationalist Writings, 1895–1946*, edited by Karen Steele, 187–88. Dublin: Irish Academic Press, 2004.

Swift, Jonathan. "A Modest Proposal." In *The Field Day Anthology of Irish Writing*, vol. I, edited by Seamus Deane, 386–91. Derry: Field Day Publications, 1991.

Synge, John M. *The Aran Islands*. Mineola, N.Y.: Dover, 1998.

———. "Autobiography." In *J. M. Synge Collected Works*, vol. II, *Prose*, edited by Alan Price, 3–15. Gerrards Cross, Buckinghamshire: Colin Smythe, 1982.

———. "Can We Go Back into Our Mother's Womb?" In *The Politics of Language in Ireland: 1366–1922*, edited by Tony Crowley, 212–13. London and New York: Routledge, 2000.

———. *The Collected Letters of John Millington Synge*, vol. I: *1871–1907*. Edited by Ann Saddlemyer. Oxford: Clarendon, 1985.

———. *The Collected Letters of John Millington Synge*, vol. II: *1907–1909*. Edited by Ann Saddlemyer. Oxford: Clarendon, 1984.

———. *Deirdre of the Sorrows*. In *The Playboy of the Western World and Other Plays*, 147–87. Oxford: Oxford University Press, 1995.

———. "The Dramatic Movement in Ireland." In *The Abbey Theatre: Interviews and Recollections*, edited by E. H. Mikhail, 54–58. London: Macmillan, 1988.

———. "Erris." In *Travels in Wicklow, West Kerry, and Connemara*, 195–200. London: Serif, 2005.

———. "The Ferryman of Dinish Island." In *Travels in Wicklow, West Kerry, and Connemara*, 163–69. London: Serif, 2005.

———. "From Galway to Gorumna." In *Travels in Wicklow, West Kerry, and Connemara*, 144–56. London: Serif, 2005.
———. "The Homes of the Harvestmen." In *Travels in Wicklow, West Kerry, and Connemara*, 183–88. London: Serif, 2005.
———. "The Inner Lands of Mayo." In *Travels in Wicklow, West Kerry, and Connemara*, 201–6. London: Serif, 2005.
———. *In the Shadow of the Glen*. Samhain (1904): 34–44.
———. "The Kelp Makers." In *Travels in Wicklow, West Kerry, and Connemara*, 170–75. London: Serif, 2005.
———. *Letters to Molly: John Millington Synge to Maire O'Neill, 1906–1909*. Edited by Ann Saddlemyer. Cambridge, Mass.: Harvard University Press, 1971.
———. "A Note on Boucicault and Irish Drama." In *J. M. Synge Collected Works*, vol. II, Prose, edited by Alan Price, 397–98. Gerrards Cross: Colin Smythe, 1982.
———. *The Playboy of the Western World*. In *Modern Irish Drama*, edited by John P. Harrington, 73–118. New York: Norton, 1991.
———. Preface to *The Playboy of the Western World*. In *The Playboy of the Western World and Other Plays*, 96–97. Oxford: Oxford University Press, 1995.
———. *Riders to the Sea*. In *Modern Irish Drama*, edited by John P. Harrington, 63–72. New York: Norton, 1991.
———. "The Smaller Peasant Proprietors." In *Travels in Wicklow, West Kerry, and Connemara*, 189–94. London: Serif, 2005.
———. *The Tinker's Wedding*. In *The Playboy of the Western World and Other Plays*, 27–50. Oxford: Oxford University Press, 1995.
———. *The Well of Saints*. In *The Playboy of the Western World and Other Plays*, 51–94. Oxford: Oxford University Press, 1995.
Synge, John M., to Elkin Mathews. 24 January 1905. Letter in possession of the author.
"Tain Bo Cuailnge" ("The Cattle Raid of Cuailnge"). In *The Field Day Anthology of Irish Writing*, vol. I, edited by Seamus Deane, 7–13. Derry, Ireland: Field Day, 1992.
Townshend, Charles. *Easter 1916: The Irish Rebellion*. London: Allen Lane, 2005.
Ward, Margaret. *Hanna Sheehy-Skeffington: A Life*. Cork, Ireland: Attic Press, 1997.
———. *Maud Gonne: Ireland's Joan of Arc*. London: Pandora, 1990.
Weintraub, Stanley. *The Unexpected Shaw: Biographical Approaches to G.B.S. and His Work*. New York: Frederick Ungar, 1982.
Welch, Robert. *The Abbey Theatre, 1899–1999: Form and Pressure*. Oxford: Oxford University Press, 1999.
———. *The Oxford Companion to Irish Literature*. Oxford: Clarendon Press, 1996.
Wilson, A. Patrick. *Victims*. In *"Victims" and "Poached,"* 3–15. Dublin: Liberty Hall Players. c1920.
Yeates, Padraig. *Lockout Dublin 1913*. Dublin: Gill and Macmillan, 2000.
Yeats, J. B. "Correspondence." *United Irishman*, 31 October 1903, 7.
———. "Ireland Out of the Dock." *United Irishman*, 10 October 1903, 2.
Yeats, William Butler. *The Collected Letters of W. B. Yeats*, vol. III, *1901–1994*, edited by John Kelly and Ronald Schuchard. Oxford: Clarendon, 1994.

———. *Deirdre*. In *W. B. Yeats: Collected Plays*, 169–203. London: Macmillan, 1982.

———. *Dramatis Personae*. In *Autobiographies*, 383–458. London: Macmillan, 1980.

———. "J. M. Synge and the Ireland of His Time." In *J. M. Synge: Interviews and Recollections*, edited by E. H. Mikhal, 55–62. London: Macmillan, 1977.

———. *Kathleen Ni Houlihan*. *Samhain* (1902): 24–31.

———. *The Letters of W. B. Yeats*. Edited by Allan Wade. London: Rupert Hart-Davis, 1954.

———. "The Man and the Echo." In *The Collected Poems of W. B. Yeats*, 337–39. New York: Macmillan, 1956.

———. *Memoirs*. Edited by Denis Donoghue. London: Papermac, 1988.

———. "Mr. Yeats' New Play." *United Irishman*, 5 April 1902, 5.

———. *On Baile's Strand*. In *W. B. Yeats: Collected Plays*, 245–78. London: Macmillan, 1982.

———. "On Those That Hated 'The Playboy of the Western World,' 1907." In *The Collected Poems of W. B. Yeats*, 109. New York: Macmillan, 1956.

———. "Plans and Methods." *Beltaine* (1899): 6–9.

———. "Plans and Methods." *Beltaine* (1900): 3–6.

———. "September 1913." In *The Collected Poems of W. B. Yeats*, 106. New York: Macmillan, 1956.

———. "To a Shade." In *The Collected Poems of W. B. Yeats*, 108. New York: Macmillan, 1956.

Zorn, Christa. "Cosmopolitan Shaw and the Transformation of the Public Sphere." In *Shaw: The Annual of Bernard Shaw Studies*, vol. 28: *Shaw and War*, edited by Lagretta Tallent Lenker, 188–208. University Park, Pa.: Pennsylvania State University Press, 2008.

Index

Abbey Theatre, 4, 39, 47, 50, 78–79, 80, 83–84, 85, 90, 92, 93–95, 96, 97, 113, 114–15, 116, 119, 120, 123, 124, 126, 128, 130, 133–34, 159–60, 163, 181–82, 183, 188, 191, 199, 201, 206, 207, 210, 227nn18–19, 227n21, 229n1, 230n5, 231n16, 232n20, 232n22, 232nn25–27, 233n1, 233nn3–4, 233nn6–7, 235n23, 236n24, 236n29, 237n5, 238nn19–20, 240nn15–16, 241n17, 241n20 (*see also* Irish National Theatre Society; National Theatre Society Ltd.); audiences of, 54, 76, 78, 81, 92, 123, 137, 162, 164, 167, 193–94, 207; opening of, 27–30

Æ. *See* Russell, George

Allgood, Molly (Maire O'Neill), 50, 79, 85–86, 124, 227n16, 229n1, 230n3, 232n27, 235n17

Allgood, Sara, 74, 232n27, 241n17

Archer, William, 27

Arnold, Bruce, 17

Ashley, Evelyn, 125, 127, 236n4

Atkinson, Robert, 35, 228n25

Bailey, W. F., 194

Beerbohm, Max, 27

Bertolini, John, 31, 228n22

Boer War, 51, 52, 228n23, 230n4, 237n12

Booth, Handel, 135

Boucicault, Dion, 64, 201, 227n21, 242n29

Boyle, William, 133, 199, 233n4

British army (military), 61, 70, 116–17, 154, 183, 201, 203, 205–6, 207, 230n6, 237n12; and Easter Rising, 212, 215–18, 221, 244n2, 244n4; and the Great War, 4, 110, 168, 172, 179, 184, 185, 188, 193, 195, 198–200, 206–7, 239n4

British labour, 4, 115–16, 136, 151, 157–59, 171, 222, 237n13

Carney, Winifred, 207

Carson, Sir Edward, 150, 152–53, 155–56, 237nn14–15, 244n4

Catholic Church (Catholicism): on liberalism in Ireland, 94, 100–101, 115, 143; and morality, 25, 35, 41, 46, 56, 58, 68, 69, 71, 74–75, 87, 94, 98–104, 106, 117–18, 139–40, 147, 148–49, 223, 234n9, 237n7, 237n11; on Socialism in Ireland, 3, 45, 98–104, 106, 111, 117, 125, 139–40, 143, 148, 152, 235nn19–20; and trade unions, 92, 98, 102–5, 112, 113–15, 117, 125, 139–40, 143, 147, 148

Catholic Times, 102

Ceannt, Eamonn, 175, 196

Chesterton, G. K., 125, 236n3

Church Street buildings collapse, 1913 (Dublin), 138–39, 161

Clarke, Tom, 145, 174, 196, 218

Cluithcheoiri na hEireann (Theatre of Ireland), 23, 123, 233n1

Coliseum Theatre (London), 182, 191, 240n16

Colthurst, Captain Bowen, 215, 216

Conniffe, Michael, 133–34
Connolly, James: and Abbey Theatre, 92, 94–95, 233n4; background of, 225n7; and Catholic Church, 3, 94–95, 98–103, 106, 111, 122, 177–78, 223n5, 234n8, 234n11, 235n19; and Dublin Lockout, 130, 132, 133–34, 136, 138–39, 141–42, 143, 147–49, 154–57, 158–59; and Easter Rising, 7, 61, 188, 213–15, 216, 217, 220–21; execution of, 219; on the Great War, 4, 168, 169–71, 173–74, 195, 198, 239n1; with Irish Citizen Army (ICA), 5, 154–57, 176, 180–81, 195, 199, 207, 208, 215, 219, 221, 237n12, 241n27, 243n48; with Irish Socialist Republican Party (ISRP), 10, 14–16, 93, 225n3, 225n7; with Irish Transport and General Workers' Union (ITGWU), 3, 4, 103, 110, 116, 124–25, 133–34, 136, 138–39, 154, 158–59; with Irish Workers' Dramatic Company, 159, 182; London rally with Shaw, 132, 147–49, 151, 153; planning insurrection, 174–76, 180–81, 194, 195–97, 198–99, 207–12, 213, 239n7; as Socialist agitator, 2, 3, 8, 49, 92, 93–94, 95–97, 111, 112, 130, 131, 152, 168, 175, 184, 221–22, 223, 238n21, 244n3, 244n6, 245n10; Socialist Party of Ireland (SPI), 104, 110; and women's advancement, 23, 101–2, 177, 214
—books: *Labour in Irish History*, 96–97, 110, 233n5, 237n10; *Re-Conquest of Ireland*, 143, 176–78, 220, 234n7, 237n6
—editor of: *F. Sheehy-Skeffington's Speech from the Dock with Letter from George Bernard Shaw*, 179–80, 240n11; *Harp*, 97, 124; *Irish Worker*, 147, 157, 158; *Workers' Republic*, 14, 15, 97, 199, 208, 209
—essays: "Arms and the Man," 155; "Conscription," 195; "A Continental Revolution," 169, 174; "Enlist or Starve," 195; "The Irish Flag," 212; "The Isolation of Dublin," 159; "Labour in Dublin," 141–2, 144, 146; "Next to Revolution," 199; "Notes on the Front," 183; "Our Duty in the Crisis," 168, 169; "The Ties that Bind," 198; "The War Upon the German Nation," 170, 173; "Why the Citizen Army Honours Rossa," 181
—pamphlet: *Labour, Nationality, and Religion*, 3, 98–99, 100–103, 106, 108, 110, 111, 234n16
—play: *Under Which Flag?* 4, 5, 8, 199, 200–210, 212, 242n29, 242n33, 242nn36–37, 243n42
Connolly, Joseph, 137
Connolly, Lillie, 221, 245n9
Connolly, Sean, 5, 123, 124, 131, 137, 140, 163, 183, 199, 207, 210, 213–14, 240n13, 243n48, 244n2
Cummins, Geraldine, 126
—play: *Broken Faith* (coauthored with Suzanne Day), 126–28, 138

Daily Herald, 102, 136, 147, 150–53, 236n3
Dargan, William, 128, 236n27
Davis, Tracy, 8, 12–14, 17, 48
Day, Suzanne R., 126–27, 138
—plays: *Broken Faith* (coauthored with Geraldine Cummins), 126–28, 138; *Toilers*, 138
DMP. *See* Dublin Metropolitan Police
DRT. *See* Dublin Repertoire Theatre
Dublin Castle, 81, 160, 183, 194–95, 200, 208, 213–14, 219, 243n48
Dublin Employers' Federation, 125, 132, 146
Dublin Industrial Peace Committee, 146
Dublin Lockout (1913), 3–4, 7, 63, 89, 131–46, 157–60, 162–66, 171, 173, 196, 215, 222, 237n7, 238n13, 238n16, 238n18, 239n23, 241n27
Dublin Metropolitan Police (DMP), 133–36, 155, 208, 210, 214, 243n49
Dublin Municipal Art Gallery, 127, 129, 141, 147

Dublin Repertoire Theatre (DRT), 127, 130–31, 138, 163, 236n4
Dublin United Tramways Company, 117, 131

Easter Proclamation (1916), 61, 214. *See also* Easter Rising
Easter Rising (1916), 7, 52, 209, 214–21, 238n21, 244n2
Engels, Friedrich, 33
Ervine, St. John, 110, 123, 163, 182
—play: *Mixed Marriage*, 113–16, 163, 182, 235n21

Fabian Society, 1–2, 8–13, 19, 32, 45–46, 50, 54, 60, 83, 89, 91, 96, 103, 106, 109, 113, 115, 144, 162, 173, 174, 187, 191, 220, 225n3, 226n8, 233n7
Farr, Florence, 27, 84
Fay, Frank, 27, 225n5
Fay, William, 225n5, 231n16, 232n27
Fianna, 131
Fitzgerald, Mabel, 172–74, 179–80, 183
Forward, 169, 176
Freeman's Journal, 69, 74–75, 81, 103–4, 107, 111, 139, 171–76, 180, 183, 234nn14–15, 235n18, 239n2

Gaelic League, 35, 106, 109, 144, 239n23
Gahan, Peter, 8–9, 221–22, 244n8
Gibbs, A. M., 47, 143, 159, 235n17
Gifford, Muriel, 134
Gifford, Nellie, 134
Gogarty, Oliver St. John, 26, 223
Gonne, Maude, 52, 61, 227n17, 230n4
Granville-Barker, Harley, 30, 39, 91, 94, 226n8, 233n1
The Great War, 4, 8, 74, 110, 116, 153, 167–81, 184–200, 204, 208, 211, 217–18, 221–22, 239n2, 239n5, 241n19, 241n23
Gregory, Lady Augusta, 17, 29, 36, 39, 43, 50, 80, 84, 97, 120, 127, 128, 130, 137, 167, 182, 184, 188–89, 193, 199, 201, 216, 227n18, 229n3, 230n3, 233nn6–7, 238n18, 241n22
—plays: *Kathleen Ni Houlihan* (co-authored with W. B. Yeats), 10, 29, 30, 34, 36, 43, 47, 52, 62, 65, 201, 221, 227n19, 228n24, 228nn26–27, 233n4, 242n33, 242n36; *The Workhouse Ward*, 188, 238n18
Grene, Nicholas, 5, 32, 80, 182–3, 239n2, 240n10
Griffith, Arthur, 13–14, 22, 24, 26, 35, 36, 37–38, 48, 61, 63, 72, 75, 81, 116–17, 118, 129, 197–98, 221, 227nn12–13, 230nn6–7, 231n14, 231n22
Goulding, Sir William, 125, 236n27

Hackett, Rosie, 238n16
Holloway, Joseph, 56, 82, 91, 95, 108–9, 137, 166, 167, 230n5, 233n29, 235n17
Holroyd, Michael, 81, 84, 143, 174, 182
Horniman, Annie, 27–28, 97, 182, 234n7
Hyde, Douglas, 73

IAOS. *See* Irish Agricultural Organization Society
Ibsen, Henrik, 2, 9–10, 31, 39
—play: *A Doll's House*, 19, 23, 234n10
ICA. *See* Irish Citizen Army
Imperial Hotel, 133–34, 214–15, 219, 220
Independent Theatre Company (ITC, Dublin), 123–24, 127
INTS. *See* Irish National Theatre Society
Irish Agricultural Organization Society (IAOS), 143, 178
Irish Citizen, 126–27, 166, 178, 239n8, 240n9
Irish Citizen Army (ICA), 3, 4, 5, 154–57, 159, 163, 167, 176, 179, 180–81, 183, 195, 197, 199, 206–17, 219, 221–22, 237n12, 238n16, 240nn13–14, 241n25, 241n27, 242n32, 243nn48–49, 245n10
Irish Independent, 85, 103, 117–18, 129, 131, 147, 148–49, 151–53, 171, 215, 219, 237n11

Irish National Theatre Society (INTS), 2, 10, 13, 16, 17, 27–32, 36, 41, 143, 225n5, 226nn8–9, 227n20, 228n28, 229n29. *See also* Abbey Theatre; National Theatre Society Ltd.
Irish Review, 23, 141, 235n19, 236n26
Irish Socialist Republic Party (ISRP), 2, 10, 12, 14–16, 90, 93, 95, 110, 225nn2–3, 225n7
Irish Theatre Company, 242n32, 243n40
Irish Times, 107, 111, 124, 125, 129, 130, 135, 137, 138, 144, 151, 154, 165, 227n12, 234n15, 235n18
Irish Transport and General Workers' Union (ITGWU), 93, 95, 97, 103, 110, 111, 112, 116–18, 119–21, 124–25, 128, 164–65, 168, 171, 176, 177, 179, 183, 207, 208, 214, 221, 243n50; and Dublin Lockout, 63, 131–40, 143, 146, 154, 156, 158–59, 212, 216, 238n16; formation of, 92, 96, 98
Irish Volunteers (IV), 4, 157, 195, 197, 206, 208, 211, 213, 217, 241n25, 241n27, 242n32, 243n48
Irish Worker, 117, 118, 119, 120–21, 128, 147, 151, 155, 157–58, 158–59, 165, 168, 170–71, 173, 175–76, 180
Irish Workers' Dramatic Company, 119–20, 159, 167, 182–83, 188, 198, 200, 236n24, 238n18
ISRP. *See* Irish Socialist Republic Party
ITC, Dublin. *See* Independent Theatre Company
ITGWU. *See* Irish Transport and General Workers' Union
IV. *See* Irish Volunteers

Jacob's Biscuit Factory, 132, 158, 215, 236n1, 238n16
Jenckes, Norma, 33

Kane, S. J., Robert, 98, 100–104, 106, 111, 117, 155, 234n16

Kelly, Alderman Tom, 215, 243n44
Kenny, P. D., 71, 93–95, 111, 222, 233nn2–3
Kiberd, Declan, 5, 10, 21, 34, 72, 74, 146, 226n9, 231n12
Kilmainham Prison, 197, 219

Lane, Hugh, 127–30, 137, 140, 147, 221, 236n28
Larkin, Delia, 5, 119, 182, 237n9, 238n18
Larkin, James, 5, 91–92, 96, 97, 115, 117, 118–19, 124–25, 128, 159, 164–66, 223, 235n22, 236n2, 238n22, 241n27, 243n50; and Dublin Lockout, 3, 131–40, 147, 150, 152–54, 157, 171, 215, 237n7
Lenin, Vladimir, 175, 219–20, 239n7
Levitas, Ben, 17, 162, 165, 195–96, 231n13, 239nn22–23
Liberty Hall, 119–21, 123, 133–34, 140, 143, 147, 154, 163, 176, 179, 180, 183, 199, 200, 202, 206, 207, 208, 209, 210, 212, 213, 214, 215, 216, 236n2, 237n6, 238n16, 241n27, 242n32, 243n43
Lynn, Dr. Kathleen, 243

MacBride, John, 52, 227n17, 230n4
MacDiarmuid, Sean, 145, 175, 196
MacDonagh, Thomas, 5, 23, 61, 135, 141, 144, 174, 215, 218, 237n5, 242n32, 243n40
MacDonnell, Flora, 125, 127
MacKenna, Stephen, 58, 60, 63, 65, 77, 123–24, 214, 219–20, 226n10, 229n3, 238n17, 243n47
MacNeill, Eoin, 195, 211, 213, 241n25, 245n9
MacSwiney, Terence, 112
—play: *The Holocaust*, 112–13
Mahaffy, John Petland, 35, 228n25
Mallin, Michael, 199, 210, 215
Manchester Guardian, 57–60, 182
Mann, Tom, 152, 170
Markievicz, Count Casimir, 5, 123–24, 127, 130–31, 134–35, 236n4, 237n4
—play: *The Memory of the Dead*, 123

Markievicz, Countess Constance (née Gore-Booth), 5, 123, 124, 130, 131, 134–35, 140, 215, 236n4, 237n4, 241n27
Marx, Karl, 17, 100, 118, 143, 152
Maxwell, General John, 219, 244n6, 245n9
McCormack, W. J., 55, 88
McDiarmid, Lucy, 81, 232n23
McNulty, Edward, 159–60, 244n2
—play: *The Lord Mayor*, 160–63, 238nn19–20, 244n2
Moloney, Helena, 5, 123–24, 130–31, 133–34, 140, 182–83, 198–99, 207, 215, 241n17
Morrissey, S. J., Thomas J., 96, 97, 116, 118, 136, 139
Murphy, William Martin, 11, 35, 103, 117–18, 125, 128–30, 137, 141, 160, 162, 171, 195, 214–15, 219, 221, 236n27, 244n6; and Dublin Lockout, 131, 134, 137, 148, 150–52, 236n1
Murray, Christopher, 119, 120, 200, 241n27

Nathan, Sir Matthew, 182, 194–95, 213, 241n23, 244n4
National Gallery of Ireland, 127–28, 236n28
National Theatre Society Ltd., 2, 10, 36, 227n20, 233n6. See also Irish National Theatre Society; Abbey Theatre
Nevin, Donal, 14, 98, 100, 152, 242n39, 245n9
New Statesman, 171, 217, 239n3, 240n9, 244n3
Nic Shiubhlaigh, Maire, 78, 232n22

O'Brien, William, 5, 10, 14, 16, 93, 95, 96–97, 102, 104–5, 108–9, 155, 178, 236n26, 239n7, 242n30; and Abbey Theatre, 90–91, 95, 165–66, 234n14; and Dublin Lockout, 133–34, 136, 139; and Irish insurrection, 168, 174–75, 195, 213, 243n44; and Irish Socialist Party (ISP), 104; and Irish Socialist Republican Party (ISRP), 10, 14, 16, 225n2; and Irish Transport and General Workers' Union (ITGWU), 95, 103, 118, 120, 133–34, 136, 139, 155, 165–66
O'Carroll, Richard, 180, 216
O'Casey, Sean, 119, 156, 200, 238n20, 239nn22–23, 240n13, 241n27, 245n10
O'Dwyer, Delia, 37
O'Farrell, Elizabeth, 216
O'Leary, Michael, 184, 194, 200, 241n18
Oman, William, 181, 210
O'Riordan, Conal, 97, 233n7
Orpen, William, 140
Ostrovsky, Aleksandr, 23

Parnell, Charles Stewart, 35, 71, 74, 117, 137, 140, 150, 180, 214, 221, 238n15
Partridge, William, 147
Payne, Ben Iden, 78, 231n16
Pearse, Padraic, 3, 5, 198, 201, 218, 220, 240nn13–14, 242n32; on Irish Labour, 144–46, 174, 196–97, 209, 221; and Irish Volunteers (IV), 4, 195, 206, 217, 241n25; planning insurrection, 174, 181, 195–97, 206, 209, 243n44, 244n3
—essays: "The Coming Revolution," 145, 157; "From a Heritage," 146, 157, 196; "Ghosts," 241n26; "Peace and the Gael," 196; "The Sovereign People," 209
—play: *The Singer*, 196
—poem: "The Rebel," 197
Perolz, Moria, 130
Plunkett, Geraldine, 196
Plunkett, Horace, 143, 178, 194, 221, 245n9
Plunkett, Joseph Mary, 141, 175, 196, 242n32
Powers, Ambrose, 130, 236n29

Quinn, John, 28, 227n18

Raftery, Antoine, 25, 227n15, 229n32, 232n18

Redmond-Howard, L. G., 217, 220
RIC. *See* Royal Irish Constabulary
Roberts, George, 26, 28, 74, 90, 233n5
Robinson, Lennox, 134
Rooney, William, 231n14
Rossa, Jeremiah O'Donovan, 180–81, 240nn13–14
Royal Irish Constabulary (RIC), 134, 135
Russell, George (Æ), 10, 130, 143–44, 147–49, 151, 154, 178, 220, 221, 237n6, 237n10, 244n8
Ryan, Desmond, 118
Ryan, Frederick, 2, 9, 10–17, 96, 104, 110–11, 123, 221, 235n19, 236n26; and Irish Socialist Republican Party (ISRP), 2, 9
—play: *The Laying of the Foundations*, 2, 10–17, 19, 22, 90, 93, 104, 115, 138, 160–62, 176, 225nn4–5, 228n28
Ryan, W. P., 93, 95, 102, 111, 118, 205, 209, 241n24

Saddlemyer, Ann, 5, 51, 231n16, 234n13
Shaw, Charlotte, 143, 179, 222, 240n9
Shaw, George Bernard: and Abbey Theatre, 28, 47, 78, 97, 182, 188, 194, 233n7, 236n3, 241n17, 241n20; and Catholic Church, 3, 30, 41–43, 45–46, 54, 69, 80, 87, 94, 100, 105–6, 109, 111, 118, 149–50, 172, 185, 200, 229nn30–31, 229n2 (chap. 2), 235nn19–20; as dramatist, 1, 2, 4, 6, 9, 19, 27–28, 36, 112–13, 116, 120, 124, 127, 140, 146, 155, 159–60, 166, 194, 226nn8–9, 228n22, 232n23, 233n1, 234n10, 237n4, 242n33; and Dublin Lockout, 133, 136, 149, 153, 155–56, 237n13; and Dublin Municipal Art Gallery, 127–30, 236n28; and Easter Rising, 5, 7, 210, 211–12, 216, 217–19, 244nn1–2, 244n8; and Fabian philosophy, 1, 2, 8–10, 12, 31, 45, 89, 113; and the Great War, 4, 7, 169–74, 175–76, 178–80, 182–88, 189, 194, 196, 197, 199–200, 221–22; and Irish Agricultural Organization Society (IAOS), 143; and *Irish Citizen*, 178–79, 240n9; and Irish Citizen Army (ICA), 3, 5, 150, 153–56, 181, 199, 211, 221; and Irish National Theatre Society (INTS), 17, 27, 28, 31, 36; and Irish Socialism, 2, 6, 7, 82, 85, 93, 96, 110–11, 115, 118, 147–48, 155, 213; and Irish Transport and General Workers' Union (ITGWU), 7, 155; and *Irish Worker*, 128, 155, 173; as lecturer, 3, 8, 9, 92, 103–12, 122, 126, 132, 142, 154, 221, 234nn14–16, 235nn17–18, 235n20, 236n25; and *New Statesman*, 171, 217, 239n3, 240n9, 244n3; as Socialist, 1, 2, 6, 7, 17, 18, 86, 125, 141, 142, 143–44, 225n1, 236n3; as speechmaker, 147, 149–54, 167, 237n11; and women's advancement, 19, 23–24, 103–4
—books: *The Quintessence of Ibsenism*, 9; *War Issues for Irishmen*, 26, 183, 199–200, 221–22
—essays and pamphlets: "Children of the Dublin Slums," 223; "Common Sense About the War," 169, 185, 221; "The Easter Week Executions," 218–19, 244n4; "Economic," 9, 12; "Ireland and the First World War" ("Ireland and the War—the Erratic View of Mr. Bernard Shaw") 171, 172; "The Irish Players," 78; "Letter from George Bernard Shaw on Sheehy-Skeffington's Sentence," 179, 180; "My Motto Is Ireland for All," 103, 234n13; "Neglected Morals of the Irish Rising," 217–18, 244n1
—plays: *Arms and the Man*, 27, 31, 155, 226n9; *The Devil's Disciple*, 4, 130, 131, 226n9, 232n28; *Getting Married*, 23, 24; *John Bull's Other Island*, 2, 4, 7, 17, 19, 20, 27–31, 32–34, 36, 37–49, 50–51, 52–54, 56, 58, 60, 64–65, 66, 67, 68, 72–73, 76, 77, 78, 82, 83, 86, 87, 88, 90, 94, 98, 100, 106, 108, 123, 125–26, 127, 138, 143, 184, 185, 186, 187, 188, 189, 192, 193–94, 206, 213, 227n21, 228nn27–29, 229n2, 231n10, 235n21, 236n29, 236n4

(chap. 4), 242n29; *Major Barbara*, 239n1; *Man and Superman*, 91, 235n17; *Man of Destiny*, 31, 226n9; *Mrs Warren's Profession*, 13, 31, 225n6; *O'Flaherty V.C.*, 4, 8, 182, 183–94, 195, 198, 199–201, 202–7, 215, 222, 240n15, 241nn20–23, 242n28, 242n36, 243n41; *The Shewing-up of Blanco Posnet*, 3, 4, 23, 50, 80–85, 86, 89, 94, 97, 100, 105, 108, 128, 130, 162, 232nn23–28; *Widowers' Houses*, 9, 10, 12–14, 17, 31, 162, 225n6
—prefaces: "On Marriage," 23–24; "Preface for Politicians," 28–29
—speeches and lectures: "Literature in Ireland," 232n21; "Mad Dogs in Uniform," 149–53, 154–57, 162, 167, 170, 237n11, 237n13; "The Poor Law and Destitution in Ireland," 3, 82, 103–12, 142, 176, 234n12, 234n15, 239n23

Sheehy-Skeffington, Francis, 5, 23–24, 93, 96–97, 104–5, 110–12, 126–27, 136, 138, 139, 147, 150–52, 154, 166, 178–80, 184, 200, 207, 208, 210–12, 215–18, 236n26, 239n8, 240nn9–12, 243n44; and anti-recruitment, 178–80, 184, 240nn10–11; as correspondent for the *Daily Herald*, 136, 147, 150, 152, 208; death of, 215–16, 218; and Socialist Party of Ireland (SPI), 104

Sheehy-Skeffington, Hannah, 179–80, 216, 243n44

Sinn Fein, 116–17, 129, 147, 227n13, 230n7, 235n22

Socialist Party of Ireland (SPI), 104, 110, 111

SPI. *See* Socialist Party of Ireland

Swift, Jonathan, 122, 148, 236n25

Synge, John Millington: and Abbey Theatre, 39, 227n19, 229n1, 230n5, 231n16, 232n20, 232n22, 232n25, 232n27, 233n3, 233nn6–7, 237n5, 238n19; and Catholic Church (and morality), 22, 24–25, 30, 41, 46, 54, 55–56, 58, 59, 66, 68–69, 71, 74–75, 77, 79–80, 87, 94–95, 100, 101, 104, 106, 118, 140, 178, 185, 190–91, 197, 229nn30–31; as dramatist, 2, 3, 4, 5, 7, 16–17, 19–20, 22–25, 27, 30–31, 34, 36–37, 49, 50–51, 54, 56, 59–60, 63, 67, 82, 83, 84–85, 91, 93–94, 97, 111–12, 113, 116, 118, 123–24, 127, 129, 135, 140, 141, 142, 145, 149, 156–57, 167, 176, 181, 184, 188–89, 192, 201, 202, 204, 205, 209, 212, 214, 219, 223, 227nn13–14, 227n16, 227n18, 227n20, 228n5, 228n29, 229n3, 232n19, 232n25, 233nn5–7, 234n13, 237n5, 237n15, 241n24, 242n33; and Irish National Theatre Society (INTS), 27, 31, 41, 227n20, 228nn28–29; and leftist leanings, 3, 4, 5, 7, 16–19, 21, 26, 30–31, 54, 56, 57–60, 61, 63–64, 65, 69–70, 78, 82, 89–90, 92, 94–95, 110, 122, 145–46, 174, 212, 226nn10–11, 227n15, 238n17, 245n10; as *Manchester Guardian* correspondent, 56–59, 69–70, 143; and women's advancement, 19, 23–25, 77, 178
—book: *The Aran Islands*, 18–19, 24–25, 73, 76, 203, 226n11
—essays: "Autobiography," 18; "Can We Go Back into Our Mother's Womb?," 197–98, 221; "Erris," 57–58; "The Ferryman of Dinish Island," 59; "From Galway to Gorumna," 57, 69–70; "The Homes of the Harvestmen," 65; "The Inner Lands of Mayo," 57; "A Note on Boucicault and Irish Drama," 201; "The Smaller Peasant Proprietors," 58
—plays: *Deirdre of the Sorrows*, 51, 85–90, 92, 132, 146, 167, 202; *In the Shadow of the Glen*, 2, 18, 19–27, 30, 31, 34, 35, 36–37, 38, 40, 41, 43, 46, 47, 48, 51, 52, 55, 59, 61, 70–72, 75, 77, 78, 86, 87, 101, 106, 118, 124, 127, 133, 167, 171, 177, 204, 206, 227n17, 227n19, 228n26, 228n28, 229nn31–33, 229nn1–2, 232n22, 233n5, 235n17, 235n21; *The Playboy of the Western World*, 5, 19, 20, 29, 39, 49, 50, 51–54, 56, 58, 60–63, 64–77, 78–80,

—plays—*continued*
86, 87, 90–91, 92, 94, 95, 108, 113, 118, 130, 134, 140, 161, 167, 193, 195–96, 197, 204, 207, 210, 213, 216, 220–21, 229n1, 230n6, 230n8, 231nn10–13, 231nn15–18, 232nn20–22, 232n28, 233n29, 233nn2–3 (chap. 3), 235n18, 238n19, 241n24; *Riders to the Sea*, 27, 41, 59, 68, 112, 167, 190, 203, 228n26, 229n30, 229n3 (chap. 2); *The Tinker's Wedding*, 41, 59, 66; *The Well of Saints*, 27, 55–56, 59, 227n19, 230n5, 231n9
—preface: "Preface to *The Playboy of the Western World*," 19, 190

Tobin, Dr. Richard, 221

United Irishman, 13–14, 22, 36, 37, 52, 62, 72, 225n5, 227n13, 231n14
Ulster Volunteer Force (UVF), 153, 156, 244n4
UVF. *See* Ulster Volunteer Force

Walker, William, 115–16
Walsh, Archbishop William, 139–40, 148
Weintraub, Stanley, 8
White, Captain Jack, 154–56, 167, 237n12
Wilde, Oscar, 31, 228n22, 237n15
Wilson, A. Patrick, 120, 124, 130, 137, 159, 162, 182, 208, 236n24, 242n28

—plays: *A Call to Arms*, 167–68, 242n28; *The Cobbler*, 163, 238n21; *The Slough*, 163–68, 177, 238n22, 239n23; *Victims*, 120–23, 163, 167, 208
Workers' Republic, 14–16, 97, 176, 183, 195, 198, 199–200, 203, 208, 209–10, 212, 242n27

Yeates, Padraig, 117, 135, 156, 243n44
Yeats, W. B., 5, 17, 28, 31, 35, 39, 47, 50, 51, 74–75, 79, 80, 84, 85, 120, 128, 136, 146, 150, 151, 160, 167, 182, 194, 209, 225n4, 226n9, 227n18, 227n20, 228n29, 229n3, 230nn4–5, 231nn16–17, 232n20, 233n3, 233nn6–7, 234n13, 237n8, 238nn19–20, 241n20, 242n40
—plays: *Deirdre*, 51, 86; *Kathleen Ni Houlihan* (co-authored with Lady Augusta Gregory), 10, 29–30, 34, 36, 43, 47, 52, 62, 65, 201, 221, 227n19, 228n24, 228nn26–27, 233n4, 242n33, 242n36; *The King's Threshold*, 226n8; *Land of Heart's Desire*, 27; *On Baile's Strand*, 228n22
—poems: "Easter 1916," 220; "On Those That Hated 'The Playboy of the Western World,' 1907" ("On Those Who Dislike the Playboy"), 141; "September 1913" ("Romance in Ireland"), 137; "To a Friend Whose Work Has Come to Nothing," 137; "To a Shade," 137

Nelson O'Ceallaigh Ritschel is a Synge scholar who has moved into Shaw Studies. His earlier publications on Synge, Shaw, James Connolly, and Irish theater include three books since 2001 and numerous essays in journals and anthologies. He is professor at Massachusetts Maritime Academy where he teaches Irish literature and theater.

The Florida Bernard Shaw Series

This series was made possible by a generous grant from the David and Rachel Howie Foundation.

Edited by R. F. Dietrich

Pygmalion's Wordplay: The Postmodern Shaw, by Jean Reynolds (1999)
Shaw's Theater, by Bernard F. Dukore (2000)
Bernard Shaw and the French, by Michel W. Pharand (2001)
The Matter with Ireland, Second Edition, edited by Dan H. Laurence and David H. Greene (2001)
Bernard Shaw's Remarkable Religion: A Faith That Fits the Facts, by Stuart E. Baker (2002)
Bernard Shaw's The Black Girl in Search of God: The Story Behind the Story, by Leon Hugo (2003)
Shaw Shadows: Rereading the Texts of Bernard Shaw, by Peter Gahan (2004)
Bernard Shaw: A Life, by A. M. Gibbs (2005)
What Shaw Really Wrote about the War, edited by J. L. Wisenthal and Daniel O'Leary (2006)
Bernard Shaw and China: Cross-Cultural Encounters, by Kay Li (2007)
Shaw's Controversial Socialism, by James Alexander (2009)
Bernard Shaw as Artist-Fabian, by Charles A. Carpenter (2009)
Shaw, Synge, Connolly, and Socialist Provocation, by Nelson O`Ceallaigh Ritschel (2011; first paperback edition, 2012)
Who's Afraid of Bernard Shaw? Some Personalities in Shaw's Plays, by Stanley Weintraub (2011)
Shaw, Plato, and Euripides: Classical Currents in Major Barbara, by Sidney P. Albert (2012)
Shaw and Feminisms: On Stage and Off, edited by D. A. Hadfield and Jean Reynolds (2012)

www.ingramcontent.com/pod-product-compliance
Lightning Source LLC
Chambersburg PA
CBHW020833160426
43192CB00007B/631